T0100213

Get the eBooks FREE!

(PDF, ePub, Kindle, and liveBook all included)

We believe that once you buy a book from us, you should be able to read it in any format we have available. To get electronic versions of this book at no additional cost to you, purchase and then register this book at the Manning website.

Go to https://www.manning.com/freebook and follow the instructions to complete your pBook registration.

That's it!
Thanks from Manning!

Deep Learning for
Vision Systems

MOHAMED ELGENDY

MANNING
SHELTER ISLAND

For online information and ordering of this and other Manning books, please visit www.manning.com. The publisher offers discounts on this book when ordered in quantity. For more information, please contact

  Special Sales Department
  Manning Publications Co.
  20 Baldwin Road
  PO Box 761
  Shelter Island, NY 11964
  Email: orders@manning.com

Manning Publications Co.
20 Baldwin Road
PO Box 761
Shelter Island, NY 11964

Development editor:	Jenny Stout
Technical development editor:	Alain Couniot
Review editor:	Ivan Martinović
Production editor:	Lori Weidert
Copy editor:	Tiffany Taylor
Proofreader:	Keri Hales
Technical proofreader:	Al Krinker
Typesetter:	Dennis Dalinnik
Cover designer:	Marija Tudor

ISBN: 9781617296192
Printed in the United States of America

To my mom, Huda, who taught me perseverance and kindness
To my dad, Ali, who taught me patience and purpose
To my loving and supportive wife, Amanda, who always inspires me to keep climbing
To my two-year-old daughter, Emily, who teaches me every day that AI still has
a long way to go to catch up with even the tiniest humans

contents

3 *Convolutional neural networks* 92

4 *Structuring DL projects and hyperparameter tuning* 145

preface

Two years ago, I decided to write a book to teach deep learning for computer vision from an *intuitive* perspective. My goal was to develop a comprehensive resource that takes learners from knowing only the basics of machine learning to building advanced deep learning algorithms that they can apply to solve complex computer vision problems.

The problem: In short, as of this moment, there are no books out there that teach deep learning for computer vision the way I wanted to learn about it. As a beginner machine learning engineer, I wanted to read one book that would take me from point A to point Z. I planned to specialize in building modern computer vision applications, and I wished that I had a single resource that would teach me everything I needed to do two things: 1) use neural networks to build an end-to-end computer vision application, and 2) be comfortable reading and implementing research papers to stay up-to-date with the latest industry advancements.

I found myself jumping between online courses, blogs, papers, and YouTube videos to create a comprehensive curriculum for myself. It's challenging to try to comprehend what is happening under the hood on a deeper level: not just a basic understanding, but how the concepts and theories make sense mathematically. It was impossible to find one comprehensive resource that (horizontally) covered the most important topics that I needed to learn to work on complex computer vision applications while also diving deep enough (vertically) to help me understand the math that makes the magic work.

As a beginner, I searched but couldn't find anything to meet these needs. So now I've written it. My goal has been to write a book that not only teaches the content I wanted when I was starting out, but also levels up your ability to learn on your own.

My solution is a comprehensive book that dives deep both horizontally and vertically:

- *Horizontally*—This book explains most topics that an engineer needs to learn to build production-ready computer vision applications, from neural networks and how they work to the different types of neural network architectures and how to train, evaluate, and tune the network.
- *Vertically*—The book dives a level or two deeper than the code and explains intuitively (and gently) how the math works under the hood, to empower you to be comfortable reading and implementing research papers or even inventing your own techniques.

At the time of writing, I believe this is the only deep learning for vision systems resource that is taught this way. Whether you are looking for a job as a computer vision engineer, want to gain a deeper understanding of advanced neural networks algorithms in computer vision, or want to build your product or startup, I wrote this book with you in mind. I hope you enjoy it.

acknowledgments

This book was a lot of work. No, make that really a lot of work! But I hope you will find it valuable. There are quite a few people I'd like to thank for helping me along the way.

I would like to thank the people at Manning who made this book possible: publisher Marjan Bace and everyone on the editorial and production teams, including Jennifer Stout, Tiffany Taylor, Lori Weidert, Katie Tennant, and many others who worked behind the scenes.

Many thanks go to the technical peer reviewers led by Alain Couniot—Al Krinker, Albert Choy, Alessandro Campeis, Bojan Djurkovic, Burhan ul haq, David Fombella Pombal, Ishan Khurana, Ita Cirovic Donev, Jason Coleman, Juan Gabriel Bono, Juan José Durillo Barrionuevo, Michele Adduci, Millad Dagdoni, Peter Hraber, Richard Vaughan, Rohit Agarwal, Tony Holdroyd, Tymoteusz Wolodzko, and Will Fuger—and the active readers who contributed their feedback in the book forums. Their contributions included catching typos, code errors and technical mistakes, as well as making valuable topic suggestions. Each pass through the review process and each piece of feedback implemented through the forum topics shaped and molded the final version of this book.

Finally, thank you to the entire Synapse Technology team. You've created something that's incredibly cool. Thank you to Simanta Guatam, Aleksandr Patsekin, Jay Patel, and others for answering my questions and brainstorming ideas for the book.

about this book

Who should read this book

If you know the basic machine learning framework, can hack around in Python, and want to learn how to build and train advanced, production-ready neural networks to solve complex computer vision problems, I wrote this book for you. The book was written for anyone with intermediate Python experience and basic machine learning understanding who wishes to explore training deep neural networks and learn to apply deep learning to solve computer vision problems.

When I started writing the book, my primary goal was as follows: "I want to write a book to grow readers' skills, not teach them content." To achieve this goal, I had to keep an eye on two main tenets:

1. *Teach you how to learn.* I don't want to read a book that just goes through a set of scientific facts. I can get that on the internet for free. If I read a book, I want to finish it having grown my skillset so I can study the topic further. I want to learn how to think about the presented solutions and come up with my own.

2. *Go very deep.* If I'm successful in satisfying the first tenet, that makes this one easy. If you learn how to learn new concepts, that allows me to dive deep without worrying that you might fall behind. This book doesn't avoid the math part of the learning, because understanding the mathematical equations will empower you with the best skill in the AI world: the ability to read research papers, compare innovations, and make the right decisions about implementing new concepts in your own problems. But I promise to introduce only the mathematical concepts you need, and I promise to present them in a way that

doesn't interrupt your flow of understanding the concepts without the math part if you prefer.

How this book is organized: A roadmap

This book is structured into three parts. The first part explains deep leaning in detail as a foundation for the remaining topics. I strongly recommend that you not skip this section, because it dives deep into neural network components and definitions and explains all the notions required to be able to understand how neural networks work under the hood. After reading part 1, you can jump directly to topics of interest in the remaining chapters. Part 2 explains deep learning techniques to solve object classification and detection problems, and part 3 explains deep learning techniques to generate images and visual embeddings. In several chapters, practical projects implement the topics discussed.

About the code

All of this book's code examples use open source frameworks that are free to download. We will be using Python, Tensorflow, Keras, and OpenCV. Appendix A walks you through the complete setup. I also recommend that you have access to a GPU if you want to run the book projects on your machine, because chapters 6–10 contain more complex projects to train deep networks that will take a long time on a regular CPU. Another option is to use a cloud environment like Google Colab for free or other paid options.

Examples of source code occur both in numbered listings and in line with normal text. In both cases, source code is formatted in a `fixed-width font like this` to separate it from ordinary text. Sometimes code is also **in bold** to highlight code that has changed from previous steps in the chapter, such as when a new feature adds to an existing line of code.

In many cases, the original source code has been reformatted; we've added line breaks and reworked indentation to accommodate the available page space in the book. In rare cases, even this was not enough, and listings include line-continuation markers (➥). Additionally, comments in the source code have often been removed from the listings when the code is described in the text. Code annotations accompany many of the listings, highlighting important concepts.

The code for the examples in this book is available for download from the Manning website at www.manning.com/books/deep-learning-for-vision-systems and from GitHub at https://github.com/moelgendy/deep_learning_for_vision_systems.

liveBook discussion forum

Purchase of *Deep Learning for Vision Systems* includes free access to a private web forum run by Manning Publications where you can make comments about the book, ask technical questions, and receive help from the author and from other users. To access the forum, go to https://livebook.manning.com/#!/book/deep-learning-for-vision-systems/discussion. You can also learn more about Manning's forums and the rules of conduct at https://livebook.manning.com/#!/discussion.

Manning's commitment to our readers is to provide a venue where a meaningful dialogue between individual readers and between readers and the author can take place. It is not a commitment to any specific amount of participation on the part of the author, whose contribution to the forum remains voluntary (and unpaid). We suggest you try asking the author some challenging questions lest his interest stray! The forum and the archives of previous discussions will be accessible from the publisher's website as long as the book is in print.

about the author

Mohamed Elgendy is the vice president of engineering at Rakuten, where he is leading the development of its AI platform and products. Previously, he served as head of engineering at Synapse Technology, building proprietary computer vision applications to detect threats at security checkpoints worldwide. At Amazon, Mohamed built and managed the central AI team that serves as a deep learning think tank for Amazon engineering teams like AWS and Amazon Go. He also developed the deep learning for computer vision curriculum at Amazon's Machine University. Mohamed regularly speaks at AI conferences like Amazon's DevCon, O'Reilly's AI conference, and Google's I/O.

about the cover illustration

The figure on the cover of *Deep Learning for Vision Systems* depicts Ibn al-Haytham, an Arab mathematician, astronomer, and physicist who is often referred to as "the father of modern optics" due to his significant contributions to the principles of optics and visual perception. The illustration is modified from the frontispiece of a fifteenth-century edition of Johannes Hevelius's work *Selenographia*.

In his book *Kitab al-Manazir* (*Book of Optics*), Ibn al-Haytham was the first to explain that vision occurs when light reflects from an object and then passes to one's eyes. He was also the first to demonstrate that vision occurs in the brain, rather than in the eyes—and many of these concepts are at the heart of modern vision systems. You will see the correlation when you read chapter 1 of this book.

Ibn al-Haytham has been a great inspiration for me as I work and innovate in this field. By honoring his memory on the cover of this book, I hope to inspire fellow practitioners that our work can live and inspire others for thousands of years.

Part 1

Deep learning foundation

Computer vision is a technological area that's been advancing rapidly thanks to the tremendous advances in artificial intelligence and deep learning that have taken place in the past few years. Neural networks now help self-driving cars to navigate around other cars, pedestrians, and other obstacles; and recommender agents are getting smarter about suggesting products that resemble other products. Face-recognition technologies are becoming more sophisticated, too, enabling smartphones to recognize faces before unlocking a phone or a door. Computer vision applications like these and others have become a staple in our daily lives. However, by moving beyond the simple recognition of objects, deep learning has given computers the power to imagine and create new things, like art that didn't exist previously, new human faces, and other objects. Part 1 of this book looks at the foundations of deep learning, different forms of neural networks, and structured projects that go a bit further with concepts like hyperparameter tuning.

Welcome to
computer vision

1

Hello! I'm very excited that you are here. You are making a great decision—to grasp deep learning (DL) and computer vision (CV). The timing couldn't be more perfect. CV is an area that's been advancing rapidly, thanks to the huge AI and DL advances of recent years. Neural networks are now allowing self-driving cars to figure out where other cars and pedestrians are and navigate around them. We are using CV applications in our daily lives more and more with all the smart devices in our homes—from security cameras to door locks. CV is also making face recognition work better than ever: smartphones can recognize faces for unlocking, and smart locks can unlock doors. I wouldn't be surprised if sometime in the near future, your couch or television is able to recognize specific people in your house and react according to their personal preferences. It's not just about recognizing objects—DL has given computers the power to imagine and create new things like artwork; new objects; and even unique, realistic human faces.

The main reason that I'm excited about deep learning for computer vision, and what drew me to this field, is how rapid advances in AI research are enabling new applications to be built every day and across different industries, something not possible just a few years ago. The unlimited possibilities of CV research is what inspired me to write this book. By learning these tools, perhaps you will be able to invent new products and applications. Even if you end up not working on CV per se, you will find many concepts in this book useful for some of your DL algorithms and architectures. That is because while the main focus is CV applications, this book covers the most important DL architectures, such as artificial neural networks (ANNs), convolutional networks (CNNs), generative adversarial networks (GANs), transfer learning, and many more, which are transferable to other domains like natural language processing (NLP) and voice user interfaces (VUIs).

The high-level layout of this chapter is as follows:

- *Computer vision intuition*—We will start with visual perception intuition and learn the similarities between humans and machine vision systems. We will look at how vision systems have two main components: a sensing device and an interpreting device. Each is tailored to fulfill a specific task.
- *Applications of CV*—Here, we will take a bird's-eye view of the DL algorithms used in different CV applications. We will then discuss vision in general for different creatures.
- *Computer vision pipeline*—Finally, we will zoom in on the second component of vision systems: the interpreting device. We will walk through the sequence of steps taken by vision systems to process and understand image data. These are referred to as a *computer vision pipeline*. The CV pipeline is composed of four main steps: image input, image preprocessing, feature extraction, and an ML model to interpret the image. We will talk about image formation and how computers see images. Then, we will quickly review image-processing techniques and extracting features.

Ready? Let's get started!

1.1   *Computer vision*

The core concept of any AI system is that it can perceive its environment and take actions based on its perceptions. *Computer vision* is concerned with the visual perception part: it is the science of perceiving and understanding the world through images and videos by constructing a physical model of the world so that an AI system can then take appropriate actions. For humans, vision is only one aspect of perception. We perceive the world through our sight, but also through sound, smell, and our other senses. It is similar with AI systems—vision is just one way to understand the world. Depending on the application you are building, you select the sensing device that best captures the world.

1.1.1 *What is visual perception?*

Visual perception, at its most basic, is the act of observing patterns and objects through sight or visual input. With an autonomous vehicle, for example, visual perception means understanding the surrounding objects and their specific details—such as pedestrians, or whether there is a particular lane the vehicle needs to be centered in—and detecting traffic signs and understanding what they mean. That's why the word *perception* is part of the definition. We are not just looking to capture the surrounding environment. We are trying to build systems that can actually understand that environment through visual input.

1.1.2 *Vision systems*

In past decades, traditional image-processing techniques were considered CV systems, but that is not totally accurate. A machine processing an image is completely different from that machine understanding what's happening within the image, which is not a trivial task. Image processing is now just a piece of a bigger, more complex system that aims to interpret image content.

HUMAN VISION SYSTEMS

At the highest level, vision systems are pretty much the same for humans, animals, insects, and most living organisms. They consist of a sensor or an eye to capture the image and a brain to process and interpret the image. The system then outputs a prediction of the image components based on the data extracted from the image (figure 1.1).

Let's see how the human vision system works. Suppose we want to interpret the image of dogs in figure 1.1. We look at it and directly understand that the image consists of a bunch of dogs (three, to be specific). It comes pretty natural to us to classify

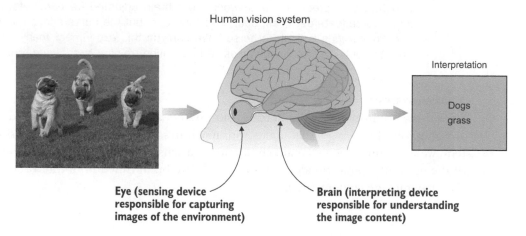

Eye (sensing device responsible for capturing images of the environment)

Brain (interpreting device responsible for understanding the image content)

Figure 1.1   The human vision system uses the eye and brain to sense and interpret an image.

and detect objects in this image because we have been trained over the years to identify dogs.

Suppose someone shows you a picture of a dog for the first time—you definitely
don't know what it is. Then they tell you that this is a dog. After a couple experiments
like this, you will have been trained to identify dogs. Now, in a follow-up exercise, they
show you a picture of a horse. When you look at the image, your brain starts analyzing
the object features: hmmm, it has four legs, long face, long ears. Could it be a dog?
"Wrong: this is a horse," you're told. Then your brain adjusts some parameters in its
algorithm to learn the differences between dogs and horses. Congratulations! You just
trained your brain to classify dogs and horses. Can you add more animals to the equation, like cats, tigers, cheetahs, and so on? Definitely. You can train your brain to identify almost anything. The same is true of computers. You can train machines to learn
and identify objects, but humans are much more intuitive than machines. It takes
only a few images for you to learn to identify most objects, whereas with machines, it
takes thousands or, in more complex cases, millions of image samples to learn to
identify objects.

The ML perspective

Let's look at the previous example from the machine learning perspective:

- You learned to identify dogs by looking at examples of several dog-labeled
  images. This approach is called *supervised learning*.
- *Labeled data* is data for which you already know the target answer. You were
  shown a sample image of a dog and told that it was a dog. Your brain learned
  to associate the features you saw with this label: dog.
- You were then shown a different object, a horse, and asked to identify it. At
  first, your brain thought it was a dog, because you hadn't seen horses before,
  and your brain confused horse features with dog features. When you were
  told that your prediction was wrong, your brain adjusted its parameters to
  learn horse features. "Yes, both have four legs, but the horse's legs are longer. Longer legs indicate a horse." We can run this experiment many times
  until the brain makes no mistakes. This is called *training by trial and error*.

AI VISION SYSTEMS

Scientists were inspired by the human vision system and in recent years have done an
amazing job of copying visual ability with machines. To mimic the human vision system, we need the same two main components: a sensing device to mimic the function
of the eye and a powerful algorithm to mimic the brain function in interpreting and
classifying image content (figure 1.2).

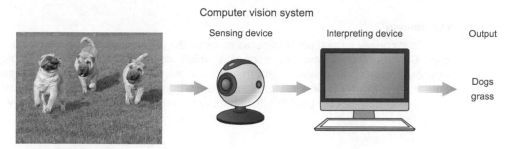

Figure 1.2 The components of the computer vision system are a sensing device and an interpreting device.

1.1.3 Sensing devices

Vision systems are designed to fulfill a specific task. An important aspect of design is selecting the best sensing device to capture the surroundings of a specific environment, whether that is a camera, radar, X-ray, CT scan, Lidar, or a combination of devices to provide the full scene of an environment to fulfill the task at hand.

Let's look at the autonomous vehicle (AV) example again. The main goal of the AV vision system is to allow the car to understand the environment around it and move from point A to point B safely and in a timely manner. To fulfill this goal, vehicles are equipped with a combination of cameras and sensors that can detect 360 degrees of movement—pedestrians, cyclists, vehicles, roadwork, and other objects—from up to three football fields away.

Here are some of the sensing devices usually used in self-driving cars to perceive the surrounding area:

- Lidar, a radar-like technique, uses invisible pulses of light to create a high-resolution 3D map of the surrounding area.
- Cameras can see street signs and road markings but cannot measure distance.
- Radar can measure distance and velocity but cannot see in fine detail.

Medical diagnosis applications use X-rays or CT scans as sensing devices. Or maybe you need to use some other type of radar to capture the landscape for agricultural vision systems. There are a variety of vision systems, each designed to perform a particular task. The first step in designing vision systems is to identify the task they are built for. This is something to keep in mind when designing end-to-end vision systems.

> **Recognizing images**
> Animals, humans, and insects all have eyes as sensing devices. But not all eyes have the same structure, output image quality, and resolution. They are tailored to the specific needs of the creature. Bees, for instance, and many other insects, have compound

(continued)

eyes that consist of multiple lenses (as many as 30,000 lenses in a single compound eye). Compound eyes have low resolution, which makes them not so good at recognizing objects at a far distance. But they are very sensitive to motion, which is essential for survival while flying at high speed. Bees don't need high-resolution pictures. Their vision systems are built to allow them to pick up the smallest movements while flying fast.

Compound eyes   How bees see afl ower

Compound eyes are low resolution but sensitive to motion.

1.1.4 *Interpreting devices*

Computer vision algorithms are typically employed as interpreting devices. The interpreter is the brain of the vision system. Its role is to take the output image from the sensing device and learn features and patterns to identify objects. So we need to build a brain. Simple! Scientists were inspired by how our brains work and tried to reverse engineer the central nervous system to get some insight on how to build an artificial brain. Thus, *artificial neural networks (ANNs)* were born (figure 1.3).

In figure 1.3, we can see an analogy between biological neurons and artificial systems. Both contain a main processing element, a *neuron*, with input signals (x_1, x_2, ..., x_n) and an output.

The learning behavior of biological neurons inspired scientists to create a network of neurons that are connected to each other. Imitating how information is processed in the human brain, each artificial neuron fires a signal to all the neurons that it's connected to when enough of its input signals are activated. Thus, neurons have a very simple mechanism on the individual level (as you will see in the next chapter); but when you have millions of these neurons stacked in layers and connected together, each neuron is connected to thousands of other neurons, yielding a learning behavior. Building a multilayer neural network is called *deep learning* (figure 1.4).

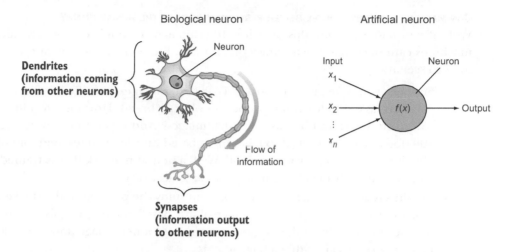

Figure 1.3 The similarities between biological neurons and artificial systems

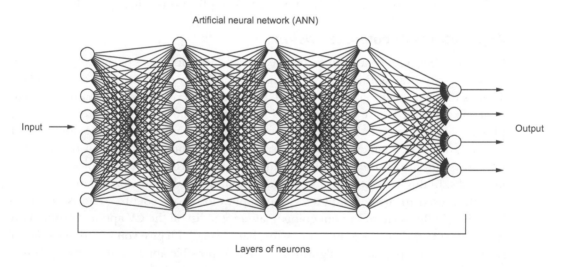

Figure 1.4 Deep learning involves layers of neurons in a network.

DL methods learn representations through a sequence of transformations of data through layers of neurons. In this book, we will explore different DL architectures, such as ANNs and convolutional neural networks, and how they are used in CV applications.

CAN MACHINE LEARNING ACHIEVE BETTER PERFORMANCE THAN THE HUMAN BRAIN?

Well, if you had asked me this question 10 years ago, I would've probably said no, machines cannot surpass the accuracy of a human. But let's take a look at the following two scenarios:

- Suppose you were given a book of 10,000 dog images, classified by breed, and you were asked to learn the properties of each breed. How long would it take you to study the 130 breeds in 10,000 images? And if you were given a test of 100 dog images and asked to label them based on what you learned, out of the 100, how many would you get right? Well, a neural network that is trained in a couple of hours can achieve more than 95% accuracy.

- On the creation side, a neural network can study the patterns in the strokes, colors, and shading of a particular piece of art. Based on this analysis, it can then transfer the style from the original artwork into a new image and create a new piece of original art within a few seconds.

Recent AI and DL advances have allowed machines to surpass human visual ability in many image classification and object detection applications, and capacity is rapidly expanding to many other applications. But don't take my word for it. In the next section, we'll discuss some of the most popular CV applications using DL technology.

1.2 *Applications of computer vision*

Computers began to be able to recognize human faces in images decades ago, but now AI systems are rivaling the ability of computers to classify objects in photos and videos. Thanks to the dramatic evolution in both computational power and the amount of data available, AI and DL have managed to achieve superhuman performance on many complex visual perception tasks like image search and captioning, image and video classification, and object detection. Moreover, deep neural networks are not restricted to CV tasks: they are also successful at natural language processing and voice user interface tasks. In this book, we'll focus on visual applications that are applied in CV tasks.

DL is used in many computer vision applications to recognize objects and their behavior. In this section, I'm not going to attempt to list all the CV applications that are out there. I would need an entire book for that. Instead, I'll give you a bird's-eye view of some of the most popular DL algorithms and their possible applications across different industries. Among these industries are autonomous cars, drones, robots, in-store cameras, and medical diagnostic scanners that can detect lung cancer in early stages.

1.2.1 *Image classification*

Image classification is the task of assigning to an image a label from a predefined set of categories. A *convolutional neural network* is a neural network type that truly shines in processing and classifying images in many different applications:

- *Lung cancer diagnosis*—Lung cancer is a growing problem. The main reason lung cancer is very dangerous is that when it is diagnosed, it is usually in the middle or late stages. When diagnosing lung cancer, doctors typically use their eyes to examine CT scan images, looking for small nodules in the lungs. In the early stages, the nodules are usually very small and hard to spot. Several CV companies decided to tackle this challenge using DL technology.

Almost every lung cancer starts as a small nodule, and these nodules appear in a variety of shapes that doctors take years to learn to recognize. Doctors are very good at identifying mid- and large-size nodules, such as 6–10 mm. But when nodules are 4 mm or smaller, sometimes doctors have difficulty identifying them. DL networks, specifically CNNs, are now able to learn these features automatically from X-ray and CT scan images and detect small nodules early, before they become deadly (figure 1.5).

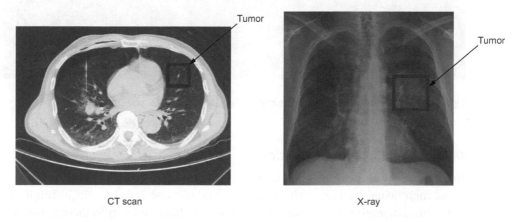

Figure 1.5 Vision systems are now able to learn patterns in X-ray images to identify tumors in earlier stages of development.

- *Traffic sign recognition*—Traditionally, standard CV methods were employed to detect and classify traffic signs, but this approach required time-consuming manual work to handcraft important features in images. Instead, by applying DL to this problem, we can create a model that reliably classifies traffic signs, learning to identify the most appropriate features for this problem by itself (figure 1.6).

NOTE Increasing numbers of image classification tasks are being solved with convolutional neural networks. Due to their high recognition rate and fast execution, CNNs have enhanced most CV tasks, both pre-existing and new. Just like the cancer diagnosis and traffic sign examples, you can feed tens or hundreds of thousands of images into a CNN to label them into as many classes as you want. Other image classification examples include identifying people and objects, classifying different animals (like cats versus dogs versus horses), different breeds of animals, types of land suitable for agriculture, and so on. In short, if you have a set of *labeled* images, convolutional networks can classify them into a set of predefined classes.

Figure 1.6   Vision systems can detect traffic signs with very high performance.

1.2.2   *Object detection and localization*

Image classification problems are the most basic applications for CNNs. In these problems, each image contains only one object, and our task is to identify it. But if we aim to reach human levels of understanding, we have to add complexity to these networks so they can recognize multiple objects and their locations in an image. To do that, we can build object detection systems like YOLO (you only look once), SSD (single-shot detector), and Faster R-CNN, which not only classify images but also can locate and detect each object in images that contain multiple objects. These DL systems can look at an image, break it up into smaller regions, and label each region with a class so that a variable number of objects in a given image can be localized and labeled (figure 1.7). You can imagine that such a task is a basic prerequisite for applications like autonomous systems.

1.2.3   *Generating art (style transfer)*

Neural style transfer, one of the most interesting CV applications, is used to transfer the style from one image to another. The basic idea of style transfer is this: you take one image—say, of a city—and then apply a style of art to that image—say, *The Starry Night* (by Vincent Van Gogh)—and output the same city from the original image, but looking as though it was painted by Van Gogh (figure 1.8).

This is actually a neat application. The astonishing thing, if you know any painters, is that it can take days or even weeks to finish a painting, and yet here is an application that can paint a new image inspired by an existing style in a matter of seconds.

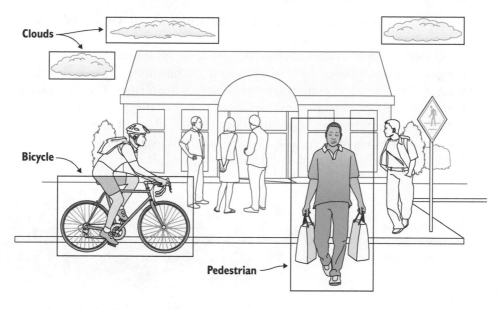

Figure 1.7 Deep learning systems can segment objects in an image.

Figure 1.8 Style transfer from Van Gogh's *The Starry Night* onto the original image, producing a piece of art that feels as though it was created by the original artist

1.2.4 Creating images

Although the earlier examples are truly impressive CV applications of AI, this is where I see the real magic happening: the magic of creation. In 2014, Ian Goodfellow invented a new DL model that can imagine new things called generative adversarial networks (GANs). The name makes them sound a little intimidating, but I promise you that they are not. A GAN is an evolved CNN architecture that is considered a major advancement in DL. So when you understand CNNs, GANs will make a lot more sense to you.

GANs are sophisticated DL models that generate stunningly accurate synthesized images of objects, people, and places, among other things. If you give them a set of images, they can make entirely new, realistic-looking images. For example, StackGAN is one of the GAN architecture variations that can use a textual description of an object to generate a high-resolution image of the object matching that description. This is not just running an image search on a database. These "photos" have never been seen before and are totally imaginary (figure 1.9).

This small blue bird has a short, pointy beak and brown on its wings.

This bird is completely red with black wings and a pointy beak.

Figure 1.9   Generative adversarial networks (GANS) can create new, "made-up" images from a set of existing images.

The GAN is one of the most promising advancements in machine learning in recent years. Research into GANs is new, and the results are overwhelmingly promising. Most of the applications of GANs so have far have been for images. But it makes you wonder: if machines are given the power of imagination to create pictures, what else can they create? In the future, will your favorite movies, music, and maybe even books be created by computers? The ability to synthesize one data type (text) to another (image) will eventually allow us to create all sorts of entertainment using only detailed text descriptions.

GANs create artwork

In October 2018, an AI-created painting called *The Portrait of Edmond Belamy* sold for $432,500. The artwork features a fictional person named Edmond de Belamy, possibly French and—to judge by his dark frock coat and plain white collar—a man of the church.

AI-generated artwork featuring a fictional person named Edmond de Belamy sold for $432,500.

The artwork was created by a team of three 25-year-old French students using GANs. The network was trained on a dataset of 15,000 portraits painted between the fourteenth and twentieth centuries, and then it created one of its own. The team printed the image, framed it, and signed it with part of a GAN algorithm.

1.2.5 Face recognition

Face recognition (FR) allows us to exactly identify or tag an image of a person. Day-to-day applications include searching for celebrities on the web and auto-tagging friends and family in images. Face recognition is a form of fine-grained classification.

The famous *Handbook of Face Recognition* (Li et al., Springer, 2011) categorizes two modes of an FR system:

- *Face identification*—Face identification involves one-to-many matches that compare a query face image against all the template images in the database to determine the identity of the query face. Another face recognition scenario involves a watchlist check by city authorities, where a query face is matched to a list of suspects (one-to-few matches).
- *Face verification*—Face verification involves a one-to-one match that compares a query face image against a template face image whose identity is being claimed (figure 1.10).

1.2.6 Image recommendation system

In this task, a user seeks to find similar images with respect to a given query image. Shopping websites provide product suggestions (via images) based on the selection of a particular product, for example, showing a variety of shoes similar to those the user selected. An example of an apparel search is shown in figure 1.11.

Face verification

Face identification

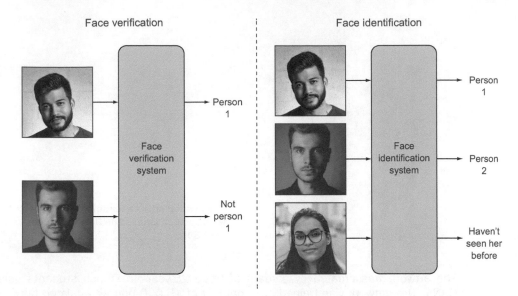

Figure 1.10   Example of face verification (left) and face recognition (right)

Query   ⟶   Retrievals

Figure 1.11   Apparel search. The leftmost image in each row is the query/clicked image, and the subsequent columns show similar apparel. (*Source*: Liu et al., 2016.)

1.3   *Computer vision pipeline: The big picture*

Okay, now that I have your attention, let's dig one level deeper into CV systems. Remember that earlier in this chapter, we discussed how vision systems are composed of two main components: sensing devices and interpreting devices (figure 1.12 offers a reminder). In this section, we will take a look at the pipeline the interpreting device component uses to process and understand images.

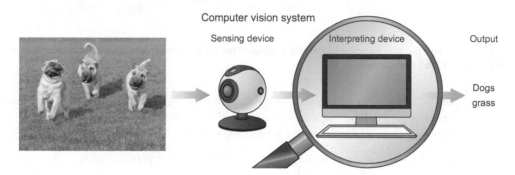

Figure 1.12   Focusing on the interpreting device in computer vision systems

Applications of CV vary, but a typical vision system uses a sequence of distinct steps to process and analyze image data. These steps are referred to as a *computer vision pipeline*. Many vision applications follow the flow of acquiring images and data, processing that data, performing some analysis and recognition steps, and then finally making a prediction based on the extracted information (figure 1.13).

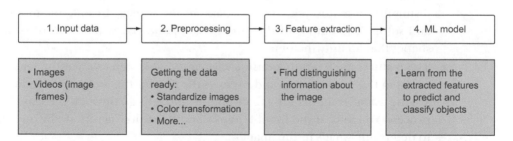

Figure 1.13   The computer vision pipeline, which takes input data, processes it, extracts information, and then sends it to the machine learning model to learn

Let's apply the pipeline in figure 1.13 to an image classifier example. Suppose we have an image of a motorcycle, and we want the model to predict the probability of the object from the following classes: motorcycle, car, and dog (see figure 1.14).

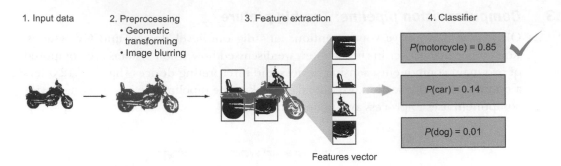

Figure 1.14   Using the machine learning model to predict the probability of the motorcycle object from the motorcycle, car, and dog classes

DEFINITIONS   An *image classifier* is an algorithm that takes in an image as input and outputs a label or "class" that identifies that image. A *class* (also called a *category*) in machine learning is the output category of your data.

Here is how the image flows through the classification pipeline:

1 A computer receives visual input from an imaging device like a camera. This input is typically captured as an image or a sequence of images forming a video.

2 Each image is then sent through some preprocessing steps whose purpose is to standardize the images. Common preprocessing steps include resizing an image, blurring, rotating, changing its shape, or transforming the image from one color to another, such as from color to grayscale. Only by standardizing the images—for example, making them the same size—can you then compare them and further analyze them.

3 We extract features. *Features* are what help us define objects, and they are usually information about object shape or color. For example, some features that distinguish a motorcycle are the shape of the wheels, headlights, mudguards, and so on. The output of this process is a *feature vector* that is a list of unique shapes that identify the object.

4 The features are fed into a *classification model.* This step looks at the feature vector from the previous step and predicts the class of the image. Pretend that you are the classifier model for a few minutes, and let's go through the classification process. You look at the list of features in the feature vector one by one and try to determine what's in the image:

   a First you see a *wheel* feature; could this be a car, a motorcycle, or a dog? Clearly it is not a dog, because dogs don't have wheels (at least, normal dogs, not robots). Then this could be an image of a car or a motorcycle.

   b You move on to the next feature, the *headlights.* There is a higher probability that this is a motorcycle than a car.

   c The next feature is *rear mudguards*—again, there is a higher probability that it is a motorcycle.

   d The object has only two wheels; this is closer to a motorcycle.

   e And you keep going through all the features like the body shape, pedal, and so on, until you arrive at a best guess of the object in the image.

The output of this process is the probability of each class. As you can see in our example, the dog has the lowest probability, 1%, whereas there is an 85% probability that this is a motorcycle. You can see that, although the model was able to predict the right class with the highest probability, it is still a little confused about distinguishing between cars and motorcycles—it predicted that there is a 14% chance this is an image of a car. Since we know that it is a motorcycle, we can say that our ML classification algorithm is 85% accurate. Not bad! To improve this accuracy, we may need to do more of step 1 (acquire more training images), or step 2 (more processing to remove noise), or step 3 (extract better features), or step 4 (change the classifier algorithm and tune some hyperparameters), or even allow more training time. The many different approaches we can take to improve the performance of our model all lie in one or more of the pipeline steps.

That was the big picture of how images flow through the CV pipeline. Next, we'll zoom in one level deeper on each of the pipeline steps.

1.4 Image input

In CV applications, we deal with images or video data. Let's talk about grayscale and color images for now, and in later chapters, we will talk about videos, since videos are just stacked sequential frames of images.

1.4.1 Image as functions

An image can be represented as a function of two variables x and y, which define a two-dimensional area. A digital image is made of a grid of pixels. The *pixel* is the raw building block of an image. Every image consists of a set of pixels in which their values represent the *intensity* of light that appears in a given place in the image. Let's take a look at the motorcycle example again after applying the pixel grid to it (figure 1.15).

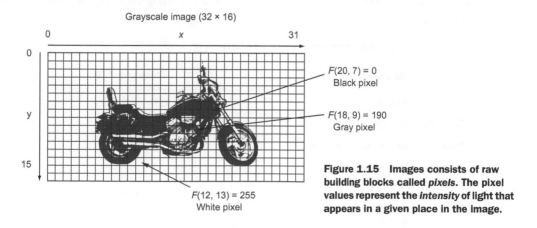

Grayscale image (32 × 16)

$F(20, 7) = 0$
Black pixel

$F(18, 9) = 190$
Gray pixel

$F(12, 13) = 255$
White pixel

Figure 1.15 **Images consists of raw building blocks called *pixels*. The pixel values represent the *intensity* of light that appears in a given place in the image.**

The image in figure 1.14 has a size of 32 × 16. This means the dimensions of the image are 32 pixels wide and 16 pixels tall. The x-axis goes from 0 to 31, and the y-axis from 0 to 16. Overall, the image has 512 (32 × 16) pixels. In this grayscale image, each pixel contains a value that represents the *intensity of light* on that specific pixel. The pixel values range from 0 to 255. Since the pixel value represents the intensity of light, the value 0 represents very dark pixels (black), 255 is very bright (white), and the values in between represent the intensity on the grayscale.

You can see that the image coordinate system is similar to the Cartesian coordinate system: images are two-dimensional and lie on the x-y plane. The origin (0, 0) is at the top left of the image. To represent a specific pixel, we use the following notations: F as a function, and x, y as the location of the pixel in x- and y-coordinates. For example, the pixel located at $x = 12$ and $y = 13$ is white; this is represented by the following function: $F(12, 13) = 255$. Similarly, the pixel (20, 7) that lies on the front of the motorcycle is black, represented as $F(20, 7) = 0$.

```
Grayscale => F(x, y) gives the intensity at position (x, y)
```

That was for grayscale images. How about color images?

In color images, instead of representing the value of the pixel by just one number, the value is represented by three numbers representing the intensity of each color in the pixel. In an RGB system, for example, the value of the pixel is represented by three numbers: the intensity of red, intensity of green, and intensity of blue. There are other color systems for images like HSV and Lab. All follow the same concept when representing the pixel value (more on color images soon). Here is the function representing color images in the RGB system:

```
Color image in RGB => F(x, y) = [ red (x, y), green (x, y), blue (x, y) ]
```

Thinking of an image as a function is very useful in image processing. We can think of an image as a function of $F(x, y)$ and operate on it mathematically to transform it to a new image function $G(x, y)$. Let's take a look at the image transformation examples in table 1.1.

Table 1.1   Image transformation example functions

Application	Transformation
Darken the image.	`G(x, y) = 0.5 * F(x, y)`
Brighten the image.	`G(x, y) = 2 * F(x, y)`
Move an object down 150 pixels.	`G(x, y) = F(x, y + 150)`
Remove the gray in an image to transform the image into black and white.	`G(x, y) = { 0 if F(x, y) < 130, 255 otherwise }`

1.4.2   How computers see images

When we look at an image, we see objects, landscape, colors, and so on. But that's not the case with computers. Consider figure 1.16. Your human brain can process it and immediately know that it is a picture of a motorcycle. To a computer, the image looks like a 2D matrix of the pixels' values, which represent intensities across the color spectrum. There is no context here, just a massive pile of data.

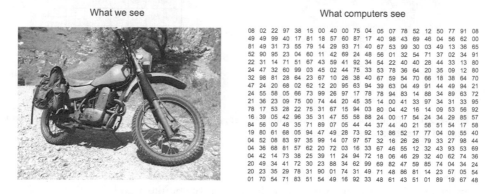

Figure 1.16   A computer sees images as matrices of values. The values represent the intensity of the pixels across the color spectrum. For example, grayscale images range between pixel values of 0 for black and 255 for white.

The image in figure 1.16 is of size 24×24. This size indicates the width and height of the image: there are 24 pixels horizontally and 24 vertically. That means there is a total of 576 (24×24) pixels. If the image is 700×500, then the dimensionality of the matrix will be (700, 500), where each pixel in the matrix represents the intensity of brightness in that pixel. Zero represents black, and 255 represents white.

1.4.3   Color images

In grayscale images, each pixel represents the intensity of only one color, whereas in the standard RGB system, color images have three channels (red, green, and blue). In other words, color images are represented by three matrices: one represents the intensity of red in the pixel, one represents green, and one represents blue (figure 1.17).

As you can see in figure 1.17, the color image is composed of three channels: red, green, and blue. Now the question is, how do computers see this image? Again, they see the matrix, unlike grayscale images, where we had only one channel. In this case, we will have three matrices stacked on top of each other; that's why it's a 3D matrix. The dimensionality of 700×700 color images is (700, 700, 3). Let's say the first matrix represents the red channel; then each element of that matrix represents an intensity of red color in that pixel, and likewise with green and blue. Each pixel in a color

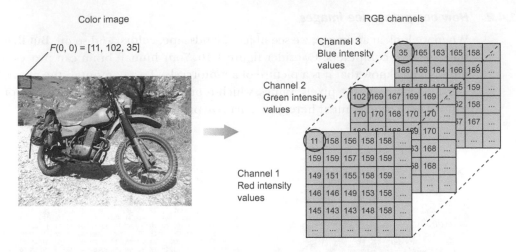

Figure 1.17   Color images are represented by red, green, and blue channels, and matrices can be used to indicate those colors' intensity.

image has three numbers (0 to 255) associated with it. These numbers represent intensity of red, green, and blue color in that particular pixel.

If we take the pixel (0,0) as an example, we will see that it represents the top-left pixel of the image of green grass. When we view this pixel in the color images, it looks like figure 1.18. The example in figure 1.19 shows some shades of the color green and their RGB values.

Figure 1.18   An image of green grass is actually made of three colors of varying intensity.

Figure 1.19   Different shades of green mean different intensities of the three image colors (red, green, blue).

How do computers see color?

Computers see an image as matrices. Grayscale images have one channel (gray); thus, we can represent grayscale images in a 2D matrix, where each element represents the intensity of brightness in that particular pixel. Remember, 0 means black and 255 means white. Grayscale images have one channel, whereas color images have three channels: red, green, and blue. We can represent color images in a 3D matrix where the depth is three.

We've also seen how images can be treated as functions of space. This concept allows us to operate on images mathematically and change or extract information from them. Treating images as functions is the basis of many image-processing techniques, such as converting color to grayscale or scaling an image. Each of these steps is just operating mathematical equations to transform an image pixel by pixel.

- Grayscale: $f(x, y)$ gives the intensity at position (x, y)
- Color image: $f(x, y) = [$ red (x, y), green (x, y), blue (x, y) $]$

1.5 *Image preprocessing*

In machine learning (ML) projects, you usually go through a data preprocessing or cleaning step. As an ML engineer, you will spend a good amount of time cleaning up and preparing the data before you build your learning model. The goal of this step is to make your data ready for the ML model to make it easier to analyze and process computationally. The same thing is true with images. Based on the problem you are solving and the dataset in hand, some data massaging is required before you feed your images to the ML model.

Image processing could involve simple tasks like image resizing. Later, you will learn that in order to feed a dataset of images to a convolutional network, the images all have to be the same size. Other processing tasks can take place, like geometric and color transformation, converting color to grayscale, and many more. We will cover various image-processing techniques throughout the chapters of this book and in the projects.

The acquired data is usually messy and comes from different sources. To feed it to the ML model (or neural network), it needs to be standardized and cleaned up. Preprocessing is used to conduct steps that will reduce the complexity and increase the accuracy of the applied algorithm. We can't write a unique algorithm for each of the conditions in which an image is taken; thus, when we acquire an image, we convert it into a form that would allow a general algorithm to solve it. The following subsections describe some data-preprocessing techniques.

1.5.1 *Converting color images to grayscale to reduce computation complexity*

Sometimes you will find it useful to remove unnecessary information from your images to reduce space or computational complexity. For example, suppose you want to convert your colored images to grayscale, because for many objects, color is not necessary to recognize and interpret an image. Grayscale can be good enough for recognizing certain objects. Since color images contain more information than black-and-white images, they can add unnecessary complexity and take up more space in memory. Remember that color images are represented in three channels, which means that converting them to grayscale will reduce the number of pixels that need to be processed (figure 1.20).

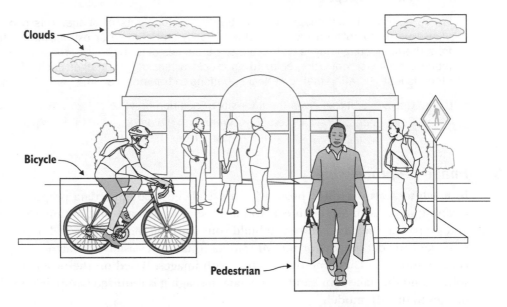

Figure 1.20   Converting color images to grayscale results in a reduced number of pixels that need to be processed. This could be a good approach for applications that do not rely a lot on the color information loss due to the conversion.

In this example, you can see how patterns of brightness and darkness (intensity) can be used to define the shape and characteristics of many objects. However, in other applications, color is important to define certain objects, like skin cancer detection, which relies heavily on skin color (red rashes).

- *Standardizing images*—As you will see in chapter 3, one important constraint that exists in some ML algorithms, such as CNNs, is the need to resize the images in your dataset to unified dimensions. This implies that your images must be preprocessed and scaled to have identical widths and heights before being fed to the learning algorithm.
- *Data augmentation*—Another common preprocessing technique involves augmenting the existing dataset with modified versions of the existing images. Scaling, rotations, and other affine transformations are typically used to enlarge your dataset and expose the neural network to a wide variety of variations of

When is color important?

Converting an image to grayscale might not be a good decision for some problems. There are a number of applications for which color is very important: for example, building a diagnostic system to identify red skin rashes in medical images. This application relies heavily on the intensity of the red color in the skin. Removing colors from the image will make it harder to solve this problem. In general, color images provide very helpful information in many medical applications.

Another example of the importance of color in images is lane-detection applications in a self-driving car, where the car has to identify the difference between yellow and white lines, because they are treated differently. Grayscale images do not provide enough information to distinguish between the yellow and white lines.

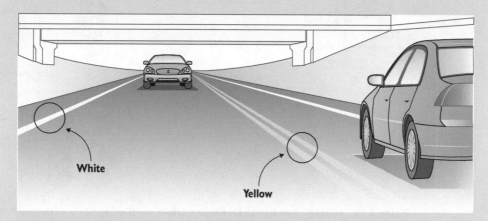

White

Yellow

Grayscale-based image processors cannot differentiate between color images.

The rule of thumb to identify the importance of colors in your problem is to look at the image with the human eye. If you are able to identify the object you are looking for in a gray image, then you probably have enough information to feed to your model. If not, then you definitely need more information (colors) for your model. The same rule can be applied for most other preprocessing techniques that we will discuss.

your images. This makes it more likely that your model will recognize objects when they appear in any form and shape. Figure 1.21 shows an example of image augmentation applied to a butterfly image.

- *Other techniques*—Many more preprocessing techniques are available to get your images ready for training an ML model. In some projects, you might need to remove the background color from your images to reduce noise. Other projects might require that you brighten or darken your images. In short, any adjustments that you need to apply to your dataset are part of preprocessing. You will select

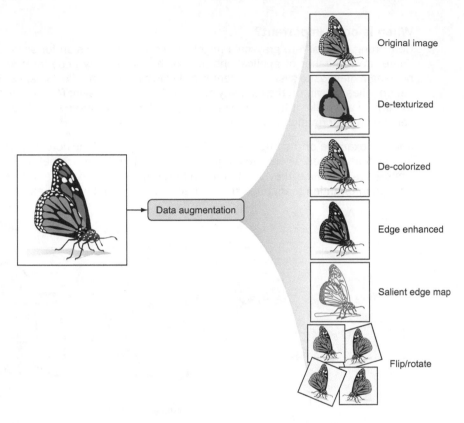

Figure 1.21   Image-augmentation techniques create modified versions of the input image to provide more examples for the ML model to learn from.

the appropriate processing techniques based on the dataset at hand and the problem you are solving. You will see many image-processing techniques throughout this book, helping you build your intuition of which ones you need when working on your own projects.

No free lunch theorem

This is a phrase that was introduced by David Wolpert and William Macready in "No Free Lunch Theorems for Optimizations" (*IEEE Transactions on Evolutionary Computation* 1, 67). You will often hear this said when a team is working on an ML project. It means that no one prescribed recipe fits all models. When working on ML projects, you will need to make many choices like building your neural network architecture, tuning hyperparameters, and applying the appropriate data preprocessing techniques. While there are some rule-of-thumb approaches to tackle certain problems, there is really no single recipe that is guaranteed to work well in all situations.

You must make certain assumptions about the dataset and the problem you are trying to solve. For some datasets, it is best to convert the colored images to grayscale, while for other datasets, you might need to keep or adjust the color images.

The good news is that, unlike traditional machine learning, DL algorithms require minimum data preprocessing because, as you will see soon, neural networks do most of the heavy lifting in processing an image and extracting features.

1.6 Feature extraction

Feature extraction is a core component of the CV pipeline. In fact, the entire DL model works around the idea of extracting useful features that clearly define the objects in the image. So we'll spend a little more time here, because it is important that you understand what a feature is, what a vector of features is, and why we extract features.

> **DEFINITION** A *feature* in machine learning is an individual measurable property or characteristic of an observed phenomenon. Features are the input that you feed to your ML model to output a prediction or classification. Suppose you want to predict the price of a house: your input features (properties) might include `square_foot`, `number_of_rooms`, `bathrooms`, and so on, and the model will output the predicted price based on the values of your features. Selecting good features that clearly distinguish your objects increases the predictive power of ML algorithms.

1.6.1 What is a feature in computer vision?

In CV, a *feature* is a measurable piece of data in your image that is unique to that specific object. It may be a distinct color or a specific shape such as a line, edge, or image segment. A good feature is used to distinguish objects from one another. For example, if I give you a feature like a wheel and ask you to guess whether an object is a motorcycle or a dog, what would your guess be? A motorcycle. Correct! In this case, the wheel is a strong feature that clearly distinguishes between motorcycles and dogs. However, if I give you the same feature (a wheel) and ask you to guess whether an object is a bicycle or a motorcycle, this feature is not strong enough to distinguish between those objects. You need to look for more features like a mirror, license plate, or maybe a pedal, that collectively describe an object. In ML projects, we want to transform the raw data (image) into a feature vector to show to our learning algorithm, which can learn the characteristics of the object (figure 1.22).

In the figure, we feed the raw input image of a motorcycle into a feature extraction algorithm. Let's treat the feature extraction algorithm as a black box for now, and we will come back to it. For now, we need to know that the extraction algorithm produces a vector that contains a list of features. This feature vector is a 1D array that makes a robust representation of the object.

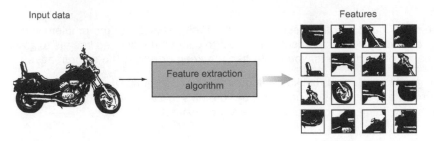

Figure 1.22   Example input image fed to a feature-extraction algorithm to find patterns within the image and create the feature vector

Feature generalizability

It is important to point out that figure 1.22 reflects features extracted from just one motorcycle. A very important characteristic of a feature is *repeatability*. The feature should be able to detect motorcycles in general, not just this specific one. So in real-world problems, a feature is not an exact copy of a piece of the input image.

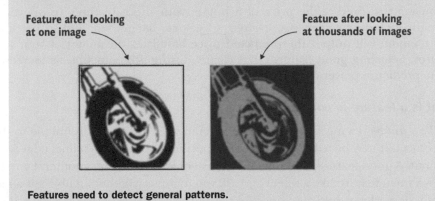

If we take the *wheel* feature, for example, the feature doesn't look exactly like the wheel of one particular motorcycle. Instead, it looks like a circular shape with some patterns that identify wheels in all images in the training dataset. When the feature extractor sees thousands of images of motorcycles, it recognizes patterns that define wheels in general, regardless of where they appear in the image and what type of motorcycle they are part of.

1.6.2   *What makes a good (useful) feature?*

Machine learning models are only as good as the features you provide. That means coming up with good features is an important job in building ML models. But what makes a good feature? And how can you tell?

Let's discuss this with an example. Suppose we want to build a classifier to tell the difference between two types of dogs: Greyhound and Labrador. Let's take two features—the dogs' height and their eye color—and evaluate them (figure 1.23).

Figure 1.23   Example of Greyhound and Labrador dogs

Let's begin with height. How useful do you think this feature is? Well, on average, Greyhounds tend to be a couple of inches taller than Labradors, but not always. There is a lot of variation in the dog world. So let's evaluate this feature across different values in both breeds' populations. Let's visualize the height distribution on a toy example in the histogram in figure 1.24.

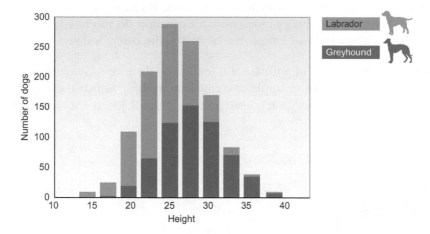

Figure 1.24   A visualization of the height distribution on a toy dogs dataset

From the histogram, we can see that if the dog's height is 20 inches or less, there is more than an 80% probability that the dog is a Labrador. On the other side of the histogram, if we look at dogs that are taller than 30 inches, we can be pretty confident the dog is a Greyhound. Now, what about the data in the middle of the histogram (heights from 20 to 30 inches)? We can see that the probability of each type of dog is pretty close. The thought process in this case is as follows:

if height ≤ 20:

   return higher probability to Labrador

if height ≥ 30:

   return higher probability to Greyhound

if 20 < height < 30:

   look for other features to classify the object

So the height of the dog in this case is a useful feature because it helps (adds information) in distinguishing between both dog types. We can keep it. But it doesn't distinguish between Greyhounds and Labradors in all cases, which is fine. In ML projects, there is usually no one feature that can classify all objects on its own. That's why, in machine learning, we almost always need multiple features, where each feature captures a different type of information. If only one feature would do the job, we could just write `if-else` statements instead of bothering with training a classifier.

> **TIP**   Similar to what we did earlier with color conversion (color versus grayscale), to figure out which features you should use for a specific problem, do a thought experiment. Pretend you are the classifier. If you want to differentiate between Greyhounds and Labradors, what information do you need to know? You might ask about the hair length, the body size, the color, and so on.

For another quick example of a non-useful feature to drive this idea home, let's look at dog eye color. For this toy example, imagine that we have only two eye colors, blue and brown. Figure 1.25 shows what a histogram might look like for this example.

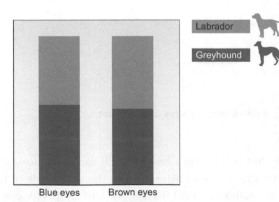

Figure 1.25   A visualization of the eye color distribution in a toy dogs dataset

It is clear that for most values, the distribution is about 50/50 for both types. So practically, this feature tells us nothing, because it doesn't correlate with the type of dog. Hence, it doesn't distinguish between Greyhounds and Labradors.

> **What makes a good feature for object recognition?**
> A good feature will help us recognize an object in all the ways it may appear. Characteristics of a good feature follow:
>
> - Identifiable
> - Easily tracked and compared
> - Consistent across different scales, lighting conditions, and viewing angles
> - Still visible in noisy images or when only part of an object is visible

1.6.3 *Extracting features (handcrafted vs. automatic extracting)*

This is a large topic in machine learning that could take up an entire book. It's typically described in the context of a topic called *feature engineering*. In this book, we are only concerned with extracting features in images. So I'll touch on the idea very quickly in this chapter and build on it in later chapters.

TRADITIONAL MACHINE LEARNING USING HANDCRAFTED FEATURES

In traditional ML problems, we spend a good amount of time in manual feature selection and engineering. In this process, we rely on our domain knowledge (or partner with domain experts) to create features that make ML algorithms work better. We then feed the produced features to a classifier like a support vector machine (SVM) or AdaBoost to predict the output (figure 1.26). Some of the handcrafted feature sets are these:

- Histogram of oriented gradients (HOG)
- Haar Cascades
- Scale-invariant feature transform (SIFT)
- Speeded-Up Robust Feature (SURF)

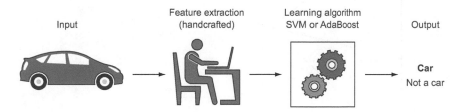

Figure 1.26 Traditional machine learning algorithms require handcrafted feature extraction.

DEEP LEARNING USING AUTOMATICALLY EXTRACTED FEATURES

In DL, however, we do not need to manually extract features from the image. The network extracts features automatically and learns their importance on the output by applying weights to its connections. You just feed the raw image to the network, and while it passes through the network layers, the network identifies patterns within the image with which to create features (figure 1.27). Neural networks can be thought of as feature extractors plus classifiers that are end-to-end trainable, as opposed to traditional ML models that use handcrafted features.

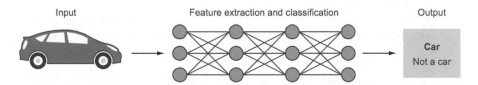

Figure 1.27   A deep neural network passes the input image through its layers to automatically extract features and classify the object. No handcrafted features are needed.

How do neural networks distinguish useful features from non-useful features?

You might get the impression that neural networks only understand the most useful features, but that's not entirely true. Neural networks scoop up all the features available and give them random weights. During the training process, the neural network adjusts these weights to reflect their importance and how they should impact the output prediction. The patterns with the highest appearance frequency will have higher weights and are considered more useful features. Features with the lowest weights will have very little impact on the output. This learning process will be discussed in deeper detail in the next chapter.

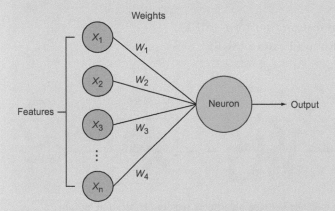

Weighting different features to reflect their importance in identifying the object

WHY USE FEATURES?

The input image has too much extra information that is not necessary for classification. Therefore, the first step after preprocessing the image is to simplify it by extracting the important information and throwing away nonessential information. By extracting important colors or image segments, we can transform complex and large image data into smaller sets of features. This makes the task of classifying images based on their features simpler and faster.

Consider the following example. Suppose we have a dataset of 10,000 images of motorcycles, each of 1,000 width by 1,000 height. Some images have solid backgrounds, and others have busy backgrounds of unnecessary data. When these thousands of images are fed to the feature extraction algorithms, we lose all the unnecessary data that is not important to identify motorcycles, and we only keep a consolidated list of useful features that can be fed directly to the classifier (figure 1.28). This process is a lot simpler than having the classifier look at the raw dataset of 10,000 images to learn the properties of motorcycles.

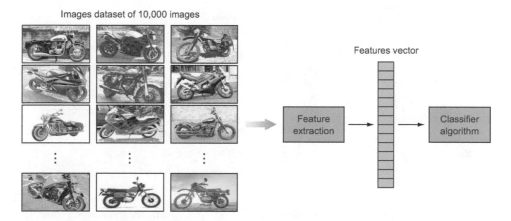

Figure 1.28   Extracting and consolidating features from thousands of images in one feature vector to be fed to the classifier

1.7   *Classifier learning algorithm*

Here is what we have discussed so far regarding the classifier pipeline:

- *Input image*—We've seen how images are represented as functions, and that computers see images as a 2D matrix for grayscale images and a 3D matrix (three channels) for colored images.
- *Image preprocessing*—We discussed some image-preprocessing techniques to clean up our dataset and make it ready as input to the ML algorithm.
- *Feature extraction*—We converted our large dataset of images into a vector of useful features that uniquely describe the objects in the image.

Now it is time to feed the extracted feature vector to the classifier to output a class label for the images (for example, motorcycle or otherwise).

As we discussed in the previous section, the classification task is done one of these ways: traditional ML algorithms like SVMs, or deep neural network algorithms like CNNs. While traditional ML algorithms might get decent results for some problems, CNNs truly shine in processing and classifying images in the most complex problems.

In this book, we will discuss neural networks and how they work in detail. For now, I want you to know that neural networks *automatically* extract useful features from your dataset, and they act as a classifier to output class labels for your images. Input images pass through the layers of the neural network to learn their features layer by layer (figure 1.29). The deeper your network is (the more layers), the more it will learn the features of the dataset: hence the name *deep learning*. More layers come with some trade-offs that we will discuss in the next two chapters. The last layer of the neural network usually acts as the classifier that outputs the class label.

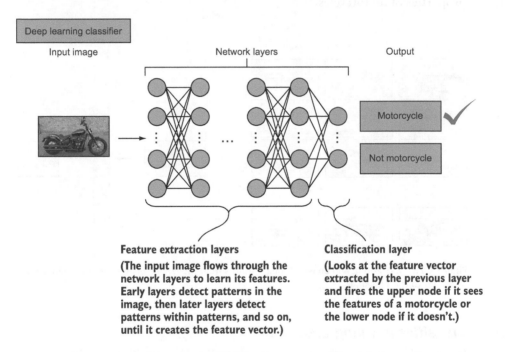

Figure 1.29 **Input images pass through the layers of a neural network so it can learn features layer by layer.**

Summary

- Both human and machine vision systems contain two basic components: a sensing device and an interpreting device.
- The interpreting process consists of four steps: input the data, preprocess it, do feature extraction, and produce a machine learning model.

- An image can be represented as a function of x and y. Computers see an image as a matrix of pixel values: one channel for grayscale images and three channels for color images.
- Image-processing techniques vary for each problem and dataset. Some of these techniques are converting images to grayscale to reduce complexity, resizing images to a uniform size to fit your neural network, and data augmentation.
- Features are unique properties in the image that are used to classify its objects. Traditional ML algorithms use several feature-extraction methods.

Deep learning
and neural networks

This chapter covers

- Understanding perceptrons and multilayer perceptrons

- Working with the different types of activation functions

- Training networks with feedforward, error functions, and error optimization

- Performing backpropagation

In the last chapter, we discussed the computer vision (CV) pipeline components: the input image, preprocessing, extracting features, and the learning algorithm (classifier). We also discussed that in traditional ML algorithms, we manually extract features that produce a vector of features to be classified by the learning algorithm, whereas in deep learning (DL), neural networks act as both the feature extractor and the classifier. A neural network automatically recognizes patterns and extracts features from the image and classifies them into labels (figure 2.1).

In this chapter, we will take a short pause from the CV context to open the DL algorithm box from figure 2.1. We will dive deeper into how neural networks learn features and make predictions. Then, in the next chapter, we will come

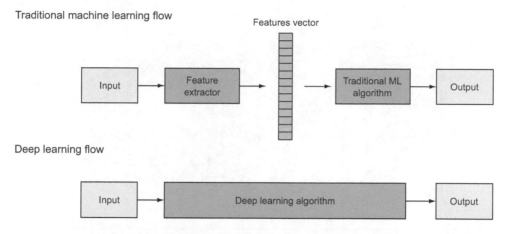

Figure 2.1 Traditional ML algorithms require manual feature extraction. A deep neural network automatically extracts features by passing the input image through its layers.

back to CV applications with one of the most popular DL architectures: convolutional neural networks.

The high-level layout of this chapter is as follows:

- We will begin with the most basic component of the neural network: the *perceptron*, a neural network that contains only one neuron.
- Then we will move on to a more complex neural network architecture that contains hundreds of neurons to solve more complex problems. This network is called a *multilayer perceptron* (MLP), where neurons are stacked in *hidden layers*. Here, you will learn the main components of the neural network architecture: the input layer, hidden layers, weight connections, and output layer.
- You will learn that the network training process consists of three main steps:
  1 Feedforward operation
  2 Calculating the error
  3 Error optimization: using backpropagation and gradient descent to select the most optimum parameters that minimize the error function

We will dive deep into each of these steps. You will see that building a neural network requires making necessary design decisions: choosing an optimizer, cost function, and activation functions, as well as designing the architecture of the network, including how many layers should be connected to each other and how many neurons should be in each layer. Ready? Let's get started!

2.1 *Understanding perceptrons*

Let's take a look at the artificial neural network (ANN) diagram from chapter 1 (figure 2.2). You can see that ANNs consist of many neurons that are structured in layers to perform some kind of calculations and predict an output. This architecture can be

Artificial neural network (ANN)

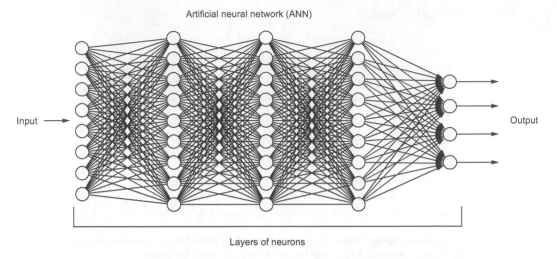

Input →

Output

Layers of neurons

Figure 2.2   An artificial neural network consists of layers of nodes, or neurons connected with edges.

also called a *multilayer perceptron*, which is more intuitive because it implies that the network consists of perceptrons structured in multiple layers. Both terms, MLP and ANN, are used interchangeably to describe this neural network architecture.

In the MLP diagram in figure 2.2, each node is called a *neuron*. We will discuss how MLP networks work soon, but first let's zoom in on the most basic component of the neural network: the perceptron. Once you understand how a single perceptron works, it will become more intuitive to understand how multiple perceptrons work together to learn data features.

2.1.1   *What is a perceptron?*

The most simple neural network is the perceptron, which consists of a single neuron. Conceptually, the perceptron functions in a manner similar to a biological neuron (figure 2.3). A biological neuron receives electrical signals from its *dendrites*, modulates the electrical signals in various amounts, and then fires an output signal through its *synapses* only when the total strength of the input signals exceeds a certain threshold. The output is then fed to another neuron, and so forth.

To model the biological neuron phenomenon, the artificial neuron performs two consecutive functions: it calculates the *weighted sum* of the inputs to represent the total strength of the input signals, and it applies a *step function* to the result to determine whether to fire the output 1 if the signal exceeds a certain threshold or 0 if the signal doesn't exceed the threshold.

As we discussed in chapter 1, not all input features are equally useful or important. To represent that, each input node is assigned a weight value, called its *connection weight*, to reflect its importance.

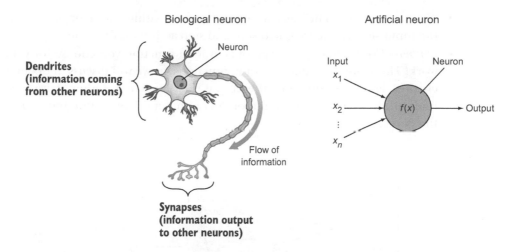

Figure 2.3 Artificial neurons were inspired by biological neurons. Different neurons are connected to each other by synapses that carry information.

Connection weights

Not all input features are equally important (or useful) features. Each input feature (x_1) is assigned its own weight (w_1) that reflects its importance in the decision-making process. Inputs assigned greater weight have a greater effect on the output. If the weight is high, it amplifies the input signal; and if the weight is low, it diminishes the input signal. In common representations of neural networks, the weights are represented by lines or edges from the input node to the perceptron.

For example, if you are predicting a house price based on a set of features like size, neighborhood, and number of rooms, there are three input features (x_1, x_2, and x_3). Each of these inputs will have a different weight value that represents its effect on the final decision. For example, if the size of the house has double the effect on the price compared with the neighborhood, and the neighborhood has double the effect compared with the number of rooms, you will see weights something like 8, 4, and 2, respectively.

How the connection values are assigned and how the learning happens is the core of the neural network training process. This is what we will discuss for the rest of this chapter.

In the perceptron diagram in figure 2.4, you can see the following:

- *Input vector*—The feature vector that is fed to the neuron. It is usually denoted with an uppercase X to represent a vector of inputs (x_1, x_2, . . ., x_n).
- *Weights vector*—Each x_1 is assigned a weight value w_1 that represents its importance to distinguish between different input datapoints.

- *Neuron functions*—The calculations performed within the neuron to modulate the input signals: the weighted sum and step activation function.
- *Output*—Controlled by the type of activation function you choose for your network. There are different activation functions, as we will discuss in detail in this chapter. For a step function, the output is either 0 or 1. Other activation functions produce probability output or float numbers. The output node represents the perceptron prediction.

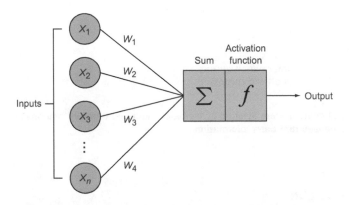

Figure 2.4 Input vectors are fed to the neuron, with weights assigned to represent importance. Calculations performed within the neuron are weighted sum and activation functions.

Let's take a deeper look at the weighted sum and step function calculations that happen inside the neuron.

WEIGHTED SUM FUNCTION

Also known as a *linear combination*, the weighted sum function is the sum of all inputs multiplied by their weights, and then added to a bias term. This function produces a straight line represented in the following equation:

$$z = \sum x_i \cdot w_i + b \text{ (bias)}$$

$$z = x_1 \cdot w_1 + x_2 \cdot w_2 + x_3 \cdot w_3 + \cdots + x_n \cdot w_n + b$$

Here is how we implement the weighted sum in Python:

```
z = np.dot(w.T,X) + b
```
◁— **X is the input vector (uppercase X), w is the weights vector, and b is the y-intercept.**

What is a bias in the perceptron, and why do we add it?

Let's brush up our memory on some linear algebra concepts to help understand what's happening under the hood. Here is the function of the straight line:

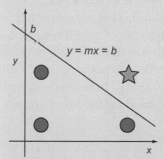

The equation of a straight line

The function of a straight line is represented by the equation ($y = mx + b$), where b is the y-intercept. To be able to define a line, you need two things: the slope of the line and a point on the line. The bias is that point on the y-axis. Bias allows you to move the line up and down on the y-axis to better fit the prediction with the data. Without the bias (b), the line always has to go through the origin point (0,0), and you will get a poorer fit. To visualize the importance of bias, look at the graph in the above figure and try to separate the circles from the star using a line that passes through the origin (0,0). It is not possible.

The input layer can be given biases by introducing an extra input node that always has a value of 1, as you can see in the next figure. In neural networks, the value of the bias (b) is treated as an extra weight and is learned and adjusted by the neuron to minimize the cost function, as we will learn in the following sections of this chapter.

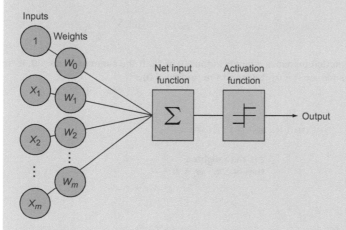

The input layer can be given biases by introducing an extra input that always has a value of 1.

STEP ACTIVATION FUNCTION

In both artificial and biological neural networks, a neuron does not just output the bare input it receives. Instead, there is one more step, called an *activation function*; this is the decision-making unit of the brain. In ANNs, the activation function takes the same weighted sum input from before ($z = \Sigma x_i \cdot w_i + b$) and activates (fires) the neuron if the weighted sum is higher than a certain threshold. This activation happens based on the activation function calculations. Later in this chapter, we'll review the different types of activation functions and their general purpose in the broader context of neural networks. The simplest activation function used by the perceptron algorithm is the step function that produces a binary output (0 or 1). It basically says that if the summed input ≥ 0, it "fires" (output = 1); else (summed input < 0), it doesn't fire (output = 0) (figure 2.5).

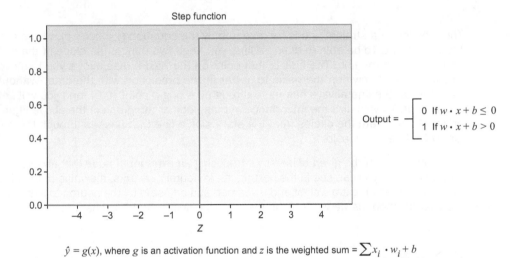

$\hat{y} = g(x)$, where g is an activation function and z is the weighted sum $= \sum x_i \cdot w_i + b$

Figure 2.5 **The step function produces a binary output (0 or 1). If the summed input $\geq$ 0, it "fires" (output = 1); else (summed input < 0) it doesn't fire (output = 0).**

This is how the step function looks in Python:

```python
def step_function(z):
    if z <= 0:
        return 0
    else:
        return 1
```

z is the weighted sum = $\Sigma x_i \cdot w_i + b$

2.1.2 How does the perceptron learn?

The perceptron uses trial and error to learn from its mistakes. It uses the weights as knobs by tuning their values up and down until the network is trained (figure 2.6).

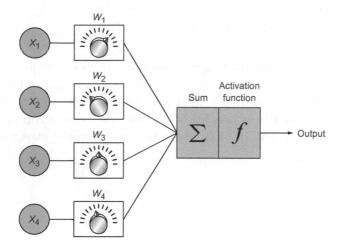

Figure 2.6 **Weights are tuned up and down during the learning process to optimize the value of the loss function.**

The perceptron's learning logic goes like this:

1 The neuron calculates the weighted sum and applies the activation function to make a prediction $\hat{y}$. This is called the feedforward process:

$$\hat{y} = \text{activation}\left(\sum x_i \cdot w_i + b\right)$$

2 It compares the output prediction with the correct label to calculate the error:

$$\text{error} = y - \hat{y}$$

3 It then updates the weight. If the prediction is too high, it adjusts the weight to make a lower prediction the next time, and vice versa.

4 Repeat!

This process is repeated many times, and the neuron continues to update the weights to improve its predictions until step 2 produces a very small error (close to zero), which means the neuron's prediction is very close to the correct value. At this point, we can stop the training and save the weight values that yielded the best results to apply to future cases where the outcome is unknown.

2.1.3 Is one neuron enough to solve complex problems?

The short answer is no, but let's see why. The perceptron is a linear function. This means the trained neuron will produce a straight line that separates our data.

Suppose we want to train a perceptron to predict whether a player will be accepted into the college squad. We collect all the data from previous years and train the perceptron to predict whether players will be accepted based on only two features (height and weight). The trained perceptron will find the best weights and bias values to produce the *straight line* that best separates the accepted from non-accepted (best fit). The line has this equation:

$$z = \text{height} \cdot w_1 + \text{age} \cdot w_2 + b$$

After the training is complete on the training data, we can start using the perceptron to predict with new players. When we get a player who is 150 cm in height and 12 years old, we compute the previous equation with the values (150, 12). When plotted in a graph (figure 2.7), you can see that it falls below the line: the neuron is predicting that this player will not be accepted. If it falls above the line, then the player will be accepted.

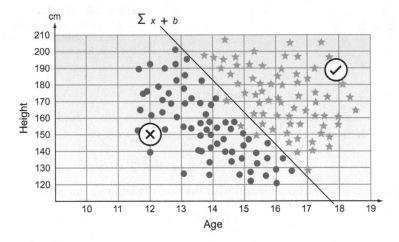

Figure 2.7   Linearly separable data can be separated by a straight line.

In figure 2.7, the single perceptron works fine because our data was *linearly separable*. This means the training data can be separated by a straight line. But life isn't always that simple. What happens when we have a more complex dataset that cannot be separated by a straight line (*nonlinear dataset*)?

As you can see in figure 2.8, a single straight line will not separate our training data. We say that it does not *fit* our data. We need a more complex network for more complex data like this. What if we built a network with two perceptrons? This would produce two lines. Would that help us separate the data better?

Okay, this is definitely better than the straight line. But, I still see some color mispredictions. Can we add more neurons to make the function fit better? Now you are getting it. Conceptually, the more neurons we add, the better the network will fit our

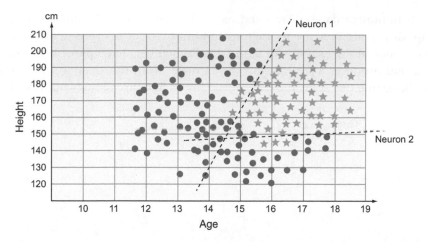

Figure 2.8   In a nonlinear dataset, a single straight line cannot separate the training data. A network with two perceptrons can produce two lines and help separate the data further in this example.

training data. In fact, if we add too many neurons, this will make the network *overfit* the training data (not good). But we will talk about this later. The general rule here is that the more complex our network is, the better it learns the features of our data.

2.2   *Multilayer perceptrons*

We saw that a single perceptron works great with simple datasets that can be separated by a line. But, as you can imagine, the real world is much more complex than that. This is where neural networks can show their full potential.

Linear vs. nonlinear problems
- *Linear datasets*—The data can be split with a single straight line.
- *Nonlinear datasets*—The data cannot be split with a single straight line. We need more than one line to form a shape that splits the data.

Look at this 2D data. In the linear problem, the stars and dots can be easily classified by drawing a single straight line. In nonlinear data, a single line will not separate both shapes.

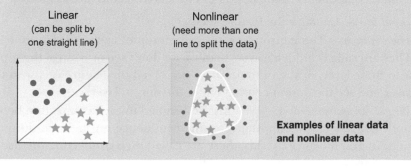

Examples of linear data and nonlinear data

To split a nonlinear dataset, we need more than one line. This means we need to come up with an architecture to use tens and hundreds of neurons in our neural network. Let's look at the example in figure 2.9. Remember that a perceptron is a linear function that produces a straight line. So in order to fit this data, we try to create a triangle-like shape that splits the dark dots. It looks like three lines would do the job.

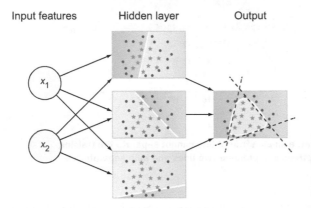

Figure 2.9   A perceptron is a linear function that produces a straight line. So to fit this data, we need three perceptrons to create a triangle-like shape that splits the dark dots.

Figure 2.9 is an example of a small neural network that is used to model nonlinear data. In this network, we used three neurons stacked together in one layer called a *hidden layer*, so called because we don't see the output of these layers during the training process.

2.2.1 *Multilayer perceptron architecture*

We've seen how a neural network can be designed to have more than one neuron. Let's expand on this idea with a more complex dataset. The diagram in figure 2.10 is from the Tensorflow playground website (https://playground.tensorflow.org). We try to model a spiral dataset to distinguish between two classes. In order to fit this dataset, we need to build a neural network that contains tens of neurons. A very common neural network architecture is to stack the neurons in layers on top of each other, called *hidden layers*. Each layer has *n* number of neurons. Layers are connected to each other by weight connections. This leads to the multilayer perceptron (MLP) architecture in the figure.

The main components of the neural network architecture are as follows:

- *Input layer*—Contains the feature vector.
- *Hidden layers*—The neurons are stacked on top of each other in hidden layers. They are called "hidden" layers because we don't see or control the input going into these layers or the output. All we do is feed the feature vector to the input layer and see the output coming out of the output layer.
- *Weight connections (edges)*—Weights are assigned to each connection between the nodes to reflect the importance of their influence on the final output prediction. In graph network terms, these are called *edges* connecting the *nodes*.

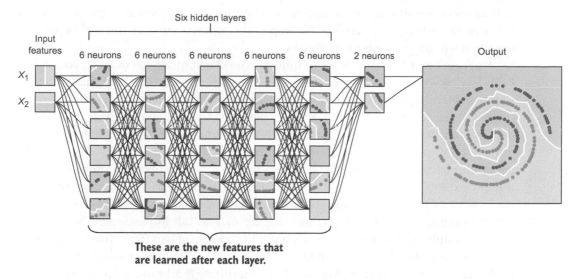

Figure 2.10 Tensorflow playground example representation of the feature learning in a deep neural network

- *Output layer*—We get the answer or prediction from our model from the output layer. Depending on the setup of the neural network, the final output may be a real-valued output (regression problem) or a set of probabilities (classification problem). This is determined by the type of activation function we use in the neurons in the output layer. We'll discuss the different types of activation functions in the next section.

We discussed the input layer, weights, and output layer. The next area of this architecture is the hidden layers.

2.2.2 What are hidden layers?

This is where the core of the feature-learning process takes place. When you look at the hidden layer nodes in figure 2.10, you see that the early layers detect simple patterns to learn low-level features (straight lines). Later layers detect patterns within patterns to learn more complex features and shapes, then patterns within patterns within patterns, and so on. This concept will come in handy when we discuss convolutional networks in later chapters. For now, know that, in neural networks, we stack hidden layers to learn complex features from each other until we fit our data. So when you are designing your neural network, if your network is not fitting the data, the solution could be adding more hidden layers.

2.2.3 How many layers, and how many nodes in each layer?

As a machine learning engineer, you will mostly be designing your network and tuning its hyperparameters. While there is no single prescribed recipe that fits all models, we will try throughout this book to build your hyperparameter tuning intuition, as well as recommend some starting points. The number of layers and the number of neurons in each layer are among the important hyperparameters you will be designing when working with neural networks.

A network can have one or more hidden layers (technically, as many as you want). Each layer has one or more neurons (again, as many as you want). Your main job, as a machine learning engineer, is to design these layers. Usually, when we have two or more hidden layers, we call this a *deep neural network*. The general rule is this: the deeper your network is, the more it will fit the training data. But too much depth is not a good thing, because the network can fit the training data so much that it fails to generalize when you show it new data (overfitting); also, it becomes more computationally expensive. So your job is to build a network that is not too simple (one neuron) and not too complex for your data. It is recommended that you read about different neural network architectures that are successfully implemented by others to build an intuition about what is too simple for your problem. Start from that point, maybe three to five layers (if you are training on a CPU), and observe the network performance. If it is performing poorly (underfitting), add more layers. If you see signs of overfitting (discussed later), then decrease the number of layers. To build a sense of how neural networks perform when you add more layers, play around with the Tensorflow playground (https://playground.tensorflow.org).

Fully connected layers

It is important to call out that the layers in classical MLP network architectures are fully connected to the next hidden layer. In the following figure, notice that each node in a layer is connected to all nodes in the previous layer. This is called a *fully connected network*. These edges are the weights that represent the importance of this node to the output value.

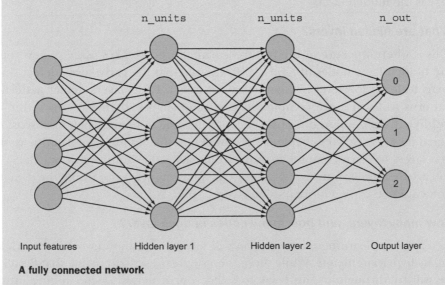

A fully connected network

In later chapters, we will discuss other variations of neural network architecture (like convolutional and recurrent networks). For now, know that this is the most basic neural network architecture, and it can be referred to by any of these names: ANN, MLP, fully connected network, or feedforward network.

Let's do a quick exercise to find out how many edges we have in our example. Suppose that we designed an MLP network with two hidden layers, and each has five neurons:

- `Weights_0_1`: (4 nodes in the input layer) × (5 nodes in layer 1) + 5 biases [1 bias per neuron] = 25 edges
- `Weights_1_2`: 5 × 5 nodes + 5 biases = 30 edges
- `Weights_2_output`: 5 × 3 nodes + 3 bias = 18 edges
- Total edges (weights) in this network = 73

We have a total of 73 weights in this very simple network. The values of these weights are randomly initialized, and then the network performs feedforward and backpropagation to learn the best values of weights that most fit our model to the training data.

To see the number of weights in this network, try to build this simple network in Keras as follows:

```
model = Sequential([
    Dense(5, input_dim=4),
    Dense(5),
    Dense(3)
])
```

And print the model summary:

```
model.summary()
```

The output will be as follows:

```
Layer (type)              Output Shape           Param #
=================================================================
dense (Dense)             (None, 5)              25

dense_1 (Dense)           (None, 5)              30

dense_2 (Dense)           (None, 3)              18
=================================================================
Total params: 73
Trainable params: 73
Non-trainable params: 0
```

2.2.4   *Some takeaways from this section*

Let's recap what we've discussed so far:

- We talked about the analogy between biological and artificial neurons: both have inputs and a neuron that does some calculations to modulate the input signals and create output.
- We zoomed in on the artificial neuron's calculations to explore its two main functions: weighted sum and the activation function.
- We saw that the network assigns random weights to all the edges. These weight parameters reflect the usefulness (or importance) of these features on the output prediction.
- Finally, we saw that perceptrons contain a single neuron. They are linear functions that produce a straight line to split linear data. In order to split more complex data (nonlinear), we need to apply more than one neuron in our network to form a multilayer perceptron.
- The MLP architecture contains input features, connection weights, hidden layers, and an output layer.
- We discussed the high-level process of how the perceptron learns. The learning process is a repetition of three main steps: feedforward calculations to produce a prediction (weighted sum and activation), calculating the error, and backpropagating the error and updating the weights to minimize the error.

We should also keep in mind some of the important points about neural network hyperparameters:

- *Number of hidden layers*—You can have as many layers as you want, each with as many neurons as you want. The general idea is that the more neurons you have, the better your network will learn the training data. But if you have too many neurons, this might lead to a phenomenon called *overfitting*: the network learned the training set so much that it memorized it instead of learning its features. Thus, it will fail to generalize. To get the appropriate number of layers, start with a small network, and observe the network performance. Then start adding layers until you get satisfying results.
- *Activation function*—There are many types of activation functions, the most popular being ReLU and softmax. It is recommended that you use ReLU activation in the hidden layers and Softmax for the output layer (you will see how this is implemented in most projects in this book).
- *Error function*—Measures how far the network's prediction is from the true label. Mean square error is common for regression problems, and cross-entropy is common for classification problems.
- *Optimizer*—Optimization algorithms are used to find the optimum weight values that minimize the error. There are several optimizer types to choose from. In this chapter, we discuss batch gradient descent, stochastic gradient descent, and

mini-batch gradient descent. Adam and RMSprop are two other popular optimizers that we don't discuss.

- *Batch size*—Mini-batch size is the number of sub-samples given to the network, after which parameter update happens. Bigger batch sizes learn faster but require more memory space. A good default for batch size might be 32. Also try 64, 128, 256, and so on.
- *Number of epochs*—The number of times the entire training dataset is shown to the network while training. Increase the number of epochs until the validation accuracy starts decreasing even when training accuracy is increasing (overfitting).
- *Learning rate*—One of the optimizer's input parameters that we tune. Theoretically, a learning rate that is too small is guaranteed to reach the minimum error (if you train for infinity time). A learning rate that is too big speeds up the learning but is not guaranteed to find the minimum error. The default `lr` value of the optimizer in most DL libraries is a reasonable start to get decent results. From there, go down or up by one order of magnitude. We will discuss the learning rate in detail in chapter 4.

More on hyperparameters

Other hyperparameters that we have not discussed yet include dropout and regularization. We will discuss hyperparameter tuning in detail in chapter 4, after we cover convolutional neural networks in chapter 3.

In general, the best way to tune hyperparameters is by trial and error. By getting your hands dirty with your own projects as well as learning from other existing neural network architectures, you will start to develop intuition about good starting points for your hyperparameters.

Learn to analyze your network's performance and understand which hyperparameter you need to tune for each symptom. And this is what we are going to do in this book. By understanding the reasoning behind these hyperparameters and observing the network performance in the projects at the end of the chapters, you will develop a feel for which hyperparameter to tune for a particular effect. For example, if you see that your error value is not decreasing and keeps oscillating, then you might fix that by reducing the learning rate. Or, if you see that the network is performing poorly in learning the training data, this might mean that the network is underfitting and you need to build a more complex model by adding more neurons and hidden layers.

2.3 Activation functions

When you are building your neural network, one of the design decisions that you will need to make is what activation function to use for your neurons' calculations. Activation functions are also referred to as *transfer functions* or *nonlinearities* because they transform the linear combination of a weighted sum into a nonlinear model. An activation function is placed at the end of each perceptron to decide whether to activate this neuron.

Why use activation functions at all? Why not just calculate the weighted sum of our network and propagate that through the hidden layers to produce an output?

The purpose of the activation function is to introduce nonlinearity into the network. Without it, a multilayer perceptron will perform similarly to a single perceptron no matter how many layers we add. Activation functions are needed to restrict the output value to a certain finite value. Let's revisit the example of predicting whether a player gets accepted (figure 2.11).

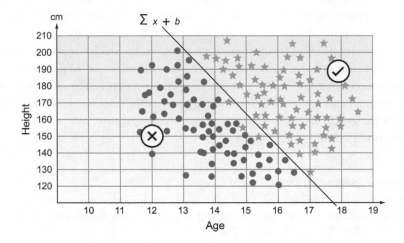

Figure 2.11   This example revisits the prediction of whether a player gets accepted from section 2.1.

First, the model calculates the weighted sum and produces the linear function (z):

$$z = \text{height} \cdot w_1 + \text{age} \cdot w_2 + b$$

The output of this function has no bound. z could literally be any number. We use an activation function to wrap the prediction values to a finite value. In this example, we use a step function where if $z > 0$, then above the line (accepted) and if $z < 0$, then below the line (rejected). So without the activation function, we just have a linear function that produces a number, but no decision is made in this perceptron. The activation function is what decides whether to fire this perceptron.

There are infinite activation functions. In fact, the last few years have seen a lot of progress in the creation of state-of-the-art activations. However, there are still relatively few activations that account for the vast majority of activation needs. Let's dive deeper into some of the most common types of activation functions.

2.3.1 Linear transfer function

A *linear transfer function*, also called an *identity function*, indicates that the function passes a signal through unchanged. In practical terms, the output will be equal to the input, which means we don't actually have an activation function. So no matter how many layers our neural network has, all it is doing is computing a linear activation function or, at most, scaling the weighted average coming in. But it doesn't transform input into a nonlinear function.

$$\text{activation}(z) = z = wx + b$$

The composition of two linear functions is a linear function, so unless you throw a nonlinear activation function in your neural network, you are not computing any interesting functions no matter how deep you make your network. No learning here!

To understand why, let's calculate the derivative of the activation $z(x) = w \cdot x + b$, where $w = 4$ and $b = 0$. When we plot this function, it looks like figure 2.12. Then the derivative of $z(x) = 4x$ is $z'(x) = 4$ (figure 2.13).

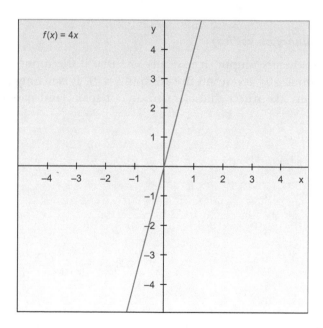

Figure 2.12 The plot for the activation function $f(x) = 4x$

The derivative of a linear function is constant: it does not depend on the input value x. This means that every time we do a backpropagation, the gradient will be the same. And this is a big problem: we are not really improving the error, since the gradient is pretty much the same. This will be clearer when we discuss backpropagation later in this chapter.

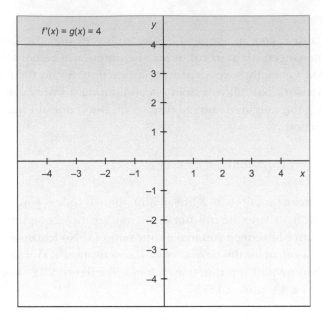

Figure 2.13   The plot for the derivative of $z(x) = 4x$ is $z'(x) = 4$.

2.3.2   *Heaviside step function (binary classifier)*

The *step function* produces a binary output. It basically says that if the input $x > 0$, it fires (output $y = 1$); else (input < 0), it doesn't fire (output $y = 0$). It is mainly used in binary classification problems like true or false, spam or not spam, and pass or fail (figure 2.14).

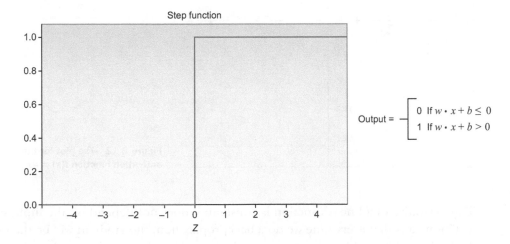

Figure 2.14   Step functions are commonly used in binary classification problems because they transform the input into zero or one.

2.3.3 *Sigmoid/logistic function*

This is one of the most common activation functions. It is often used in binary classifiers to predict the *probability* of a class when you have two classes. The sigmoid squishes all the values to a probability between 0 and 1, which reduces extreme values or outliers in the data without removing them. Sigmoid or logistic functions convert infinite continuous variables (range between $-\infty$ to $+\infty$) into simple probabilities between 0 and 1. It is also called the *S-shape curve* because when plotted in a graph, it produces an S-shaped curve. While the step function is used to produce a discrete answer (pass or fail), sigmoid is used to produce the probability of passing and probability of failing (figure 2.15):

$$\sigma(z) = \frac{1}{1 + e^{-z}}$$

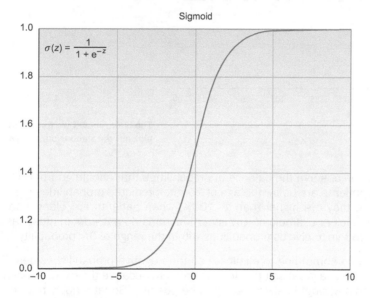

Figure 2.15 **While the step function is used to produce a discrete answer (pass or fail), sigmoid is used to produce the probability of passing or failing.**

Here is how sigmoid is implemented in Python:

```
import numpy as np          ⊲⎯ Imports numpy

def sigmoid(x):             ⊲⎯ Sigmoid activation
    return 1 / (1 + np.exp(-x))    function
```

Just-in-time linear algebra (optional)

Let's take a deeper dive into the math side of the sigmoid function to understand the problem it helps solve and how the sigmoid function equation is driven. Suppose that we are trying to predict whether patients have diabetes based on only one feature: their age. When we plot the data we have about our patients, we get the linear model shown in the figure:

$$z = \beta_0 + \beta_1 \, age$$

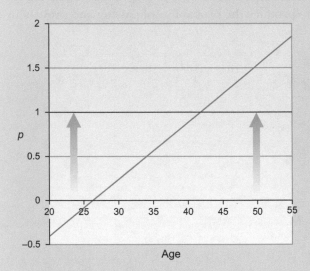

The linear model we get when we plot our data about our patients

In this plot, you can observe the balance of probabilities that should go from 0 to 1. Note that when patients are below the age of 25, the predicted probabilities are negative; meanwhile, they are higher than 1 (100%) when patients are older than 43 years old. This is a clear example of why linear functions do not work in most cases. Now, how do we fix this to give us probabilities within the range of 0 < probability < 1?

First, we need to do something to eliminate all the negative probability values. The exponential function is a great solution for this problem because the exponent of any-thing (and I mean *anything*) is always going to be positive. So let's apply that to our linear equation to calculate the probability (*p*):

$$p = \exp(z) = \exp(\beta_0 + \beta_1 \, age)$$

This equation ensures that we always get probabilities greater than 0. Now, what about the values that are higher than 1? We need to do something about them. With proportions, any given number divided by a number that is greater than it will give us a number smaller than 1. Let's do exactly that to the previous equation. We divide the equation by its value plus a small value: either 1 or a (in some cases very small) value—let's call it epsilon (ε):

$$p = \frac{\exp(z)}{\exp(z) + \varepsilon}$$

If you divide the equation by exp(z), you get

$$p = \frac{1}{1 + \exp(-z)}$$

When we plot the probability of this equation, we get the S shape of the sigmoid function, where probability is no longer below 0 or above 1. In fact, as patients' ages grow, the probability asymptotically gets closer to 1; and as the weights move down, the function asymptotically gets closer to 0 but is never outside the 0 < p < 1 range. This is the plot of the sigmoid function and logistic regression.

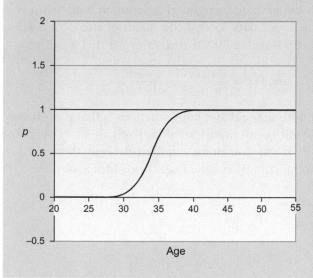

As patients get older, the probability asymptotically gets closer to 1. This is the plot of the sigmoid function and logistic regression.

2.3.4 Softmax function

The softmax function is a generalization of the sigmoid function. It is used to obtain classification probabilities when we have more than two classes. It forces the outputs of a neural network to sum to 1 (for example, 0 < output < 1). A very common use case in deep learning problems is to predict a single class out of many options (more than two).

The softmax equation is as follows:

$$\sigma(x_j) = \frac{e^{x_j}}{\sum_i e^{x_i}}$$

Figure 2.16 shows an example of the softmax function.

Figure 2.16   The softmax function transforms the input values to probability values between 0 and 1.

TIP Softmax is the go-to function that you will often use at the output layer of a classifier when you are working on a problem where you need to predict a class between more than two classes. Softmax works fine if you are classifying two classes, as well. It will basically work like a sigmoid function. By the end of this section, I'll tell you my recommendations about when to use each activation function.

2.3.5 *Hyperbolic tangent function (tanh)*

The hyperbolic tangent function is a shifted version of the sigmoid version. Instead of squeezing the signal values between 0 and 1, tanh squishes all values to the range –1 to 1. Tanh almost always works better than the sigmoid function in hidden layers because it has the effect of centering your data so that the mean of the data is close to zero rather than 0.5, which makes learning for the next layer a little bit easier:

$$\tanh(x) = \frac{\sinh(x)}{\cosh(x)} = \frac{e^x - e^{-x}}{e^x + e^{-x}}$$

One of the downsides of both sigmoid and tanh functions is that if (z) is very large or very small, then the gradient (or derivative or slope) of this function becomes very small (close to zero), which will slow down gradient descent (figure 2.17). This is when the ReLU activation function (explained next) provides a solution.

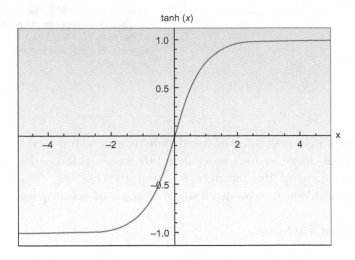

Figure 2.17   If (z) is very large or very small, then the gradient (or derivative or slope) of this function becomes very small (close to zero).

2.3.6 *Rectified linear unit*

The rectified linear unit (ReLU) activation function activates a node only if the input is above zero. If the input is below zero, the output is always zero. But when the input is higher than zero, it has a linear relationship with the output variable. The ReLU function is represented as follows:

$$f(x) = \max(0, x)$$

At the time of writing, ReLU is considered the state-of-the-art activation function because it works well in many different situations, and it tends to train better than sigmoid and tanh in hidden layers (figure 2.18).

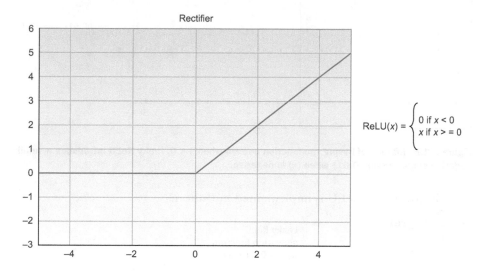

Figure 2.18   The ReLU function eliminates all negative values of the input by transforming them into zeros.

Here is how ReLU is implemented in Python:

```
def relu(x):          ◁─┐  ReLU activation
    if x < 0:           │  function
        return 0
    else:
return x
```

2.3.7   *Leaky ReLU*

One disadvantage of ReLU activation is that the derivative is equal to zero when (x) is negative. Leaky ReLU is a ReLU variation that tries to mitigate this issue. Instead of having the function be zero when $x < 0$, leaky ReLU introduces a small negative slope (around 0.01) when (x) is negative. It usually works better than the ReLU function, although it's not used as much in practice. Take a look at the leaky ReLU graph in figure 2.19; can you see the leak?

$$f(x) = \max(0.01x, \, x)$$

Why 0.01? Some people like to use this as another hyperparameter to tune, but that would be overkill, since you already have other, bigger problems to worry about. Feel free to try different values (0.1, 0.01, 0.002) in your model and see how they work.

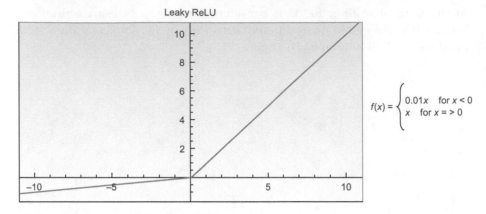

Figure 2.19   Instead of having the function be zero when x < 0, leaky ReLU introduces a small negative slope (around 0.01) when (x) is negative.

Here is how Leaky ReLU is implemented in Python:

```
def leaky_relu(x):
    if x < 0:
        return x * 0.01
    else:
return x
```

← **Leaky ReLU activation function with a 0.01 leak**

Table 2.1 summarizes the various activation functions we've discussed in this section.

Table 2.1   A cheat sheet of the most common activation functions

Activation function	Description	Plot	Equation
Linear transfer function (identity function)	The signal passes through it unchanged. It remains a linear function. Almost never used.		$f(x) = x$
Heaviside step function (binary classifier)	Produces a binary output of 0 or 1. Mainly used in binary classification to give a discrete value.		$\text{output} = \begin{cases} 0 \text{ if } w \cdot x + b \leq 0 \\ 1 \text{ if } w \cdot x + b > 0 \end{cases}$

Table 2.1 A cheat sheet of the most common activation functions

Activation function	Description	Plot	Equation
Sigmoid/ logistic function	Squishes all the values to a probability between 0 and 1, which reduces extreme values or outliers in the data. Usually used to classify two classes.		$\sigma(z) = \dfrac{1}{1 + e^{-z}}$
Softmax function	A generalization of the sigmoid function. Used to obtain classification probabilities when we have more than two classes.		$\sigma(x_j) = \dfrac{e^{x_j}}{\sum_i e^{x_i}}$
Hyperbolic tangent function (tanh)	Squishes all values to the range of –1 to 1. Tanh almost always works better than the sigmoid function in hidden layers.		$\tanh(x) = \dfrac{\sinh(x)}{\cosh(x)}$ $= \dfrac{e^x - e^{-x}}{e^x + e^{-x}}$
Rectified linear unit (ReLU)	Activates a node only if the input is above zero. Always recommended for hidden layers. Better than tanh.		$f(x) = \max(0, x)$
Leaky ReLU	Instead of having the function be zero when $x < 0$, leaky ReLU introduces a small negative slope (around 0.01) when (x) is negative.		$f(x) = \max(0.01x, x)$

Hyperparameter alert

Due to the number of activation functions, it may appear to be an overwhelming task to select the appropriate activation function for your network. While it is important to select a good activation function, I promise this is not going to be a challenging task when you design your network. There are some rules of thumb that you can start with, and then you can tune the model as needed. If you are not sure what to use, here are my two cents about choosing an activation function:

- *For hidden layers*—In most cases, you can use the ReLU activation function (or leaky ReLU) in hidden layers, as you will see in the projects that we will build throughout this book. It is increasingly becoming the default choice because it is a bit faster to compute than other activation functions. More importantly, it reduces the likelihood of the gradient vanishing because it does not saturate for large input values—as opposed to the sigmoid and tanh activation functions, which saturate at ~ 1. Remember, the gradient is the slope. When the function plateaus, this will lead to no slope; hence, the gradient starts to vanish. This makes it harder to *descend* to the minimum error (we will talk more about this phenomenon, called *vanishing/exploding gradients*, in later chapters).
- *For the output layer*—The softmax activation function is generally a good choice for most classification problems when the classes are mutually exclusive. The sigmoid function serves the same purpose when you are doing binary classification. For regression problems, you can simply use no activation function at all, since the weighted sum node produces the continuous output that you need: for example, if you want to predict house pricing based on the prices of other houses in the same neighborhood.

2.4   *The feedforward process*

Now that you understand how to stack perceptrons in layers, connect them with weights/edges, perform a weighted sum function, and apply activation functions, let's implement the complete forward-pass calculations to produce a prediction output. The process of computing the linear combination and applying the activation function is called *feedforward*. We briefly discussed feedforward several times in the previous sections; let's take a deeper look at what happens in this process.

The term *feedforward* is used to imply the forward direction in which the information flows from the input layer through the hidden layers, all the way to the output layer. This process happens through the implementation of two consecutive functions: the weighted sum and the activation function. In short, the forward pass is the calculations through the layers to make a prediction.

Let's take a look at the simple three-layer neural network in figure 2.20 and explore each of its components:

- *Layers*—This network consists of an input layer with three input features, and three hidden layers with 3, 4, 1 neurons in each layer.

- *Weights and biases (w, b)*—The edges between nodes are assigned random weights denoted as $W_{ab}^{(n)}$, where (n) indicates the layer number and (ab) indicates the weighted edge connecting the ath neuron in layer (n) to the bth neuron in the previous layer $(n-1)$. For example, $W_{23}^{(2)}$ is the weight that connects the second node in layer 2 to the third node in layer 1 (a_2^2 to a_1^3). (Note that you can see different denotations of $W_{ab}^{(n)}$ in other DL literature, which is fine as long as you follow one convention for your entire network.)

  The biases are treated similarly to weights because they are randomly initialized, and their values are learned during the training process. So, for convenience, from this point forward we are going to represent the basis with the same notation that we gave for the weights (w). In DL literature, you will mostly find all weights and biases represented as (w) for simplicity.

- *Activation functions $\sigma(x)$*—In this example, we are using the sigmoid function $\sigma(x)$ as an activation function.

- *Node values (a)*—We will calculate the weighted sum, apply the activation function, and assign this value to the node a_m^n, where n is the layer number and m is the node index in the layer. For example, a_2^3 means node number 2 in layer 3.

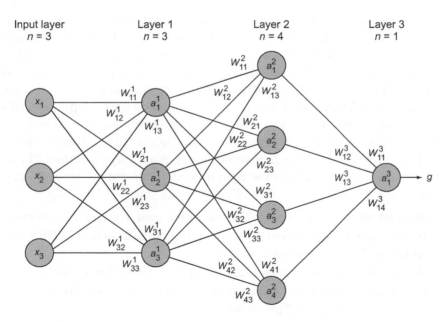

Figure 2.20   A simple three-layer neural network

2.4.1 *Feedforward calculations*

We have all we need to start the feedforward calculations:

$$a_1^{(1)} = \sigma(w_{11}^{(1)} x_1 + w_{21}^{(1)} x_2 + w_{31}^{(1)} x_3)$$

$$a_2^{(1)} = \sigma(w_{12}^{(1)} x_1 + w_{22}^{(1)} x_2 + w_{32}^{(1)} x_3)$$

$$a_3^{(1)} = \sigma(w_{13}^{(1)} x_1 + w_{23}^{(1)} x_2 + w_{33}^{(1)} x_3)$$

Then we do the same calculations for layer 2

$$a_1^{(2)}, a_2^{(2)}, a_3^{(2)}, \text{and } a_4^{(2)}$$

all the way to the output prediction in layer 3:

$$\hat{y} = a_1^{(2)} = \sigma\ (w_{11}^{(3)} a_1^{(2)} + w_{12}^{(3)} a_2^{(2)} + w_{13}^{(3)} a_3^{(2)} + w_{14}^{(3)} a_4^{(2)})$$

And there you have it! You just calculated the feedforward of a two-layer neural network. Let's take a moment to reflect on what we just did. Take a look at how many equations we need to solve for such a small network. What happens when we have a more complex problem with hundreds of nodes in the input layer and hundreds more in the hidden layers? It is more efficient to use matrices to pass through multiple inputs at once. Doing this allows for big computational speedups, especially when using tools like NumPy, where we can implement this with one line of code.

Let's see how the matrices computation looks (figure 2.21). All we did here is simply stack the inputs and weights in matrices and multiply them together. The intuitive way to read this equation is from the right to the left. Start at the far right and follow with me:

- We stack all the inputs together in one vector (row, column), in this case (3, 1).
- We multiply the input vector by the weights matrix from layer 1 ($W^{(1)}$) and then apply the sigmoid function.
- We multiply the result for layer 2 $\Rightarrow \sigma \cdot W^{(2)}$ and layer 3 $\Rightarrow \sigma \cdot W^{(3)}$.
- If we have a fourth layer, you multiply the result from step 3 by $\sigma \cdot W^{(4)}$, and so on, until we get the final prediction output $\hat{y}$!

Here is a simplified representation of this matrices formula:

$$\hat{y} = \sigma \cdot W^{(3)} \cdot \sigma \cdot W^{(2)} \cdot \sigma \cdot W^{(1)} \cdot (x)$$

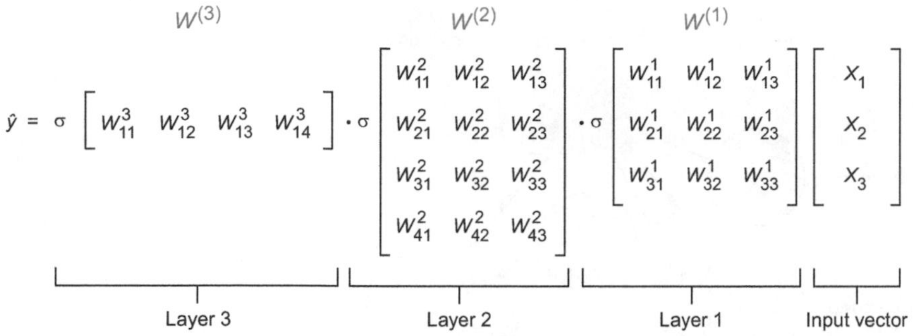

$$\hat{y} = \sigma \begin{bmatrix} w_{11}^3 & w_{12}^3 & w_{13}^3 & w_{14}^3 \end{bmatrix} \cdot \sigma \begin{bmatrix} w_{11}^2 & w_{12}^2 & w_{13}^2 \\ w_{21}^2 & w_{22}^2 & w_{23}^2 \\ w_{31}^2 & w_{32}^2 & w_{33}^2 \\ w_{41}^2 & w_{42}^2 & w_{43}^2 \end{bmatrix} \cdot \sigma \begin{bmatrix} w_{11}^1 & w_{12}^1 & w_{13}^1 \\ w_{21}^1 & w_{22}^1 & w_{23}^1 \\ w_{31}^1 & w_{32}^1 & w_{33}^1 \end{bmatrix} \begin{bmatrix} x_1 \\ x_2 \\ x_3 \end{bmatrix}$$

$W^{(3)}$ $W^{(2)}$ $W^{(1)}$

Layer 3   Layer 2   Layer 1   Input vector

Figure 2.21 **Reading from left to right, we stack the inputs together in one vector, multiply the input vector by the weights matrix from layer 1, apply the sigmoid function, and multiply the result.**

2.4.2 Feature learning

The nodes in the hidden layers (a_i) are the new features that are learned after each layer. For example, if you look at figure 2.20, you see that we have three feature inputs (x_1, x_2, and x_3). After computing the forward pass in the first layer, the network learns patterns, and these features are transformed to three new features with different values ($a_1^{(1)}, a_2^{(1)}, a_3^{(1)}$). Then, in the next layer, the network learns patterns within the patterns and produces new features ($a_1^{(2)}, a_2^{(2)}, a_3^{(2)}$, and $a_4^{(2)}$, and so forth). The produced features after each layer are not totally understood, and we don't see them, nor do we have much control over them. It is part of the neural network magic. That's why they are called *hidden* layers. What we do is this: we look at the final output prediction and keep tuning some parameters until we are satisfied by the network's performance.

To reiterate, let's see this in a small example. In figure 2.22, you see a small neural network to estimate the price of a house based on three features: how many bedrooms it has, how big it is, and which neighborhood it is in. You can see that the original input feature values 3, 2000, and 1 were transformed into new feature values after performing the feedforward process in the first layer ($a_1^{(2)}, a_2^{(2)}, a_3^{(2)}, a_4^{(2)}$). Then they were transformed again to a prediction output value ($\hat{y}$). When training a neural network, we see the prediction output and compare it with the true price to calculate the error and repeat the process until we get the minimum error.

To help visualize the feature-learning process, let's take another look at figure 2.9 (repeated here in figure 2.23) from the Tensorflow playground. You can see that the first layer learns basic features like lines and edges. The second layer begins to learn more complex features like corners. The process continues until the last layers of the network learn even more complex feature shapes like circles and spirals that fit the dataset.

Input
features

Hidden layer

Output
prediction ($\hat{y}$)

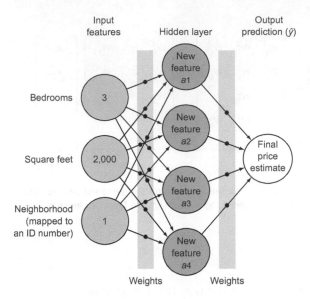

Bedrooms

Square feet

Neighborhood
(mapped to
an ID number)

Weights   Weights

**Figure 2.22   A small neural network
to estimate the price of a house
based on three features: how many
bedrooms it has, how big it is, and
which neighborhood it is in**

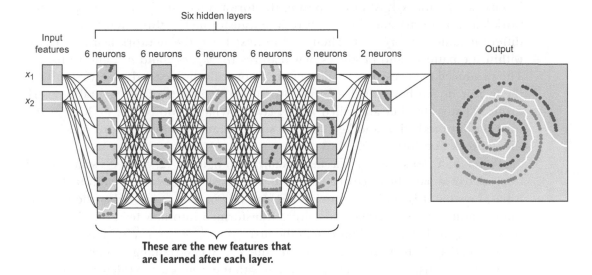

**These are the new features that
are learned after each layer.**

Figure 2.23   Learning features in multiple hidden layers

That is how a neural network learns new features: via the network's hidden layers.
First, they recognize patterns in the data. Then, they recognize patterns within patterns;
then patterns within patterns within patterns, and so on. The deeper the network is,
the more it learns about the training data.

Vectors and matrices refresher

If you understood the matrix calculations we just did in the feedforward discussion, feel free to skip this sidebar. If you are still not convinced, hang tight: this sidebar is for you.

The feedforward calculations are a set of matrix multiplications. While you will not do these calculations by hand, because there are a lot of great DL libraries that do them for you with just one line of code, it is valuable to understand the mathematics that happens under the hood so you can debug your network. Especially because this is very trivial and interesting, let's quickly review matrix calculations.

Let's start with some basic definitions of matrix dimensions:

- A *scalar* is a single number.
- A *vector* is an array of numbers.
- A *matrix* is a 2D array.
- A *tensor* is an n-dimensional array with $n > 2$.

Scalar   Vector   Matrix   Tensor

$$1 \qquad \begin{bmatrix} 1 \\ 2 \end{bmatrix} \qquad \begin{bmatrix} 1 & 2 \\ 3 & 4 \end{bmatrix} \qquad \begin{bmatrix} [1\ 2] & [3\ 2] \\ [1\ 7] & [5\ 4] \end{bmatrix}$$

Matrix dimensions: a scalar is a single number, a vector is an array of numbers, a matrix is a 2D array, and a tensor is an n-dimensional array.

We will follow the conventions used in most mathematical literature:

- Scalars are written in lowercase and italics: for instance, n.
- Vectors are written in lowercase, italics, and bold type: for instance, $\boldsymbol{x}$.
- Matrices are written in uppercase, italics, and bold: for instance, $\boldsymbol{X}$.
- Matrix dimensions are written as follows: (row × column).

Multiplication:

- *Scalar multiplication*—Simply multiply the scalar number by all the numbers in the matrix. Note that scalar multiplications don't change the matrix dimensions:

$$2 \cdot \begin{bmatrix} 10 & 6 \\ 4 & 3 \end{bmatrix} = \begin{bmatrix} 2 \cdot 10 & 2 \cdot 6 \\ 2 \cdot 4 & 2 \cdot 3 \end{bmatrix}$$

- *Matrix multiplication*—When multiplying two matrices, such as in the case of $(\text{row}_1 \times \text{column}_1) \times (\text{row}_2 \times \text{column}_2)$, column_1 and row_2 must be equal to each other, and the product will have the dimensions $(\text{row}_1 \times \text{column}_2)$. For example,

$$\begin{bmatrix} 3 & 4 & 2 \end{bmatrix} \cdot \begin{bmatrix} 13 & 9 & 7 \\ 8 & 7 & 4 \\ 6 & 4 & 0 \end{bmatrix} = \begin{bmatrix} x & y & z \end{bmatrix}$$

Same

$1 \times 3 \qquad 3 \times 3 \qquad\qquad 1 \times 3$

Product

where $x = 3 \cdot 13 + 4 \cdot 8 + 2 \cdot 6 = 83$, and the same for $y = 63$ and $z = 37$.

Now that you know the matrices multiplication rules, pull out a piece of paper and work through the dimensions of matrices in the earlier neural network example. The following figure shows the matrix equation again for your convenience.

$$\hat{y} = \sigma \overbrace{\begin{bmatrix} w_{11}^3 & w_{12}^3 & w_{13}^3 & w_{14}^3 \end{bmatrix}}^{W^{(3)}} \cdot \sigma \overbrace{\begin{bmatrix} w_{11}^2 & w_{12}^2 & w_{13}^2 \\ w_{21}^2 & w_{22}^2 & w_{23}^2 \\ w_{31}^2 & w_{32}^2 & w_{33}^2 \\ w_{41}^2 & w_{42}^2 & w_{43}^2 \end{bmatrix}}^{W^{(2)}} \cdot \sigma \overbrace{\begin{bmatrix} w_{11}^1 & w_{12}^1 & w_{13}^1 \\ w_{21}^1 & w_{22}^1 & w_{23}^1 \\ w_{31}^1 & w_{32}^1 & w_{33}^1 \end{bmatrix}}^{W^{(1)}} \begin{bmatrix} x_1 \\ x_2 \\ x_3 \end{bmatrix}$$

| Layer 3 | Layer 2 | Layer 1 | Input vector |

The matrix equation from the main text. Use it to work through matrix dimensions.

The last thing I want you to understand about matrices is *transposition*. With transposition, you can convert a row vector to a column vector and vice versa, where the shape $(m \times n)$ is inverted and becomes $(n \times m)$. The superscript (A^T) is used for transposed matrices:

$$A = \begin{bmatrix} 2 \\ 8 \end{bmatrix} \Rightarrow A^T = [2 \ 8]$$

$$A = \begin{bmatrix} 1 & 2 & 3 \\ 4 & 5 & 6 \\ 7 & 8 & 9 \end{bmatrix} \Rightarrow A^T = \begin{bmatrix} 1 & 4 & 7 \\ 2 & 5 & 8 \\ 3 & 6 & 9 \end{bmatrix}$$

$$A = \begin{bmatrix} 0 & 1 \\ 2 & 4 \\ 1 & -1 \end{bmatrix} \Rightarrow A^T = \begin{bmatrix} 0 & 2 & 1 \\ 1 & 4 & -1 \end{bmatrix}$$

2.5   *Error functions*

So far, you have learned how to implement the forward pass in neural networks to produce a prediction that consists of the weighted sum plus activation operations. Now, how do we evaluate the prediction that the network just produced? More importantly, how do we know how far this prediction is from the correct answer (the label)? The answer is this: measure the error. The selection of an error function is another important aspect of the design of a neural network. Error functions can also be referred to as *cost functions* or *loss functions,* and these terms are used interchangeably in DL literature.

2.5.1 What is the error function?

The *error function* is a measure of how "wrong" the neural network prediction is with respect to the expected output (the label). It quantifies how far we are from the correct solution. For example, if we have a high loss, then our model is not doing a good job. The smaller the loss, the better the job the model is doing. The larger the loss, the more our model needs to be trained to increase its accuracy.

2.5.2 Why do we need an error function?

Calculating error is an optimization problem, something all machine learning engineers love (mathematicians, too). Optimization problems focus on defining an error function and trying to optimize its parameters to get the minimum error (more on optimization in the next section). But for now, know that, in general, when we are working on an optimization problem, if we are able to define the error function for the problem, we have a very good shot at solving it by running optimization algorithms to minimize the error function.

In optimization problems, our ultimate goal is to find the optimum variables (weights) that would minimize the error function as much as we can. If we don't know how far from the target we are, how will we know what to change in the next iteration? The process of minimizing this error is called *error function optimization*. We will review several optimization methods in the next section. But for now, all we need to know from the error function is how far we are from the correct prediction, or how much we missed the desired degree of performance.

2.5.3 Error is always positive

Consider this scenario: suppose we have two data points that we are trying to get our network to predict correctly. If the first gives an error of 10 and the second gives an error of –10, then our average error is zero! This is misleading because "error = 0" means our network is producing perfect predictions, when, in fact, it missed by 10 twice. We don't want that. We want the error of each prediction to be positive, so the errors don't cancel each other when we take the average error. Think of an archer aiming at a target and missing by 1 inch. We are not really concerned about which direction they missed; all we need to know is how far each shot is from the target.

A visualization of loss functions of two separate models plotted over time is shown in figure 2.24. You can see that model #1 is doing a better job of minimizing error, whereas model #2 starts off better until epoch 6 and then plateaus.

Different loss functions will give different errors for the same prediction, and thus have a considerable effect on the performance of the model. A thorough discussion of loss functions is outside the scope of this book. Instead, we will focus on the two most commonly used loss functions: mean squared error (and its variations), usually used for regression problems, and cross-entropy, used for classification problems.

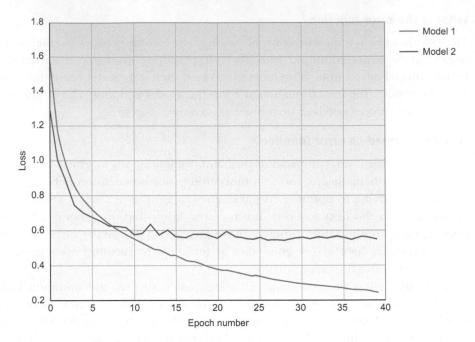

Figure 2.24   A visualization of the loss functions of two separate models plotted over time

2.5.4   *Mean square error*

Mean squared error (MSE) is commonly used in regression problems that require the output to be a real value (like house pricing). Instead of just comparing the prediction output with the label $(\hat{y}_i - y_i)$, the error is squared and averaged over the number of data points, as you see in this equation:

$$E(W, b) = \frac{1}{N}\sum_{i=1}^{N} (\hat{y}_i - y_i)^2$$

MSE is a good choice for a few reasons. The square ensures the error is always positive, and larger errors are penalized more than smaller errors. Also, it makes the math nice, which is always a plus. The notations in the formula are listed in table 2.2.

MSE is quite sensitive to outliers, since it squares the error value. This might not be an issue for the specific problem that you are solving. In fact, this sensitivity to outliers might be beneficial in some cases. For example, if you are predicting a stock price, you would want to take outliers into account, and sensitivity to outliers would be a good thing. In other scenarios, you wouldn't want to build a model that is skewed by outliers, such as predicting a house price in a city. In that case, you are more interested in the median and less in the mean. A variation error function of MSE called

Table 2.2   Meanings of notation used in regression problems

Notation	Meaning
$E(W, b)$	The loss function. Is also annotated as $J(W, b)$ in other literature.
W	Weights matrix. In some literature, the weights are denoted by the theta sign (θ).
b	Biases vector.
N	Number of training examples.
$\hat{y}_i$	Prediction output. Also notated as $h_{w, b}(X)$ in some DL literature.
y_i	The correct output (the label).
$(\hat{y}_i - y_i)$	Usually called the *residual*.

mean absolute error (MAE) was developed just for this purpose. It averages the absolute error over the entire dataset without taking the square of the error:

$$E(W, b) = \frac{1}{N}\sum_{i=1}^{N} |\hat{y}_i - y_i|$$

2.5.5   *Cross-entropy*

Cross-entropy is commonly used in classification problems because it quantifies the difference between two probability distributions. For example, suppose that for a specific training instance, we are trying to classify a dog image out of three possible classes (dogs, cats, fish). The true distribution for this training instance is as follows:

```
Probability(cat)      P(dog)          P(fish)
    0.0                1.0              0.0
```

We can interpret this "true" distribution to mean that the training instance has 0% probability of being class A, 100% probability of being class B, and 0% probability of being class C. Now, suppose our machine learning algorithm predicts the following probability distribution:

```
Probability(cat)      P(dog)          P(fish)
    0.2                0.3              0.5
```

How close is the predicted distribution to the true distribution? That is what the cross-entropy loss function determines. We can use this formula:

$$E(W, b) = -\sum_{i=1}^{m} \hat{y}_i \log(p_i)$$

where (y) is the target probability, (p) is the predicted probability, and (m) is the number of classes. The sum is over the three classes: cat, dog, and fish. In this case, the loss is 1.2:

```
E = - (0.0 * log(0.2) + 1.0 * log(0.3) + 0.0 * log(0.5)) = 1.2
```

So that is how "wrong" or "far away" our prediction is from the true distribution.

Let's do this one more time, just to show how the loss changes when the network makes better predictions. In the previous example, we showed the network an image of a dog, and it predicted that the image was 30% likely to be a dog, which was very far from the target prediction. In later iterations, the network learns some patterns and gets the predictions a little better, up to 50%:

```
Probability(cat)      P(dog)           P(fish)
     0.3               0.5               0.2
```

Then we calculate the loss again:

```
E = - (0.0*log(0.3) + 1.0*log(0.5) + 0.0*log(0.2)) = 0.69
```

You see that when the network makes a better prediction (dog is up to 50% from 30%), the loss decreases from 1.2 to 0.69. In the ideal case, when the network predicts that the image is 100% likely to be a dog, the cross-entropy loss will be 0 (feel free to try the math).

To calculate the cross-entropy error across all the training examples (n), we use this general formula:

$$E(W, b) = -\sum_{i=1}^{n}\sum_{i=1}^{m} \hat{y}_{ij} \log(p_{ij})$$

NOTE It is important to note that you will not be doing these calculations by hand. Understanding how things work under the hood gives you better intuition when you are designing your neural network. In DL projects, we usually use libraries like Tensorflow, PyTorch, and Keras where the error function is generally a parameter choice.

2.5.6   *A final note on errors and weights*

As mentioned before, in order for the neural network to learn, it needs to minimize the error function as much as possible (0 is ideal). The lower the errors, the higher the accuracy of the model in predicting values. How do we minimize the error?

Let's look at the following perceptron example with a single input to understand the relationship between the weight and the error:

Suppose the input $x = 0.3$, and its label (goal prediction) $y = 0.8$. The prediction output ($\hat{y}$) of this perception is calculated as follows:

$$\hat{y}_i = w \cdot x = w \cdot 0.3$$

And the error, in its simplest form, is calculated by comparing the prediction $\hat{y}$ and the label y:

$$\text{error} = |\hat{y} - y|$$

$$= |(w \cdot x) - y|$$

$$= |w \cdot 0.3 - 0.8|$$

If you look at this error function, you will notice that the input (x) and the goal prediction (y) are fixed values. They will never change for these specific data points. The only two variables that we can change in this equation are the error and the weight. Now, if we want to get to the minimum error, which variable can we play with? Correct: the weight! The weight acts as a knob that the network needs to adjust up and down until it gets the minimum error. This is how the network learns: by adjusting weight. When we plot the error function with respect to the weight, we get the graph shown in figure 2.25.

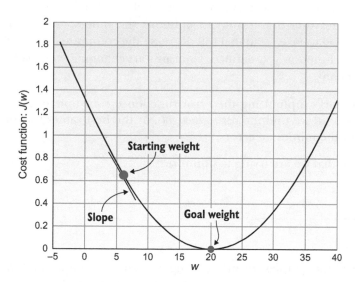

Figure 2.25 The network learns by adjusting weight. When we plot the error function with respect to weight, we get this type of graph.

As mentioned before, we initialize the network with random weights. The weight lies somewhere on this curve, and our mission is to make it *descend* this curve to its optimal value with the minimum error. The process of finding the goal weights of the neural network happens by adjusting the weight values in an iterative process using an *optimization algorithm*.

2.6   *Optimization algorithms*

Training a neural network involves showing the network many examples (a training dataset); the network makes predictions through feedforward calculations and compares them with the correct labels to calculate the error. Finally, the neural network needs to *adjust the weights* (on all edges) until it gets the minimum error value, which means maximum accuracy. Now, all we need to do is build algorithms that can find the optimum weights for us.

2.6.1   *What is optimization?*

Ahh, optimization! A topic that is dear to my heart, and dear to every machine learning engineer (mathematicians too). Optimization is a way of framing a problem to maximize or minimize some value. The best thing about computing an error function is that we turn the neural network into an optimization problem where our goal is to *minimize the error.*

Suppose you want to optimize your commute from home to work. First, you need to define the metric that you are optimizing (the error function). Maybe you want to optimize the cost of the commute, or the time, or the distance. Then, based on that specific loss function, you work on minimizing its value by changing some parameters. Changing the parameters to minimize (or maximize) a value is called *optimization.* If you choose the loss function to be the cost, maybe you will choose a longer commute that will take two hours, or (hypothetically) you might walk for five hours to minimize the cost. On the other hand, if you want to optimize the time spent commuting, maybe you will spend $50 to take a cab that will decrease the commute time to 20 minutes. Based on the loss function you defined, you can start changing your parameters to get the results you want.

> **TIP**   In neural networks, optimizing the error function means updating the weights and biases until we find the *optimal weights*, or the best values for the weights to produce the minimum error.

Let's look at the space that we are trying to optimize:

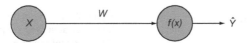

In a neural network of the simplest form, a perceptron with one input, we have only one weight. We can easily plot the error (that we are trying to minimize) with respect to this weight, represented by the 2D curve in figure 2.26 (repeated from earlier).

But what if we have two weights? If we graph all the possible values of the two weights, we get a 3D plane of the error (figure 2.27).

What about more than two weights? Your network will probably have hundreds or thousands of weights (because each edge in your network has its own weight value).

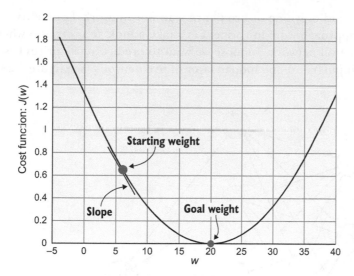

Figure 2.26 The error function with respect to its weight for a single perceptron is a 2D curve.

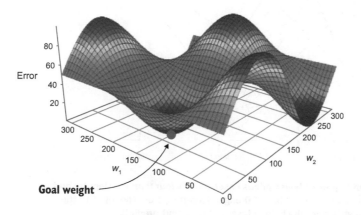

Figure 2.27 Graphing all possible values of two weights gives a 3D error plane.

Since we humans are only equipped to understand a maximum of 3 dimensions, it is impossible for us to visualize error graphs when we have 10 weights, not to mention hundreds or thousands of weight parameters. So, from this point on, we will study the error function using the 2D or 3D plane of the error. In order to optimize the model, our goal is to search this space to find the best weights that will achieve the lowest possible error.

Why do we need an optimization algorithm? Can't we just brute-force through a lot of weight values until we get the minimum error?

Suppose we used a brute-force approach where we just tried a lot of different possible weights (say 1,000 values) and found the weight that produced the minimum error. Could that work? Well, theoretically, yes. This approach might work when we have very few inputs and only one or two neurons in our network. Let me try to convince you that this approach wouldn't scale. Let's take a look at a scenario where we have a very simple neural network. Suppose we want to predict house prices based on only four features (inputs) and one hidden layer of five neurons (see figure 2.28).

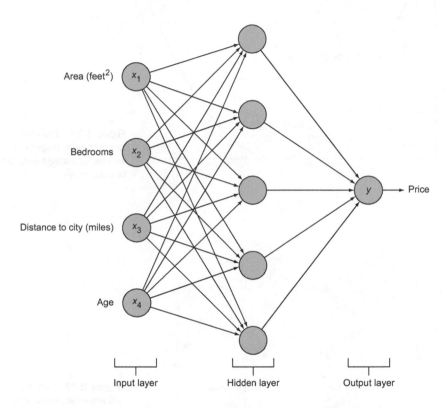

Figure 2.28   **If we want to predict house prices based on only four features (inputs) and one hidden layer of five neurons, we'll have 20 edges (weights) from the input to the hidden layer, plus 5 weights from the hidden layer to the output prediction.**

As you can see, we have 20 edges (weights) from the input to the hidden layer, plus 5 weights from the hidden layer to the output prediction, totaling 25 weight variables that need to be adjusted for optimum values. To brute-force our way through a simple neural network of this size, if we are trying 1,000 different values for each weight, then we will have a total of 10^{75} combinations:

$$1,000 \times 1,000 \times \ldots \times 1,000 = 1,000^{25} = 10^{75} \text{ combinations}$$

Let's say we were able to get our hands on the fastest supercomputer in the world: Sunway TaihuLight, which operates at a speed of 93 petaflops $\Rightarrow 93 \times 10^{15}$ floating-point operations per second (FLOPs). In the best-case scenario, this supercomputer would need

$$\frac{10^{75}}{93 \times 10^{15}} = 1.08 \times 10^{58} \text{ seconds} = 3.42 \times 10^{50} \text{ years}$$

That is a huge number: it's longer than the universe has existed. Who has that kind of time to wait for the network to train? Remember that this is a very simple neural network that usually takes a few minutes to train using smart optimization algorithms. In the real world, you will be building more complex networks that have thousands of inputs and tens of hidden layers, and you will be required to train them in a matter of hours (or days, or sometimes weeks). So we have to come up with a different approach to find the optimal weights.

Hopefully I have convinced you that brute-forcing through the optimization process is not the answer. Now, let's study the most popular optimization algorithm for neural networks: gradient descent. Gradient descent has several variations: batch gradient descent (BGD), stochastic gradient descent (SGD), and mini-batch GD (MB-GD).

2.6.2 *Batch gradient descent*

The general definition of a *gradient* (also known as a *derivative*) is that it is the function that tells you the slope or rate of change of the line that is tangent to the curve at any given point. It is just a fancy term for the slope or steepness of the curve (figure 2.29).

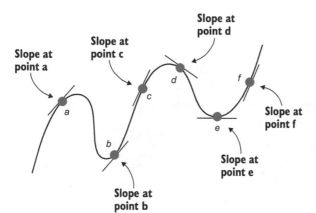

Figure 2.29 A gradient is the function that describes the rate of change of the line that is tangent to a curve at any given point.

Gradient descent simply means updating the weights iteratively to descend the slope of the error curve until we get to the point with minimum error. Let's take a look at the error function that we introduced earlier with respect to the weights. At the initial weight point, we calculate the derivative of the error function to get the slope (direction) of the next step. We keep repeating this process to take steps down the curve until we reach the minimum error (figure 2.30).

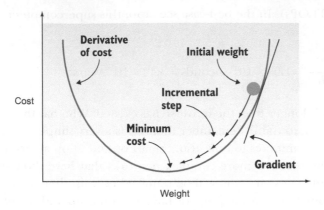

Figure 2.30   **Gradient descent takes incremental steps to descend the error function.**

HOW DOES GRADIENT DESCENT WORK?

To visualize how gradient descent works, let's plot the error function in a 3D graph (figure 2.31) and go through the process step by step. The random initial weight (starting weight) is at point A, and our goal is to descend this error mountain to the goal w_1 and w_2 weight values, which produce the minimum error value. The way we do that is by taking a series of steps *down* the curve until we get the minimum error. In order to descend the error mountain, we need to determine two things for each step:

- The step direction (gradient)
- The step size (learning rate)

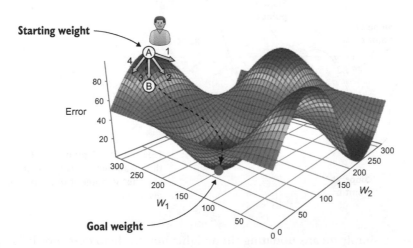

Figure 2.31   **The random initial weight (starting weight) is at point A. We descend the error mountain to the w_1 and w_2 weight values that produce the minimum error value.**

THE DIRECTION (GRADIENT)

Suppose you are standing on the top of the error mountain at point A. To get to the bottom, you need to determine the step direction that results in the deepest descent (has the steepest slope). And what is the slope, again? It is the derivative of the curve. So if you are standing on top of that mountain, you need to look at all the directions around you and find out which direction will result in the deepest descent (1, 2, 3, or 4, for example). Let's say it is direction 3; we choose that way. This brings us to point B, and we restart the process (calculate feedforward and error) and find the direction of deepest descent, and so forth, until we get to the bottom of the mountain.

This process is called *gradient descent*. By taking the derivative of the error with respect to the weight ($\frac{dE}{dw}$), we get the direction that we should take. Now there's one thing left. The gradient only determines the direction. How large should the size of the step be? It could be a 1-foot step or a 100-foot jump. This is what we need to determine next.

THE STEP SIZE (LEARNING RATE α)

The *learning rate* is the size of each step the network takes when it descends the error mountain, and it is usually denoted by the Greek letter alpha (α). It is one of the most important hyperparameters that you tune when you train your neural network (more on that later). A larger learning rate means the network will learn faster (since it is descending the mountain with larger steps), and smaller steps mean slower learning. Well, this sounds simple enough. Let's use large learning rates and complete the neural network training in minutes instead of waiting for hours. Right? Not quite. Let's take a look at what could happen if we set a very large learning rate value.

In figure 2.32, you are starting at point A. When you take a large step in the direction of the arrow, instead of descending the error mountain, you end up at point B, on the other side. Then another large step takes you to C, and so forth. The error will keep *oscillating* and will never descend. We will talk more later about tuning the learning rate and how to determine if the error is oscillating. But for now, you need to know this: if you use a very small learning rate, the network will eventually descend the

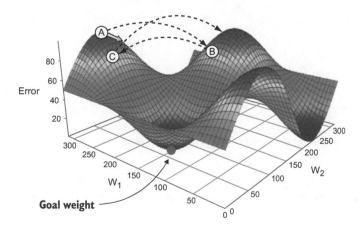

Figure 2.32 Setting a very large learning rate causes the error to oscillate and never descend.

mountain and will get to the minimum error. But this training will take longer (maybe weeks or months). On the other hand, if you use a very large learning rate, the network might keep oscillating and never train. So we usually initialize the learning rate value to 0.1 or 0.01 and see how the network performs, and then tune it further.

PUTTING DIRECTION AND STEP TOGETHER

By multiplying the direction (derivative) by the step size (learning rate), we get the change of the weight for each step:

$$\Delta w_i = -\alpha \frac{dE}{dw_i}$$

We add the minus sign because the derivative always calculates the slope in the upward direction. Since we need to descend the mountain, we go in the opposite direction of the slope:

$$w_{\text{next-step}} = w_{\text{current}} + \Delta w$$

Calculus refresher: Calculating the partial derivative

The derivative is the study of change. It measures the steepness of a curve at a particular point on a graph.

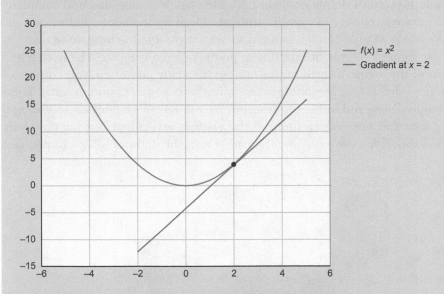

We want to find the steepness of the curve at the exact weight point.

It looks like mathematics has given us just what we are looking for. On the error graph, we want to find the steepness of the curve at the exact weight point. Thank you, math!

Other terms for *derivative* are *slope* and *rate of change*. If the error function is denoted as $E(x)$, then the derivative of the error function *with respect to the weight* is denoted as

$$\frac{d}{dw} E(x) \quad \text{or just} \quad \frac{dE(x)}{dw}$$

This formula shows how much the total error will change when we change the weight.

Luckily, mathematicians created some rules for us to calculate the derivative. Since this is not a mathematics book, we will not discuss the proof of the rules. Instead, we will start applying these rules at this point to calculate our gradient. Here are the basic derivative rules:

Constant Rule: $\frac{d}{dx}(c) = 0$	Difference Rule: $\frac{d}{dx}[f(x) - g(x)] - f'(x) - g'(x)$
Constant Multiple Rule: $\frac{d}{dx}[cf(x)] = cf'(x)$	Product Rule: $\frac{d}{dx}[f(x)g(x)] = f(x)g'(x) + g(x)f'(x)$
Power Rule: $\frac{d}{dx}(x^n) = x^{n-1}$	Quotient Rule: $\frac{d}{dx}\left[\frac{f(x)}{g(x)}\right] = \frac{g(x)f'(x) - f(x)g'(x)}{[g(x)]^2}$
Sum Rule: $\frac{d}{dx}[f(x) - g(x)] = f'(x) - g'(x)$	Chain Rule: $\frac{d}{dx}f(g(x)) = f'(g(x))g'(x)$

Let's take a look at a simple function to apply the derivative rules:

$$f(x) = 10x^5 + 4x^7 + 12x$$

We can apply the power, constant, and sum rules to get $\frac{df}{dx}$ also denoted as $f'(x)$:

$$\text{then, } f'(x) = 50x^4 + 28x^6 + 12$$

To get an intuition of what this means, let's plot $f(x)$:

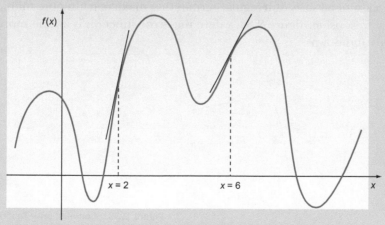

Using a simple function to apply derivative rules. To get the slope at any point, we can compute $f'(x)$ at that point.

(continued)

If we want to get the slope at any point, we can compute $f'(x)$ at that point. So $f'(2)$ gives us the slope of the line on the left, and $f'(6)$ gives the slope of the second line. Get it?

For a last example of derivatives, let's apply the power rule to calculate the derivative of the sigmoid function:

$$\frac{d}{dx}\,\sigma(x) = \frac{d}{dx}\left[\frac{1}{1 + e^{-x}}\right]$$

$$= \frac{d}{dx}\,(1 + e^{-x}) \quad \longleftarrow \text{ power rule}$$

$$= -(1 + e^{-x})^{-2}(-e^{-x})$$

$$= \frac{e^{-x}}{(1 + e^{-x})^2}$$

$$= \frac{1}{1 + e^{-x}} \cdot \frac{e^{-x}}{1 + e^{-x}}$$

$$= \sigma(x) \cdot (1 - \sigma(x))$$

If you want to write out the derivative of the sigmoid activation function in code, it will look like this:

```
def sigmoid(x):
    return 1/(1+np.exp(-x))

def sigmoid_derivative(x):
    return sigmoid(x) * (1 - sigmoid(x))
```

Note that you don't need to memorize the derivative rules, nor do you need to calculate the derivatives of the functions yourself. Thanks to the awesome DL community, we have great libraries that will compute these functions for you in just one line of code. But it is valuable to understand how things are happening under the hood.

PITFALLS OF BATCH GRADIENT DESCENT

Gradient descent is a very powerful algorithm to get to the minimum error. But it has two major pitfalls.

First, not all cost functions look like the simple bowls we saw earlier. There may be holes, ridges, and all sorts of irregular terrain that make reaching the minimum error very difficult. Consider figure 2.33, where the error function is a little more complex and has ups and downs.

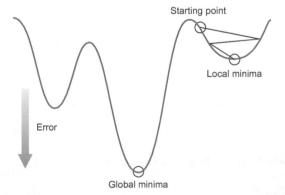

Figure 2.33 Complex error functions are represented by more complex curves with many local minima values. Our goal is to reach the global minimum value.

Remember that during weight initialization, the starting point is randomly selected. What if the starting point of the gradient descent algorithm is as shown in this figure? The error will start descending the small mountain on the right and will indeed reach a minimum value. But this minimum value, called the *local minima*, is not the lowest possible error value for this error function. It is the minimum value for the local mountain where the algorithm randomly started. Instead, we want to get to the lowest possible error value, the *global minima*.

Second, batch gradient descent uses the entire training set to compute the gradients at every step. Remember this loss function?

$$L(W, b) = \frac{1}{N} \sum_{i=1}^{N} (\hat{y}_i - y_i)^2$$

This means that if your training set (N) has 100,000,000 (100 million) records, the algorithm needs to sum over 100 million records just to take *one step*. That is computationally very expensive and slow. And this is why this algorithm is also called *batch gradient descent*—because it uses the entire training data in one batch.

One possible approach to solving these two problems is stochastic gradient descent. We'll take a look at SGD in the next section.

2.6.3 *Stochastic gradient descent*

In stochastic gradient descent, the algorithm randomly selects data points and goes through the gradient descent one data point at a time (figure 2.34). This provides many different weight starting points and descends all the mountains to calculate their local minimas. Then the minimum value of all these local minimas is the global minima. This sounds very intuitive; that is the concept behind the SGD algorithm.

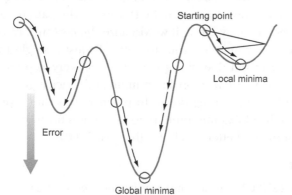

Figure 2.34 The stochastic gradient descent algorithm randomly selects data points across the curve and descends all of them to find the local minima.

Stochastic is just a fancy word for *random*. Stochastic gradient descent is probably the most-used optimization algorithm for machine learning in general and for deep learning in particular. While gradient descent measures the loss and gradient over the full training set to take one step toward the minimum, SGD *randomly* picks *one instance* in the training set for each one step and calculates the gradient based only on that single instance. Let's take a look at the pseudocode of both GD and SGD to get a better understanding of the differences between these algorithms:

GD	Stochastic GD
1 Take all the data. 2 Compute the gradient. 3 Update the weights and take a step down. 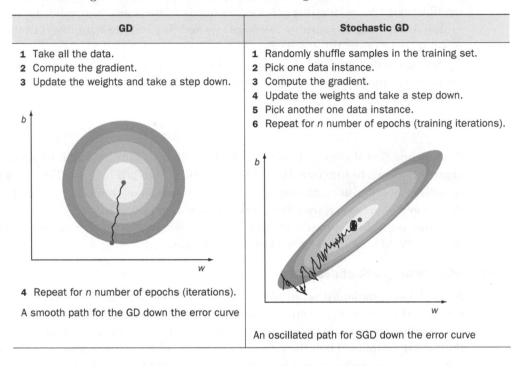 4 Repeat for *n* number of epochs (iterations). A smooth path for the GD down the error curve	1 Randomly shuffle samples in the training set. 2 Pick one data instance. 3 Compute the gradient. 4 Update the weights and take a step down. 5 Pick another one data instance. 6 Repeat for *n* number of epochs (training iterations). An oscillated path for SGD down the error curve

Because we take a step after we compute the gradient for the entire training data in batch GD, you can see that the path down the error is smooth and almost a straight line. In contrast, due to the stochastic (random) nature of SGD, you see the path toward the global cost minimum is not direct but may zigzag if we visualize the cost surface in a 2D space. That is because in SGD, every iteration tries to better fit just a single training example, which makes it a lot faster but does not guarantee that every step takes us a step down the curve. It will arrive close to the global minimum and, once it gets there, it will continue to bounce around, never settling down. In practice, this isn't a problem because ending up very close to the global minimum is good enough for most practical purposes. SGD almost always performs better and faster than batch GD.

2.6.4 *Mini-batch gradient descent*

Mini-batch gradient descent (MB-GD) is a compromise between BGD and SGD. Instead of computing the gradient from one sample (SGD) or all samples (BGD), we divide the training sample into *mini-batches* from which to compute the gradient (a common mini-batch size is $k = 256$). MB-GD converges in fewer iterations than BGD because we update the weights more frequently; however, MB-GD lets us use vectorized operations, which typically result in a computational performance gain over SGD.

2.6.5   *Gradient descent takeaways*

There is a lot going on here, so let's sum it up, shall we? Here is how gradient descent is summarized in my head:

- Three types: batch, stochastic, and mini-batch.
- All follow the same concept:
  - Find the direction of the steepest slope: the derivative of the error with respect to the weight $\frac{dE}{dw_i}$.
  - Set the learning rate (or step size). The algorithm will compute the slope, but you will set the learning rate as a hyperparameter that you will tune by trial and error.
  - Start the learning rate at 0.01, and then go down to 0.001, 0.0001, 0.00001. The lower you set your learning rate, the more guaranteed you are to descend to the minimum error (if you train for an infinite time). Since we don't have infinite time, 0.01 is a reasonable start, and then we go down from there.
- Batch GD updates the weights after computing the gradient of *all* the training data. This can be computationally very expensive when the data is huge. It doesn't scale well.
- Stochastic GD updates the weights after computing the gradient of a single instance of the training data. SGD is faster than BGD and usually reaches very close to the global minimum.
- Mini-batch GD is a compromise between batch and stochastic, using neither all the data nor a single instance. Instead, it takes a group of training instances (called a mini-batch), computes the gradient on them and updates the weights, and then repeats until it processes all the training data. In most cases, MB-GD is a good starting point.
  - batch_size is a hyperparameter that you will tune. This will come up again in the hyperparameter-tuning section in chapter 4. But typically, you can start experimenting with batch_size = 32, 64, 128, 256.
  - Don't get *batch_size* confused with *epochs*. An *epoch* is the full cycle over all the training data. The batch is the number of training samples in the group for which we are computing the gradient. For example, if we have 1,000 samples in our training data and set batch_size = 256, then epoch 1 = batch 1 of 256 samples plus batch 2 (256 samples) plus batch 3 (256 samples) plus batch 4 (232 samples).

Finally, you need to know that a lot of variations to gradient descent have been used over the years, and this is a very active area of research. Some of the most popular enhancements are

- Nesterov accelerated gradient
- RMSprop

- Adam
- Adagrad

Don't worry about these optimizers now. In chapter 4, we will discuss tuning techniques to improve your optimizers in more detail.

I know that was a lot, but stay with me. These are the main things I want to you remember from this section:

- How gradient descent works (slope plus step size)
- The difference between batch, stochastic, and mini-batch GD
- The GD hyperparameters that you will tune: learning rate and batch_size

If you've got this covered, you are good to move to the next section. And don't worry a lot about hyperparameter tuning. I'll cover network tuning in more detail in coming chapters and in almost all the projects in this book.

2.7   *Backpropagation*

Backpropagation is the core of how neural networks learn. Up until this point, you learned that training a neural network typically happens by the repetition of the following three steps:

- Feedforward: get the linear combination (weighted sum), and apply the activation function to get the output prediction ($\hat{y}$):

$$\hat{y} = \sigma \cdot W^{(3)} \cdot \sigma \cdot W^{(2)} \cdot \sigma \cdot W^{(1)} \cdot (x)$$

- Compare the prediction with the label to calculate the error or loss function:

$$E(W, b) = \frac{1}{N} \sum_{i=1}^{N} |\hat{y}_i - y_i|$$

- Use a gradient descent optimization algorithm to compute the Δw that optimizes the error function:

$$\Delta w_i = -\alpha \frac{dE}{dw_i}$$

Backpropagate the Δw through the network to update the weights:

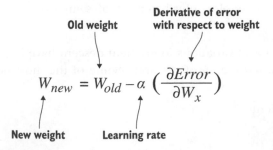

In this section, we will dive deeper into the final step: backpropagation.

2.7.1 What is backpropagation?

Backpropagation, or *backward pass*, means propagating derivatives of the error with respect to each specific weight

$$\frac{dE}{dw_i}$$

from the last layer (output) back to the first layer (inputs) to adjust weights. By propagating the Δw backward from the prediction node ($\hat{y}$) all the way through the hidden layers and back to the input layer, the weights get updated:

$$(w_{\text{next–step}} = w_{\text{current}} + \Delta w)$$

This will take the error one step down the error mountain. Then the cycle starts again (steps 1 to 3) to update the weights and take the error another step down, until we get to the minimum error.

Backpropagation might sound clearer when we have only one weight. We simply adjust the weight by adding the Δw to the old weight $w_{\text{new}} = w - \alpha \frac{dE}{dw_i}$.

But it gets complicated when we have a multilayer perceptron (MLP) network with many weight variables. To make this clearer, consider the scenario in figure 2.35.

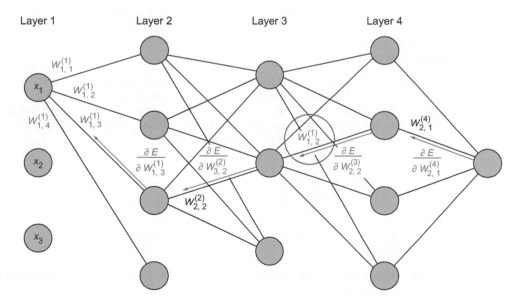

Figure 2.35 **Backpropagation becomes complicated when we have a multilayer perceptron (MLP) network with many weight variables.**

How do we compute the change of the total error with respect to w_{13} $\frac{dE}{dw_{13}}$? Remember that $\frac{dE}{dw_{13}}$ basically says, "How much will the total error change when we change the parameter w_{13}?"

We learned how to compute $\frac{dE}{dw_{21}}$ by applying the derivative rules on the error function. That is straightforward because w_{21} is directly connected to the error function. But to compute the derivatives of the total error with respect to the weights all the way back to the input, we need a calculus rule called *the chain rule*.

Calculus refresher: Chain rule in derivatives

Back again to calculus. Remember the derivative rules that we listed earlier? One of the most important rules is the chain rule. Let's dive deep into it to see how it is implemented in backpropagation:

Chain Rule: $\frac{d}{dx} f(g(x)) = f'(g(x))g'(x)$

The chain rule is a formula for calculating the derivatives of functions that are composed of functions inside other functions. It is also called the *outside-inside rule*. Look at this:

$$\frac{d}{dx} f(g(x)) = \frac{d}{dx} \text{ outside function} \times \frac{d}{dx} \text{ inside function}$$

$$= \frac{d}{dx} f(g(x)) \times \frac{d}{dx} g(x)$$

The chain rule says, "When composing functions, the derivatives just multiply." That is going to be very useful for us when implementing backpropagation, because feed-forwarding is just composing a bunch of functions, and backpropagation is taking the derivative at each piece of this function.

To implement the chain rule in backpropagation, all we are going to do is multiply a bunch of partial derivatives to get the effect of errors all the way back to the input. Here is how it works—but first, remember that our goal is to propagate the error backward all the way to the input layer. So in the following example, we want to calculate $\frac{dE}{dx}$, which is the effect of total error on input (x):

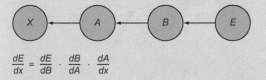

$$\frac{dE}{dx} = \frac{dE}{dB} \cdot \frac{dB}{dA} \cdot \frac{dA}{dx}$$

All we do here is multiply the upstream gradient by the local gradient all the way until we get to the target value.

Figure 2.36 shows how backpropagation uses the chain rule to flow the gradients in the backward direction through the network. Let's apply the chain rule to calculate the derivative of the error with respect to the third weight on the first input $w_{1,3}^{(1)}$, where the (1) means layer 1, and $w_{1,3}$ means node number 1 and weight number 3:

$$\frac{dE}{dw_{1,3}^{(1)}} = \frac{dE}{dw_{2,1}^{(4)}} \times \frac{dw_{2,1}^{(4)}}{dw_{2,2}^{(3)}} \times \frac{dw_{2,2}^{(3)}}{dw_{3,2}^{(2)}} \times \frac{dw_{3,2}^{(2)}}{dw_{1,3}^{(1)}}$$

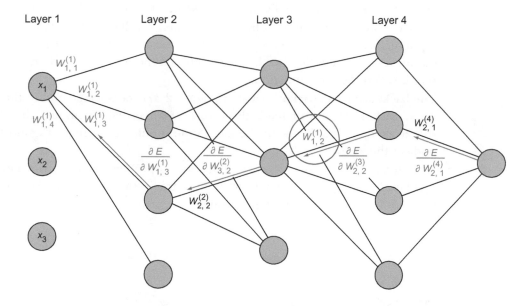

Figure 2.36 Backpropagation uses the chain rule to flow gradients back through the network.

The equation might look complex at the beginning, but all we are doing really is multiplying the partial derivative of the edges starting from the output node all the way backward to the input node. All the notations are what makes this look complex, but once you understand how to read $w_{1,3}^{(1)}$, the backward-pass equation looks like this:

The error backpropagated to the edge $w_{1,3}^{(1)}$ = effect of error on edge 4 · effect on edge 3 · effect on edge 2 · effect on target edge

There you have it. That is the backpropagation technique used by neural networks to update the weights to best fit our problem.

2.7.2 *Backpropagation takeaways*

- Backpropagation is a learning procedure for neurons.
- Backpropagation repeatedly adjusts weights of the connections (weights) in the network to minimize the cost function (the difference between the actual output vector and the desired output vector).
- As a result of the weight adjustments, hidden layers come to represent important features other than the features represented in the input layer.
- For each layer, the goal is to find a set of weights that ensures that for each input vector, the output vector produced is the same as (or close to) the desired output vector. The difference in values between the produced and desired outputs is called the error function.
- The backward pass (backpropagation; figure 2.37) starts at the end of the network, backpropagates or feeds the errors back, recursively applies the chain rule to compute gradients all the way to the inputs of the network, and then updates the weights.
- To reiterate, the goal of a typical neural network problem is to discover a model that best fits our data Ultimately, we want to minimize the cost or loss function by choosing the best set of weight parameters.

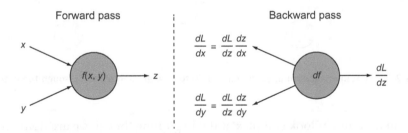

Figure 2.37   The forward pass calculates the output prediction (left). The backward pass passes the derivative of the error backward to update its weights (right).

Summary

- Perceptrons work fine for datasets that can be separated by one straight line (linear operation).
- Nonlinear datasets that cannot be modeled by a straight line need a more complex neural network that contains many neurons. Stacking neurons in layers creates a multilayer perceptron.
- The network learns by the repetition of three main steps: feedforward, calculate error, and optimize weights.

- Parameters are variables that are updated by the network during the training process, like weights and biases. These are tuned automatically by the model during training.
- Hyperparameters are variables that you tune, such as number of layers, activation functions, loss functions, optimizers, early stopping, and learning rate. We tune these before training the model.

Convolutional
neural networks

3

This chapter covers

- Classifying images using MLP
- Working with the CNN architecture to classify images
- Understanding convolution on color images

Previously, we talked about artificial neural networks (ANNs), also known as multilayer perceptrons (MLPs), which are basically layers of neurons stacked on top of each other that have learnable weights and biases. Each neuron receives some inputs, which are multiplied by their weights, with nonlinearity applied via activation functions. In this chapter, we will talk about convolutional neural networks (CNNs), which are considered an evolution of the MLP architecture that performs a lot better with images.

The high-level layout of this chapter is as follows:

1 *Image classification with MLP*—We will start with a mini project to classify images using MLP topology and examine how a regular neural network architecture processes images. You will learn about the MLP architecture's drawbacks when processing images and why we need a new, creative neural network architecture for this task.

2 *Understanding CNNs*—We will explore convolutional networks to see how they extract features from images and classify objects. You will learn about the three main components of CNNs: the convolutional layer, the pooling layer, and the fully connected layer. Then we will apply this knowledge in another mini project to classify images with CNNs.

3 *Color images*—We will compare how computers see color images versus grayscale images, and how convolution is implemented over color images.

4 *Image classification project*—We will apply all that you learn in this chapter in an end-to-end image classification project to classify color images with CNNs.

The basic concepts of how the network learns and optimizes parameters are the same with both MLPs and CNNs:

- *Architecture*—MLPs and CNNs are composed of layers of neurons that are stacked on top of each other. CNNs have different structures (convolutional versus fully connected layers), as we are going to see in the coming sections.
- *Weights and biases*—In convolutional and fully connected layers, inference works the same way. Both have weights and biases that are initially randomly generated, and their values are learned by the network. The main difference between them is that the weights in MLPs are in a vector form, whereas in convolutional layers, weights take the form of convolutional filters or kernels.
- *Hyperparameters*—As with MLPs, when we design CNNs we will always specify the error function, activation function, and optimizer. All hyperparameters explained in the previous chapters remain the same; we will add some new ones that are specific to CNNs.
- *Training*—Both networks learn the same way. First they perform a forward pass to get predictions; second, they compare the prediction with the true label to get the loss function ($y - \hat{y}$); and finally, they optimize parameters using gradient descent, backpropagate the error to all the weights, and update their values to minimize the loss function.

Ready? Let's get started!

3.1 *Image classification using MLP*

Let's recall the MLP architecture from chapter 2. Neurons are stacked in layers on top of each other, with weight connections. The MLP architecture consists of an input layer, one or more hidden layers, and an output layer (figure 3.1).

This section uses what you know about MLPs from chapter 2 to solve an image classification problem using the MNIST dataset. The goal of this classifier will be to classify images of digits from 0 to 9 (10 classes). To begin, let's look at the three main components of our MLP architecture (input layer, hidden layers, and output layer).

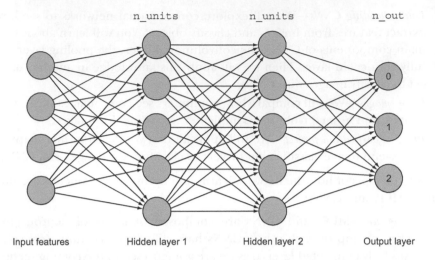

Figure 3.1   The MLP architecture consists of layers of neurons connected by weight connections.

3.1.1   *Input layer*

When we work with 2D images, we need to preprocess them into something the network can understand before feeding them to the network. First, let's see how computers perceive images. In figure 3.2, we have an image 28 pixels wide × 28 pixels high. This image is seen by the computer as a 28 × 28 matrix, with pixel values ranging from 0 to 255 (0 for black, 255 for white, and the range in between for grayscale).

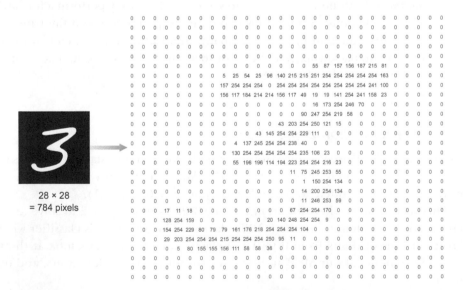

Figure 3.2   The computer sees this image as a 28 × 28 matrix of pixel values ranging from 0 to 255.

Since MLPs only take as input 1D vectors with dimensions $(1, n)$, they cannot take a raw 2D image matrix with dimensions (x, y). To fit the image in the input layer, we first need to transform our image into one large vector with the dimensions $(1, n)$ that contains all the pixel values in the image. This process is called *image flattening*. In this example, the total number (n) of pixels in this image is $28 \times 28 = 784$. Then, in order to feed this image to our network, we need to flatten the (28×28) matrix into one long vector with dimensions $(1, 784)$. The input vector looks like this:

$$x = [row1, row2, row3, ..., row28]$$

That said, the input layer in this example will have a total of 784 nodes: $x_1, x_2, ..., x_{784}$.

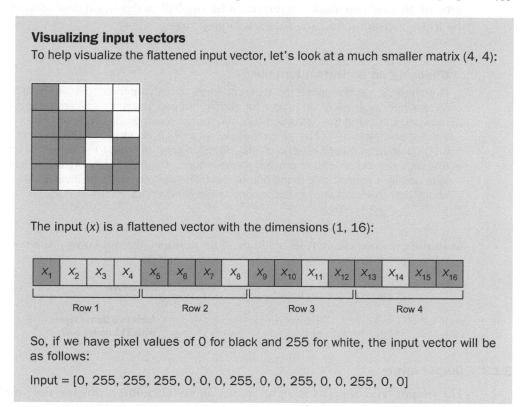

Visualizing input vectors

To help visualize the flattened input vector, let's look at a much smaller matrix (4, 4):

The input (x) is a flattened vector with the dimensions (1, 16):

So, if we have pixel values of 0 for black and 255 for white, the input vector will be as follows:

Input = [0, 255, 255, 255, 0, 0, 0, 255, 0, 0, 255, 0, 0, 255, 0, 0]

Here is how we flatten an input image in Keras:

```
from keras.models import Sequential
from keras.layers import Flatten

model = Sequential()
model.add( Flatten(input_shape = (28,28) ))
```

Defines the model →

As before, imports the Keras library

Imports a layer called Flatten to convert the image matrix into a vector

Adds the Flatten layer, also known as the input layer

The Flatten layer in Keras handles this process for us. It takes the 2D image matrix input and converts it into a 1D vector. Note that the Flatten layer must be supplied a parameter value of the shape of the input image. Now the image is ready to be fed to the neural network.

What's next? Hidden layers.

3.1.2   Hidden layers

As discussed in the previous chapter, the neural network can have one or more hidden layers (technically, as many as you want). Each layer has one or more neurons (again, as many as you want). Your main job as a neural network engineer is to design these layers. For the sake of this example, let's say you decided to arbitrarily design the network to have two hidden layers, each having 512 nodes—and don't forget to add the ReLU activation function for each hidden layer.

> **Choosing an activation function**
>
> In chapter 2, we discussed the different types of activation functions in detail. As a DL engineer, you will often have a lot of different choices when you are building your network. Choosing the activation function that is the most suitable for the problem you are solving is one of these choices. While there is no single best answer that fits all problems, in most cases, the ReLU function performs best in the hidden layers; and for most classification problems where classes are mutually exclusive, softmax is generally a good choice in the output layer. The softmax function gives us the probability that the input image depicts one of the (n) classes.

As in the previous chapter, let's add two fully connected (also known as *dense*) layers, using Keras:

```
from keras.layers import Dense          ◁—  Imports the Dense layer

model.add(Dense(512, activation = 'relu'))     Adds two Dense layers
model.add(Dense(512, activation = 'relu'))     with 512 nodes each
```

3.1.3   Output layer

The output layer is pretty straightforward. In classification problems, the number of nodes in the output layer should be equal to the number of classes that you are trying to detect. In this problem, we are classifying 10 digits (0, 1, 2, 3, 4, 5, 6, 7, 8, 9). Then we need to add one last Dense layer that contains 10 nodes:

```
model.add(Dense(10, activation = 'softmax'))
```

3.1.4 Putting it all together

When we put all these layers together, we get a neural network like the one in figure 3.3.

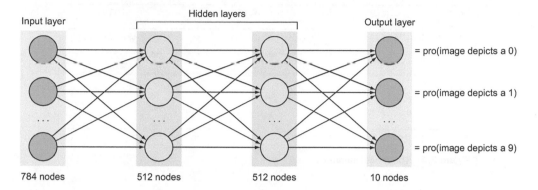

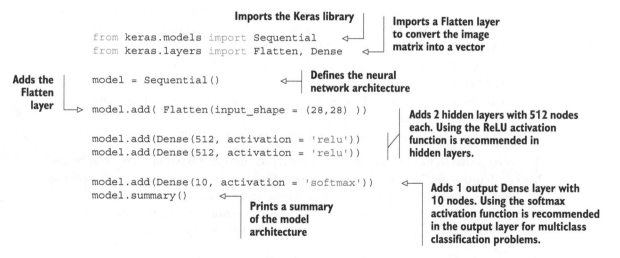

Figure 3.3 The neural network we create by combining the input, hidden, and output layers

Here is how it looks in Keras:

Imports the Keras library

Imports a Flatten layer to convert the image matrix into a vector

```
from keras.models import Sequential
from keras.layers import Flatten, Dense
```

Adds the Flatten layer

Defines the neural network architecture

```
model = Sequential()

model.add( Flatten(input_shape = (28,28) ))

model.add(Dense(512, activation = 'relu'))
model.add(Dense(512, activation = 'relu'))

model.add(Dense(10, activation = 'softmax'))
model.summary()
```

Adds 2 hidden layers with 512 nodes each. Using the ReLU activation function is recommended in hidden layers.

Prints a summary of the model architecture

Adds 1 output Dense layer with 10 nodes. Using the softmax activation function is recommended in the output layer for multiclass classification problems.

When you run this code, you will see the model summary printed as shown in figure 3.4.

You can see that the output of the flatten layer is a vector with 784 nodes, as discussed before, since we have 784 pixels in each 28 × 28 images. As designed, the hidden layers produce 512 nodes each; and, finally, the output layer (dense_3) produces a layer with 10 nodes.

```
┌─────────────────────────────────────────────────────────────────┐
│ Layer (type)                 Output Shape             Param #     │
│ =================================================================│
│ Flatten_1 (Flatten)          (None, 784)              0           │
│ ────────────────────────────────────────────────────────────────│
│ dense_1 (Dense)              (None, 512)              401920      │
│ ────────────────────────────────────────────────────────────────│
│ dense_2 (Dense)              (None, 512)              262656      │
│ ────────────────────────────────────────────────────────────────│
│ dense_3 (Dense)              (None, 10)               5130        │
│ =================================================================│
│ Total params: 669,706                                             │
│ Trainable params: 669,706                                         │
│ Non-trainable params: 0                                           │
└─────────────────────────────────────────────────────────────────┘
```

Figure 3.4   The model summary

The Param # field represents the number of parameters (weights) produced at each layer. These are the weights that will be adjusted and learned during the training process. They are calculated as follows:

1 Params after the flatten layer = 0, because this layer only flattens the image to a vector for feeding into the input layer. The weights haven't been added yet.

2 Params after layer 1 = (784 nodes in input layer) × (512 in hidden layer 1) + (512 connections to biases) = 401,920.

3 Params after layer 2 = (512 nodes in hidden layer 1) × (512 in hidden layer 2) + (512 connections to biases) = 262,656.

4 Params after layer 3= (512 nodes in hidden layer 2) × (10 in output layer) + (10 connections to biases) = 5,130.

5 Total params in the network = 401,920 + 262,656 + 5,130 = 669,706.

This means that in this tiny network, we have a total of 669,706 parameters (weights and biases) that the network needs to learn and whose values it needs to tune to optimize the error function. This is a huge number for such a small network. You can see how this number would grow out of control if we added more nodes and layers or used bigger images. This is one of the two major drawbacks of MLPs that we will discuss next.

MLPs vs. CNNs

If you train the example MLP on the MNIST dataset, you will get pretty good results (close to 96% accuracy compared to 99% with CNNs). But MLPs and CNNs do not usually yield comparable results. The MNIST dataset is special because it is very clean and perfectly preprocessed. For example, all images have the same size and are centered in a 28 × 28 pixel grid. Also, the MNIST dataset contains only grayscale images. It would be a much harder task if the images had color or the digits were skewed or not centered.

If you try the example MLP architecture with a slightly more complex dataset like CIFAR-10, as we will do in the project at the end of this chapter, the network will perform very poorly (around 30–40% accuracy). It performs even worse with more complex datasets. In messy real-world image data, CNNs truly outshine MLPs.

3.1.5 Drawbacks of MLPs for processing images

We are nearly ready to talk about the topic of this chapter: CNNs. But first, let's discuss the two major problems in MLPs that convolutional networks are designed to fix.

SPATIAL FEATURE LOSS

Flattening a 2D image to a 1D vector input results in losing the spatial features of the image. As we saw in the mini project earlier, before feeding an image to the hidden layers of an MLP, we must flatten the image matrix to a 1D vector. This means throwing away all the 2D information contained in the image. Treating an input as a simple vector of numbers with no special structure might work well for 1D signals; but in 2D images, it will lead to information loss because the network doesn't relate the pixel values to each other when trying to find patterns. MLPs have no knowledge of the fact that these pixel numbers were originally spatially arranged in a grid and that they are connected to each other. CNNs, on the other hand, do not require a flattened image. We can feed the raw image matrix of pixels to a CNN network, and the CNN will understand that pixels that are close to each other are more heavily related than pixels that are far apart.

Let's oversimplify things to learn more about the importance of spatial features in an image. Suppose we are trying to teach a neural network to identify the shape of a square, and suppose the pixel value 1 is white and 0 is black. When we draw a white square on a black background, the matrix will look like figure 3.5.

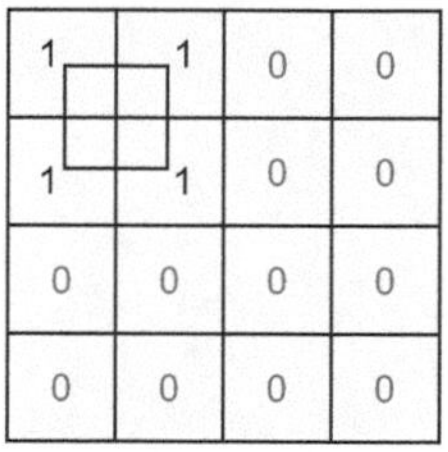

Figure 3.5 **If the pixel value 1 is white and 0 is black, this is what our matrix looks like for identifying a square.**

Since MLPs take a 1D vector as an input, we have to flatten the 2D image to a 1D vector. The input vector of figure 3.5 looks like this:

Input vector = [1, 1, 0, 0, 1, 1, 0, 0, 0, 0, 0, 0, 0, 0, 0, 0]

When the training is complete, the network will learn to identify a square *only* when the input nodes x_1, x_2, x_5, and x_6 are fired. But what happens when we have new images with square shapes located in different areas in the image, as shown in figure 3.6?

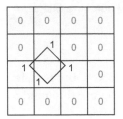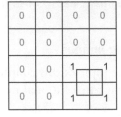

Figure 3.6   Square shapes in different areas of the image

The MLP will have no idea that these are the shapes of squares because the network didn't learn the square shape as a feature. Instead, it learned the input nodes that, when fired, might lead to a square shape. If we want our network to learn squares, we need a lot of square shapes located everywhere in the image. You can see how this solution won't scale for complex problems.

Another example of feature learning is this: if we want to teach a neural network to recognize cats, then ideally, we want the network to learn all the shapes of cat features regardless of where they appear on the image (ears, nose, eyes, and so on). This only happens when the network looks at the image as a set of pixels that, when close to each other, are heavily related.

The mechanism of how CNNs learn will be explained in detail in this chapter. But figure 3.7 shows how the network learns features throughout its layers.

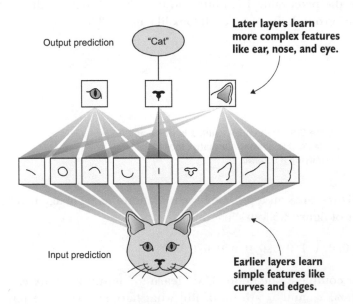

Output prediction

Later layers learn more complex features like ear, nose, and eye.

Input prediction

Earlier layers learn simple features like curves and edges.

Figure 3.7   CNNs learn the image features through its layers.

FULLY CONNECTED (DENSE) LAYERS

MLPs are composed of dense layers that are fully connected to each other. *Fully connected* means every node in one layer is connected to *all* nodes of the previous layer and *all* nodes in the next layer. In this scenario, each neuron has parameters (weights) to train per neuron from the previous layer. While this is not a big problem for the MNIST dataset because the images are really small in size (28 × 28), what happens when we try to process larger images? For example, if we have an image with dimensions 1,000 × 1,000, it will yield 1 million parameters for each node in the first hidden layer. So if the first hidden layer has 1,000 neurons, this will yield 1 billion parameters even in such a small network. You can imagine the computational complexity of optimizing 1 billion parameters after only the first layer. This number will increase drastically when we have tens or hundreds of layers. This can get out of control pretty fast and will not scale.

CNNs, on the other hand, are *locally connected* layers, as figure 3.8 shows: nodes are connected to only a small subset of the previous layers' nodes. Locally connected layers use far fewer parameters than densely connected layers, as you will see.

Fully connected neural net   Locally connected neural net

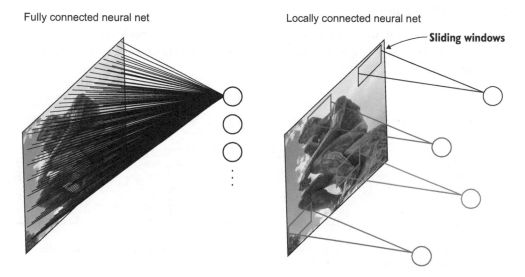

Figure 3.8 **(Left) Fully connected neural network where all neurons are connected to all pixels of the image. (Right) Locally connected network where only a subset of pixels is connected to each neuron. These subsets are called** *sliding windows.*

WHAT DOES IT ALL MEAN?

The loss of information caused by flattening a 2D image matrix to a 1D vector and the computational complexity of fully connected layers with larger images suggest that we need an entirely new way of processing image input, one where 2D information is not entirely lost. This is where convolutional networks come in. CNNs accept the full image matrix as input, which significantly helps the network understand the patterns contained in the pixel values.

3.2   CNN architecture

Regular neural networks contain multiple layers that allow each layer to find successively complex features, and this is the way CNNs work. The first layer of convolutions learns some basic features (edges and lines), the next layer learns features that are a little more complex (circles, squares, and so on), the following layer finds even more complex features (like parts of the face, a car wheel, dog whiskers, and the like), and so on. You will see this demonstrated shortly. For now, know that the CNN architecture follows the same pattern as neural networks: we stack neurons in hidden layers on top of each other; weights are randomly initiated and learned during network training; and we apply activation functions, calculate the error $(y - \hat{y})$, and backpropagate the error to update the weights. This process is the same. The difference is that we use convolutional layers instead of regular fully connected layers for the feature-learning part.

3.2.1   The big picture

Before we look in detail at the CNN architecture, let's back up for a moment to see the big picture (figure 3.9). Remember the image classification pipeline we discussed in chapter 1?

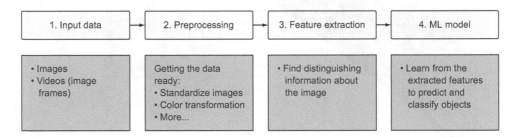

Figure 3.9   The image classification pipeline consists of four components: data input, data preprocessing, feature extraction, and the ML algorithm.

Before deep learning (DL), we used to manually extract features from images and then feed the resulting feature vector to a classifier (a regular ML algorithm like SVM). With the magic that neural networks provide, we can replace the manual work of step 3 in figure 3.9 with a neural network (MLP or CNN) that does both feature learning and classification (steps 3 and 4).

We saw earlier, in the digit-classification project, how to use MLP to learn features and classify an image (steps 3 and 4 together). It turned out that our issue with fully connected layers was not the classification part—fully connected layers do that very well. Our issue was in the way fully connected layers process the image to learn features. Let's get a little creative: we'll keep what's working and make modifications to what's not working. The fully connected layers aren't doing a good job of feature extraction (step 3), so let's replace that with locally connected layers (convolutional layers). On the other hand, fully connected layers do a great job of classifying the extracted features (step 4), so let's keep them for the classification part.

The high-level architecture of CNNs looks like figure 3.10:

- Input layer
- Convolutional layers for feature extraction
- Fully connected layers for classification
- Output prediction

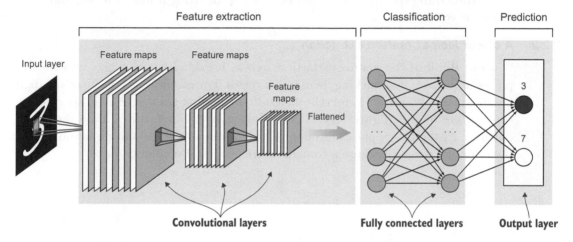

Figure 3.10 **The CNN architecture consists of the following: input layer, convolutional layers, fully connected layers, and output prediction.**

Remember, we are still talking about the big picture. We will dive into each of these components soon. In figure 3.10, suppose we are building a CNN to classify images into two classes: the numbers 3 and 7. Look at the figure, and follow along with these steps:

1 Feed the raw image to the convolutional layers.
2 The image passes through the CNN layers to detect patterns and extract features called *feature maps*. The output of this step is then flattened to a vector of the learned features of the image. Notice that the image dimensions shrink after each layer, and the number of feature maps (the layer depth) increases until we have a long array of small features in the last layer of the feature-extraction part. Conceptually, you can think of this step as the neural network learning to represent more abstract features of the original image.

3 The flattened feature vector is fed to the fully connected layers to classify the extracted features of the image.

4 The neural network fires the node that represents the correct prediction of the image. Note that in this example, we are classifying two classes (3 and 7). Thus the output layer will have two nodes: one to represent the digit 3, and one for the digit 7.

DEFINITION   The basic idea of neural networks is that neurons learn features from the input. In CNNs, a *feature map* is the output of one filter applied to the previous layer. It is called a feature map because it is a mapping of where a certain kind of feature is found in the image. CNNs look for features such as straight lines, edges, or even objects. Whenever they spot these features, they report them to the feature map. Each feature map is looking for something specific: one could be looking for straight lines and another for curves.

3.2.2   *A closer look at feature extraction*

You can think of the feature-extraction step as breaking large images into smaller pieces of features and stacking them into a vector. For example, an image of the digit 3 is one image (depth = 1) and is broken into smaller images that contain specific features of the digit 3 (figure 3.11). If it is broken into four features, then the depth equals 4. As the image passes through the CNN layers, it shrinks in dimensions, and the layer gets deeper because it contains more images of smaller features.

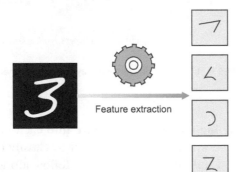

Feature extraction

Figure 3.11   An image is broken into smaller images that contain distinctive features.

Note that this is just a metaphor to help visualize the feature-extraction process. CNNs don't literally break an image into pieces. Instead, they *extract meaningful features* that separate this object from other images in the training set, and stack them in an array of features.

3.2.3 *A closer look at classification*

After feature extraction is complete, we add fully connected layers (a regular MLP) to look at the features vector and say, "The first feature (top) has what looks like an edge: this could be 3, or 7, or maybe an ugly 2. I'm not sure; let's look at the second feature. Hmm, this is definitely not a 7 because it has a curve," and so on until the MLP is confident that the image is the digit 3.

How CNNs learn patterns

It is important to note that a CNN doesn't go from the image input to the features vector directly in one layer. This usually happens in tens or hundreds of layers, as you will see later in this chapter. The feature-learning process happens step by step after each hidden layer. So the first layer usually learns very basic features like lines and edges, and the second assembles those lines into recognizable shapes, corners, and circles. Then, in the deeper layers, the network learns more complex shapes such as human hands, eyes, ears, and so on. For example, here is a simplified version of how CNNs learn faces.

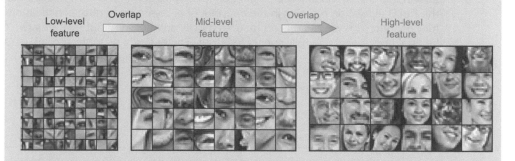

A simplified version of how CNNs learn faces

You can see that the early layers detect patterns in the image to learn low-level features like edges, and the later layers detect *patterns within patterns* to learn more complex features like parts of the face, then *patterns within patterns within patterns*, and so on:

> Input image
>
> + Layer 1 ⇒ patterns
>
> + Layer 2 ⇒ patterns within patterns
>
> + Layer 3 ⇒ patterns within patterns within patterns
>
> ... and so on

This concept will come in handy when we discuss more advanced CNN architectures in later chapters. For now, know that in neural networks, we stack hidden layers to learn patterns from each other until we have an array of meaningful features to identify the image.

3.3 Basic components of a CNN

Without further ado, let's discuss the main components of a CNN architecture. There are three main types of layers that you will see in almost every convolutional network (figure 3.12):

1 Convolutional layer (CONV)
2 Pooling layer (POOL)
3 Fully connected layer (FC)

CNN text representation

The text representation of the architecture in figure 3.12 goes like this:

CNN architecture: INPUT ⇒ CONV ⇒ RELU ⇒ POOL ⇒ CONV ⇒ RELU ⇒ POOL ⇒ FC ⇒ SOFTMAX

Note that the ReLU and softmax activation functions are not really standalone layers—they are the activation functions used in the previous layer. The reason they are shown this way in the text representation is to call out that the CNN designer is using the ReLU activation function in the convolutional layers and softmax activation in the fully connected layer. So this represents a CNN architecture that contains two convolutional layers plus one fully connected layer. You can add as many convolutional and fully connected layers as you see fit. The convolutional layers are for feature learning or extraction, and the fully connected layers are for classification.

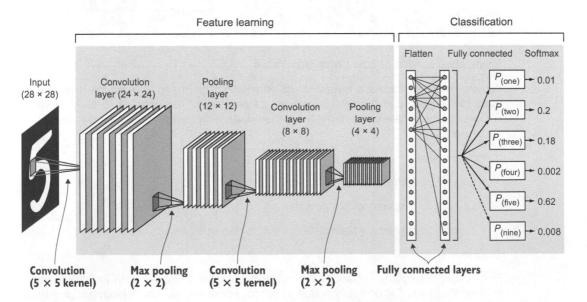

Figure 3.12 The basic components of convolutional networks are convolutional layers and pooling layers to perform feature extraction, and fully connected layers for classification.

Now that we've seen the full architecture of a convolutional network, let's dive deeper into each of the layer types to get a deeper understanding of how they work. Then at the end of this section, we will put them all back together.

3.3.1 Convolutional layers

A convolutional layer is the core building block of a convolutional neural network. Convolutional layers act like a feature finder window that slides over the image pixel by pixel to extract meaningful features that identify the objects in the image.

WHAT IS CONVOLUTION?

In mathematics, convolution is the operation of two functions to produce a third modified function. In the context of CNNs, the first function is the input image, and the second function is the convolutional filter. We will perform some mathematical operations to produce a modified image with new pixel values.

Let's zoom in on the first convolutional layer to see how it processes an image (figure 3.13). By sliding the convolutional filter over the input image, the network breaks the image into little chunks and processes those chunks individually to assemble the modified image, a feature map.

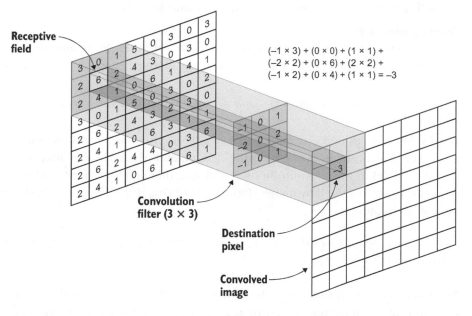

$$(-1 \times 3) + (0 \times 0) + (1 \times 1) +$$
$$(-2 \times 2) + (0 \times 6) + (2 \times 2) +$$
$$(-1 \times 2) + (0 \times 4) + (1 \times 1) = -3$$

Figure 3.13 A 3 × 3 convolutional filter is sliding over the input image.

Keeping this diagram in mind, here are some facts about convolution filters:

- The small 3 × 3 matrix in the middle *is* the convolution filter, also called a *kernel.*
- The kernel slides over the original image pixel by pixel and does some math calculations to get the values of the new "convolved" image on the next layer.

The area of the image that the filter convolves is called the *receptive field* (see figure 3.14).

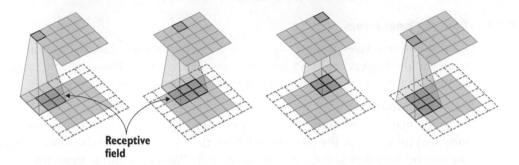

Figure 3.14   The kernel slides over the original image pixel by pixel and calculates the convolved image on the next layer. The convolved area is called the *receptive field*.

What are the kernel values? In CNNs, the convolution matrix *is* the weights. This means they are also *randomly initialized* and the values are *learned* by the network (so you will not have to worry about assigning its values).

CONVOLUTIONAL OPERATIONS

The math should look familiar from our discussion of MLPs. Remember how we multiplied the input by the weights and summed them all together to get the weighted sum?

$$\text{weighted sum} = x_1 \cdot w_1 + x_2 \cdot w_2 + x_3 \cdot w_3 + \dots + x_n \cdot w_n + b$$

We do the same thing here, except that in CNNs, the neurons and weights are structured in a matrix shape. So we multiply each pixel in the receptive field by the corresponding pixel in the convolution filter and sum them all together to get the value of the center pixel in the new image (figure 3.15). This is the same matrix dot product we saw in chapter 2:

$(93 \times -1) + (139 \times 0) + (101 \times 1) + (26 \times -2) + (252 \times 0) + (196 \times 2) + (135 \times -1) + (240 \times 0) + (48 \times 1) = 243$

The filter (or kernel) slides over the whole image. Each time, we multiply every corresponding pixel element-wise and then add them all together to create a new image with new pixel values. This convolved image is called a *feature map* or *activation map*.

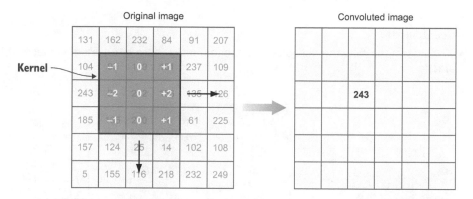

Figure 3.15 Multiplying each pixel in the receptive field by the corresponding pixel in the convolution filter and summing them gives the value of the center pixel in the new image.

Applying filters to learn features

Let's not lose focus of the initial goal. We are doing all this so the network extracts features from the image. How does applying filters lead toward this goal? In image processing, filters are used to filter out unwanted information or amplify features in an image. These filters are matrices of numbers that convolve with the input image to modify it. Look at this edge-detection filter:

0	−1	0
−1	4	−1
0	−1	0

When this kernel (K) is convolved with the input image $F(x,y)$, it creates a new convolved image (a feature map) that amplifies the edges.

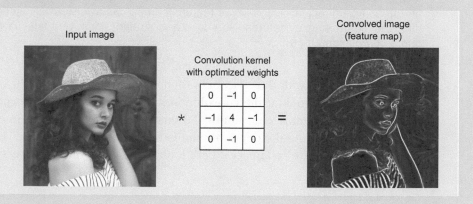

Applying an edge detection kernel on an image

(continued)

To understand how the convolution happens, let's zoom in on a small piece of the image.

Input image

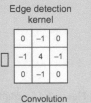

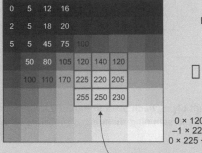

Edge detection kernel

0	−1	0
−1	4	−1
0	−1	0

Convolution
$0 \times 120 + -1 \times 140 + 0 \times 120 +$
$-1 \times 225 + 4 \times 220 + -1 \times 205 +$
$0 \times 225 + -1 \times 250 + 0 \times 230 = 60$

Calculations for applying an edge kernel on an input image

The new value of the middle pixel in the convolved image is 60. The pixel value is > 0, which means that a small edge has been detected.

This image shows the convolution calculations in one area of the image to compute the value of one pixel. We compute the values of all the pixels by sliding the kernel over the input image pixel by pixel and applying the same convolution process.

These kernels are often called *weights* because they determine how important a pixel is in forming a new output image. Similar to what we discussed about MLP and weights, these weights represent the importance of the feature on the output. In images, the input features are the pixel values.

Other filters can be applied to detect different types of features. For example, some filters detect horizontal edges, others detect vertical edges, still others detect more complex shapes like corners, and so on. The point is that these filters, when applied in the convolutional layers, yield the feature-learning behavior we discussed earlier: first they learn simple features like edges and straight lines, and later layers learn more complex features.

We are basically done with the concept of filter. That is all there is to it!

Now, let's take a look at the convolutional layer as a whole: Each convolutional layer contains one or more convolutional filters. The number of filters in each convolutional layer determines the depth of the next layer, because each filter produces its own feature map (convolved image). Let's look at the convolutional layers in Keras to see how they work:

```
from keras.layers import Conv2D

model.add(Conv2D(filters=16, kernel_size=2, strides='1', padding='same',
        activation='relu'))
```

And there you have it. One line of code creates the convolutional layer. We will see where this line fits in the full code later in this chapter. Let's stay focused on the convolutional layer. As you can see from the code, the convolutional layer takes five main arguments. As mentioned in chapter 2, it is recommended that we use the ReLU activation function in the neural networks' hidden layers. That's one argument out of the way. Now, let's explain the remaining four hyperparameters that control the size and depth of the output volume:

- Filters: the number of convolutional filters in each layer. This represents the depth of its output.
- Kernel size: the size of the convolutional filter matrix. Sizes vary: 2×2, 3×3, 5×5.
- Stride.
- Padding.

We will discuss strides and padding in the next section. But now, let's look at each of these four hyperparameters.

> **NOTE** As you learned in chapter 2 on deep learning, hyperparameters are the knobs you tune (increase and decrease) when configuring your neural network to improve performance.

NUMBER OF FILTERS IN THE CONVOLUTIONAL LAYER

Each convolutional layer has one or more filters. To understand this, let's review MLPs from chapter 2. Remember how we stacked neurons in hidden layers, and each hidden layer has *n* number of neurons (also called *hidden units*)? Figure 3.16 shows the MLP diagram from chapter 2.

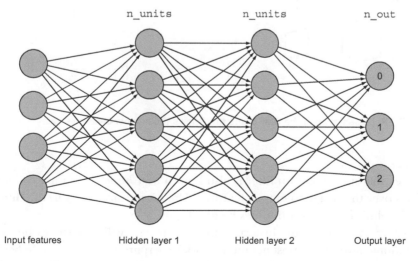

Figure 3.16 Neurons are stacked in hidden layers, and each hidden layer has *n* neurons (hidden units).

Similarly, with CNNs, the convolutional layers are the hidden layers. And to increase the number of neurons in hidden layers, we increase the number of kernels in convolutional layers. Each kernel unit is considered a neuron. For example, if we have a 3×3 kernel in the convolutional layer, this means we have 9 hidden units in this layer. When we add another 3×3 kernel, we have 18 hidden units. Add another one, and we have 27, and so on. So, by increasing the number of kernels in a convolutional layer, we increase the number of hidden units, which makes our network more complex and able to detect more complex patterns. The same was true when we added more neurons (hidden units) to the hidden layers in the MLP. Figure 3.17 provides a representation of the CNN layers that shows the number-of-kernels idea.

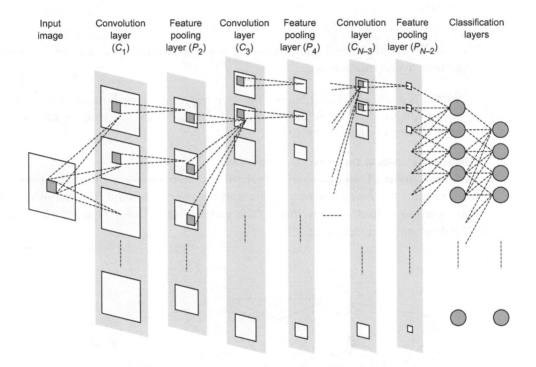

Figure 3.17   Representation of the CNN layers that shows the number-of-kernels idea

KERNEL SIZE

Remember that a convolution filter is also known as a *kernel*. It is a matrix of weights that slides over the image to extract features. The kernel size refers to the dimensions of the convolution filter (width times height; figure 3.18).

`kernel_size` is one of the hyperparameters that you will be setting when building a convolutional layer. Like most neural network hyperparameters, no single best answer fits all problems. The intuition is that smaller filters will capture very fine details of the image, and bigger filters will miss minute details in the image.

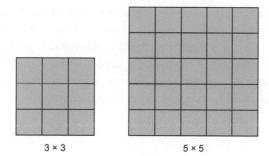

3 × 3   5 × 5

Figure 3.18   The kernel size refers to the dimensions of the convolution filter.

Remember that filters contain the weights that will be learned by the network. So, theoretically, the bigger the `kernel_size`, the deeper the network, which means the better it learns. However, this comes with higher computational complexity and might lead to overfitting.

Kernel filters are almost always square and range from the smallest at 2 × 2 to the largest at 5 × 5. Theoretically, you can use bigger filters, but this is not preferred because it results in losing important image details.

> **Tuning**
>
> I don't want you to get overwhelmed with all the hyperparameter tuning. Deep learning is really an art as well as a science. I can't emphasize this enough: most of your work as a DL engineer will be spent not building the actual algorithms, but rather building your network architecture and setting, experimenting, and tuning your hyperparameters. A great deal of research today is focused on trying to find the optimal topologies and parameters for a CNN, given a type of problem. Fortunately, the problem of tuning hyperparameters doesn't have to be as hard as it might seem. Throughout the book, I will indicate good starting points for using hyperparameters and help you develop an instinct for evaluating your model and analyzing its results to know which knob (hyperparameter) you need to tune (increase or decrease).

STRIDES AND PADDING

You will usually think of these two hyperparameters together, because they both control the shape of the output of a convolutional layer. Let's see how:

- *Strides*—The amount by which the filter slides over the image. For example, to slide the convolution filter one pixel at a time, the strides value is 1. If we want to jump two pixels at a time, the strides value is 2. Strides of 3 or more are uncommon and rare in practice. Jumping pixels produces smaller output volumes spatially.

  Strides of 1 will make the output image roughly the same height and width of the input image, while strides of 2 will make the output image roughly half of the input image size. I say "roughly" because it depends on what you set the padding parameter to do with the edge of the image.

■ *Padding*—Often called *zero-padding* because we add zeros around the border of an image (figure 3.19). Padding is most commonly used to allow us to preserve the spatial size of the input volume so the input and output width and height are the same. This way, we can use convolutional layers without necessarily shrinking the height and width of the volumes. This is important for building deeper networks, since, otherwise, the height/width would shrink as we went to deeper layers.

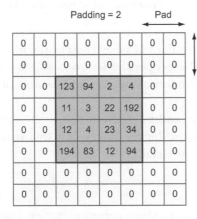

Figure 3.19   Zero-padding adds zeros around the border of the image. Padding = 2 adds two layers of zeros around the border.

NOTE The goal when using strides and padding hyperparameters is one of two things: keep all the important details of the image and transfer them to the next layer (when the `strides` value is 1 and the `padding` value is `same`); or ignore some of the spatial information of the image to make the processing computationally more affordable. Note that we will be adding the pooling layer (discussed next) to reduce the size of the image to focus on the extracted features. For now, know that strides and padding hyperparameters are meant to control the behavior of the convolutional layer and the size of its output: whether to pass on all image details or ignore some of them.

3.3.2 *Pooling layers or subsampling*

Adding more convolutional layers increases the depth of the output layer, which leads to increasing the number of parameters that the network needs to optimize (learn). You can see that adding several convolutional layers (usually tens or even hundreds) will produce a huge number of parameters (weights). This increase in network dimensionality increases the time and space complexity of the mathematical operations that take place in the learning process. This is when pooling layers come in handy. *Subsampling* or *pooling* helps reduce the size of the network by reducing the number of parameters passed to the next layer. The pooling operation resizes its input by applying a summary statistical function, such as a maximum or average, to reduce the overall number of parameters passed on to the next layer.

The goal of the pooling layer is to downsample the feature maps produced by the convolutional layer into a smaller number of parameters, thus reducing computational complexity. It is a common practice to add pooling layers after every one or two convolutional layers in the CNN architecture (figure 3.20).

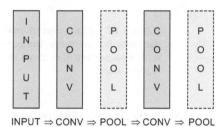

INPUT ⇒ CONV ⇒ POOL ⇒ CONV ⇒ POOL

Figure 3.20 Pooling layers are commonly added after every one or two convolutional layers.

MAX POOLING VS. AVERAGE POOLING

There are two main types of pooling layers: max pooling and average pooling. We will discuss max pooling first.

Similar to convolutional kernels, max pooling kernels are windows of a certain size and strides value that slide over the image. The difference with max pooling is that the windows don't have weights or any values. All they do is slide over the feature map created by the previous convolutional layer and select the max pixel value to pass along to the next layer, ignoring the remaining values. In figure 3.21, you see a pooling filter with a size of 2×2 and strides of 2 (the filter jumps 2 pixels when sliding over the image). This pooling layer reduces the feature map size from 4×4 down to 2×2.

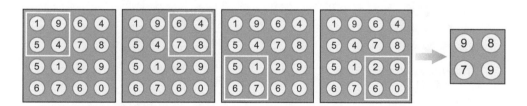

Figure 3.21 A 2 × 2 pooling filter and strides of 2, reducing the feature map from 4 × 4 to 2 × 2

When we do that to all the feature maps in the convolutional layer, we get maps of smaller dimensions (width times height), but the depth of the layer is kept the same because we apply the pooling filter to each of the feature maps from the previous filter. So if the convolutional layer has three feature maps, the output of the pooling layer will also have three feature maps, but of smaller size (figure 3.22).

Global average pooling is a more extreme type of dimensionality reduction. Instead of setting a window size and strides, global average pooling calculates the average

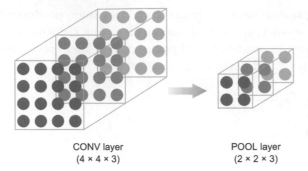

CONV layer
(4 × 4 × 3)

POOL layer
(2 × 2 × 3)

**Figure 3.22   If the convolutional layer
has three feature maps, the pooling
layer's output will have three smaller
feature maps.**

values of all pixels in the feature map (figure 3.23). You can see in figure 3.24 that the
global average pooling layer takes a 3D array and turns it into a vector.

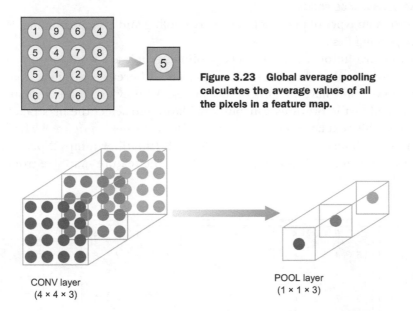

**Figure 3.23   Global average pooling
calculates the average values of all
the pixels in a feature map.**

CONV layer
(4 × 4 × 3)

POOL layer
(1 × 1 × 3)

Figure 3.24   The global average pooling layer turns a 3D array into a vector.

WHY USE A POOLING LAYER?

As you can see from the examples we have discussed, pooling layers reduce the dimensionality of our convolutional layers. The reason it is important to reduce dimensionality
is that in complex projects, CNNs contain many convolutional layers, and each has tens
or hundreds of convolutional filters (kernels). Since the kernel contains the parameters
(weights) that the network learns, this can get out of control very quickly, and the dimensionality of our convolutional layers can get very large. So adding pooling layers helps
keep the important features and pass them along to the next layer, while shrinking image

dimensionality. Think of pooling layers as image-compressing programs. They reduce the image resolution while keeping its important features (figure 3.25).

Original   Downsampled

Figure 3.25 Pooling layers reduce image resolution and keep the image's important features.

Pooling vs. strides and padding

The main purpose of pooling and strides is to reduce the number of parameters in the neural network. The more parameters we have, the more computationally expensive the training process will be. Many people dislike the pooling operation and think that we can get away without it in favor of tuning strides and padding the convolutional layer. For example, "Striving for Simplicity: The All Convolutional Net"[a] proposes discarding the pooling layer in favor of architecture that only consists of repeated convolutional layers. To reduce the size of the representation, the authors suggest occasionally using larger strides in the convolutional layer. Discarding pooling layers has also been found helpful in training good generative models, such as generative adversarial networks (GANs), which we will discuss in chapter 10. It seems likely that future architectures will feature very few to no pooling layers. But for now, pooling layers are still widely used to downsample images from one layer to the next.

[a] Jost Tobias Springenberg, Alexey Dosovitskiy, Thomas Brox, and Martin Riedmiller, "Striving for Simplicity: The All Convolutional Net," https://arxiv.org/abs/1412.6806.

CONVOLUTIONAL AND POOLING LAYERS RECAP

Let's review what we have done so far. Up until this point, we used a series of convolutional and pooling layers to process an image and extract meaningful features that are specific to the images in the training dataset. To summarize how we got here:

1 The raw image is fed to the convolutional layer, which is a set of kernel filters that slide over the image to extract features.

2 The convolutional layer has the following attributes that we need to configure:

```
from keras.layers import Conv2D

model.add(Conv2D(filters=16, kernel_size=2, strides='1',
    padding='same', activation='relu'))
```

– `filters` is the number of kernel filters in each layer (the depth of the hidden layer).
– `kernel_size` is the size of the filter (aka kernel). Usually 2, or 3, or 5.
– `strides` is the amount by which the filter slides over the image. A `strides` value of 1 or 2 is usually recommended as a good start.

 – `padding` adds columns and rows of zero values around the border of the image to reserve the image size in the next layer.
 – `activation` of `relu` is strongly recommended in the hidden layers.

3 The pooling layer has the following attributes that we need to configure:

```
from keras.layers import MaxPooling2D

model.add(MaxPooling2D(pool_size=(2, 2), strides = 2))
```

And we keep adding pairs of convolutional and pooling layers to achieve the required depth for our "deep" neural network.

Visualize what happens after each layer

After the convolutional layers, the image keeps its width and height dimensions (usually), but it gets deeper and deeper after each layer. Why? Remember the cutting-the-image-into-pieces-of-features analogy we mentioned earlier? That is what's happening after the convolutional layer.

For example, suppose the input image is 28 × 28 (like in the MNIST dataset). When we add a CONV_1 layer (with `filters` of 4, `strides` of 1, and `padding` of same), the output will be the same width and height dimensions but with `depth` of 4 (28 × 28 × 4). Now we add a CONV_2 layer with the same hyperparameters but more filters (12), and we get deeper output: 28 × 28 × 12.

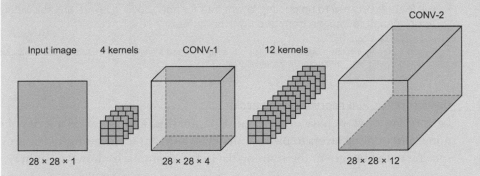

After the pooling layers, the image keeps its depth but shrinks in width and height:

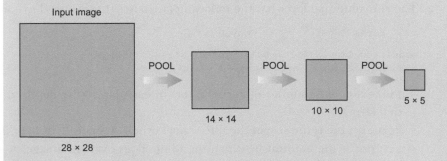

Putting the convolutional and pooling together, we get something like this:

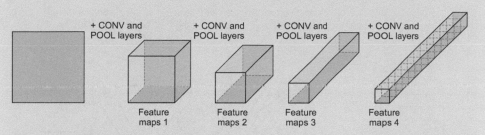

This keeps happening until we have, at the end, a long tube of small shaped images that contain all the features in the original image.

The output of the convolutional and pooling layers produces a feature tube ($5 \times 5 \times 40$) that is *almost* ready to be classified. We use 40 here as an example for the depth of the feature tube, as in 40 feature maps. The last step is to flatten this tube before feeding it to the fully connected layer for classification. As discussed earlier, the flattened layer will have the dimensions of $(1, m)$ where $m = 5 \times 5 \times 40 = 1,000$ neurons.

3.3.3 Fully connected layers

After passing the image through the feature-learning process using convolutional and pooling layers, we have extracted all the features and put them in a long tube. Now it is time to use these extracted features to classify images. We will use the regular neural network architecture, MLP, that we discussed in chapter 2.

WHY USE FULLY CONNECTED LAYERS?

MLPs work great in classification problems. The reason we used convolutional layers in this chapter is that MLPs lose a lot of valuable information when extracting features from an image—we have to flatten the image before feeding it to the network— whereas convolutional layers can process raw images. Now we have the features extracted, and after we flatten them, we can use regular MLPs to classify them.

We discussed the MLP architecture thoroughly in chapter 2: nothing new here. To reiterate, here are the fully connected layers (figure 3.26):

- *Input flattened vector*—As illustrated in figure 3.26, to feed the features tube to the MLP for classification, we flatten it to a vector with the dimensions $(1, n)$. For example, if the features tube has the dimensions of $5 \times 5 \times 40$, the flattened vector will be $(1, 1000)$.
- *Hidden layer*—We add one or more fully connected layers, and each layer has one or more neurons (similar to what we did when we built regular MLPs).
- *Output layer*—Chapter 2 recommended using the softmax activation function for classification problems involving more than two classes. In this example, we are classifying digits from 0 to 9: 10 classes. The number of neurons in the output layer is equal to the number of classes; thus, the output layer will have 10 nodes.

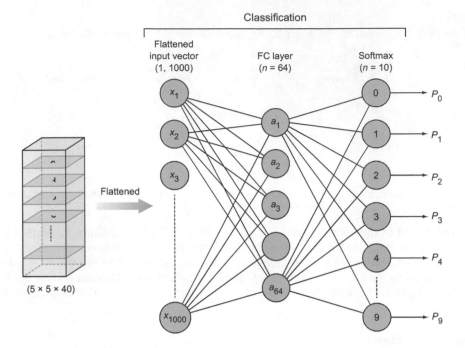

Figure 3.26 Fully connected layers for an MLP

MLPs and fully connected layers

Remember from chapter 2 that multilayer perceptrons (MLPs) are also called fully connected layers, because all the nodes from one layer are connected to all the nodes in the previous and next layers. They are also called *dense layers*. The terms *MLP*, *fully connected*, *dense*, and sometimes *feedforward* are used interchangeably to refer to the regular neural network architecture.

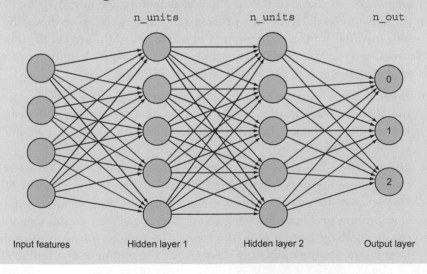

3.4 Image classification using CNNs

Okay, you are now fully equipped to build your own CNN model to classify images. For this mini project, which is a simple problem but which will help build the foundation to more complex problems in the following chapters, we will use the MNIST dataset. (The MNIST dataset is like "Hello World" for deep learning.)

> **NOTE** Regardless of which DL library you decide to use, the concepts are pretty much the same. You start with designing the CNN architecture in your mind or on a piece of paper, and then you begin stacking layers on top of each other and setting their parameters. Both Keras and MXNet (along with Tensor-Flow, PyTorch, and other DL libraries) have pros and cons that we will discuss later, but the concepts are similar. So for the rest of this book, we will be working mostly with Keras with a little overview of other libraries here and there.

3.4.1 Building the model architecture

This is the part in your project where you define and build the CNN model architecture. To look at the full code of the project that includes image preprocessing, training, and evaluating the model, go to the book's GitHub repo at https://github.com/moelgendy/deep_learning_for_vision_systems and open the mnist_cnn notebook or go to the book's website: www.manning.com/books/deep-learning-for-vision-systems or www.computerVisionBook.com. At this point, we are concerned with the code that builds the model architecture. At the end of this chapter, we will build an end-to-end image classifier and dive deeper into the other pieces:

```
from keras.models import Sequential
from keras.layers import Conv2D, MaxPooling2D, Flatten, Dense, Dropout

model = Sequential()          ◁——  Builds the
                                    model object

                                                         CONV_1: adds a convolutional
                                                         layer with ReLU activation and
                                                         depth = 32 kernels

model.add(Conv2D(32, kernel_size=(3, 3), strides=1, padding='same',
          activation='relu', input_shape=(28,28,1)))      ◁——
model.add(MaxPooling2D(pool_size=(2, 2)))      ◁——  POOL_1: downsamples the image
                                                    to choose the best features
CONV_2:
increases
the depth
to 64  ┕—▷ model.add(Conv2D(64, (3, 3), strides=1, padding='same', activation='relu'))
           model.add(MaxPooling2D(pool_size=(2, 2)))      ◁——

                                                    POOL_2: more
                                                    downsampling
           model.add(Flatten())      ◁——

                                                    Flatten, since there are too
           model.add(Dense(64, activation='relu'))      ◁——   many dimensions; we only
                                                               want a classification output

           model.add(Dense(10, activation='softmax'))      ◁——

  ┌—▷ model.summary()          FC_2: Outputs a softmax        FC_1: Fully connected to
  │                            to squash the matrix into       get all relevant data
  │   Prints the model         output probabilities for
  │   architecture summary     the 10 classes
```

```
Layer (type)                 Output Shape              Param #
=================================================================
conv2d_1 (Conv2D)            (None, 28, 28, 32)        320

max_pooling2d_1 (MaxPooling2 (None, 14, 14, 32)        0

conv2d_2 (Conv2D)            (None, 14, 14, 64)        18496

max_pooling2d_2 (MaxPooling2 (None, 7, 7, 64)          0

flatten_1 (Flatten)          (None, 3136)              0

dense_1 (Dense)              (None, 64)                200768

dense_2 (Dense)              (None, 10)                650
=================================================================
Total params: 220,234
Trainable params: 220,234
Non-trainable params: 0
```

Figure 3.27   The printed model summary

When you run this code, you will see the model summary printed as in figure 3.27. Following are some general observations before we look at the model summary:

- We need to pass the input_shape argument to the first convolutional layer only. Then we don't need to declare the input shape to the model, since the output of the previous layer is the input of the current layer—it is already known to the model.

- You can see that the output of every convolutional and pooling layer is a 3D tensor of shape (None, height, width, channels). The height and width values are pretty straightforward: they are the dimensions of the image at this layer. The channels value represents the depth of the layer. This is the number of feature maps in each layer. The first value in this tuple, set to None, is the number of images that are processed in this layer. Keras sets this to None, which means this dimension is variable and accepts any number of batch_size.

- As you can see in the Output Shape columns, as you go deeper through the network, the image dimensions shrink and the depth increases, as we discussed earlier in this chapter.

- Notice the number of total params (weights) that the network needs to optimize: 220,234, compared to the number of params from the MLP network we created earlier in this chapter (669,706). We were able to cut it down to almost a third.

Let's take a look at the model summary line by line:

- CONV_1—We know the input shape: (28 × 28 × 1). Look at the output shape of conv2d: (28 × 28 × 32). Since we set the strides parameter to 1 and padding to same, the dimensions of the input image did not change. But depth increased to 32. Why? Because we added 32 filters in this layer. Each filter produces one feature map.

- POOL_1—The input of this layer is the output of its previous layer: (28 × 28 × 32). After the pooling layer, the image dimensions shrink, and depth stays the same. Since we used a 2 × 2 pool, the output shape is (14 × 14 × 32).

- CONV_2— Same as before, convolutional layers increase depth and keep dimensions. The input from the previous layer is (14 × 14 × 32). Since the filters in this layer are set to 64, the output is (14 × 14 × 64).

- POOL_2—Same 2 × 2 pool, keeping the depth and shrinking the dimensions. The output is (7 × 7 × 64).

- Flatten—Flattening a features tube that has dimensions of (7 × 7 × 64) converts it into a flat vector of dimensions (1, 3136).

- Dense_1—We set this fully connected layer to have 64 neurons, so the output is 64.

- Dense_2—This is the output layer that we set to 10 neurons, since we have 10 classes.

3.4.2 *Number of parameters (weights)*

Okay, now we know how to build the model and read the summary line by line to see how the image shape changes as it passes through the network layers. One important thing remains: the Param # column on the right in the model summary.

WHAT ARE THE PARAMETERS?

Parameters is just another name for weights. These are the things that your network learns. As we discussed in chapter 2, the network's goal is to update the weight values during the gradient descent and backpropagation processes until it finds the optimal parameter values that minimize the error function.

HOW ARE THESE PARAMETERS CALCULATED?

In MLP, we know that the layers are fully connected to each other, so the weight connections or edges are simply calculated by multiplying the number of neurons in each layer. In CNNs, weight calculations are not as straightforward. Fortunately, there is an equation for this:

number of params = filters × kernel size × depth of the previous layer + number of filters (for biases)

Let's apply this equation in an example. Suppose we want to calculate the parameters at the second layer of the previous mini project. Here is the code for CONV_2 again:

```
model.add(Conv2D(64, (3, 3), strides=1, padding='same', activation='relu'))
```

Since we know that the depth of the previous layer is 32, then

$$\Rightarrow \text{Params} = 64 \times 3 \times 3 \times 32 + 64 = 18{,}496$$

Note that the pooling layers *do not* add any parameters. Hence, you will see the Param # value is 0 after the pooling layers in the model summary. The same is true for the flatten layer: no extra weights are added (figure 3.28).

Layer (type)	Output Shape	Param #
max_pooling2d_1 (MaxPooling2	(None, 14, 14, 32)	0
conv2d_2 (Conv2D)	(None, 14, 14, 64)	18496
max_pooling2d_2 (MaxPooling2	(None, 7, 7, 64)	0
flatten_1 (Flatten)	(None, 3136)	0

Figure 3.28   **Pooling and flatten layers don't add parameters, so Param # is 0 after pooling and flattening layers in the model summary.**

When we add all the parameters in the Param # column, we get the total number of parameters that this network needs to optimize: 220,234.

TRAINABLE AND NON-TRAINABLE PARAMS
In the model summary, you will see the total number of params and, below it, the number of trainable and non-trainable params. The trainable params are the weights that this neural network needs to optimize during the training process. In this example, all our params are trainable (figure 3.29).

```
=================================================================
Total params: 220,234
Trainable params: 220,234
Non-trainable params: 0
```

Figure 3.29   **All of our params are trainable and need to be optimized during training.**

In later chapters, we will talk about using a pretrained network and combining it with your own network for faster and more accurate results: in such a case, you may decide to freeze some layers because they are pretrained. So, not all of the network params will be trained. This is useful for understanding the memory and space complexity of your model before starting the training process; but more on that later. As far as we know now, all our params are trainable.

3.5   *Adding dropout layers to avoid overfitting*

So far, you have been introduced to the three main layers of CNNs: convolution, pooling, and fully connected. You will find these three layer types in almost every CNN architecture. But that's not all of them—there are additional layers that you can add to avoid overfitting.

3.5.1 What is overfitting?

The main cause of poor performance in machine learning is either overfitting or underfitting the data. *Underfitting* is as the name implies: the model fails to fit the training data. This happens when the model is too simple to fit the data: for example, using one perceptron to classify a nonlinear dataset.

Overfitting, on the other hand, means fitting the data too much: memorizing the training data and not really learning the features. This happens when we build a super network that fits the training dataset perfectly (very low error while training) but fails to generalize to other data samples that it hasn't seen before. You will see that, in overfitting, the network performs very well in the training dataset but performs poorly in the test dataset (figure 3.30).

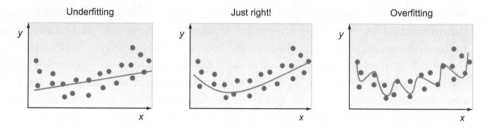

Figure 3.30 Underfitting (left): the model doesn't represent the data very well. Just right (middle): the model fits the data very well. Overfitting (right): the model fits the data too much, so it won't be able to generalize for unseen examples.

In machine learning, we don't want to build models that are too simple and so underfit the data or are too complex and overfit it. We want to use other techniques to build a neural network that is just right for our problem. To address that, we will discuss dropout layers next.

3.5.2 What is a dropout layer?

A dropout layer is one of the most commonly used layers to prevent overfitting. Dropout turns off a percentage of neurons (nodes) that make up a layer of your network (figure 3.31). This percentage is identified as a hyperparameter that you tune when you build your network. By "turns off," I mean these neurons are not included in a particular forward or backward pass. It may seem counterintuitive to throw away a connection in your network, but as a network trains, some nodes can dominate others or end up making large mistakes. Dropout gives you a way to balance your network so that every node works equally toward the same goal, and if one makes a mistake, it won't dominate the behavior of your model. You can think of dropout as a technique that makes a network resilient; it makes all the nodes work well as a team by making sure no node is too weak or too strong.

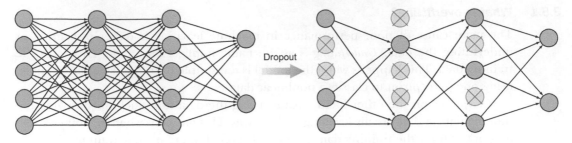

Figure 3.31   Dropout turns off a percentage of the neurons that make up a network layer.

3.5.3   *Why do we need dropout layers?*

Neurons develop codependency among each other during training, which controls the individual power of each neuron, leading to overfitting of training data. To really understand why dropouts are effective, let's take a closer look at the MLP in figure 3.31 and think about what the nodes in each layer really represent. The first layer (far left) is the input layer that contains the input features. The second layer contains the features learned from the patterns of the previous layer when multiplied by the weights. Then the following layer is patterns learned within patterns, and so on. Each neuron represents a certain feature that, when multiplied by a weight, is transformed into another feature. When we randomly turn off some of these nodes, we force the other nodes to learn patterns without relying on only one or two features, because any feature can be randomly dropped out at any point. This results in spreading out the weights among all the features, leading to more trained neurons.

Dropout helps reduce interdependent learning among the neurons. In that sense, it helps to view dropout as a form of ensemble learning. In ensemble learning, we train a number of weaker classifiers separately, and then we use them at test time by averaging the responses of all ensemble members. Since each classifier has been trained separately, it has learned different aspects of the data, and their mistakes (errors) are different. Combining them helps to produce a stronger classifier, which is less prone to overfitting.

Intuition

An analogy that helps me understand dropout is training your biceps with a bar. When lifting a bar with both arms, we tend to rely on our stronger arm to lift a little more weight than our weaker arm. Our stronger arm will end up getting more training than the other and develop a larger muscle:

Dropout means mixing up our workout (training) a little. We tie our right arm and train our left arm only. Then we tie the left arm and train the right arm only. Then we mix it up and go back to the bar with both arms, and so on. After some time, you will see that you have developed both of your biceps:

This is exactly what happens when we train neural networks. Sometimes part of the network has very large weights and dominates all the training, while another part of the network doesn't get much training. What dropout does is turn off some neurons and let the rest of the neurons train. Then, in the next epoch, it turns off other neurons, and the process continues.

3.5.4 Where does the dropout layer go in the CNN architecture?

As you have learned in this chapter, a standard CNN consists of alternating convolutional and pooling layers, ending with fully connected layers. To prevent overfitting, it's become standard practice after you flatten the image to inject a few dropout layers between the fully connected layers at the end of the architecture. Why? Because dropout is known to work well in the fully connected layers of convolutional neural nets. Its effect in convolutional and pooling layers is, however, not well studied yet:

CNN architecture: ... $CONV \Rightarrow POOL \Rightarrow Flatten \Rightarrow DO \Rightarrow FC \Rightarrow DO \Rightarrow FC$

Let's see how we use Keras to add a dropout layer to our previous model:

```
# CNN and POOL layers
# ...
# ...                                    Flatten layer
model.add(Flatten())            ◄─┘

                                         Dropout layer with
                                         30% probability
model.add(Dropout(rate=0.3))    ◄─┘

                                         FC_1: fully connected
model.add(Dense(64, activation='relu'))  ◄─  to get all relevant data

model.add(Dropout(rate=0.5))    ◄─┐
                                         Dropout layer with
                                         50% probability
model.add(Dense(10, activation='softmax'))  ◄─┐
                                         FC_2: outputs a softmax to squash
                                         the matrix into output probabilities
model.summary()    ◄─  Prints the model   for the 10 classes
                       architecture summary
```

As you can see, the dropout layer takes `rate` as an argument. The rate represents the fraction of the input units to drop. For example, if we set `rate` to 0.3, it means 30% of the neurons in this layer will be randomly dropped in each epoch. So if we have 10 nodes in a layer, 3 of these neurons will be turned off, and 7 will be trained. The three neurons are randomly selected, and in the next epoch other randomly selected neurons are turned off, and so on. Since we do this randomly, some neurons may be turned off more than others, and some may never be turned off. This is okay, because we do this many times so that, on average, each neuron will get almost the same treatment. Note that this rate is another hyperparameter that we tune when building our CNN.

3.6   *Convolution over color images (3D images)*

Remember from chapter 1 that computers see grayscale images as 2D matrices of pixels (figure 3.32). To a computer, the image looks like a 2D matrix of the pixels' values, which represent intensities across the color spectrum. There is no context here, just a massive pile of data.

Color images, on the other hand, are interpreted by the computer as 3D matrices with height, width, and depth. In the case of RGB images (red, green, and blue) the depth is three: one channel for each color. For example, a color 28 × 28 image will be seen by the computer as a 28 × 28 × 3 matrix. Think of this as a stack of three 2D matrices—one each for the red, green, and blue channels of the image. Each of the

What we see

What computers see

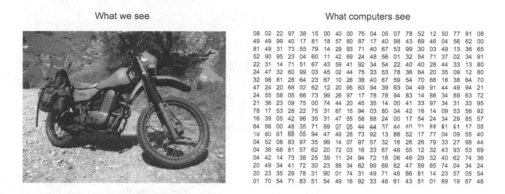

Figure 3.32 To a computer, an image looks like a 2D matrix of pixel values.

three matrices represents the value of intensity of its color. When they are stacked, they create a complete color image (figure 3.33).

NOTE For generalization, we represent images as a 3D array: height × width × depth. For grayscale images, depth is 1; and for color images, depth is 3.

Color image

RGB channels

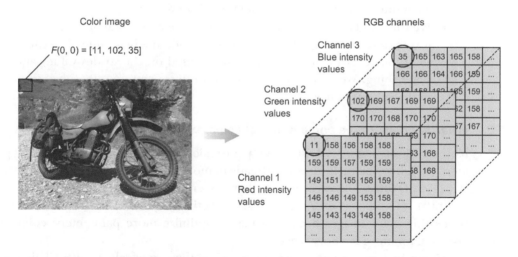

Figure 3.33 Color images are represented by three matrices. Each matrix represents the value of its color's intensity. Stacking them creates a complete color image.

3.6.1 How do we perform a convolution on a color image?

Similar to what we did with grayscale images, we slide the convolutional kernel over the image and compute the feature maps. Now the kernel is itself three-dimensional: one dimension for each color channel (figure 3.34).

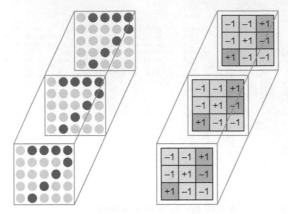

Figure 3.34   We slide the convolutional kernel over the image and compute the feature maps, resulting in a 3D kernel.

To perform convolution, we will do the same thing we did before, except that now, our sum is three times as many terms. Let's see how (figure 3.35):

- Each of the color channels has its own corresponding filter.
- Each filter will slide over its image, multiply every corresponding pixel element-wise, and then add them all together to compute the convolved pixel value of each filter. This is similar to what we did previously.
- We then add the three values to get the value of a single node in the convolved image or feature map. And don't forget to add the bias value of 1. Then we slide the filters over by one or more pixels (based on the strides value) and do the same thing. We continue this process until we compute the pixel values of all nodes in the feature map.

3.6.2   *What happens to the computational complexity?*

Note that if we pass a 3×3 filter over a grayscale image, we will have a total of 9 parameters (weights) for each filter (as already demonstrated). In color images, every filter is itself a 3D filter. This means every filter has a number of parameters: (height × width × depth) = $(3 \times 3 \times 3)$ = 27. You can see how the network complexity increases when processing color images because it has to optimize more parameters; color images also take up more memory space.

Color images contain more information than grayscale images. This can add unnecessary computational complexity and take up memory space. However, color images are also really useful for certain classification tasks. That's why in some use cases, you, as a computer vision engineer, will use your judgement as to whether to convert your color images to grayscale where color doesn't really matter. This is because for many objects, color is not needed to recognize and interpret an image: grayscale could be enough to recognize objects.

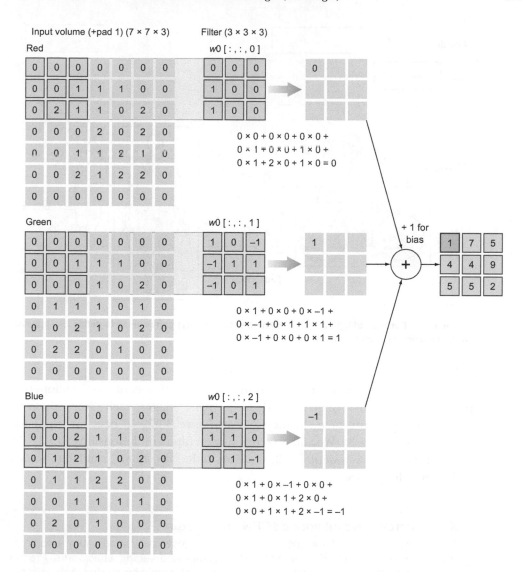

Figure 3.35 Performing convolution

In figure 3.36, you can see how patterns of light and dark in an object (intensity) can be used to define its shape and characteristics. However, in other applications, color is important to define certain objects: for example, skin cancer detection relies heavily on skin color (red rashes). In general, when it comes to CV applications like identifying cars, people, or skin cancer, you can decide whether color information is important or not by thinking about your own vision. If the identification problem is easier in color for us humans, it's likely easier for an algorithm to see color images, too.

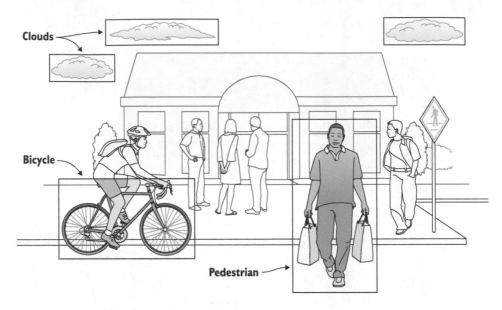

Figure 3.36   Patterns of light and dark in an object (intensity) can be used to define its shape and characteristics in a grayscale image.

Note that in figure 3.36, we added only one filter (that contains 3 channels), which produced one feature map. Similarly to grayscale images, each filter we add will produce its own feature map. In the CNN in figure 3.37, we have an input image of dimensions ($7 \times 7 \times 3$). We add two convolution filters of dimensions (3×3). The output feature map has a depth of 2, since we added two filters, similar to what we did with grayscale images.

An important closing note on CNN architecture

I strongly recommend looking at existing architectures, since many people have already done the work of throwing things together and seeing what works. Practically speaking, unless you are working on research problems, you should start with a CNN architecture that has already been built by other people to solve problems similar to yours. Then tune it further to fit your data.

In chapter 4, we will explain how to diagnose your network's performance and discuss tuning strategies to improve it. In chapter 5, we will discuss the most popular CNN architectures and examine how other researchers built them. What I want you to take from this section is, first, a conceptual understanding of how a CNN is built; and, second, that more layers lead to more neurons, which lead to more learning behavior. But this comes with computational cost. So you should always consider the size and complexity of your training data (many layers may not be necessary for a simple task).

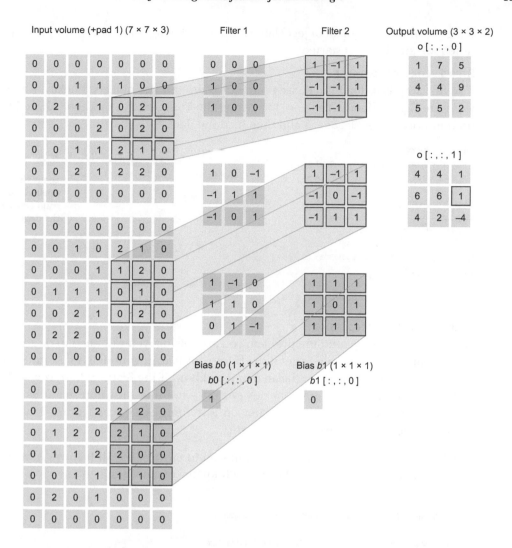

Figure 3.37 Our input image has dimensions (7 × 7 × 3), and we add two convolution filters of dimensions (3 × 3). The output feature map has a depth of 2.

3.7 Project: Image classification for color images

Let's take a look at an end-to-end image classification project. In this project, we will train a CNN to classify images from the CIFAR-10 dataset (www.cs.toronto.edu/ ~kriz/cifar.html). CIFAR-10 is an established CV dataset used for object recognition. It is a subset of the 80 Million Tiny Images dataset[1] and consists of 60,000 (32 × 32) color

---

[1] Antonio Torralba, Rob Fergus, and William T. Freeman, "80 Million Tiny Images: A Large Data Set for Non-parametric Object and Scene Recognition," *IEEE Transactions on Pattern Analysis and Machine Intelligence* (November 2008), https://doi.org/10.1109/TPAMI.2008.128.

images containing 1 of 10 object classes, with 6,000 images per class. Now, fire up your notebook and let's get started.

STEP 1: LOAD THE DATASET

The first step is to load the dataset into our train and test objects. Luckily, Keras provides the CIFAR dataset for us to load using the `load_data()` method. All we have to do is import `keras.datasets` and then load the data:

```
import keras
from keras.datasets import cifar10
(x_train, y_train), (x_test, y_test) = cifar10.load_data()
```
⟵ **Loads the preshuffled train and tests the data**

```
import numpy as np
import matplotlib.pyplot as plt
%matplotlib inline

fig = plt.figure(figsize=(20,5))
for i in range(36):
    ax = fig.add_subplot(3, 12, i + 1, xticks=[], yticks=[])
    ax.imshow(np.squeeze(x_train[i]))
```

STEP 2: IMAGE PREPROCESSING

Based on your dataset and the problem you are solving, you will need to do some data cleanup and preprocessing to get it ready for your learning model. A cost function has the shape of a bowl, but it can be an elongated bowl if the features have very different scales. Figure 3.38 shows gradient descent on a training set where features 1 and 2 have the same scale (on the left), and on a training set where feature 1 has much smaller values than feature 2 (on the right).

TIP   When using gradient descent, you should ensure that all features have a similar scale; otherwise, it will take much longer to converge.

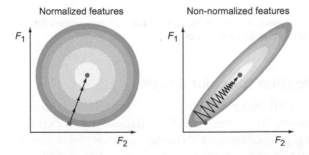

Gradient descent with and without feature scaling

Figure 3.38   Normalized features are on the same scale represented by a uniform bowl (left). Non-normalized features are not on the same scale and are represented by an elongated bowl (right). Gradient descent on a training set with features that have the same scale (left) and on a training set where feature 1's values are much smaller than feature 2's (right).

Rescale the images

Rescale the input images as follows:

```
x_train = x_train.astype('float32')/255
x_test = x_test.astype('float32')/255
```
◁─┐ **Rescales the images by dividing the pixel values by 255: [0,255] ⇒ [0,1]**

Prepare the labels (one-hot encoding)

In this chapter and throughout the book, we will discuss how computers process input data (images) by converting it into numeric values in the form of matrices of pixel intensities. But what about the labels? How are the labels understood by computers? Every image in our dataset has a specific label that explains (in text) how this image is categorized. In this particular dataset, for example, the labels are categorized by the following 10 classes: ['airplane', 'automobile', 'bird', 'cat', 'deer', 'dog', 'frog', 'horse', 'ship', 'truck']. We need to convert these text labels into a form that can be processed by computers. Computers are good with numbers, so we will do something called *one-hot encoding*. One-hot encoding is a process by which categorical variables are converted into a numeric form.

Suppose the dataset looks like the following:

Image	Label
image_1	dog
image_2	automobile
image_3	airplane
image_4	truck
image_5	bird

After one-hot encoding, we have the following:

	airplane	bird	cat	deer	dog	frog	horse	ship	truck	automobile
image_1	0	0	0	0	1	0	0	0	0	0
image_2	0	0	0	0	0	0	0	0	0	1
image_3	1	0	0	0	0	0	0	0	0	0
image_4	0	0	0	0	0	0	0	0	1	0
image_5	0	1	0	0	0	0	0	0	0	0

Luckily, Keras has a method that does just that for us:

```
from keras.utils import np_utils

num_classes = len(np.unique(y_train))
y_train = keras.utils.to_categorical(y_train, num_classes)
y_test = keras.utils.to_categorical(y_test, num_classes)
```
◁─┐ **One-hot encodes the labels**

Split the dataset for training and validation

In addition to splitting our data into train and test datasets, it is a standard practice to further split the training data into training and validation datasets (figure 3.39). Why? Because each split is used for a different purpose:

- *Training dataset*—The sample of data used to train the model.
- *Validation dataset*—The sample of data used to provide an unbiased evaluation of model fit on the training dataset while tuning model hyperparameters. The evaluation becomes more biased as skill on the validation dataset is incorporated into the model configuration.
- *Test dataset*—The sample of data used to provide an unbiased evaluation of final model fit on the training dataset.

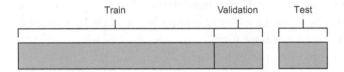

Figure 3.39 Splitting the data into training, validation, and test subsets

Here is the Keras code:

```
(x_train, x_valid) = x_train[5000:], x_train[:5000]
(y_train, y_valid) = y_train[5000:], y_train[:5000]
```
Breaks the training set into training and validation sets

```
print('x_train shape:', x_train.shape)
```
⟵ **Prints the shape of the training set**

```
print(x_train.shape[0], 'train samples')
print(x_test.shape[0], 'test samples')
print(x_valid.shape[0], 'validation samples')
```
Prints the number of training, validation, and test images

The label matrix

One-hot encoding converts the $(1 \times n)$ label vector to a label matrix of dimensions $(10 \times n)$, where n is the number of sample images. So, if we have 1,000 images in our dataset, the label vector will have the dimensions (1×1000). After one-hot encoding, the label matrix dimensions will be (1000×10). That's why, when we define our network architecture in the next step, we will make the output softmax layer contain 10 nodes, where each node represents the probability of each class we have.

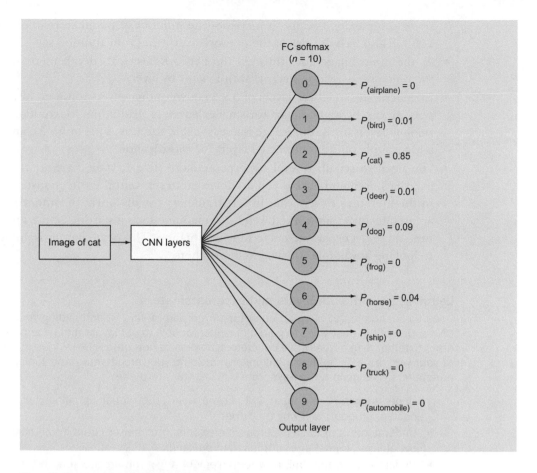

STEP 3: DEFINE THE MODEL ARCHITECTURE

You learned that the core building block of CNNs (and neural networks in general) is the layer. Most DL projects consist of stacking together simple layers that implement a form of *data distillation*. As you learned in this chapter, the main CNN layers are convolution, pooling, fully connected, and activation functions.

How do you decide on the network architecture?

How many convolutional layers should you create? How many pooling layers? In my opinion, it is very helpful to read about some of the most popular architectures (AlexNet, ResNet, Inception) and extract the key ideas leading to the design decisions. Looking at how these state-of-the-art architectures are built and playing with your own projects will help you build an intuition about the CNN architecture that most suits the problem you are solving. We will discuss the most popular CNN architectures in chapter 5. Until then, here is what you need to know:

- The more layers you add, the better (at least theoretically) your network will learn; but this will come at the cost of increasing the computational and memory space complexity, because it increases the number of parameters to optimize. You will also face the risk of the network overfitting your training set.

- As the input image goes through the network layers, its depth increases, and the dimensions (width, height) shrink, layer by layer.

- In general, two or three layers of 3 × 3 convolutional layers followed by a 2 × 2 pooling can be a good start for smaller datasets. Add more convolutional and pooling layers until your image is a reasonable size (say, 4 × 4 or 5 × 5), and then add a couple of fully connected layers for classification.

- You need to set up several hyperparameters (like `filter`, `kernel_size`, and `padding`). Remember that you do not need to reinvent the wheel: instead, look in the literature to see what hyperparameters usually work for others. Choose an architecture that worked well for someone else as a starting point, and then tune these hyperparameters to fit your situation. The next chapter is dedicated to looking at what has worked well for others.

Learning to work with layers and hyperparameters

I don't want you to get hung up on setting hyperparameters when building your first CNNs. One of the best ways to gain an instinct for how to put layers and hyperparameters together is to actually see concrete examples of how others have done it. Most of your work as a DL engineer will involve building your architecture and tuning the parameters. The main takeaways from this chapter are these:

- Understand how the main CNN layers work (convolution, pooling, fully connected, dropout) and why they exist.
- Understand what each hyperparameter does (number of filters in the convolutional layer, kernel size, strides, and padding).
- Understand, in the end, how to implement any given architecture in Keras. If you are able to replicate this project on your own dataset, you are good to go.

In chapter 5, we will review several state-of-the-art architectures and see what worked for them.

The architecture shown in figure 3.40 is called AlexNet: it's a popular CNN architecture that won the ImageNet challenges in 2011 (more details on AlexNet in chapter 5). The AlexNet CNN architecture is composed of five convolutional and pooling layers, and three fully connected layers.

Let's try a smaller version of AlexNet and see how it performs with our dataset (figure 3.41). Based on the results, we might add more layers. Our architecture will stack three convolutional layers and two fully connected (dense) layers as follows:

CNN: INPUT $\Rightarrow$ CONV_1 $\Rightarrow$ POOL_1 $\Rightarrow$ CONV_2 $\Rightarrow$ POOL_2 $\Rightarrow$ CONV_3 $\Rightarrow$ POOL_3 $\Rightarrow$ DO $\Rightarrow$ FC $\Rightarrow$ DO $\Rightarrow$ FC (softmax)

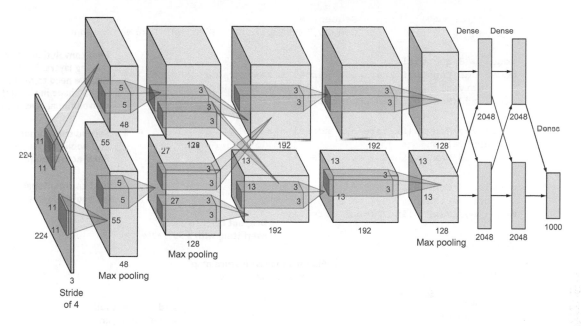

Figure 3.40   AlexNet architecture

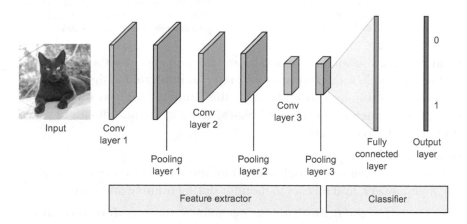

Figure 3.41   We will build a small CNN consisting of three convolutional layers and two dense layers.

Note that we will use the ReLU activation function for all the hidden layers. In the last dense layer, we will use a softmax activation function with 10 nodes to return an array of 10 probability scores (summing to 1). Each score will be the probability that the current image belongs to our 10 image classes:

```
from keras.models import Sequential
from keras.layers import Conv2D, MaxPooling2D, Flatten, Dense, Dropout

model = Sequential()
model.add(Conv2D(filters=16, kernel_size=2, padding='same',
    activation='relu', input_shape=(32, 32, 3)))
model.add(MaxPooling2D(pool_size=2))

model.add(Conv2D(filters=32, kernel_size=2, padding='same',
    activation='relu'))
model.add(MaxPooling2D(pool_size=2))

model.add(Conv2D(filters=64, kernel_size=2, padding='same',
    activation='relu'))
model.add(MaxPooling2D(pool_size=2))

model.add(Dropout(0.3))

model.add(Flatten())

model.add(Dense(500, activation='relu'))
model.add(Dropout(0.4))

model.add(Dense(10, activation='softmax'))

model.summary()
```

First convolutional and pooling layers. Note that we need to define input_shape in the first convolutional layer only.

Second convolutional and pooling layers with a ReLU activation function

Third convolutional and pooling layers

Dropout layer to avoid overfitting with a 30% rate

Flattens the last feature map into a vector of features

Adds the first fully connected layer

Another dropout layer with a 40% rate

Prints a summary of the model architecture

The output layer is a fully connected layer with 10 nodes and softmax activation to give probabilities to the 10 classes.

When you run this cell, you will see the model architecture and how the dimensions of the feature maps change with every successive layer, as illustrated in figure 3.42.

We discussed previously how to understand this summary. As you can see, our model has 528,054 parameters (weights and biases) to train. We also discussed previously how this number was calculated.

STEP 4: COMPILE THE MODEL

The last step before training our model is to define three more hyperparameters—a loss function, an optimizer, and metrics to monitor during training and testing:

- *Loss function*—How the network will be able to measure its performance on the training data.
- *Optimizer*—The mechanism that the network will use to optimize its parameters (weights and biases) to yield the minimum loss value. It is usually one of the variants of stochastic gradient descent, explained in chapter 2.
- *Metrics*—List of metrics to be evaluated by the model during training and testing. Typically we use `metrics=['accuracy']`.

Feel free to revisit chapter 2 for more details on the exact purpose and different types of loss functions and optimizers.

```
Layer (type)                     Output Shape             Param #
=================================================================
conv2d_1  (Conv2D)               (None, 32, 32, 16)       208

max_pooling2d_1  (MaxPooling 2 (None, 16, 16, 16)        0

conv2d_2  (Conv2D)               (None, 16, 16, 32)       2080

max_pooling2d_2  (MaxPooling 2 (None, 0, 0, 32)          0

conv2d_3  (Conv2D)               (None, 8, 8, 64)         8256

max_pooling2d_3  (MaxPooling 2 (None, 4, 4, 64)          0

dropout_1  (Dropout)             (None, 4, 4, 64)         0

flatten_1  (Flatten)             (None, 1024)             0

dense_1  (Dense)                 (None, 500)              512500

dropout_2  (Dropout)             (None, 500)              0

dense_2  (Dense)                 (None, 10)               5010
=================================================================
Total params: 528,054
Trainable params: 528,054
Non-trainable params: 0
```

Figure 3.42   Model summary

Here is the code to compile the model:

```
model.compile(loss='categorical_crossentropy', optimizer='rmsprop',
    metrics=['accuracy'])
```

STEP 5: TRAIN THE MODEL

We are now ready to train the network. In Keras, this is done via a call to the network's
.fit() method (as in fitting the model to the training data):

```
from keras.callbacks import ModelCheckpoint

checkpointer = ModelCheckpoint(filepath='model.weights.best.hdf5', verbose=1,
    save_best_only=True)

hist = model.fit(x_train, y_train, batch_size=32, epochs=100,
    validation_data=(x_valid, y_valid), callbacks=[checkpointer],
    verbose=2, shuffle=True)
```

When you run this cell, the training will start, and the verbose output shown in figure 3.43 will show one epoch at a time. Since 100 epochs of display do not fit on one
page, the screenshot shows the first 13 epochs. But when you run this on your notebook, the display will keep going for 100 epochs.

```
Train on 45000 amples, validation 5000 samples
Epoch 1/100
Epoch 00000: val_loss improved from inf to 1.35820, saving model to model.weights.best.hdf5
46s - loss: 1.6192 - acc: 0.4140 - val_loss: 1.3582 - val_acc: 0.5166
Epoch 2/100
Epoch 00001: val_loss improved from 1.35820 to 1.22245, saving model to model.weights.best.hdf5
53s - loss: 1.2881 - acc: 0.5402 - val_loss: 1.2224 - val_acc: 0.5644
Epoch 3/100
Epoch 00002: val_loss improved from 1.22245 to 1.12096, saving model to model.weights.best.hdf5
49s - loss: 1.1630 - acc: 0.5879 - val_loss: 1.1210 - val_acc: 0.6046
Epoch 4/100
Epoch 00003: val_loss improved from 1.12096 to 1.10724, saving model to model.weights.best.hdf5
56s - loss: 1.0928 - acc: 0.6160 - val_loss: 1.1072 - val_acc: 0.6134
Epoch 5/100
Epoch 00004: val_loss improved from 1.10724 to 0.97377, saving model to model.weights.best.hdf5
52s - loss: 1.0413 - acc: 0.6382 - val_loss: 0.9738 - val_acc: 0.6596
Epoch 6/100
Epoch 00005: val_loss improved from 0.97377 to 0.95501, saving model to model.weights.best.hdf5
50s - loss: 1.0090 - acc: 0.6484 - val_loss: 0.9550 - val_acc: 0.6768
Epoch 7/100
Epoch 00006: val_loss improved from 0.95501 to 0.94448, saving model to model.weights.best.hdf5
49s - loss: 0.9967 - acc: 0.6561 - val_loss: 0.9445 - val_acc: 0.6828
Epoch 8/100
Epoch 00007: val_loss did not improve
61s - loss: 0.9934 - acc: 0.6604 - val_loss: 1.1300 - val_acc: 0.6376
Epoch 9/100
Epoch 00008: val_loss improved from 0.94448 to 0.91779, saving model to model.weights.best.hdf5
49s - loss: 0.9858 - acc: 0.6672 - val_loss: 0.9178 - val_acc: 0.6882
Epoch 10/100
Epoch 00009: val_loss did not improve
50s - loss: 0.9839 - acc: 0.6658 - val_loss: 0.9669 - val_acc: 0.6748
Epoch 11/100
Epoch 00010: val_loss improved from 0.91779 to 0.91570, saving model to model.weights.best.hdf5
49s - loss: 1.0002 - acc: 0.6624 - val_loss: 0.9157 - val_acc: 0.6936
Epoch 12/100
Epoch 00011: val_loss did not improve
54s - loss: 1.0001 - acc: 0.6659 - val_loss: 1.1442 - val_acc: 0.6646
Epoch 13/100
Epoch 00012: val_loss did not improve
56s - loss: 1.0161 - acc: 0.6633 - val_loss: 0.9702 - val_acc: 0.6788
```

Figure 3.43   The first 13 epochs of training

Looking at the verbose output in figure 3.43 will help you analyze how your network is performing and suggest which knobs (hyperparameter) to tune. We will discuss this in detail in chapter 4. For now, let's look at the most important takeaways:

- `loss` and `acc` are the error and accuracy values for the training data. `val_loss` and `val_acc` are the error and accuracy values for the validation data.
- Look at the `val_loss` and `val_acc` values after each epoch. Ideally, we want `val_loss` to be decreasing and `val_acc` to be increasing, indicating that the network is actually learning after each epoch.
- From epochs 1 through 6, you can see that the model is saving the weights after each epoch, because the validation loss value is improving. So at the end of each epoch, we save the weights that are considered the best weights so far.

- At epoch 7, `val_loss` went up to 1.1300 from 0.9445, which means that it did not improve. So the network did not save the weights at this epoch. If you stop the training now and load the weights from epoch 6, you will get the best results that you achieved during the training.
- The same is true for epoch 8: `val_loss` decreases, so the network saves the weights as best values. And at epoch 9, there is no improvement, and so forth.
- If you stop your training after 12 epochs and load the best weights, the network will load the weights saved after epoch 10 at (`val_loss` = 0.9157) and (`val_acc` = 0.6936). This means you can expect to get accuracy on the test data close to 69%.

Keep your eye on these common phenomena

- `val_loss` *is oscillating.* If `val_loss` is oscillating up and down, you might want to decrease the learning-rate hyperparameter. For example, if you see `val_loss` going from 0.8 to 0.9, to 0.7, to 1.0, and so on, this might mean that your learning rate is too high to descend the error mountain. Try decreasing the learning rate and letting the network train for a longer time.

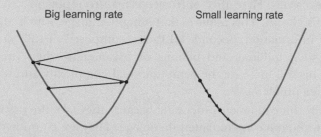

If `val_loss` oscillates, the learning rate may be too high.

- `val_loss` *is not improving (underfitting).* If `val_loss` is not decreasing, this might mean your model is too simple to fit the data (underfitting). Then you may want to build a more complex model by adding more hidden layers to help the network fit the data.
- `loss` *is decreasing and* `val_loss` *stopped improving.* This means your network started to overfit the training data and failed to decrease the error for the validation data. In this case, consider using a technique to prevent overfitting, like dropout layers. There are other techniques to avoid overfitting, as we will discuss in the next chapter.

STEP 6: LOAD THE MODEL WITH THE BEST VAL_ACC

Now that the training is complete, we use the Keras method `load_weights()` to load into our model the weights that yielded the best validation accuracy score:

```
model.load_weights('model.weights.best.hdf5')
```

STEP 7: EVALUATE THE MODEL

The last step is to evaluate our model and calculate the accuracy value as a percentage indicating how often our model correctly predicts the image classification:

```
score = model.evaluate(x_test, y_test, verbose=0)
print('\n', 'Test accuracy:', score[1])
```

When you run this cell, you will get an accuracy of about 70%. That is not bad. But we can do a lot better. Try playing with the CNN architecture by adding more convolutional and pooling layers, and see if you can improve your model.

In the next chapter, we will discuss strategies to set up your DL project and hyperparameter tuning to improve the model's performance. At the end of chapter 4, we will revisit this project to apply these strategies and improve the accuracy to above 90%.

Summary

- MLPs, ANNs, dense, and feedforward all refer to the regular fully connected neural network architecture that we discussed in chapter 2.
- MLPs usually work well for 1D inputs, but they perform poorly with images for two main reasons. First, they only accept feature inputs in a vector form with dimensions $(1 \times n)$. This requires flattening the image, which will lead to losing its spatial information. Second, MLPs are composed of fully connected layers that will yield millions and billions of parameters when processing bigger images. This will increase the computational complexity and will not scale for many image problems.
- CNNs really shine in image processing because they take the raw image matrix as an input without having to flatten the image. They are composed of locally connected layers called convolution filters, as opposed to the MLPs' dense layers.
- CNNs are composed of three main layers: the convolutional layer for feature extraction, the pooling layer to reduce network dimensionality, and the fully connected layer for classification.
- The main cause of poor prediction performance in machine learning is either overfitting or underfitting the data. Underfitting means that the model is too simple and fails to fit (learn) the training data. Overfitting means that the model is so complex that it memorizes the training data and fails to generalize for test data that it hasn't seen before.
- A dropout layer is added to prevent overfitting. Dropout turns off a percentage of neurons (nodes) that make up a layer of our network.

Structuring DL projects
and hyperparameter tuning

This chapter covers

- Defining performance metrics
- Designing baseline models
- Preparing training data
- Evaluating a model and improving its performance

This chapter concludes the first part of this book, providing a foundation for deep learning (DL). In chapter 2, you learned how to build a multilayer perceptron (MLP). In chapter 3, you learned about a neural network architecture topology that is very commonly used in computer vision (CV) problems: convolutional neural networks (CNNs). In this chapter, we will wrap up this foundation by discussing how to structure your machine learning (ML) project from start to finish. You will learn strategies to quickly and efficiently get your DL systems working, analyze the results, and improve network performance.

As you might have already noticed from the previous projects, DL is a very empirical process. It relies on running experiments and observing model performance more than having one go-to formula for success that fits all problems. We often have an initial idea for a solution, code it up, run the experiment to see how it did, and then use the outcome of this experiment to refine our ideas. When building and tuning a neural network, you will find yourself making many seemingly arbitrary decisions:

- What is a good architecture to start with?
- How many hidden layers should you stack?
- How many hidden units or filters should go in each layer?
- What is the learning rate?
- Which activation function should you use?
- Which yields better results, getting more data or tuning hyperparameters?

In this chapter, you will learn the following:

- *Defining the performance metrics for your system*—In addition to model accuracy, you will use other metrics like precision, recall, and F-score to evaluate your network.
- *Designing a baseline model*—You will choose an appropriate neural network architecture to run your first experiment.
- *Getting your data ready for training*—In real-world problems, data comes in messy, not ready to be fed to a neural network. In this section, you will massage your data to get it ready for learning.
- *Evaluating your model and interpreting its performance*—When training is complete, you analyze your model's performance to identify bottlenecks and narrow down improvement options. This means diagnosing which of the network components are performing worse than expected and identifying whether poor performance is due to overfitting, underfitting, or a defect in the data.
- *Improving the network and tuning hyperparameters*—Finally, we will dive deep into the most important hyperparameters to help develop your intuition about which hyperparameters you need to tune. You will use tuning strategies to make incremental changes based on your diagnosis from the previous step.

TIP   With more practice and experimentation, DL engineers and researchers build their intuition over time as to the most effective ways to make improvements. My advice is to get your hands dirty and try different architectures and approaches to develop your hyperparameter-tuning skills.

Ready? Let's get started!

4.1   Defining performance metrics

Performance metrics allow us to evaluate our system. When we develop a model, we want to find out how well it is working. The simplest way to measure the "goodness" of our model is by measuring its accuracy. The accuracy metric measures how many times our model made the correct prediction. So, if we test the model with 100 input samples, and it made the correct prediction 90 times, this means the model is 90% accurate.

Here is the equation used to calculate model accuracy:

$$\text{accuracy} = \frac{\text{correct predictions}}{\text{total number of examples}}$$

4.1.1 Is accuracy the best metric for evaluating a model?

We have been using accuracy as a metric for evaluating our model in earlier projects, and it works fine in many cases. But let's consider the following problem: you are designing a medical diagnosis test for a rare disease. Suppose that only one in every million people has this disease. Without any training or even building a system at all, if you hardcode the output to be always negative (no disease found), your system will always achieve 99.999% accuracy. Is that good? The system is 99.999% accurate, which might sound fantastic, but it will never capture the patients with the disease. This means the accuracy metric is not suitable to measure the "goodness" of this model. We need other evaluation metrics that measure different aspects of the model's prediction ability.

4.1.2 Confusion matrix

To set the stage for other metrics, we will use a *confusion matrix*: a table that describes the performance of a classification model. The confusion matrix itself is relatively simple to understand, but the related terminology can be a little confusing at first. Once you understand it, you'll find that the concept is really intuitive and makes a lot of sense. Let's go through it step by step.

The goal is to describe model performance from different angles other than prediction accuracy. For example, suppose we are building a classifier to predict whether a patient is sick or healthy. The expected classifications are either *positive* (the patient is sick) or *negative* (the patient is healthy). We run our model on 1,000 patients and enter the model predictions in table 4.1.

Table 4.1   Running our model to predict healthy vs. sick patients

	Predicted sick (positive)	Predicted healthy (negative)
Sick patients (positive)	100 True positives (TP)	30 False negative (FN)
Healthy patients (negative)	70 False positives (FP)	800 True negatives (TN)

Let's now define the most basic terms, which are whole numbers (not rates):

- *True positives (TP)*—The model correctly predicted yes (the patient has the disease).
- *True negatives (TN)*—The model correctly predicted no (the patient does not have the disease).

- *False positives (FP)*—The model falsely predicted yes, but the patient actually does not have the disease (in some literature known as a *Type I error* or *error of the first kind*).
- *False negatives (FN)*—The model falsely predicted no, but the patient actually does have the disease (in some literature known as a *Type II error* or *error of the second kind*).

The patients that the model predicts are negative (no disease) are the ones that the model believes are healthy, and we can send them home without further care. The patients that the model predicts are positive (have disease) are the ones that we will send for further investigation. Which mistake would we rather make? Mistakenly diagnosing someone as positive (has disease) and sending them for more investigation is not as bad as mistakenly diagnosing someone as negative (healthy) and sending them home at risk to their life. The obvious choice of evaluation metric here is that we care more about the number of false negatives (FN). We want to find all the sick people, even if the model accidentally classifies some healthy people as sick. This metric is called *recall*.

4.1.3 *Precision and recall*

Recall (also known as *sensitivity*) tells us how many of the sick patients our model incorrectly diagnosed as well. In other words, how many times did the model *incorrectly* diagnose a sick patient as negative (false negative, FN)? Recall is calculated by the following equation:

$$\text{Recall} = \frac{\text{true positive}}{\text{true positive} + \text{false negative}}$$

Precision (also known as *specificity*) is the opposite of recall. It tells us how many of the well patients our model incorrectly diagnosed as sick. In other words, how many times did the model *incorrectly* diagnose a well patient as positive (false positive, FP)? Precision is calculated by the following equation:

$$\text{Precision} = \frac{\text{true positive}}{\text{true positive} + \text{false positive}}$$

Identifying an appropriate metric

It is important to note that although in the example of health diagnostics we decided that recall is a better metric, other use cases require different metrics, like precision. To identify the most appropriate metric for your problem, ask yourself which of the two possible false predictions is more consequential: false positive or false negative. If your answer is FP, then you are looking for precision. If FN is more significant, then recall is your answer.

Consider a spam email classifier, for example. Which of the two false predictions would you care about more: falsely classifying a non-spam email as spam, in which case it gets lost, or falsely classifying a spam email as non-spam, after which it makes its way to the inbox folder? I believe you would care more about the former. You don't want the receiver to lose an email because your model misclassified it as spam. We want to catch all spam, but it is very bad to lose a non-spam email. In this example, precision is a suitable metric to use.

In some applications, you might care about both precision and recall at the same time. That's called an F-score, as explained next.

4.1.4   F-score

In many cases, we want to summarize the performance of a classifier with a single metric that represents both recall and precision. To do so, we can convert precision (p) and recall (r) into a single F-score metric. In mathematics, this is called the *harmonic mean* of p and r:

$$\text{F-score} = \frac{2pr}{p+r}$$

The F-score gives a good overall representation of how your model is performing. Let's take a look at the health-diagnostics example again. We agreed that this is a *high-recall* model. But what if the model is doing really well on the FN and giving us a high recall score, but it's performing poorly on the FP and giving us a low precision score? Doing poorly on FP means, in order to not miss any sick patients, it is mistakenly diagnosing a lot of patients as sick, to be on the safe side. So, while recall might be more important for this problem, it is good to look at the model from both scores—precision and recall—together:

	Precision	Recall	F-score
Classifier A	95%	90%	92.4%
Classifier B	98%	85%	91%

NOTE   Defining the model evaluation metric is a necessary step because it will guide your approach to improving the system. Without clearly defined metrics, it can be difficult to tell whether changes to a ML system result in progress or not.

4.2   Designing a baseline model

Now that you have selected the metrics you will use to evaluate your system, it is time to establish a reasonable end-to-end system for training your model. Depending on the problem you are solving, you need to design the baseline to suit your network type and architecture. In this step, you will want to answer questions like these:

- Should I use an MLP or CNN network (or RNN, explained later in the book)?
- Should I use other object detection techniques like YOLO or SSD (explained in later chapters)?
- How deep should my network be?
- Which activation type will I use?
- What kind of optimizer do I use?
- Do I need to add any other regularization layers like dropout or batch normalization to avoid overfitting?

If your problem is similar to another problem that has been studied extensively, you will do well to first copy the model and algorithm already known to perform the best for that task. You can even use a model that was trained on a different dataset for your own problem without having to train it from scratch. This is called *transfer learning* and will be discussed in detail in chapter 6.

For example, in the last chapter's project, we used the architecture of the popular AlexNet as a baseline model. Figure 4.1 shows the architecture of an AlexNet deep CNN, with the dimensions of each layer. The input layer is followed by five convolutional layers (CONV1 through CONV5), the output of the fifth convolutional layer is fed into two fully connected layers (FC6 through FC7), and the output layer is a fully connected layer (FC8) with a softmax function:

INPUT $\Rightarrow$ CONV1 $\Rightarrow$ POOL1 $\Rightarrow$ CONV2 $\Rightarrow$ POOL2 $\Rightarrow$ CONV3 $\Rightarrow$ CONV4 $\Rightarrow$ CONV5 $\Rightarrow$ POOL3 $\Rightarrow$ FC6 $\Rightarrow$ FC7 $\Rightarrow$ SOFTMAX_8

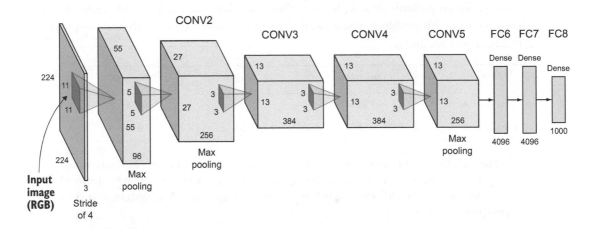

Figure 4.1   The AlexNet architecture consists of five convolutional layers and three FC layers.

Looking at the AlexNet architecture, you will find all the network hyperparameters that you need to get started with your own model:

- Network depth (number of layers): 5 convolutional layers plus 3 fully connected layers
- Layers' depth (number of filters): CONV1 = 96, CONV2 = 256, CONV3 = 384, CONV4 = 385, CONV5 = 256
- Filter size: 11×11, 5×5, 3×3, 3×3, 3×3
- ReLU as the activation function in the hidden layers (CONV1 all the way to FC7)
- Max pooling layers after CONV1, CONV2, and CONV5
- FC6 and FC7 with 4,096 neurons each
- FC8 with 1000 neurons, using a softmax activation function

NOTE In the next chapter, we will discuss some of the most popular CNN architectures along with their code implementations in Keras. We will look at networks like LeNet, AlexNet, VGG, ResNet, and Inception that will build your understanding of what architecture works best for different problems and perhaps inspire you to invent your own CNN architecture.

4.3 Getting your data ready for training

We have defined the performance metrics that we will use to evaluate our model and have built the architecture of our baseline model. Let's get our data ready for training. It is important to note that this process varies a lot based on the problem and data you have. Here, I'll explain the basic data-massaging techniques that you need to perform before training your model. I'll also help you develop an instinct for what "ready data" looks like so you can determine which preprocessing techniques you need.

4.3.1 Splitting your data for train/validation/test

When we train a ML model, we split the data into train and test datasets (figure 4.2). We use the training dataset to train the model and update the weights, and then we evaluate the model against the test dataset that it hasn't seen before. The golden rule here is this: *never use the test data for training*. The reason we should never show the test samples to the model while training is to make sure the model is not cheating. We show the model the training samples to learn their features, and then we test how it generalizes on a dataset that it has never seen, to get an unbiased evaluation of its performance.

Figure 4.2   Splitting the data into training and testing datasets

WHAT IS THE VALIDATION DATASET?

After each epoch during the training process, we need to evaluate the model's accuracy and error to see how it is performing and tune its parameters. If we use the test dataset to evaluate the model during training, we will break our golden rule of never using the testing data during training. The test data is only used to evaluate the final performance of the model *after* training is complete. So we make an additional split called a *validation dataset* to evaluate and tune parameters *during* training (figure 4.3). Once the model has completed training, we test its final performance over the test dataset.

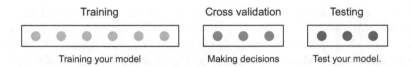

Figure 4.3   An additional split called a *validation dataset* to evaluate the model during training while keeping the test subset for the final test after training

Take a look at this pseudo code for model training:

```
for each epoch for each training data instance
        propagate error through the network
        adjust the weights
        calculate the accuracy and error over training data
for each validation data instance
        calculate the accuracy and error over the validation data
```

As we saw in the project in chapter 3, when we train the model, we get train_loss, train_acc, val_loss, and val_acc after each epoch (figure 4.4). We use this data to analyze the network's performance and diagnose overfitting and underfitting, as you will see in section 4.4.

```
Epoch 1/100
Epoch 00000: val_loss improved from inf to 1.35820, saving model to model.weights.best.hdf5
46s - loss: 1.6192 - acc: 0.4140 - val_loss: 1.3582 - val_acc: 0.5166
Epoch 2/100
Epoch 00001: val_loss improved from 1.35820 to 1.22245, saving model to model.weights.best.hdf5
53s - loss: 1.2881 - acc: 0.5402 - val_loss: 1.2224 - val_acc: 0.5644
```

Figure 4.4   Training results after each epoch

WHAT IS A GOOD TRAIN/VALIDATION/TEST DATA SPLIT?

Traditionally, an 80/20 or 70/30 split between train and test datasets is used in ML projects. When we add the validation dataset, we went with 60/20/20 or 70/15/15. But that was back when an entire dataset was just tens of thousands of samples. With the huge amount of data we have now, sometimes 1% for both the validation and the test set is enough. For example, if our dataset contains 1 million samples, 10,000 samples is very reasonable for each of the test and validation sets, because it doesn't make sense to hold back several hundred thousand samples of your dataset. It is better to use this data for model training.

So, to recap, if you have a relatively small dataset, the traditional ratios might be okay. But if you are dealing with a large dataset, then it is fine to set your train and validation sets to much smaller values.

Be sure datasets are from the same distribution

An important thing to be aware of when splitting your data is to make sure your train/validation/test datasets come from the same distribution. Suppose you are building a car classifier that will be deployed on cell phones to detect car models. Keep in mind that DL networks are data-hungry, and the common rule of thumb is that the more data you have, the better your model will perform. So, to source your data, you decide to crawl the internet for car images that are all high-quality, professionally-framed images. You train your model and tune it, you achieve satisfying results on your test dataset, and you are ready to release the model to the world—only to discover that it is performing poorly on real-life images taken by phone cameras. This happens because your model has been trained and tuned to achieve good results on high-quality images, so it fails to generalize on real-life images that may be blurry or lower resolution or have different characteristics.

In more technical words, your training and validation datasets are composed of high-quality images, whereas the production images (real life) are lower-quality images. Thus it is very important that you add lower-quality images to your train and validate datasets. Hence, the train/validate/test datasets should come from the same distribution.

4.3.2 Data preprocessing

Before you feed your data to the neural network, you will need to do some data cleanup and processing to get it ready for your learning model. There are several preprocessing techniques to choose from, based on the state of your dataset and the problem you are solving. The good news about neural networks is that they require minimal data preprocessing. When given a large amount of training data, they are able to extract and learn features from raw data, unlike the other traditional ML techniques.

With that said, preprocessing still might be required to improve performance or work within specific limitations on the neural network, such as converting images to grayscale, image resizing, normalization, and data augmentation. In this section, we'll go through these preprocessing concepts; we'll see their code implementations in the project at the end of the chapter.

IMAGE GRAYSCALING

We talked in chapter 3 about how color images are represented in three matrices versus only one matrix for grayscale images; color images add computational complexity with their many parameters. You can make a judgment call about converting all your images to grayscale, if your problem doesn't require color, to save on the computational complexity. A good rule of thumb here is to use the human-level performance rule: if you are able to identify the object with your eyes in grayscale images, then a neural network will probably be able to do the same.

IMAGE RESIZING

One limitation for neural networks is that they require all images to be the same shape. If you are using MLPs, for example, the number of nodes in the input layer must be equal to the number of pixels in the image (remember how, in chapter 3, we flattened the image to feed it to the MLP). The same is true for CNNs. You need to set the input shape of the first convolutional layer. To demonstrate this, let's look at the Keras code to add the first CNN layer:

```
model.add(Conv2D(filters=16, kernel_size=2, padding='same',
    activation='relu', input_shape=(32, 32, 3)))
```

As you can see, we have to define the shape of the image at the first convolutional layer. For example, if we have three images with dimensions of 32×32, 28×28, and 64×64, we have to resize all the images to one size before feeding them to the model.

DATA NORMALIZATION

Data normalization is the process of rescaling your data to ensure that each input feature (pixel, in the image case) has a similar data distribution. Often, raw images are composed of pixels with varying scales (ranges of values). For example, one image may have a pixel value range from 0 to 255, and another may have a range of 20 to 200. Although not required, it is preferred to normalize the pixel values to the range of 0 to 1 to boost learning performance and make the network converge faster.

To make learning faster for your neural network, your data should have the following characteristics:

- *Small values*—Typically, most values should be in the [0, 1] range.
- *Homogenous*—All pixels should have values in the same range.

Data normalization is done by subtracting the mean from each pixel and then dividing the result by the standard deviation. The distribution of such data resembles a Gaussian curve centered at zero. To demonstrate the normalization process, figure 4.5 illustrates the operation in a scatterplot.

> TIP Make sure you normalize your training and test data by using the same mean and standard deviation, because you want your data to go through the same transformation and rescale exactly the same way. You will see how this is implemented in the project at the end of this chapter.

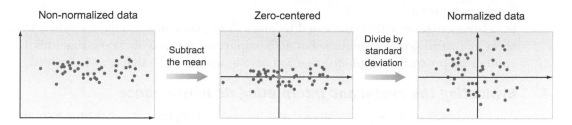

Figure 4.5 **To normalize data, we subtract the mean from each pixel and divide the result by the standard deviation.**

In non-normalized data, the cost function will likely look like a squished, elongated bowl. After you normalize your features, your cost function will look more symmetric. Figure 4.6 shows the cost function of two features, F_1 and F_2.

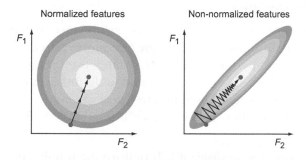

Figure 4.6 **Normalized features help the GD algorithm go straight forward toward the minimum error, thereby reaching it quickly (left). With non-normalized features, the GD oscillates toward the direction of the minimum error and reaches the minimum more slowly (right).**

As you can see, for normalized features, the GD algorithm goes straight forward toward the minimum error, thereby reaching it quickly. But for non-normalized features, it oscillates toward the direction of the minimum error and ends with a long march down the error mountain. It will eventually reach the minimum, but it will take longer to converge.

> **TIP** Why does GD oscillate for non-normalized features? If we don't normalize our data, the range of distribution of feature values will likely be different for each feature, and thus the learning rate will cause corrections in each dimension that differ proportionally from one another. This forces GD to oscillate to the direction of the minimum error and ends up with a longer path down the error.

IMAGE AUGMENTATION

Data augmentation will be discussed in more detail later in this chapter, when we cover regularization techniques. But it is important for you to know that this is another preprocessing technique that you have in your toolbelt to use when needed.

4.4   *Evaluating the model and interpreting its performance*

After the baseline model is established and the data is preprocessed, it is time to train the model and measure its performance. After training is complete, you need to determine if there are bottlenecks, diagnose which components are performing poorly, and determine whether the poor performance is due to overfitting, underfitting, or a defect in the training data.

One of the main criticisms of neural networks is that they are "black boxes." Even when they work very well, it is hard to understand *why* they work so well. Many efforts are being made to improve the interpretability of neural networks, and this field is likely to evolve rapidly in the next few years. In this section, I'll show you how to diagnose neural networks and analyze their behavior.

4.4.1   *Diagnosing overfitting and underfitting*

After running your experiment, you want to observe its performance, determine if bottlenecks are impacting its performance, and look for indicators of areas you need to improve. The main cause of poor performance in ML is either overfitting or underfitting the training dataset. We talked about overfitting and underfitting in chapter 3, but now we will dive a little deeper to understand how to detect when the system is fitting the training data too much (overfitting) and when it is too simple to fit the data (underfitting):

- *Underfitting* means the model is *too simple*: it fails to learn the training data, so it performs poorly on the training data. One example of underfitting is using a single perceptron to classify the ● and ★ shapes in figure 4.7. As you can see, a straight line does not split the data accurately.

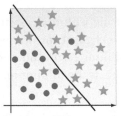

Figure 4.7   **An example of underfitting**

- *Overfitting* is when the model is *too complex* for the problem at hand. Instead of learning features that fit the training data, it actually memorizes the training data. So it performs very well on the training data, but it fails to *generalize* when tested with new data that it hasn't seen before. In figure 4.8, you see that the model fits the data too well: it splits the training data, but this kind of fitting will fail to generalize.

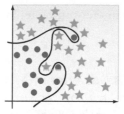

Figure 4.8   An example of overfitting

- We want to build a model that is *just right* for the data: not too complex, causing overfit, or too simple, causing underfit. In figure 4.9, you see that the model missed on a data sample of the shape O, but it looks much more likely to generalize on new data.

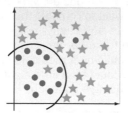

Figure 4.9   A model that is just right for the data and will generalize

TIP   The analogy I like to use to explain overfitting and underfitting is a student studying for an exam. Underfitting is when the student doesn't study very well and so fails the exam. Overfitting is when the student *memorizes* the book and can answer correctly when asked questions from the book, but answers poorly when asked questions from outside the book. The student failed to generalize. What we want is a student to *learn* from the book (training data) well enough to be able to generalize when asked questions related to the book material.

To diagnose underfitting and overfitting, the two values to focus on while training are the training error and the validation error:

- If the model is doing very well on the training set but relatively poorly on the validation set, then it is overfitting. For example, if train_error is 1% and val_error is 10%, it looks like the model has memorized the training dataset but is failing to generalize on the validation set. In this case, you might consider tuning your hyperparameters to avoid overfitting and iteratively train, test, and evaluate until you achieve an acceptable performance.
- If the model is performing poorly on the training set, then it is underfitting. For example, if the train_error is 14% and val_error is 15%, the model

might be too simple and is failing to learn the training set. You might want to consider adding more hidden layers or training longer (more epochs), or try different neural network architectures.

In the next section, we will discuss several hyperparameter-tuning techniques to avoid overfitting and underfitting.

Using human-level performance to identify a Bayes error rate

We talked about achieving a satisfying performance, but how can we know whether performance is good or not? We need a realistic baseline to compare the training and validation errors to, in order to know whether we are improving. Ideally, a 0% error rate is great, but it is not a realistic target for all problems and may even be impossible. That is why we need to define a *Bayes error rate*.

A Bayes error rate represents the best possible error our model can achieve (theoretically). Since humans are usually very good with visual tasks, we can use human-level performance as a proxy to measure Bayes error. For example, if you are working on a relatively simple task like classifying dogs and cats, humans are very accurate. The human error rate will be very low: say, 0.5%. Then we want to compare the `train_error` of our model with this value. If our model accuracy is 95%, that's not satisfying performance, and the model might be underfitting. On the other hand, suppose we are working on a more complex task for humans, like building a medical image classification model for radiologists. The human error rate could be a little higher here: say, 5%. Then a model that is 95% accurate is actually doing a good job.

Of course, this is not to say that DL models can never surpass human performance: on the contrary. But it is a good way to draw a baseline to gauge whether a model is doing well. (Note that the example error percentages are just arbitrary numbers for the sake of the example.)

4.4.2   Plotting the learning curves

Instead of looking at the training verbose output and comparing the error numbers, one way to diagnose overfitting and underfitting is to plot your training and validation errors throughout the training, as you see in figure 4.10.

Figure 4.10A shows that the network improves the loss value (aka learns) on the training data but fails to generalize on the validation data. Learning on the validation data progresses in the first couple of epochs and then flattens out and maybe decreases. This is a form of overfitting. Note that this graph shows that the network is actually learning on the training data, a good sign that training is happening. So you don't need to add more hidden units, nor do you need to build a more complex model. If anything, your network is too complex for your data, because it is learning *so much* that it is actually memorizing the data and failing to generalize to new data. In this case, your next step might be to collect more data or apply techniques to avoid overfitting.

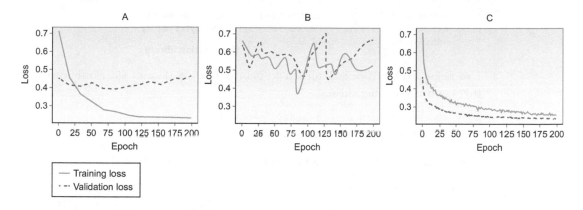

Figure 4.10 **(A)** The network improves the loss value on the training data but fails to generalize on the validation data. **(B)** The network performs poorly on both the training and validation data. **(C)** The network learns the training data and generalizes to the validation data.

Figure 4.10B shows that the network performs poorly on both training and validation data. In this case, your network is not learning. You don't need more data, because the network is too simple to learn from the data you already have. Your next step is to build a more complex model.

Figure 4.10C shows that the network is doing a good job of learning the training data and generalizing to the validation data. This means there is a good chance that the network will have good performance out in the wild on test data.

4.4.3 Exercise: Building, training, and evaluating a network

Before we move on to hyperparameter tuning, let's run a quick experiment to see how we split the data and build, train, and visualize the model results. You can see an exercise notebook for this at www.manning.com/books/deep-learning-for-vision-systems or www.computervisionbook.com.

In this exercise, we will do the following:

- Create toy data for our experiment
- Split the data into 80% training and 20% testing datasets
- Build the MLP neural network
- Train the model
- Evaluate the model
- Visualize the results

Here are the steps:

1 Import the dependencies:

```
from sklearn.datasets import make_blobs
from keras.utils import to_categorical
```

> The scikit-learn library to generate sample data

> Keras method that converts a class vector to a binary class matrix (one-hot encoding)

```
from keras.models import Sequential        Neural networks
from keras.layers import Dense             and layers library
from matplotlib import pyplot      ◄────   Visualization library
```

2 Use `make_blobs` from scikit-learn to generate a toy dataset with only two features and three label classes:

```
X, y = make_blobs(n_samples=1000, centers=3, n_features=2,
    cluster_std=2, random_state=2)
```

3 Use `to_categorical` from Keras to one-hot-encode the label:

```
y = to_categorical(y)
```

4 Split the dataset into 80% training data and 20% test data. Note that we did not create a validation dataset in this example, for simplicity:

```
n_train = 800
train_X, test_X = X[:n_train, :], X[n_train:, :]
train_y, test_y = y[:n_train], y[n_train:]
print(train_X.shape, test_X.shape)

>> (800, 2) (200, 2)
```

5 Develop the model architecture—here, a very simple, two-layer MLP network (figure 4.11 shows the model summary):

                                    **Two input dimensions because we
                                    have two features. ReLU activation
                                    function for hidden layers.**

```
model = Sequential()
model.add(Dense(25, input_dim=2, activation='relu'))  ◄──┘
model.add(Dense(3, activation='softmax'))           ◄──────────┐
model.compile(loss='categorical_crossentropy', optimizer='adam',
    metrics=['accuracy'])        ◄────────────┐
model.summary()
```

**Cross-entropy loss function (explained in chapter 2)
and adam optimizer (explained in the next section)**

**Softmax activation for the
output layer with three
nodes because we have
three classes**

Layer (type)	Output Shape	Param #
dense_1 (Dense)	(None, 25)	75
dense_2 (Dense)	(None, 3)	78

```
Total params: 153
Trainable params: 153
Non-trainable params: 0
```

Figure 4.11   Model summary

6 Train the model for 1,000 epochs:

```
history = model.fit(train_X, train_y, validation_data=(test_X, test_y),
    epochs=1000, verbose=1)
```

7 Evaluate the model:

```
_, train_acc = model.evaluate(train_X, train_y)
_, test_acc = model.evaluate(test_X, test_y)
print('Train: %.3f, Test: %.3f' % (train_acc, test_acc))

>> Train: 0.825, Test: 0.819
```

8 Plot the learning curves of model accuracy (figure 4.12):

```
pyplot.plot(history.history['accuracy'], label='train')
pyplot.plot(history.history['val_accuracy'], label='test')
pyplot.legend()
pyplot.show()
```

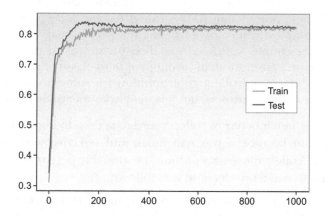

Figure 4.12   The learning curves: both train and test curves fit the data with similar behavior.

Let's evaluate the network. Looking at the learning curve in figure 4.12, you can see that both train and test curves fit the data with a similar behavior. This means the network is not overfitting, which would be indicated if the train curve was doing well but the test curve was not. But could the network be underfitting? Maybe: 82% on a very simple dataset like this is considered poor performance. To improve the performance of this neural network, I would try to build a more complex network and experiment with other underfitting techniques.

4.5   *Improving the network and tuning hyperparameters*

After you run your training experiment and diagnose for overfitting and underfitting, you need to decide whether it is more effective to spend your time tuning the network, cleaning up and processing your data, or collecting more data. The last thing you want to do is to spend a few months working in one direction only to find out that it barely improves network performance. So, before discussing the different hyperparameters to tune, let's answer this question first: should you collect more data?

4.5.1   *Collecting more data vs. tuning hyperparameters*

We know that deep neural networks thrive on lots of data. With that in mind, ML novices often throw more data to the learning algorithm as their first attempt to improve its performance. But collecting and labeling more data is not always a feasible option and, depending on your problem, could be very costly. Plus, it might not even be that effective.

> **NOTE** While efforts are being made to automate some of the data-labeling process, at the time of writing, most labeling is done manually, especially in CV problems. By *manually*, I mean that actual human beings look at each image and label them one by one (this is called *human in the loop*). Here is another layer of complexity: if you are labeling lung X-ray images to detect a certain tumor, for example, you need qualified physicians to diagnose the images. This will cost a lot more than hiring people to classify dogs and cats. So collecting more data might be a good solution for some accuracy issues and increase the model's robustness, but it is not always a feasible option.

In other scenarios, it is much better to collect more data than to improve the learning algorithm. So it would be nice if you had quick and effective ways to figure out whether it is better to collect more data or tune the model hyperparameters.

The process I use to make this decision is as follows:

1 Determine whether the performance on the training set is acceptable as-is.
2 Visualize and observe the performance of these two metrics: training accuracy (train_acc) and validation accuracy (val_acc).
3 If the network yields poor performance on the training dataset, this is a sign of underfitting. There is no reason to gather more data, because the learning algorithm is not using the training data that is already available. Instead, try tuning the hyperparameters or cleaning up the training data.
4 If performance on the training set is acceptable but is much worse on the test dataset, then the network is overfitting your training data and failing to generalize to the validation set. In this case, collecting more data could be effective.

> **TIP** When evaluating model performance, the goal is to categorize the high-level problem. If it's a *data problem*, spend more time on data preprocessing or collecting more data. If it's a *learning algorithm problem*, try to tune the network.

4.5.2   *Parameters vs. hyperparameters*

Let's not get parameters confused with hyperparameters. *Hyperparameters* are the variables that we set and tune. *Parameters* are the variables that the network updates with no direct manipulation from us. Parameters are variables that are learned and updated by the network during training, and we do not adjust them. In neural networks, parameters are the weights and biases that are optimized automatically during the backpropagation process to produce the minimum error. In contrast, hyperparameters are variables that are not learned by the network. They are set by the ML engineer before training the model and then tuned. These are variables that define the network structure and determine how the network is trained. Hyperparameter examples include learning rate, batch size, number of epochs, number of hidden layers, and others discussed in the next section.

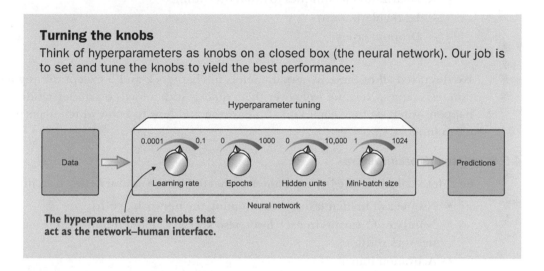

Turning the knobs
Think of hyperparameters as knobs on a closed box (the neural network). Our job is to set and tune the knobs to yield the best performance:

4.5.3   *Neural network hyperparameters*

DL algorithms come with several hyperparameters that control many aspects of the model's behavior. Some hyperparameters affect the time and memory cost of running the algorithm, and others affect the model's prediction ability.

The challenge with hyperparameter tuning is that there are no magic numbers that work for every problem. This is related to the *no free lunch theorem* that we referred to in chapter 1. Good hyperparameter values depend on the dataset and the task at hand. Choosing the best hyperparameters and knowing how to tune them require an understanding of what each hyperparameter does. In this section, you will build your intuition about why you would want to nudge a hyperparameter one way or another, and I'll propose good starting values for some of the most effective hyperparameters.

Generally speaking, we can categorize neural network hyperparameters into three main categories:

- Network architecture
  - Number of hidden layers (network depth)
  - Number of neurons in each layer (layer width)
  - Activation type
- Learning and optimization
  - Learning rate and decay schedule
  - Mini-batch size
  - Optimization algorithms
  - Number of training iterations or epochs (and early stopping criteria)
- Regularization techniques to avoid overfitting
  - L2 regularization
  - Dropout layers
  - Data augmentation

We discussed all of these hyperparameters in chapters 2 and 3 except the regularization techniques. Next, we will cover them quickly with a focus on understanding what happens when we tune each knob up or down and how to know which hyperparameter to tune.

4.5.4 *Network architecture*

First, let's talk about the hyperparameters that define the neural network architecture:

- Number of hidden layers (representing the network depth)
- Number of neurons in each layer, also known as hidden units (representing the network width)
- Activation functions

DEPTH AND WIDTH OF THE NEURAL NETWORK

Whether you are designing an MLP, CNN, or other neural network, you need to decide on the number of hidden layers in your network (depth) and the number of neurons in each layer (width). The number of hidden layers and units describes the learning capacity of the network. The goal is to set the number large enough for the network to learn the data features. A smaller network might underfit, and a larger network might overfit. To know what is a "large enough" network, you pick a starting point, observe the performance, and then tune up or down.

The more complex the dataset, the more learning capacity the model will need to learn its features. Take a look at the three datasets in figure 4.13.

If you provide the model with too much learning capacity (too many hidden units), it might tend to overfit the data and memorize the training set. If your model is overfitting, you might want to decrease the number of hidden units.

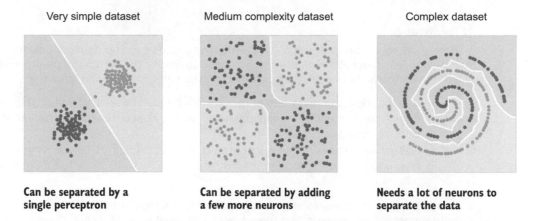

Very simple dataset | Medium complexity dataset | Complex dataset

Can be separated by a single perceptron

Can be separated by adding a few more neurons

Needs a lot of neurons to separate the data

Figure 4.13   The more complex the dataset, the more learning capacity the model will need to learn its features.

Generally, it is good to add hidden neurons until the validation error no longer improves. The trade-off is that it is computationally expensive to train deeper networks. Having a small number of units may lead to underfitting, while having more units is usually not harmful, with appropriate regularization (like dropout and others discussed later in this chapter).

Try playing around with the Tensorflow playground (https://playground.tensorflow .org) to develop more intuition. Experiment with different architectures, and gradually add more layers and more units in hidden layers while observing the network's learning behavior.

ACTIVATION TYPE

Activation functions (discussed extensively in chapter 2) introduce nonlinearity to our neurons. Without activations, our neurons would pass linear combinations (weighted sums) to each other and not solve any nonlinear problems. This is a very active area of research: every few weeks, we are introduced to new types of activations, and there are many available. But at the time of writing, ReLU and its variations (like Leaky ReLU) perform the best in hidden layers. And in the output layer, it is very common to use the softmax function for classification problems, with the number of neurons equal to the number of classes in your problem.

Layers and parameters

When considering the number of hidden layers and units in your neural network architecture, it is useful to think in terms of the number of parameters in the network and their effect on computational complexity. The more neurons in your network, the more parameters the network has to optimize. (In chapter 3, we learned how to print the model summary to see the total number of parameters that will be trained.)

(continued)

Based on your hardware setup for the training process (computational power and memory), you can determine whether you need to reduce the number of parameters. To reduce the number of training parameters, you can do one of the following:

- Reduce the depth and width of the network (hidden layers and units). This will reduce the number of training parameters and, hence, reduce the neural network complexity.
- Add pooling layers, or tweak the strides and padding of the convolutional layers to reduce the feature map dimensions. This will lower the number of parameters.

These are just examples to help you see how you will look at the number of training parameters in real projects and the trade-offs you will need to make. Complex networks lead to a large number of training params, which in turn lead to high needs for computational power and memory.

The best way to build your baseline architecture is to look at the popular architectures available to solve specific problems and start from there; evaluate its performance, tune its hyperparameters, and repeat. Remember how we were inspired by AlexNet to design our CNN in the image classification project in chapter 3. In the next chapter, we will explore some of the most popular CNN architectures like LeNet, AlexNet, VGG, ResNet, and Inception.

4.6 Learning and optimization

Now that we have built our network architecture, it is time to discuss the hyperparameters that determine how the network learns and optimize its parameter to achieve the minimum error.

4.6.1 Learning rate and decay schedule

> *The learning rate is the single most important hyperparameter, and one should always make sure that it has been tuned. If there is only time to optimize one hyperparameter, then this is the hyperparameter that is worth tuning.*
>
> —Yoshua Bengio

The learning rate (lr value) was covered extensively in chapter 2. As a refresher, let's think about how gradient descent (GD) works. The GD optimizer searches for the optimal values of weights that yield the lowest error possible. When setting up our optimizer, we need to define the step size that it takes when it descends the error mountain. This step size is the learning rate. It represents how fast or slow the optimizer descends the error curve. When we plot the cost function with only one weight, we get the oversimplified U-curve in figure 4.14, where the weight is randomly initialized at a point on the curve.

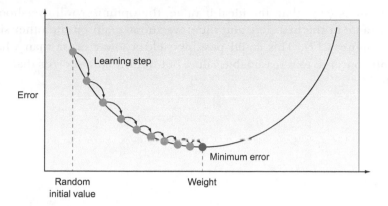

Figure 4.14   When we plot the cost function with only one weight, we get an oversimplified U-curve.

The GD calculates the gradient to find the direction that reduces the error (derivative). In figure 4.14, the descending direction is to the right. The GD starts taking steps down after each iteration (epoch). Now, as you can see in figure 4.15, if we make a *miraculously* correct choice of the learning rate value, we land on the best weight value that minimizes the error in only one step. This is an impossible case that I'm using for elaboration purposes. Let's call this the *ideal lr value.*

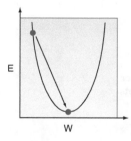

Figure 4.15   if we make a *miraculously* correct choice of the learning rate value, we land on the best weight value that minimizes the error in only one step.

If the learning rate is *smaller* than the ideal lr value, then the model can continue to learn by taking smaller steps down the error curve until it finds the most optimal value for the weight (figure 4.16). *Much smaller* means it will eventually converge but will take longer.

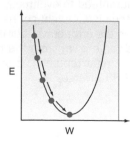

Figure 4.16   A learning rate *smaller* than the ideal lr value: the model takes smaller steps down the error curve.

If the learning rate is *larger* than the ideal lr value, the optimizer will overshoot the optimal weight value in the first step, and then overshoot again on the other side in the next step (figure 4.17). This could possibly yield a lower error than what we started with and converge to a reasonable value, but not the lowest error that we are trying to reach.

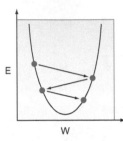

Figure 4.17   A learning rate *larger* than the ideal lr value: the optimizer overshoot the optimal weight value.

If the learning rate is *much larger* than the ideal lr value (more than twice as much), the optimizer will not only overshoot the ideal weight, but get farther and farther from the min error (figure 4.18). This phenomenon is called *divergence*.

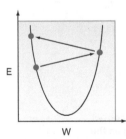

Figure 4.18   A learning rate *much larger* than the ideal lr value: the optimizer gets farther from the min error.

Too-high vs. too-low learning rate

Setting the learning rate high or low is a trade-off between the optimizer speed versus performance. Too-low lr requires many epochs to converge, often too many. Theoretically, if the learning rate is too small, the algorithm is guaranteed to eventually converge if kept running for infinity time. On the other hand, too-high lr might get us to a lower error value faster because we take bigger steps down the error curve, but there is a better chance that the algorithm will oscillate and diverge away from the minimum value. So, ideally, we want to pick the lr that is just right (optimal): it swiftly reaches the minimum point without being so big that it might diverge.

When plotting the loss value against the number of training iterations (epochs), you will notice the following:

- *Much smaller lr*—The loss keeps decreasing but needs a lot more time to converge.
- *Larger lr*—The loss achieves a better value than what we started with, but is still far from optimal.
- *Much larger lr*—The loss might initially decrease, but it starts to increase as the weight values get farther and farther away from the optimal values.
- *Good lr*—The loss decreases consistently until it reaches the minimum possible value.

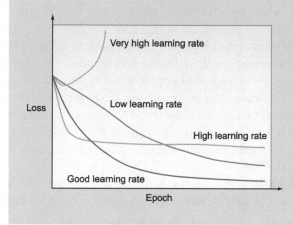

The difference between very high, high, good, and low learning rates

4.6.2 *A systematic approach to find the optimal learning rate*

The optimal learning rate will be dependent on the topology of your loss landscape, which in turn is dependent on both your model architecture and your dataset. Whether you are using Keras, Tensorflow, PyTorch, or any other DL library, using the default learning rate value of the optimizer is a good start leading to decent results. Each optimizer type has its own default value. Read the documentation of the DL library that you are using to find out the default value of your optimizer. If your model doesn't train well, you can play around with the lr variable using the usual suspects— 0.1, 0.01, 0.001, 0.0001, 0.00001, and 0.000001—to improve performance or speed up training by searching for an optimal learning rate.

The way to debug this is to look at the validation loss values in the training verbose:

- If `val_loss` decreases after each step, that's good. Keep training until it stops improving.
- If training is complete and `val_loss` is still decreasing, then maybe the learning rate was so small that it didn't converge yet. In this case, you can do one of two things:

– Train again with the same learning rate but with more training iterations (epochs) to give the optimizer more time to converge.
– Increase the lr value a little and train again.

■ If `val_loss` starts to increase or oscillate up and down, then the learning rate is too high and you need to decrease its value.

4.6.3 *Learning rate decay and adaptive learning*

Finding the learning rate value that is just right for your problem is an iterative process. You start with a static lr value, wait until training is complete, evaluate, and then tune. Another way to go about tuning your learning rate is to set a learning rate decay: a method by which the learning rate changes *during* training. It often performs better than a static value, and drastically reduces the time required to get optimal results.

By now, it's clear that when we try lower learning values, we have a better chance to get to a lower error point. But training it will take longer. In some cases, training takes so long it becomes infeasible. A good trick is to implement a decay rate in our learning rate. The decay rate tells our network to automatically decrease the lr throughout the training process. For example, we can decrease the lr by a constant value of (x) for each (n) number of steps. This way, we can start with the higher value to take bigger steps toward the minimum, and then gradually decrease the learning rate every (n) epochs to avoid overshooting the ideal lr.

One way to accomplish this is by reducing the learning rate linearly (*linear decay*). For example, you can decrease it by half every five epochs, as shown in figure 4.19.

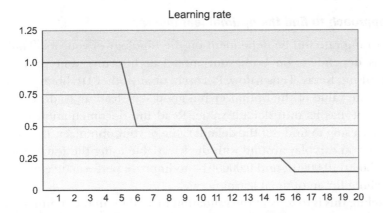

Figure 4.19   Decreasing the lr by half every five epochs

Another way is to decrease the lr exponentially (*exponential decay*). For example, you can multiply it by 0.1 every eight epochs (figure 4.20). Clearly, the network will converge a lot slower than with linear decay, but it will eventually converge.

Learning rate

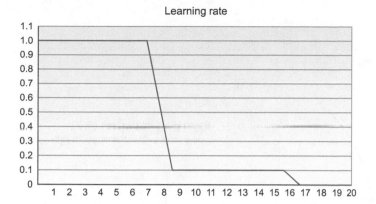

Figure 4.20 Multiplying the lr by 0.1 every eight epochs

Other clever learning algorithms have an adaptive learning rate (*adaptive learning*). These algorithms use a heuristic approach that automatically updates the lr when the training stops. This means not only decreasing the lr when needed, but also increasing it when improvements are too slow (too-small lr). Adaptive learning usually works better than other learning rate–setting strategies. Adam and Adagrad are examples of adaptive learning optimizers: more on adaptive optimizers later in this chapter.

4.6.4 *Mini-batch size*

Mini-batch size is another hyperparameter that you need to set and tune in the optimizer algorithm. The `batch_size` hyperparameter has a big effect on resource requirements of the training process and speed.

In order to understand the mini-batch, let's back up to the three GD types that we explained in chapter 2—batch, stochastic, and mini-batch:

- *Batch gradient descent (BGD)*—We feed the entire dataset to the network all at once, apply the feedforward process, calculate the error, calculate the gradient, and backpropagate to update the weights. The optimizer calculates the gradient by looking at the error generated after it sees *all* the training data, and the weights are updated *only once* after each epoch. So, in this case, the mini-batch size equals the entire training dataset. The main advantage of BGD is that it has relatively low noise and bigger steps toward the minimum (see figure 4.21). The main disadvantage is that it can take too long to process the entire training dataset at each step, especially when training on big data. BGD also requires a huge amount of memory for training large datasets, which might not be available. BGD might be a good option if you are training on a small dataset.

- *Stochastic gradient descent (SGD)*—Also called *online learning*. We feed the network a single instance of the training data at a time and use this one instance to do the forward pass, calculate error, calculate the gradient, and backpropagate to

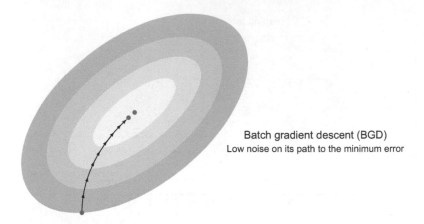

Batch gradient descent (BGD)
Low noise on its path to the minimum error

Figure 4.21   Batch GD with low noise on its path to the minimum error

update the weights (figure 4.22). In SGD, the weights are updated after it sees each single instance (as opposed to processing the entire dataset before each step for BGD). SGD can be extremely noisy as it oscillates on its way to the global minimum because it takes a step down after each single instance, which could sometimes be in the wrong direction. This noise can be reduced by using a smaller learning rate, so, on average, it takes you in a good direction and almost always performs better than BGD. With SGD you get to make progress quickly and usually reach very close to the global minimum. The main disadvantage is that by calculating the GD for one instance at a time, you lose the speed gain that comes with matrix multiplication in the training calculations.

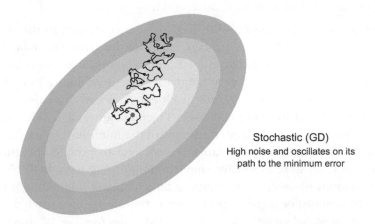

Stochastic (GD)
High noise and oscillates on its
path to the minimum error

**Figure 4.22   Stochastic GD with high noise that oscillates on its path
to the minimum error**

To recap BGD and SGD, on one extreme, if you set your mini-batch size to 1 (stochastic training), the optimizer will take a step down the error curve after computing the gradient for every single instance of the training data. This is good, but you lose the increased speed of using matrix multiplication. On the other extreme, if your mini-batch size is your entire training dataset, then you are using BGD. It takes too long to make a step toward the minimum error when processing large datasets. Between the two extremes, there is mini-batch GD.

- *Mini-batch gradient descent (MB-GD)*—A compromise between batch and stochastic GD. Instead of computing the gradient from one sample (SGD) or all training samples (BGD), we divide the training sample into mini-batches to compute the gradient from. This way, we can take advantage of matrix multiplication for faster training and start making progress instead of having to wait to train the entire training set.

Guidelines for choosing mini-batch size

First, if you have a small dataset (around less than 2,000), you might be better off using BGD. You can train the entire dataset quite fast.

For large datasets, you can use a scale of mini-batch size values. A typical starting value for the mini-batch is 64 or 128. You can then tune it up and down on this scale: 32, 64, 128, 256, 512, 1024, and keep doubling it as needed to speed up training. But make sure that your mini-batch size fits in your CPU/GPU memory. Mini-batch sizes of 1024 and larger are possible but quite rare. A larger mini-batch size allows a computational boost that uses matrix multiplication in the training calculations. But that comes at the expense of needing more memory for the training process and generally more computational resources. The following figure shows the relationship between batch size, computational resources, and number of epochs needed for neural network training:

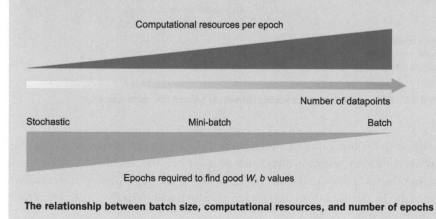

The relationship between batch size, computational resources, and number of epochs

4.7   *Optimization algorithms*

In the history of DL, many researchers proposed optimization algorithms and showed that they work well with some problems. But most of them subsequently proved to not generalize well to the wide range of neural networks that we might want to train. In time, the DL community came to feel that the GD algorithm and some of its variants work well. So far, we have discussed batch, stochastic, and mini-batch GD.

We learned that choosing a proper learning rate can be challenging because a too-small learning rate leads to painfully slow convergence, while a too-large learning rate can hinder convergence and cause the loss function to fluctuate around the minimum or even diverge. We need more creative solutions to further optimize GD.

> **NOTE**   Optimizer types are well explained in the documentation of most DL frameworks. In this section, I'll explain the concepts of two of the most popular gradient-descent-based optimizers—Momentum and Adam—that really stand out and have been shown to work well across a wide range of DL architectures. This will help you build a good foundation to dive deeper into other optimization algorithms. For more about optimization algorithms, read "An overview of gradient descent optimization algorithms" by Sebastian Ruder (https://arxiv.org/pdf/1609.04747.pdf).

4.7.1   *Gradient descent with momentum*

Recall that SGD ends up with some oscillations in the vertical direction toward the minimum error (figure 4.23). These oscillations slow down the convergence process and make it harder to use larger learning rates, which could result in your algorithm overshooting and diverging.

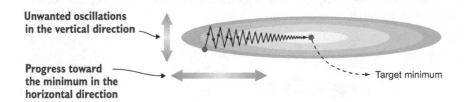

Figure 4.23   SGD oscillates in the vertical direction toward the minimum error.

To reduce these oscillations, a technique called *momentum* was invented that lets the GD navigate along relevant directions and softens the oscillation in irrelevant directions. In other words, it makes learning slower in the vertical-direction oscillations and faster in the horizontal-direction progress, which will help the optimizer reach the target minimum much faster.

This is similar to the idea of momentum from classical physics: when a snowball rolls down a hill, it accumulates momentum, going faster and faster. In the same way, our momentum term increases for dimensions whose gradients point in the same direction and reduces updates for dimensions whose gradients change direction. This leads to faster convergence and reduces oscillations.

> **How the math works in momentum**
> The math here is really simple and straightforward. The momentum is built by adding a velocity term to the equation that updates the weight:
>
> $$w_{new} = w_{old} - \alpha \frac{dE}{dw_i}$$ ◁———— **Original update rule**
>
> $w_{new} = w_{old} -$ learning rate × gradient + velocity term ◁—│ **New rule after adding velocity**
>
> The velocity term equals the weighted average of the past gradients.

4.7.2 Adam

Adam stands for *adaptive moment estimation*. Adam keeps an exponentially decaying average of past gradients, similar to momentum. Whereas momentum can be seen as a ball rolling down a slope, Adam behaves like a heavy ball with *friction* to slow down the momentum and control it. Adam usually outperforms other optimizers because it helps train a neural network model much more quickly than the techniques we have seen earlier.

Again, we have new hyperparameters to tune. But the good news is that the default values of major DL frameworks often work well, so you may not need to tune at all—except for the learning rate, which is not an Adam-specific hyperparameter:

```
keras.optimizers.Adam(lr=0.001, beta_1=0.9, beta_2=0.999, epsilon=None,
    decay=0.0)
```

The authors of Adam propose these default values:

- The learning rate needs to be tuned.
- For the momentum term β1, a common choice is 0.9.
- For the RMSprop term β2, a common choice is 0.999.
- ε is set to 10^{-8}.

4.7.3 Number of epochs and early stopping criteria

A training iteration, or *epoch*, is when the model goes a full cycle and sees the entire training dataset at once. The epoch hyperparameter is set to define how many iterations our network continues training. The more training iterations, the more our model learns the features of our training data. To diagnose whether your network needs more or fewer training epochs, keep your eyes on the training and validation error values.

The intuitive way to think about this is that we want to continue training as long as the error value is decreasing. Correct? Let's take a look at the sample verbose output from a network training in figure 4.24.

Epoch 1, Training Error: 5.4353, Validation Error: 5.6394

Epoch 2, Training Error: 5.1364, Validation Error: 5.2216

Epoch 3, Training Error: 4.7343, Validation Error: 4.8337

Figure 4.24   Sample verbose output of the first five epochs. Both training and validation errors are improving.

You can see that both training and validation errors are decreasing. This means the network is still learning. It doesn't make sense to stop the training at this point. The network is clearly still making progress toward the minimum error. Let's let it train for six more epochs and observe the results (figure 4.25).

Epoch 6, Training Error: 3.7312, Validation Error: 3.8324

Epoch 7, Training Error: 3.5324, Validation Error: 3.7215

Epoch 8, Training Error: 3.7343, Validation Error: 3.8337

Figure 4.25   The training error is still improving, but the validation error started oscillating from epoch 8 onward.

It looks like the training error is doing well and still improving. That's good. This means the network is improving on the training set. However, if you look at epochs 8 and 9, you will see that val_error started to oscillate and increase. Improving train_error while not improving val_error means the network is starting to overfit the training data and failing to generalize to the validation data.

Let's plot the training and validation errors (figure 4.26). You can see that both the training and validation errors were improving at first, but then the validation

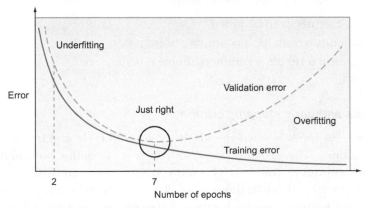

Figure 4.26   Improving train_error while not improving val_error means the network is starting to overfit.

error started to increase, leading to overfitting. We need to find a way to stop the training just before it starts to overfit. This technique is called *early stopping*.

4.7.4   *Early stopping*

Early stopping is an algorithm widely used to determine the right time to stop the training process before overfitting happens. It simply monitors the validation error value and stops the training when the value starts to increase. Here is the early stopping function in Keras:

```
EarlyStopping(monitor='val_loss', min_delta=0,  patience=20)
```

The `EarlyStopping` function takes the following arguments:

- `monitor`—The metric you monitor during training. Usually we want to keep an eye on `val_loss` because it represents our internal testing of model performance. If the network is doing well on the validation data, it will probably do well on test data and production.
- `min_delta`—The minimum change that qualifies as an improvement. There is no standard value for this variable. To decide the `min_delta` value, run a few epochs and see the change in error and validation accuracy. Define `min_delta` according to the rate of change. The default value of 0 works pretty well in many cases.
- `patience`—This variable tells the algorithm how many epochs it should wait before stopping the training if the error does not improve. For example, if we set `patience` equal to 1, the training will stop at the epoch where the error increases. We must be a little flexible, though, because it is very common for the error to oscillate a little and continue improving. We can stop the training if it hasn't improved in the last 10 or 20 epochs.

> **TIP**   The good thing about early stopping is that it allows you to worry less about the epochs hyperparameter. You can set a high number of epochs and let the stopping algorithm take care of stopping the training when error stops improving.

4.8   *Regularization techniques to avoid overfitting*

If you observe that your neural network is overfitting the training data, your network might be too complex and need to be simplified. One of the first techniques you should try is regularization. In this section, we will discuss three of the most common regularization techniques: L2, dropout, and data augmentation.

4.8.1   *L2 regularization*

The basic idea of L2 regularization is that it penalizes the error function by adding a *regularization term* to it. This, in turn, reduces the weight values of the hidden units and makes them too small, very close to zero, to help simplify the model.

Let's see how regularization works. First, we update the error function by adding the regularization term:

$$\text{error function}_{\text{new}} = \text{error function}_{\text{old}} + \text{regularization term}$$

Note that you can use any of the error functions explained in chapter 2, like MSE or cross entropy. Now, let's take a look at the regularization term

$$\text{L2 regularization term} = \frac{\lambda}{2m} \times \sum \|w\|^2$$

where lambda (λ) is the regularization parameter, m is the number of instances, and w is the weight. The updated error function looks like this:

$$\text{error function}_{\text{new}} = \text{error function}_{\text{old}} + \frac{\lambda}{2m} \times \sum \|w\|^2$$

Why does L2 regularization reduce overfitting? Well, let's look at how the weights are updated during the backpropagation process. We learned from chapter 2 that the optimizer calculates the derivative of the error, multiplies it by the learning rate, and subtracts this value from the old weight. Here is the backpropagation equation that updates the weights:

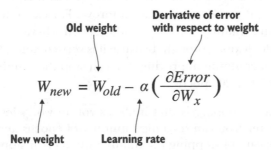

Since we add the regularization term to the error function, the new error becomes larger than the old error. This means its derivative ($\partial Error/\partial W_x$) is also bigger, leading to a smaller W_{new}. L2 regularization is also known as *weight decay*, as it forces the weights to decay toward zero (but not exactly zero).

Reducing weights leads to a simpler neural network

To see how this works, consider: if the regularization term is so large that, when multiplied with the learning rate, it will be equal to W_{old}, then this will make the new weight equal to zero. This cancels the effect of this neuron, leading to a simpler neural network with fewer neurons.

In practice, L2 regularization does not make the weights equal to zero. It just makes them smaller to reduce their effect. A large regularization parameter (λ) lead to negligible weights. When the weights are negligible, the model will not learn much from these units. This will make the network simpler and thus reduce overfitting

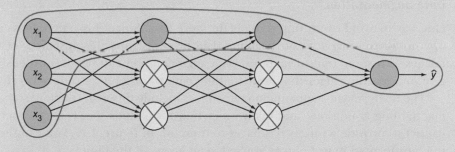

L2 regularization reduces the weights and simplifies the network to reduce overfitting.

This is what L2 regularization looks like in Keras:

```
model.add(Dense(units=16, kernel_regularizer=regularizers.l2(λ),
    activation='relu'))
```
When adding a hidden layer to your network, add the kernel_regularization argument with the L2 regularizer

The lambda value is a hyperparameter that you can tune. The default value of your DL library usually works well. If you still see signs of overfitting, increase the lambda hyperparameter to reduce the model complexity.

4.8.2   *Dropout layers*

Dropout is another regularization technique that is very effective for simplifying a neural network and avoiding overfitting. We discussed dropout extensively in chapter 3. The dropout algorithm is fairly simple: at every training iteration, every neuron has a probability p of being temporarily ignored (dropped out) during this training iteration. This means it may be active during subsequent iterations. While it is counterintuitive to intentionally pause the learning on some of the network neurons, it is quite surprising how well this technique works. The probability p is a hyperparameter that is called *dropout rate* and is typically set in the range of 0.3 to 0.5. Start with 0.3, and if you see signs of overfitting, increase the rate.

> **TIP**   I like to think of dropout as tossing a coin every morning with your team to decide who will do a specific critical task. After a few iterations, all your team members will learn how to do this task and not rely on a single member to get it done. The team would become much more resilient to change.

Both L2 regularization and dropout aim to reduce network complexity by reducing its neurons' effectiveness. The difference is that dropout completely *cancels* the effect of some neurons with every iteration, while L2 regularization just reduces the weight values to *reduce* the neurons' effectiveness. Both lead to a more robust, resilient neural network and reduce overfitting. It is recommended that you use both types of regularization techniques in your network.

4.8.3   Data augmentation

One way to avoid overfitting is to obtain more data. Since this is not always a feasible option, we can augment our training data by generating new instances of the same images with some transformations. Data augmentation can be an inexpensive way to give your learning algorithm more training data and therefore reduce overfitting.

The many image-augmentation techniques include flipping, rotation, scaling, zooming, lighting conditions, and many other transformations that you can apply to your dataset to provide a variety of images to train on. In figure 4.27, you can see some of the transformation techniques applied to an image of the digit 6.

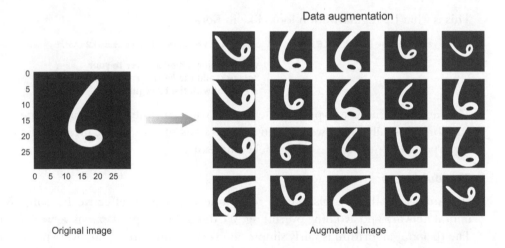

Figure 4.27   Various image augmentation techniques applied to an image of the digit 6

In figure 4.27, we created 20 new images that the network can learn from. The main advantage of synthesizing images like this is that now you have more data (20×) that tells your algorithm that if an image is the digit 6, then even if you flip it vertically or horizontally or rotate it, it's still the digit 6. This makes the model more robust to detect the number 6 in any form and shape.

Data augmentation is considered a regularization technique because allowing the network to see many variants of the object reduces its dependence on the original form of the object during feature learning. This makes the network more resilient when tested on new data.

Data augmentation in Keras looks like this:

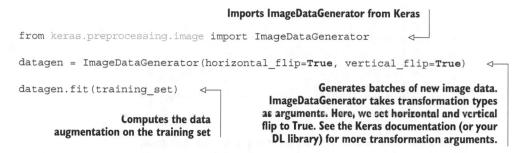

Imports ImageDataGenerator from Keras

```
from keras.preprocessing.image import ImageDataGenerator
```

```
datagen = ImageDataGenerator(horizontal_flip=True, vertical_flip=True)
```

```
datagen.fit(training_set)
```

Computes the data augmentation on the training set

Generates batches of new image data. ImageDataGenerator takes transformation types as arguments. Here, we set horizontal and vertical flip to True. See the Keras documentation (or your DL library) for more transformation arguments.

4.9   Batch normalization

Earlier in this chapter, we talked about data normalization to speed up learning. The normalization techniques we discussed were focused on preprocessing the training set before feeding it to the input layer. If the input layer benefits from normalization, why not do the same thing for the *extracted features* in the hidden units, which are changing all the time and get much more improvement in training speed and network resilience (figure 4.28)? This process is called *batch normalization* (BN).

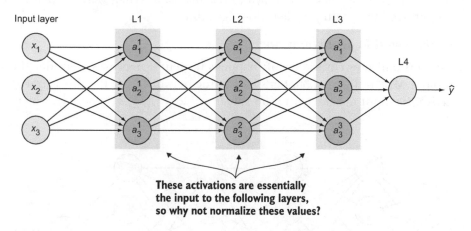

These activations are essentially the input to the following layers, so why not normalize these values?

Figure 4.28   *Batch normalization* is normalizing the extracted features in hidden units.

4.9.1   The covariate shift problem

Before we define covariate shift, let's take a look at an example to illustrate the problem that batch normalization (BN) confronts. Suppose you are building a cat classifier, and you train your algorithm on images of white cats only. When you test this classifier on images with cats that are different colors, it will not perform well. Why? Because the model has been trained on a training set with a specific distribution (white cats). When the distribution changes in the test set, it confuses the model (figure 4.29).

Covariance shift

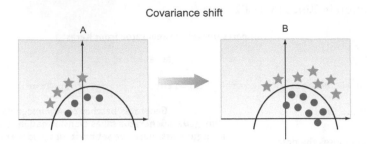

Figure 4.29   Graph A is the training set of only white cats, and graph B is the testing set with cats of various colors. The circles represent the cat images, and the stars represent the non-cat images.

We should not expect that the model trained on the data in graph A will do very well with the new distribution in graph B. The idea of the change in data distribution goes by the fancy name *covariate shift*.

DEFINITION   If a model is learning to map dataset *X* to label *y*, then if the distribution of *X* changes, it's known as *covariate shift*. When that happens, you might need to retrain your learning algorithm.

4.9.2   *Covariate shift in neural networks*

To understand how covariate shift happens in neural networks, consider the simple four-layer MLP in figure 4.30. Let's look at the network from the third-layer (L3) perspective. Its input are the activation values in L2 (a_1^2, a_2^2, a_3^2, and a_4^2), which are the

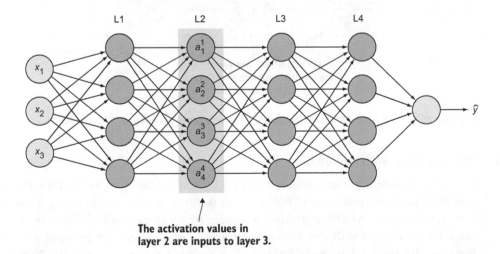

The activation values in layer 2 are inputs to layer 3.

Figure 4.30   A simple four-layer MLP. L1 features are input to the L2 layer. The same is true for layers 2, 3, and 4.

features extracted from the previous layers. L3 is trying to map these inputs to $\hat{y}$ to make it as close as possible to the label y. While the third layer is doing that, the network is adapting the values of the parameters from previous layers. As the parameters (w, b) are changing in layer 1, the activation values in the second layer are changing, too. So from the perspective of the third hidden layer, the values of the second hidden layer are changing all the time: the MLP is suffering from the problem of covariate shift. Batch norm reduces the degree of change in the distribution of the hidden unit values, causing these values to become more stable so that the later layers of the neural network have firmer ground to stand on.

> **NOTE** It is important to realize that batch normalization does not cancel or reduce the change in the hidden unit values. What it does is ensure that the distribution of that change remains the same: even if the exact values of the units change, the mean and variance do not change.

4.9.3   *How does batch normalization work?*

In their 2015 paper "Batch Normalization: Accelerating Deep Network Training by Reducing Internal Covariate Shift" (https://arxiv.org/abs/1502.03167), Sergey Ioffe and Christian Szegedy proposed the BN technique to reduce covariate shift. Batch normalization adds an operation in the neural network just before the activation function of each layer to do the following:

1. Zero-center the inputs
2. Normalize the zero-centered inputs
3. Scale and shift the results

This operation lets the model learn the optimal scale and mean of the inputs for each layer.

How the math works in batch normalization

1. To zero-center the inputs, the algorithm needs to calculate the input mean and standard deviation (the input here means the current mini-batch: hence the term *batch normalization*):

$$\mu_B \leftarrow \frac{1}{m}\sum_{i=1}^{m} x_i \qquad \longleftarrow \text{ Mini-batch mean}$$

$$\sigma_B^2 \leftarrow \frac{1}{m}\sum_{i=1}^{m} (x_i - \mu_B)^2 \qquad \longleftarrow \text{ Mini-batch variance}$$

where m is the number of instances in the mini-batch, μ_B is the mean, and σ_B is the standard deviation over the current mini-batch.

2. Normalize the input:

$$\hat{x}_i \leftarrow \frac{x_i - \mu_B}{\sqrt{\sigma_B^2 + \varepsilon}}$$

where $\hat{x}$ is the zero-centered and normalized input. Note that there is a variable here that we added (ε). This is a tiny number (typically 10^{-5}) to avoid division by zero if σ is zero in some estimates.

3   Scale and shift the results. We multiply the normalized output by a variable γ to scale it and add (β) to shift it

$$y_i \leftarrow \gamma X_i + \beta$$

where y_i is the output of the BN operation, scaled and shifted.

Notice that BN introduces two new learnable parameters to the network: γ and β. So our optimization algorithm will update the parameters of γ and β just like it updates weights and biases. In practice, this means you may find that training is rather slow at first, while GD is searching for the optimal scales and offsets for each layer, but it accelerates once it's found reasonably good values.

4.9.4   *Batch normalization implementation in Keras*

It is important to know how batch normalization works so you can get a better understanding of what your code is doing. But when using BN in your network, you don't have to implement all these details yourself. Implementing BN is often done by adding one line of code, using any DL framework. In Keras, the way you add batch normalization to your neural network is by adding a BN layer after the hidden layer, to normalize its results before they are fed to the next layer.

The following code snippet shows you how to add a BN layer when building your neural network:

```
from keras.models import Sequential
from keras.layers import Dense, Dropout
from keras.layers.normalization import BatchNormalization

model = Sequential()

model.add(Dense(hidden_units, activation='relu'))

model.add(BatchNormalization())

model.add(Dropout(0.5))

model.add(Dense(units, activation='relu'))

model.add(BatchNormalization())

model.add(Dense(2, activation='softmax'))
```

Imports the BatchNormalization layer from the Keras library

Initiates the model

Adds the first hidden layer

Adds the batch norm layer to normalize the results of layer 1

If you are adding dropout to your network, it is preferable to add it after the batch norm layer because you don't want the nodes that are randomly turned off to miss the normalization step.

Adds the second hidden layer

Output layer

Adds the batch norm layer to normalize the results of layer 2

4.9.5 *Batch normalization recap*

The intuition that I hope you'll take away from this discussion is that BN applies the normalization process not just to the input layer, but also to the values in the hidden layers in a neural network. This weakens the coupling of the learning process between earlier and later layers, allowing each layer of the network to learn more independently.

From the perspective of the later layers in the network, the earlier layers don't get to shift around as much because they are constrained to have the same mean and variance. This makes the job of learning easier in the later layers. The way this happens is by ensuring that the hidden units have a standardized distribution (mean and variance) controlled by two explicit parameters, γ and β, which the learning algorithm sets during training.

4.10 *Project: Achieve high accuracy on image classification*

In this project, we will revisit the CIFAR-10 classification project from chapter 3 and apply some of the improvement techniques from this chapter to increase the accuracy from ~65% to ~90%. You can follow along with this example by visiting the book's website, www.manning.com/books/deep-learning-for-vision-systems or www.computervisionbook.com, to see the code notebook.

We will accomplish the project by following these steps:

1 Import the dependencies.
2 Get the data ready for training:
  – Download the data from the Keras library.
  – Split it into train, validate, and test datasets.
  – Normalize the data.
  – One-hot encode the labels.
3 Build the model architecture. In addition to regular convolutional and pooling layers, as in chapter 3, we add the following layers to our architecture:
  – Deeper neural network to increase learning capacity
  – Dropout layers
  – L2 regularization to our convolutional layers
  – Batch normalization layers
4 Train the model.
5 Evaluate the model.
6 Plot the learning curve.

Let's see how this is implemented.

STEP 1: IMPORT DEPENDENCIES

Here's the Keras code to import the needed dependencies:

```
import keras                                          ⟵   Keras library to download
from keras.datasets import cifar10                          the datasets, preprocess
from keras.preprocessing.image import ImageDataGenerator    images, and network
                                                            components
```

```
from keras.models import Sequential
from keras.utils import np_utils
from keras.layers import Dense, Activation, Flatten, Dropout, BatchNormalization,
    Conv2D, MaxPooling2D
from keras.callbacks import ModelCheckpoint
from keras import regularizers, optimizers

import numpy as np                    ⟵ ⎤ Imports numpy for
                                         ⎦ math operations

from matplotlib import pyplot         ⟵ ⎤ Imports the matplotlib
                                         ⎦ library to visualize results
```

STEP 2: GET THE DATA READY FOR TRAINING

Keras has some datasets available for us to download and experiment with. These datasets are usually preprocessed and almost ready to be fed to the neural network. In this project, we use the CIFAR-10 dataset, which consists of 50,000 32 × 32 color training images, labeled over 10 categories, and 10,000 test images. Check the Keras documentation for more datasets like CIFAR-100, MNIST, Fashion-MNIST, and more.

Keras provides the CIFAR-10 dataset already split into training and testing sets. We will load them and then split the training dataset into 45,000 images for training and 5,000 images for validation, as explained in this chapter:

```
(x_train, y_train), (x_test, y_test) = cifar10.load_data()    ⎤ Downloads and
x_train = x_train.astype('float32')                           ⎦ splits the data
x_test = x_test.astype('float32')

(x_train, x_valid) = x_train[5000:], x_train[:5000]    ⎤ Breaks the training set into
(y_train, y_valid) = y_train[5000:], y_train[:5000]    ⎦ training and validation sets
```

Let's print the shape of x_train, x_valid, and x_test:

```
print('x_train =', x_train.shape)
print('x_valid =', x_valid.shape)
print('x_test =', x_test.shape)

>> x_train = (45000, 32, 32, 3)
>> x_valid = (5000, 32, 32, 3)
>> x_test = (1000, 32, 32, 3)
```

The format of the shape tuple is as follows: (number of instances, width, height, channels).

Normalize the data

Normalizing the pixel values of our images is done by subtracting the mean from each pixel and then dividing the result by the standard deviation:

```
mean = np.mean(x_train,axis=(0,1,2,3))
std = np.std(x_train,axis=(0,1,2,3))
x_train = (x_train-mean)/(std+1e-7)
x_valid = (x_valid-mean)/(std+1e-7)
x_test = (x_test-mean)/(std+1e-7)
```

One-hot encode the labels

To one-hot encode the labels in the train, valid, and test datasets, we use the `to_categorical` function in Keras:

```
num_classes = 10
y_train = np_utils.to_categorical(y_train,num_classes)
y_valid = np_utils.to_categorical(y_valid,num_classes)
y_test = np_utils.to_categorical(y_test,num_classes)
```

Data augmentation

For augmentation techniques, we will arbitrarily go with the following transformations: rotation, width and height shift, and horizontal flip. When you are working on problems, view the images that the network missed or provided poor detections for and try to understand why it is not performing well on them. Then create your hypothesis and experiment with it. For example, if the missed images were of shapes that are rotated, you might want to try the rotation augmentation. You would apply that, experiment, evaluate, and repeat. You will come to your decisions purely from analyzing your data and understanding the network performance:

```
datagen = ImageDataGenerator(          ◁──┐ Data
    rotation_range=15,                      │ augmentation
    width_shift_range=0.1,
    height_shift_range=0.1,
    horizontal_flip=True,              ┌── Computes the data
    vertical_flip=False                │   augmentation on the
    )                                  │   training set
datagen.fit(x_train)           ◁──────┘
```

STEP 3: BUILD THE MODEL ARCHITECTURE

In chapter 3, we built an architecture inspired by AlexNet (3 CONV + 2 FC). In this project, we will build a deeper network for increased learning capacity (6 CONV + 1 FC).

The network has the following configuration:

- Instead of adding a pooling layer after each convolutional layer, we will add one after every two convolutional layers. This idea was inspired by VGGNet, a popular neural network architecture developed by the Visual Geometry Group (University of Oxford). VGGNet will be explained in chapter 5.
- Inspired by VGGNet, we will set the `kernel_size` of our convolutional layers to 3 × 3 and the `pool_size` of the pooling layer to 2 × 2.
- We will add dropout layers every other convolutional layer, with (p) ranges from 0.2 and 0.4.
- A batch normalization layer will be added after each convolutional layer to normalize the input for the following layer.
- In Keras, L2 regularization is added to the convolutional layer code.

Here's the code:

L2 regularization hyperparameter (λ)

Number of hidden units variable. We declare this variable here and use it in our convolutional layers to make it easier to update from one place.

Notice that we define the input_shape here because this is the first convolutional layer. We don't need to do that for the remaining layers.

```
base_hidden_units = 32
weight_decay = 1e-4
model = Sequential()
```

Creates a sequential model (a linear stack of layers)

```
# CONV1
model.add(Conv2D(base_hidden_units, kernel_size= 3, padding='same',
        kernel_regularizer=regularizers.l2(weight_decay),
input_shape=x_train.shape[1:]))
model.add(Activation('relu'))
model.add(BatchNormalization())
```

Adds a batch normalization layer

Uses a ReLU activation function for all hidden layers

Adds L2 regularization to the convolutional layer

```
# CONV2
model.add(Conv2D(base_hidden_units, kernel_size= 3, padding='same',
        kernel_regularizer=regularizers.l2(weight_decay)))
model.add(Activation('relu'))
model.add(BatchNormalization())
```

Dropout layer with 20% probability

```
# POOL + Dropout
model.add(MaxPooling2D(pool_size=(2,2)))
model.add(Dropout(0.2))
```

Number of hidden units = 64

```
# CONV3
model.add(Conv2D(base_hidden_units * 2, kernel_size= 3, padding='same',
        kernel_regularizer=regularizers.l2(weight_decay)))
model.add(Activation('relu'))
model.add(BatchNormalization())
```

```
# CONV4
model.add(Conv2D(base_hidden_units * 2, kernel_size= 3, padding='same',
        kernel_regularizer=regularizers.l2(weight_decay)))
model.add(Activation('relu'))
model.add(BatchNormalization())
```

```
# POOL + Dropout
model.add(MaxPooling2D(pool_size=(2,2)))
model.add(Dropout(0.3))
```

```
# CONV5
model.add(Conv2D(base_hidden_units * 4, kernel_size= 3, padding='same',
        kernel_regularizer=regularizers.l2(weight_decay)))
model.add(Activation('relu'))
model.add(BatchNormalization())
```

```
# CONV6
model.add(Conv2D(base_hidden_units * 4, kernel_size= 3, padding='same',
        kernel_regularizer=regularizers.l2(weight_decay)))
model.add(Activation('relu'))
model.add(BatchNormalization())
```

```
# POOL + Dropout
model.add(MaxPooling2D(pool_size=(2,2)))
model.add(Dropout(0.4))
```

```
# FC7
model.add(Flatten())                           ◄─┤ Flattens the feature map into a ID
model.add(Dense(10, activation='softmax'))   ◄─  features vector (explained in chapter 3)

model.summary()    ◄─┐ Prints the model         10 hidden units because the
                       summary                    dataset has 10 class labels. Softmax
                                                   activation function is used for the
                                                   output layer (explained in chapter 2).
```

The model summary is shown in figure 4.31.

Layer (type)	Output Shape	Param #
conv2d_1 (Conv2D)	(None, 32, 32, 32)	896
activation_1 (Activation)	(None, 32, 32, 32)	0
batch_normalization_1 (batch	(None, 32, 32, 32)	128
conv2d_2 (Conv2D)	(None, 32, 32, 32)	9248
activation_2 (Activation)	(None, 32, 32, 32)	0
batch_normalization_2 (batch	(None, 32, 32, 32)	128
max_pooling2d_1 (MaxPooling2	(None, 16, 16, 32)	0
dropout_1 (Dropout)	(None, 16, 16, 32)	0
conv2d_3 (Conv2D)	(None, 16, 16, 64)	18496
activation_3 (Activation)	(None, 16, 16, 64)	0
batch_normalization_3 (batch	(None, 16, 16, 64)	256
conv2d_4 (Conv2D)	(None, 16, 16, 64)	36928
activation_4 (Activation)	(None, 16, 16, 64)	0
batch_normalization_4 (batch	(None, 16, 16, 64)	256
max_pooling2d_2 (MaxPooling2	(None, 8, 8, 64)	0
dropout_2 (Dropout)	(None, 8, 8, 64)	0
conv2d_5 (Conv2D)	(None, 8, 8, 128)	73856
activation_5 (Activation)	(None, 8, 8, 128)	0
batch_normalization_5 (batch	(None, 8, 8, 128)	512
conv2d_6 (Conv2D)	(None, 8, 8, 128)	147584
activation_6 (Activation)	(None, 8, 8, 128)	0
batch_normalization_6 (batch	(None, 8, 8, 128)	512
max_pooling2d_3 (MaxPooling2	(None, 4, 4, 128)	0
dropout_3 (Dropout)	(None, 4, 4, 128)	0
flatten_1 (Flatten)	(None, 2048	0
dense_1 (Dense)	(None, 10)	20490

Figure 4.31
Model summary

STEP 4: TRAIN THE MODEL

Before we jump into the training code, let's discuss the strategy behind some of the hyperparameter settings:

- batch_size—This is the mini-batch hyperparameter that we covered in this chapter. The higher the batch_size, the faster your algorithm learns. You can start with a mini-batch of 64 and double this value to speed up training. I tried 256 on my machine and got the following error, which means my machine was running out of memory. I then lowered it back to 128:

```
Resource exhausted: OOM when allocating tensor with shape[256,128,4,4]
```

- epochs—I started with 50 training iterations and found that the network was still improving. So I kept adding more epochs and observing the training results. In this project, I was able to achieve >90% accuracy after 125 epochs. As you will see soon, there is still room for improvement if you let it train longer.
- *Optimizer*—I used the Adam optimizer. See section 4.7 to learn more about optimization algorithms.

NOTE   It is important to note that I'm using a GPU for this experiment. The training took around 3 hours. It is recommended that you use your own GPU or any cloud computing service to get the best results. If you don't have access to a GPU, I recommend that you try a smaller number of epochs or plan to leave your machine training overnight or even for a couple of days, depending on your CPU specifications.

Let's see the training code:

Adam optimizer with a learning rate = 0.0001

Path of the file where the best weights will be saved, and a Boolean True to save the weights only when there is an improvement

Mini-batch size

Number of training iterations

```
batch_size = 128
epochs = 125

checkpointer = ModelCheckpoint(filepath='model.100epochs.hdf5', verbose=1,
                               save_best_only=True )
optimizer = keras.optimizers.adam(lr=0.0001,decay=1e-6)

model.compile(loss='categorical_crossentropy', optimizer=optimizer,
      metrics=['accuracy'])

history = model.fit_generator(datagen.flow(x_train, y_train,
      batch_size=batch_size), callbacks=[checkpointer],
      steps_per_epoch=x_train.shape[0] // batch_size, epochs=epochs,
      verbose=2, validation_data=(x_valid, y_valid))
```

Cross-entropy loss function (explained in chapter 2)

Allows you to do real-time data augmentation on images on CPU in parallel to training your model on GPU. The callback to the checkpointer saves the model weights; you can add other callbacks like an early stopping function.

When you run this code, you will see the verbose output of the network training for each epoch. Keep your eyes on the `loss` and `val_loss` values to analyze the network and diagnose bottlenecks. Figure 4.32 shows the verbose output of epochs 121 to 125.

```
Epoch 121/125
Epoch 00120: val_loss did not improve
30s - loss: 0.4471 - acc: 0.8741 - val_loss: 0.4124 - val_acc: 0.8886
Epoch 122/125
Epoch 00121: val_loss improved from 0.40342 to 0.40327, saving model to model.125epochs.hdf5
31s - loss: 0.4510 - acc: 0.8719 - val_loss: 0.4033 - val_acc: 0.8934
Epoch 123/125
Epoch 00122: val_loss improved from 0.40327 to 0.40112, saving model to model.125epochs.hdf5
30s - loss: 0.4497 - acc: 0.8735 - val_loss: 0.4031 - val_acc: 0.8959
Epoch 124/125
Epoch 00122: val_loss did not improve
30s - loss: 0.4497 - acc: 0.8725 - val_loss: 0.4162 - val_acc: 0.8894
Epoch 125/125
Epoch 00122: val_loss did not improve
30s - loss: 0.4471 - acc: 0.8734 - val_loss: 0.4025 - val_acc: 0.8959
```

Figure 4.32   Verbose output of epochs 121 to 125

STEP 5: EVALUATE THE MODEL

To evaluate the model, we use a Keras function called `evaluate` and print the results:

```
scores = model.evaluate(x_test, y_test, batch_size=128, verbose=1)
print('\nTest result: %.3f loss: %.3f' % (scores[1]*100,scores[0]))

>> Test result: 90.260 loss: 0.398
```

Plot learning curves

Plot the learning curves to analyze the training performance and diagnose overfitting and underfitting (figure 4.33):

```
pyplot.plot(history.history['acc'], label='train')
pyplot.plot(history.history['val_acc'], label='test')
pyplot.legend()
pyplot.show()
```

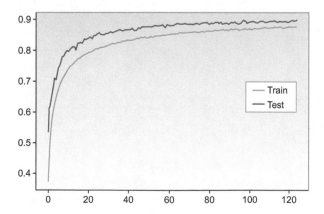

Figure 4.33   Learning curves

Further improvements

Accuracy of 90% is pretty good, but you can still improve further. Here are some ideas you can experiment with:

- *More training epochs*—Notice that the network was improving until epoch 123. You can increase the number of epochs to 150 or 200 and let the network train longer.
- *Deeper network*—Try adding more layers to increase the model complexity, which increases the learning capacity.
- *Lower learning rate*—Decrease the lr (you should train longer if you do so).
- *Different CNN architecture*—Try something like Inception or ResNet (explained in detail in the next chapter). You can get up to 95% accuracy with the ResNet neural network after 200 epochs of training.
- *Transfer learning*—In chapter 6, we will explore the technique of using a pre-trained network on your dataset to get higher results with a fraction of the learning time.

Summary

- The general rule of thumb is that the deeper your network is, the better it learns.
- At the time of writing, ReLU performs best in hidden layers, and softmax performs best in the output layer.
- Stochastic gradient descent usually succeeds in finding a minimum. But if you need fast convergence and are training a complex neural network, it's safe to go with Adam.
- Usually, the more you train, the better.
- L2 regularization and dropout work well together to reduce network complexity and overfitting.

Part 2

Image classification and detection

Rapid advances in AI research are enabling new applications to be built every day and across different industries that weren't possible just a few years ago. By learning these tools, you will be empowered to invent new products and applications yourself. Even if you end up not working on computer vision per se, many concepts here are useful for deep learning algorithms and architectures.

After working our way through the foundations of deep learning in part 1, it's time to build a machine learning project to see what you've learned. Here, we'll cover strategies to quickly and efficiently get deep learning systems working, analyze results, and improve network performance, specifically by digging into advanced convolutional neural networks, transfer learning, and object detection.

Advanced CNN architectures

This chapter covers

- Working with CNN design patterns
- Understanding the LeNet, AlexNet, VGGNet, Inception, and ResNet network architectures

Welcome to part 2 of this book. Part 1 presented the foundation of neural networks architectures and covered multilayer perceptrons (MLPs) and convolutional neural networks (CNNs). We wrapped up part 1 with strategies to structure your deep neural network projects and tune their hyperparameters to improve network performance. In part 2, we will build on this foundation to develop computer vision (CV) systems that solve complex image classification and object detection problems.

In chapters 3 and 4, we talked about the main components of CNNs and setting up hyperparameters such as the number of hidden layers, learning rate, optimizer, and so on. We also talked about other techniques to improve network performance, like regularization, augmentation, and dropout. In this chapter, you will see how these elements come together to build a convolutional network. I will walk you through five of the most popular CNNs that were cutting edge in their time, and you will see how their designers thought about building, training, and improving networks. We will start with LeNet, developed in 1998, which performed fairly well at recognizing handwritten characters. You will see how CNN architectures have evolved since then to deeper CNNs like AlexNet and VGGNet, and beyond to more advanced and super-deep networks like Inception and ResNet, developed in 2014 and 2015, respectively.

For each CNN architecture, you will learn the following:

- *Novel features*—We will explore the novel features that distinguish these networks from others and what specific problems their creators were trying to solve.
- *Network architecture*—We will cover the architecture and components of each network and see how they come together to form the end-to-end network.
- *Network code implementation*—We will walk step-by-step through the network implementations using the Keras deep learning (DL) library. The goal of this section is for you to learn how to read research papers and implement new architectures as the need arises.
- *Setting up learning hyperparameters*—After you implement a network architecture, you need to set up the hyperparameters of the learning algorithms that you learned in chapter 4 (optimizer, learning rate, weight decay, and so on). We will implement the learning hyperparameters as presented in the original research paper of each network. In this section, you will see how performance evolved from one network to another over the years.
- *Network performance*—Finally, you will see how each network performed on benchmark datasets like MNIST and ImageNet, as represented in their research papers.

The three main objectives of this chapter follow:

- Understanding the architecture and learning hyperparameters of advanced CNNs. You will be implementing simpler CNNs like AlexNet and VGGNet for simple- to medium-complexity problems. For very complex problems, you might want to use deeper networks like Inception and ResNet.
- Understanding the novel features of each network and the reasons they were developed. Each succeeding CNN architecture solves a specific limitation in the previous one. After reading about the five networks in this chapter (and their research papers), you will build a strong foundation for reading and understanding new networks as they emerge.
- Learning how CNNs have evolved and their designers' thought processes. This will help you build an instinct for what works well and what problems may arise when building your own network.

In chapter 3, you learned about the basic building blocks of convolutional layers, pooling layers, and fully connected layers of CNNs. As you will see in this chapter, in recent years a lot of CV research has focused on how to put together these basic building blocks to form effective CNNs. One of the best ways for you to develop your intuition is to examine and learn from these architectures (similar to how most of us may have learned to write code by reading other people's code).

To get the most out of this chapter, you are encouraged to read the research papers linked in each section before you read my explanation. What you have learned in part 1 of this book fully equips you to start reading research papers written by pioneers in the AI field. Reading and implementing research papers is by far one of the most valuable skills that you will build from reading this book.

> **TIP** Personally, I feel the task of going through a research paper, interpreting the crux behind it, and implementing the code is a very important skill every DL enthusiast and practitioner should possess. Practically implementing research ideas brings out the thought process of the author and also helps transform those ideas into real-world industry applications. I hope that, by reading this chapter, you will get comfortable reading research papers and implementing their findings in your own work. The fast-paced evolution in this field requires us to always stay up-to-date with the latest research. What you will learn in this book (or in other publications) now will not be the latest and greatest in three or four years—maybe even sooner. The most valuable asset that I want you to take away from this book is a strong DL foundation that empowers you to get out in the real world and be able to read the latest research and implement it yourself.

Are you ready? Let's get started!

5.1 CNN design patterns

Before we jump into the details of the common CNN architectures, we are going to look at some common design choices when it comes to CNNs. It might seem at first that there are way too many choices to make. Every time we learn about something new in deep learning, it gives us more hyperparameters to design. So it is good to be able to narrow down our choices by looking at some common patterns that were created by pioneer researchers in the field so we can understand their motivation and start from where they ended rather than doing things completely randomly:

- *Pattern 1: Feature extraction and classification*—Convolutional nets are typically composed of two parts: the feature extraction part, which consists of a series of convolutional layers; and the classification part, which consists of a series of fully connected layers (figure 5.1). This is pretty much always the case with ConvNets, starting from LeNet and AlexNet to the very recent CNNs that have come out in the past few years, like Inception and ResNet.

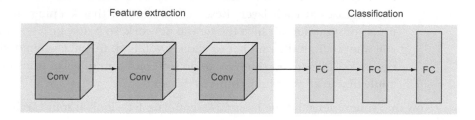

Figure 5.1   Convolutional nets generally include feature extraction and classification.

- *Pattern 2: Image depth increases, and dimensions decrease*—The input data at each layer is an image. With each layer, we apply a new convolutional layer over a new image. This pushes us to think of an image in a more generic way. First, you see that each image is a 3D object that has a height, width, and depth. Depth is referred to as the *color channel*, where depth is 1 for grayscale images and 3 for color images. In the later layers, the images still have depth, but they are not colors per se: they are feature maps that represent the features extracted from the previous layers. That's why the depth increases as we go deeper through the network layers. In figure 5.2, the depth of an image is equal to 96; this represents the number of feature maps in the layer. So, that's one pattern you will always see: the image depth increases, and the dimensions decrease.

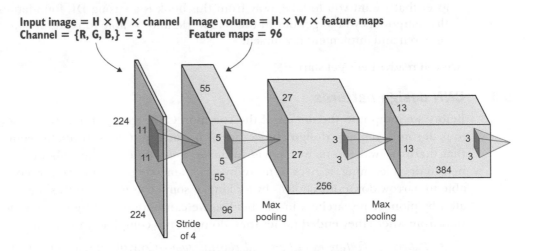

Figure 5.2   Image depth increases, and the dimensions decrease.

- *Pattern 3: Fully connected layers*—This generally isn't as strict a pattern as the previous two, but it's very helpful to know. Typically, all fully connected layers in a network either have the same number of hidden units or decrease at each layer. It is rare to find a network where the number of units in the fully connected layers increases at each layer. Research has found that keeping the number of units constant doesn't hurt the neural network, so it may be a good approach if you want to limit the number of choices you have to make when designing your network. This way, all you have to do is to pick a number of units per layer and apply that to all your fully connected layers.

Now that you understand the basic CNN patterns, let's look at some architectures that have implemented them. Most of these architectures are famous because they performed well in the ImageNet competition. ImageNet is a famous benchmark that contains millions of images; DL and CV researchers use the ImageNet dataset to compare algorithms. More on that later.

> **NOTE** The snippets in this chapter are not meant to be runnable. The goal is to show you how to implement the specifications that are defined in a research paper. Visit the book's website (www.manning.com/books/deep-learning-for-vision-systems) or Github repo (https://github.com/moelgendy/deep_learning _for_vision_systems) for the full executable code.

Now, let's get started with the first network we are going to discuss in this chapter: LeNet.

5.2 LeNet-5

In 1998, Lecun et al. introduced a pioneering CNN called *LeNet-5*.[1] The LeNet-5 architecture is straightforward, and the components are not new to you (they were new back in 1998); you learned about convolutional, pooling, and fully connected layers in chapter 3. The architecture is composed of five weight layers, and hence the name LeNet-5: three convolutional layers and two fully connected layers.

> **DEFINITION** We refer to the convolutional and fully connected layers as *weight layers* because they contain trainable weights as opposed to pooling layers that don't contain any weights. The common convention is to use the number of weight layers to describe the depth of the network. For example, AlexNet (explained next) is said to be eight layers deep because it contains five convolutional and three fully connected layers. The reason we care more about weight layers is mainly because they reflect the model's computational complexity.

5.2.1 LeNet architecture

The architecture of LeNet-5 is shown in figure 5.3:

INPUT IMAGE ⇒ C1 ⇒ TANH ⇒ S2 ⇒ C3 ⇒ TANH ⇒ S4 ⇒ C5 ⇒ TANH ⇒ FC6 ⇒ SOFTMAX7

where C is a convolutional layer, S is a subsampling or pooling layer, and FC is a fully connected layer.

Notice that Yann LeCun and his team used tanh as an activation function instead of the currently state-of-the-art ReLU. This is because in 1998, ReLU had not yet been used in the context of DL, and it was more common to use tanh or sigmoid as an activation function in the hidden layers. Without further ado, let's implement LeNet-5 in Keras.

---

[1] Y. Lecun, L. Bottou, Y. Bengio, and P. Haffner, "Gradient-Based Learning Applied to Document Recognition," *Proceedings of the IEEE* 86 (11): 2278–2324, http://yann.lecun.com/exdb/publis/pdf/lecun-01a.pdf.

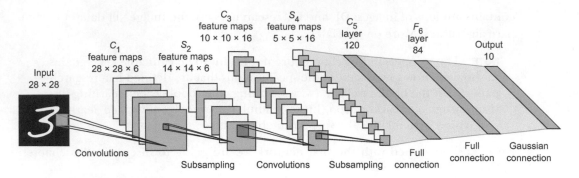

Figure 5.3   LeNet architecture

5.2.2   *LeNet-5 implementation in Keras*

To implement LeNet-5 in Keras, read the original paper and follow the architecture information from pages 6–8. Here are the main takeaways for building the LeNet-5 network:

- *Number of filters in each convolutional layer*—As you can see in figure 5.3 (and as defined in the paper), the depth (number of filters) of each convolutional layer is as follows: C1 has 6, C3 has 16, C5 has 120 layers.
- *Kernel size of each convolutional layer*—The paper specifies that the kernel_size is 5 × 5.
- *Subsampling (pooling) layers*—A subsampling (pooling) layer is added after each convolutional layer. The receptive field of each unit is a 2 × 2 area (for example, pool_size is 2). Note that the LeNet-5 creators used *average pooling*, which computes the average value of its inputs, instead of the *max pooling* layer that we used in our earlier projects, which passes the maximum value of its inputs. You can try both if you are interested, to see the difference. For this experiment, we are going to follow the paper's architecture.
- *Activation function*—As mentioned before, the creators of LeNet-5 used the tanh activation function for the hidden layers because symmetric functions are believed to yield faster convergence compared to sigmoid functions (figure 5.4).

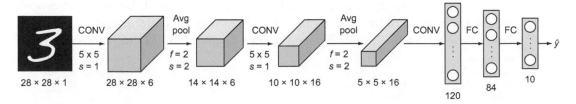

Figure 5.4   The LeNet architecture consists of convolutional kernels of size 5 × 5; pooling layers; an activation function (tanh); and three fully connected layers with 120, 84, and 10 neurons, respectively.

Now let's put that in code to build the LeNet-5 architecture:

```python
from keras.models import Sequential                                      Imports the Keras
from keras.layers import Conv2D, AveragePooling2D, Flatten, Dense        model and layers

model = Sequential()            ◄─┤  Instantiates an empty
                                     sequential model

# C1 Convolutional Layer
model.add(Conv2D(filters = 6, kernel_size = 5, strides = 1, activation = 'tanh',
                 input shape = (28,28,1), padding = 'same'))

# S2 Pooling Layer
model.add(AveragePooling2D(pool_size = 2, strides = 2, padding = 'valid'))

# C3 Convolutional Layer
model.add(Conv2D(filters = 16, kernel_size = 5, strides = 1,activation = 'tanh',
                 padding = 'valid'))

# S4 Pooling Layer
model.add(AveragePooling2D(pool_size = 2, strides = 2, padding = 'valid'))

# C5 Convolutional Layer
model.add(Conv2D(filters = 120, kernel_size = 5, strides = 1,activation = 'tanh',
                 padding = 'valid'))

model.add(Flatten())            ◄─┤  Flattens the CNN output to
                                     feed it fully connected layers

# FC6 Fully Connected Layer
model.add(Dense(units = 84, activation = 'tanh'))

# FC7 Output layer with softmax activation
model.add(Dense(units = 10, activation = 'softmax'))

model.summary()      ◄─┐  Prints the model summary (figure 5.5)
```

LeNet-5 is a small neural network by today's standards. It has 61,706 parameters, compared to millions of parameters in more modern networks, as you will see later in this chapter.

> **A note when reading the papers discussed in this chapter**
>
> When you read the LeNet-5 paper, just know that it is harder to read than the others we will cover in this chapter. Most of the ideas that I mention in this section are in sections 2 and 3 of the paper. The later sections of the paper talk about something called the *graph transformer network*, which isn't widely used today. So if you do try to read the paper, I recommend focusing on section 2, which talks about the LeNet architecture and the learning details; then maybe take a quick look at section 3, which includes a bunch of experiments and results that are pretty interesting.
>
> I recommend starting with the AlexNet paper (discussed in section 5.3), followed by the VGGNet paper (section 5.4), and then the LeNet paper. It is a good classic to look at once you go over the other ones.

```
Layer (type)                    Output Shape           Param #
=================================================================
conv2d_1 (Conv2D)               (None, 28, 28, 6)      156
_____
average_pooling2d_1 (Average    (None, 14, 14, 6)      0
_____
conv2d_2 (Conv2D)               (None, 10, 10, 16)     2416
_____
average_pooling2d_2 (Average    (None, 5, 5, 16)       0
_____
conv2d_3 (Conv2D)               (None, 1, 1, 120)      48120
_____
flatten_1 (Flatten)             (None, 120)            0
_____
dense_1 (Dense)                 (None, 84)             10164
_____
dense_2 (Dense)                 (None, 10)             850
=================================================================
Total params: 61,706
Trainable params: 61,706
Non-trainable params: 0
```

Figure 5.5   LeNet-5 model summary

5.2.3   *Setting up the learning hyperparameters*

LeCun and his team used scheduled decay learning where the value of the learning rate was decreased using the following schedule: 0.0005 for the first two epochs, 0.0002 for the next three epochs, 0.00005 for the next four, and then 0.00001 thereafter. In the paper, the authors trained their network for 20 epochs.

Let's build a `lr_schedule` function with this schedule. The method takes an integer epoch number as an argument and returns the learning rate (`lr`):

```
def lr_schedule(epoch):
    if epoch <= 2:                          ◁──────────   lr is 0.0005 for the first two
        lr = 5e-4                                         epochs, 0.0002 for the next three
    elif epoch > 2 and epoch <= 5:                        epochs (3 to 5), 0.00005 for the
        lr = 2e-4                                         next four (6 to 9), then 0.00001
    elif epoch > 5 and epoch <= 9:                        thereafter (more than 9).
        lr = 5e-5
    else:
        lr = 1e-5
    return lr
```

We use the `lr_schedule` function in the following code snippet to compile the model:

```
from keras.callbacks import ModelCheckpoint, LearningRateScheduler

lr_scheduler = LearningRateScheduler(lr_schedule)
checkpoint = ModelCheckpoint(filepath='path_to_save_file/file.hdf5',
                             monitor='val_acc',
```

```
                         verbose=1,
                         save_best_only=True)

callbacks = [checkpoint, lr_reducer]

model.compile(loss='categorical_crossentropy', optimizer='sgd',
              metrics=['accuracy'])
```

Now start the network training for 20 epochs, as mentioned in the paper:

```
hist = model.fit(X_train, y_train, batch_size=32, epochs=20,
            validation_data=(X_test, y_test), callbacks=callbacks,
            verbose=2, shuffle=True)
```

See the downloadable notebook included with the book's code for the full code implementation, if you want to see this in action.

5.2.4 *LeNet performance on the MNIST dataset*

When you train LeNet-5 on the MNIST dataset, you will get above 99% accuracy (see the code notebook with the book's code). Try to re-run this experiment with the ReLU activation function in the hidden layers, and observe the difference in the network performance.

5.3 *AlexNet*

LeNet performs very well on the MNIST dataset. But it turns out that the MNIST dataset is very simple because it contains grayscale images (1 channel) and classifies into only 10 classes, which makes it an easier challenge. The main motivation behind AlexNet was to build a deeper network that can learn more complex functions.

AlexNet (figure 5.6) was the winner of the ILSVRC image classification competition in 2012. Krizhevsky et al. created the neural network architecture and trained it on 1.2 million high-resolution images into 1,000 different classes of the ImageNet dataset.[2] AlexNet was state of the art at its time because it was the first real "deep" network that opened the door for the CV community to seriously consider convolutional networks in their applications. We will explain deeper networks later in this chapter, like VGGNet and ResNet, but it is good to see how ConvNets evolved and the main drawbacks of AlexNet that were the main motivation for the later networks.

As you can see in figure 5.6, AlexNet has a lot of similarities to LeNet but is much deeper (more hidden layers) and bigger (more filters per layer). They have similar building blocks: a series of convolutional and pooling layers stacked on top of each other followed by fully connected layers and a softmax. We've seen that LeNet has around 61,000 parameters, whereas AlexNet has about 60 million parameters and

---

[2] Alex Krizhevsky, Ilya Sutskever, and Geoffrey E. Hinton, "ImageNet Classification with Deep Convolutional Neural Networks," *Communications of the ACM* 60 (6): 84–90, https://dl.acm.org/doi/10.1145/3065386.

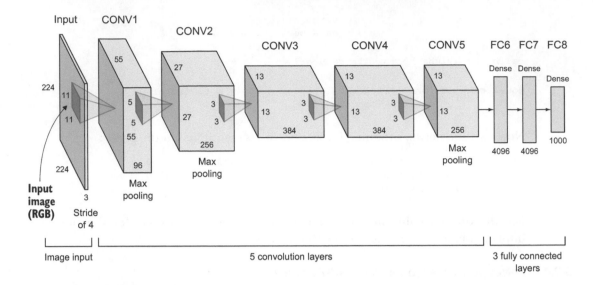

Figure 5.6   AlexNet architecture

650,000 neurons, which gives it a larger learning capacity to understand more complex features. This allowed AlexNet to achieve remarkable performance in the ILSVRC image classification competition in 2012.

ImageNet and ILSVRC

ImageNet (http://image-net.org/index) is a large visual database designed for use in visual object recognition software research. It is aimed at labeling and categorizing images into almost 22,000 categories based on a defined set of words and phrases. The images were collected from the web and labeled by humans using Amazon's Mechanical Turk crowdsourcing tool. At the time of this writing, there are over 14 million images in the ImageNet project. To organize such a massive amount of data, the creators of ImageNet followed the WordNet hierarchy where each meaningful word/ phrase in WordNet is called a *synonym set* (*synset* for short). Within the ImageNet project, images are organized according to these synsets, with the goal being to have 1,000+ images per synset.

The ImageNet project runs an annual software contest called the ImageNet Large Scale Visual Recognition Challenge (ILSVRC, www.image-net.org/challenges/LSVRC), where software programs compete to correctly classify and detect objects and scenes. We will use the ILSVRC challenge as a benchmark to compare different networks' performance.

5.3.1 AlexNet architecture

You saw a version of the AlexNet architecture in the project at the end of chapter 3. The architecture is pretty straightforward. It consists of:

- Convolutional layers with the following kernel sizes: 11×11, 5×5, and 3×3
- Max pooling layers for images downsampling
- Dropout layers to avoid overfitting
- Unlike LeNet, ReLU activation functions in the hidden layers and a softmax activation in the output layer

AlexNet consists of five convolutional layers, some of which are followed by max-pooling layers, and three fully connected layers with a final 1000-way softmax. The architecture can be represented in text as follows:

INPUT IMAGE $\Rightarrow$ CONV1 $\Rightarrow$ POOL2 $\Rightarrow$ CONV3 $\Rightarrow$ POOL4 $\Rightarrow$ CONV5 $\Rightarrow$ CONV6 $\Rightarrow$ CONV7 $\Rightarrow$ POOL8 $\Rightarrow$ FC9 $\Rightarrow$ FC10 $\Rightarrow$ SOFTMAX7

5.3.2 Novel features of AlexNet

Before AlexNet, DL was starting to gain traction in speech recognition and a few other areas. But AlexNet was the milestone that convinced a lot of people in the CV community to take a serious look at DL and demonstrate that it really works in CV. AlexNet presented some novel features that were not used in previous CNNs (like LeNet). You are already familiar with all of them from the previous chapters, so we'll go through them quickly here.

ReLU ACTIVATION FUNCTION

AlexNet uses ReLu for the nonlinear part instead of the tanh and sigmoid functions that were the earlier standard for traditional neural networks (like LeNet). ReLu was used in the hidden layers of the AlexNet architecture because it trains much faster. This is because the derivative of the sigmoid function becomes very small in the saturating region, and therefore the updates applied to the weights almost vanish. This phenomenon is called the *vanishing gradient problem*. ReLU is represented by this equation:

$$f(x) = \max(0, x)$$

It's discussed in detail in chapter 2.

> ### The vanishing gradient problem
> Certain activation functions, like the sigmoid function, squish a large input space into a small input space between 0 and 1 (–1 to 1 for tanh activations). Therefore, a large change in the input of the sigmoid function causes a small change in the output. As a result, the derivative becomes very small:

(continued)

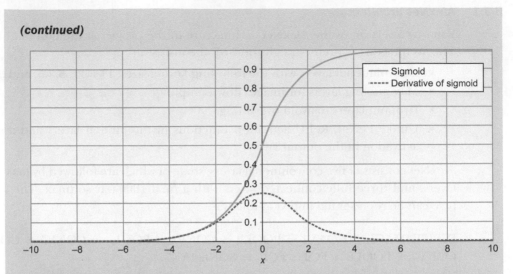

The vanishing gradient problem: a large change in the input of the sigmoid function causes a negligible change in the output.

We will talk more about the vanishing gradient phenomenon later in this chapter when we look at the ResNet architecture.

DROPOUT LAYER

As explained in chapter 3, dropout layers are used to prevent the neural network from overfitting. The neurons that are "dropped out" do not contribute to the forward pass and do not participate in backpropagation. This means every time an input is presented, the neural network samples a different architecture, but all of these architectures share the same weights. This technique reduces complex co-adaptations of neurons, since a neuron cannot rely on the presence of particular other neurons. Therefore, the neuron is forced to learn more robust features that are useful in conjunction with many different random subsets of the other neurons. Krizhevsky et al. used dropout with a probability of 0.5 in the two fully connected layers.

DATA AUGMENTATION

One popular and very effective approach to avoid overfitting is to artificially enlarge the dataset using label-preserving transformations. This happens by generating new instances of the training images with transformations like image rotation, flipping, scaling, and many more. Data augmentation is explained in detail in chapter 4.

LOCAL RESPONSE NORMALIZATION

AlexNet uses local response normalization. It is different from the batch normalization technique (explained in chapter 4). Normalization helps to speed up convergence. Nowadays, batch normalization is used instead of local response normalization; we will use BN in our implementation in this chapter.

WEIGHT REGULARIZATION

Krizhevsky et al. used a weight decay of 0.0005. Weight decay is another term for the L2 regularization technique explained in chapter 4. This approach reduces the overfitting of the DL neural network model on training data to allow the network to generalize better on new data:

```
model.add(Conv2D(32, (3,3), kernel_regularizer=l2(λ)))
```

The lambda (λ) value is a weight decay hyperparameter that you can tune. If you still see overfitting, you can reduce it by increasing the lambda value. In this case, Krizhevsky and his team found that a small decay value of 0.0005 was good enough for the model to learn.

TRAINING ON MULTIPLE GPUs

Krizhevsky et al. used a GTX 580 GPU with only 3 GB of memory. It was state-of-the-art at the time but not large enough to train the 1.2 million training examples in the dataset. Therefore, the team developed a complicated way to spread the network across two GPUs. The basic idea was that a lot of the layers were split across two different GPUs that communicated with each other. You don't need to worry about these details today: there are far more advanced ways to train deep networks on distributed GPUs, as we will discuss later in this book.

5.3.3 *AlexNet implementation in Keras*

Now that you've learned the basic components of AlexNet and its novel features, let's apply them to build the AlexNet neural network. I suggest that you read the architecture description on page 4 of the original paper and follow along.

As depicted in figure 5.7, the network contains eight weight layers: the first five are convolutional, and the remaining three are fully connected. The output of the last fully connected layer is fed to a 1000-way softmax that produces a distribution over the 1,000 class labels.

> **NOTE** AlexNet input starts with 227 × 227 × 3 images. If you read the paper, you will notice that it refers to a dimensions volume of 224 × 224 × 3 for the input images. But the numbers make sense only for 227 × 227 × 3 images (figure 5.7). I suggest that this could be a typing mistake in the paper.

The layers are stacked together as follows:

- *CONV1*—The authors used a large kernel size (11). They also used a large stride (4), which makes the input dimensions shrink by roughly a factor 4 (from 227 × 227 to 55 × 55). We calculate the dimensions of the output as follows:

$$\frac{(227 - 11)}{4} + 1 = 55$$

and the depth is the number of filters in the convolutional layer (96). The output dimensions are 55 × 55 × 96.

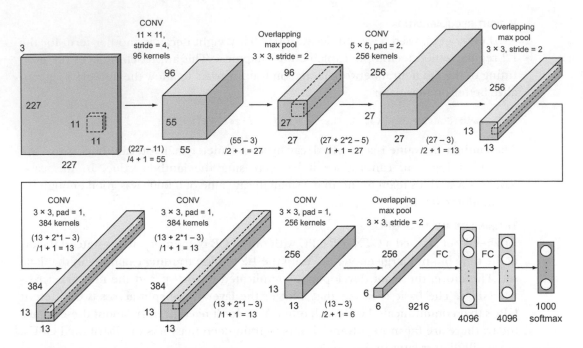

Figure 5.7 AlexNet contains eight weight layers: five convolutional and three fully connected. Two contain 4,096 neurons, and the output is fed to a 1,000-neuron softmax.

- *POOL with a filter size of 3 × 3*—This reduces the dimensions from 55 × 55 to 27 × 27:

$$\frac{(55-3)}{2} + 1 = 27$$

The pooling layer doesn't change the depth of the volume. The output dimensions are 27 × 27 × 96.

Similarly, we can calculate the output dimensions of the remaining layers:

- *CONV2*—Kernel size = 5, depth = 256, and stride = 1
- *POOL*—Size = 3 × 3, which downsamples its input dimensions from 27 × 27 to 13 × 13
- *CONV3*—Kernel size = 3, depth = 384, and stride = 1
- *CONV4*—Kernel size = 3, depth = 384, and stride = 1
- *CONV5*—Kernel size = 3, depth = 256, and stride = 1
- *POOL*—Size = 3 × 3, which downsamples its input from 13 × 13 to 6 × 6
- *Flatten layer*—Flattens the dimension volume 6 × 6 × 256 to 1 × 9,216
- *FC* with 4,096 neurons
- *FC* with 4,096 neurons
- *Softmax layer* with 1,000 neurons

NOTE You might be wondering how Krizhevsky and his team decided to implement this configuration. Setting up the right values of network hyper-parameters like kernel size, depths, stride, pooling size, etc., is tedious and requires a lot of trial and error. The idea remains the same: we want to apply many weight layers to increase the model's capacity to learn more complex functions. We also need to add pooling layers in between to downsample the input dimensions, as discussed in chapter 2. With that said, setting up the exact hyperparameters comes as one of the challenges of CNNs. VGGNet (explained next) solves this problem by implementing a uniform layer configuration to reduce the amount of trial and error when designing your network.

Note that all of the convolutional layers are followed by a batch normalization layer, and all of the hidden layers are followed by ReLU activations. Now, let's put that in code to build the AlexNet architecture:

```python
from keras.models import Sequential
from keras.regularizers import l2
from keras.layers import Conv2D, AveragePooling2D, Flatten, Dense,
    Activation,MaxPool2D, BatchNormalization, Dropout
```
Imports the Keras model, layers, and regularizers

```python
model = Sequential()
```
Instantiates an empty sequential model

```python
# 1st layer (CONV + pool + batchnorm)
model.add(Conv2D(filters= 96, kernel_size= (11,11), strides=(4,4),
    padding='valid',
                input_shape = (227,227,3)))
model.add(Activation('relu'))
model.add(MaxPool2D(pool_size=(3,3), strides=(2,2)))
model.add(BatchNormalization())
```
The activation function can be added on its own layer or within the Conv2D function as we did in previous implementations.

```python
# 2nd layer (CONV + pool + batchnorm)
model.add(Conv2D(filters=256, kernel_size=(5,5), strides=(1,1), padding='same',
                kernel_regularizer=l2(0.0005)))
model.add(Activation('relu'))
model.add(MaxPool2D(pool_size=(3,3), strides=(2,2), padding='valid'))
model.add(BatchNormalization())
```

```python
# layer 3 (CONV + batchnorm)
model.add(Conv2D(filters=384, kernel_size=(3,3), strides=(1,1), padding='same',
    kernel_regularizer=l2(0.0005)))
model.add(Activation('relu'))
model.add(BatchNormalization())
```
Note that the AlexNet authors did not add a pooling layer here.

```python
# layer 4 (CONV + batchnorm)
model.add(Conv2D(filters=384, kernel_size=(3,3), strides=(1,1), padding='same',
                kernel_regularizer=l2(0.0005)))
model.add(Activation('relu'))
model.add(BatchNormalization())
```
Similar to layer 3

```python
# layer 5 (CONV + batchnorm)
model.add(Conv2D(filters=256, kernel_size=(3,3), strides=(1,1), padding='same',
                kernel_regularizer=l2(0.0005)))
```

```
model.add(Activation('relu'))
model.add(BatchNormalization())
model.add(MaxPool2D(pool_size=(3,3), strides=(2,2), padding='valid'))

model.add(Flatten())          ◁─────  Flattens the CNN output to
                                       feed it fully connected layers

# layer 6 (Dense layer + dropout)
model.add(Dense(units = 4096, activation = 'relu'))
model.add(Dropout(0.5))

# layer 7 (Dense layers)
model.add(Dense(units = 4096, activation = 'relu'))
model.add(Dropout(0.5))

# layer 8 (softmax output layer)
model.add(Dense(units = 1000, activation = 'softmax'))

model.summary()               ◁───┤  Prints the
                                      model summary
```

When you print the model summary, you will see that the number of total parameters is 62 million:

```
------------------------------------------
Total params: 62,383, 848
Trainable params: 62,381, 096
Non-trainable params: 2,752
```

> **NOTE** Both LeNet and AlexNet have many hyperparameters to tune. The authors of those networks had to go through many experiments to set the kernel size, strides, and padding for each layer, which makes the networks harder to understand and manage. VGGNet (explained next) solves this problem with a very simple, uniform architecture.

5.3.4 *Setting up the learning hyperparameters*

AlexNet was trained for 90 epochs, which took 6 days on two Nvidia Geforce GTX 580 GPUs simultaneously. This is why you will see that the network is split into two pipelines in the original paper. Krizhevsky et al. started with an initial learning rate of 0.01 with a momentum of 0.9. The `lr` is then divided by 10 when the validation error stops improving:

**Sets the SGD optimizer with lr
of 0.01 and momentum of 0.9**

**Reduces the learning rate by 0.1
when the validation error plateaus**

```
reduce_lr = ReduceLROnPlateau(monitor='val_loss', factor=np.sqrt(0.1))    ◁─

optimizer = keras.optimizers.sgd(lr = 0.01, momentum = 0.9)

model.compile(loss='categorical_crossentropy', optimizer=optimizer,
              metrics=['accuracy'])    ◁─┐
                                          Compiles the model
```

```
model.fit(X_train, y_train, batch_size=128, epochs=90,
    ┌─▷        validation_data=(X_test, y_test), verbose=2, callbacks=[reduce_lr])
```
**Trains the model and calls the reduce_lr value
using callbacks in the training method**

5.3.5 AlexNet performance

AlexNet significantly outperformed all the prior competitors in the 2012 ILSVRC challenges. It achieved a winning top-5 test error rate of 15.3%, compared to 26.2% achieved by the second-best entry that year, which used other traditional classifiers. This huge improvement in performance attracted the CV community's attention to the potential that convolutional networks have to solve complex vision problems and led to more advanced CNN architectures, as you will see in the following sections of this chapter.

Top-1 and top-5 error rates?

Top-1 and *top-5* are terms used mostly in research papers to describe the accuracy of an algorithm on a given classification task. The top-1 error rate is the percentage of the time that the classifier did not give the correct class the highest score, and the top-5 error rate is the percentage of the time that the classifier did not include the correct class among its top five guesses.

Let's apply this in an example. Suppose there are 100 classes, and we show the network an image of a cat. The classifier outputs a score or confidence value for each class as follows:

1 Cat: 70%
2 Dog: 20%
3 Horse: 5%
4 Motorcycle: 4%
5 Car: 0.6%
6 Plane: 0.4%

This means the classifier was able to correctly predict the true class of the image in the top-1. Try the same experiment for 100 images and observe how many times the classifier missed the true label, and that's your top-1 error rate.

The same idea holds for the top-5 error rate. In the example, if the true label is *Horse*, then the classifier missed the true label in the top-1 but caught it in the first five predicted classes (for example, top-5). Calculate how many times the classifier missed the true label in the top five predictions, and that's your top-5.

Ideally, we want the model to always predict the correct class in the top-1. But top-5 gives a more holistic evaluation of the model's performance by defining how close the model is to the correct prediction for the missed classes.

5.4   VGGNet

VGGNet was developed in 2014 by the Visual Geometry Group at Oxford University (hence the name VGG).[3] The building components are exactly the same as those in LeNet and AlexNet, except that VGGNet is an even deeper network with more convolutional, pooling, and dense layers. Other than that, no new components are introduced here.

VGGNet, also known as VGG16, consists of 16 weight layers: 13 convolutional layers and 3 fully connected layers. Its uniform architecture makes it appealing in the DL community because it is very easy to understand.

5.4.1   Novel features of VGGNet

We've seen how challenging it can be to set up CNN hyperparameters like kernel size, padding, strides, and so on. VGGNet's novel concept is that it has a simple architecture containing uniform components (convolutional and pooling layers). It improves on AlexNet by replacing large kernel-sized filters (11 and 5 in the first and second convolutional layers, respectively) with multiple 3×3 pool-size filters one after another.

The architecture is composed of a series of uniform convolutional building blocks followed by a unified pooling layer, where:

- All convolutional layers are 3×3 kernel-sized filters with a `strides` value of 1 and a `padding` value of `same`.
- All pooling layers have a 2×2 pool size and a `strides` value of 2.

Simonyan and Zisserman decided to use a smaller 3×3 kernel to allow the network to extract finer-level features of the image compared to AlexNet's large kernels (11×11 and 5×5). The idea is that with a given convolutional receptive field, multiple stacked smaller kernels is better than a larger kernel because having multiple nonlinear layers increases the depth of the network; this enables it to learn more complex features at a lower cost because it has fewer learning parameters.

For example, in their experiments, the authors noticed that a stack of two 3×3 convolutional layers (without spatial pooling in between) has an effective receptive field of 5×5, and three 3×3 convolutional layers have the effect of a 7×7 receptive field. So by using 3×3 convolutions with higher depth, you get the benefits of using more nonlinear rectification layers (ReLU), which makes the decision function more discriminative. Second, this decreases the number of training parameters because when you use a three-layer 3×3 convolutional with C channels, the stack is parameterised by $3^2 C^2 = 27 C^2$ weights compared to a single 7×7 convolutional layer that requires $7^2 C^2 = 49 C^2$ weights, which is 81% more parameters.

---

[3] Karen Simonyan and Andrew Zisserman, "Very Deep Convolutional Networks for Large-Scale Image Recognition," 2014, https://arxiv.org/pdf/1409.1556v6.pdf.

Receptive field

As explained in chapter 3, the *receptive field* is the effective area of the input image on which the output depends:

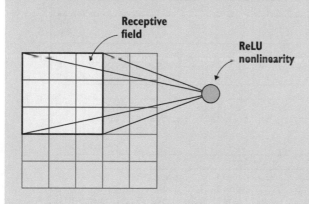

This unified configuration of the convolutional and pooling components simplifies the neural network architecture, which makes it very easy to understand and implement.

The VGGNet architecture is developed by stacking 3 × 3 convolutional layers with 2 × 2 pooling layers inserted after several convolutional layers. This is followed by the traditional classifier, which is composed of fully connected layers and a softmax, as depicted in figure 5.8.

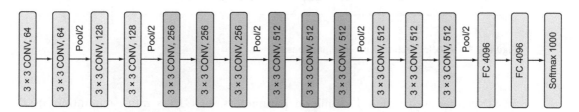

Figure 5.8   VGGNet-16 architecture

5.4.2   VGGNet configurations

Simonyan and Zisserman created several configurations for the VGGNet architecture, as shown in figure 5.9. All of the configurations follow the same generic design. Configurations D and E are the most commonly used and are called *VGG16* and *VGG19*, referring to the number of weight layers. Each block contains a series of 3 × 3 convolutional layers with similar hyperparameter configuration, followed by a 2 × 2 pooling layer.

Table 5.1 lists the number of learning parameters (in millions) for each configuration. VGG16 yields ~138 million parameters; VGG19, which is a deeper version of

ConvNet configuration					
A	A-LRN	B	C	D	E
11 weight layers	11 weight layers	13 weight layers	16 weight layers	16 weight layers	19 weight layers
Input (224 x 224 RGB image)					
conv3-64	conv3-64 LRN	conv3-64 conv3-64	conv3-64 conv3-64	conv3-64 conv3-64	conv3-64 conv3-64
maxpool					
conv3-128	conv3-128	conv3-128 conv3-128	conv3-128 conv3-128	conv3-128 conv3-128	conv3-128 conv3-128
maxpool					
conv3-256 conv3-256	conv3-256 conv3-256	conv3-256 conv3-256	conv3-256 conv3-256 conv3-256	conv3-256 conv3-256 conv3-256	conv3-256 conv3-256 conv3-256 conv3-256
maxpool					
conv3-512 conv3-512	conv3-512 conv3-512	conv3-512 conv3-512	conv3-512 conv3-512 conv3-512	conv3-512 conv3-512 conv3-512	conv3-512 conv3-512 conv3-512 conv3-512
maxpool					
conv3-512 conv3-512	conv3-512 conv3-512	conv3-512 conv3-512	conv3-512 conv3-512 conv3-512	conv3-512 conv3-512 conv3-512	conv3-512 conv3-512 conv3-512 conv3-512
maxpool					
FC-4096					
FC-4096					
FC-1000					

Figure 5.9 VGGNet architecture configurations

VGGNet, has more than 144 million parameters. VGG16 is more commonly used because it performs almost as well as VGG19 but with fewer parameters.

Table 5.1 VGGNet architecture parameters (in millions)

Network	A, A-LRN	B	C	D	E
No. of parameters	133	133	134	138	144

VGG16 IN KERAS

Configurations D (VGG16) and E (VGG19) are the most commonly used configurations because they are deeper networks that can learn more complex functions. So, in this chapter, we will implement configuration D, which has 16 weight layers. VGG19 (configuration E) can be similarly implemented by adding a fourth convolutional layer to the third, fourth, and fifth blocks as you can see in figure 5.9. This chapter's downloaded code includes a full implementation of both VGG16 and VGG19.

Note that Simonyan and Zisserman used the following regularization techniques to avoid overfitting:

- L2 regularization with weight decay of 5×10^{-4}. For simplicity, this is not added to the implementation that follows.
- Dropout regularization for the first two fully connected layers, with a dropout ratio set to 0.5.

The Keras code is as follows:

```
model = Sequential()          ◁──┐  Instantiates an empty
                                  │  sequential model
# block #1
model.add(Conv2D(filters=64, kernel_size=(3,3), strides=(1,1),
    activation='relu',
                 padding='same', input_shape=(224,224, 3)))
model.add(Conv2D(filters=64, kernel_size=(3,3), strides=(1,1),
    activation='relu',
                 padding='same'))
model.add(MaxPool2D((2,2), strides=(2,2)))

# block #2
model.add(Conv2D(filters=128, kernel_size=(3,3), strides=(1,1),
    activation='relu',
                 padding='same'))
model.add(Conv2D(filters=128, kernel_size=(3,3), strides=(1,1),
    activation='relu',
                 padding='same'))
model.add(MaxPool2D((2,2), strides=(2,2)))

# block #3
model.add(Conv2D(filters=256, kernel_size=(3,3), strides=(1,1),
    activation='relu',
                 padding='same'))
model.add(Conv2D(filters=256, kernel_size=(3,3), strides=(1,1),
    activation='relu',
                 padding='same'))
model.add(Conv2D(filters=256, kernel_size=(3,3), strides=(1,1),
    activation='relu',
                 padding='same'))
model.add(MaxPool2D((2,2), strides=(2,2)))

# block #4
model.add(Conv2D(filters=512, kernel_size=(3,3), strides=(1,1),
    activation='relu',
                 padding='same'))
model.add(Conv2D(filters=512, kernel_size=(3,3), strides=(1,1),
    activation='relu',
                 padding='same'))
model.add(Conv2D(filters=512, kernel_size=(3,3), strides=(1,1),
    activation='relu',
                 padding='same'))
model.add(MaxPool2D((2,2), strides=(2,2)))
```

```
# block #5
model.add(Conv2D(filters=512, kernel_size=(3,3), strides=(1,1),
     activation='relu',
                  padding='same'))
model.add(Conv2D(filters=512, kernel_size=(3,3), strides=(1,1),
     activation='relu',
                  padding='same'))
model.add(Conv2D(filters=512, kernel_size=(3,3), strides=(1,1),
     activation='relu',
                  padding='same'))
model.add(MaxPool2D((2,2), strides=(2,2)))

# block #6 (classifier)
model.add(Flatten())
model.add(Dense(4096, activation='relu'))
model.add(Dropout(0.5))
model.add(Dense(4096, activation='relu'))
model.add(Dropout(0.5))
model.add(Dense(1000, activation='softmax'))

model.summary()                    ⟵───  Prints the model
                                         summary
```

When you print the model summary, you will see that the number of total parameters is ~138 million:

```
--------------------------------------------
Total params: 138,357, 544
Trainable params: 138,357, 544
Non-trainable params: 0
```

5.4.3 *Learning hyperparameters*

Simonyan and Zisserman followed a training procedure similar to that of AlexNet: the training is carried out using mini-batch gradient descent with momentum of 0.9. The learning rate is initially set to 0.01 and then decreased by a factor of 10 when the validation set accuracy stops improving.

5.4.4 *VGGNet performance*

VGG16 achieved a top-5 error rate of 8.1% on the ImageNet dataset compared to 15.3% achieved by AlexNet. VGG19 did even better: it was able to achieve a top-5 error rate of ~7.4%. It is worth noting that in spite of the larger number of parameters and the greater depth of VGGNet compared to AlexNet, VGGNet required fewer epochs to converge due to the implicit regularization imposed by greater depth and smaller convolutional filter sizes.

5.5   Inception and GoogLeNet

The Inception network came to the world in 2014 when a group of researchers at Google published their paper, "Going Deeper with Convolutions."[4] The main hallmark of this architecture is building a deeper neural network while improving the utilization of the computing resources inside the network. One particular incarnation of the Inception network is called GoogLeNet and was used in the team's submission for ILSVRC 2014. It uses a network 22 layers deep (deeper than VGGNet) while reducing the number of parameters by 12 times (from ~138 million to ~13 million) and achieving significantly more accurate results. The network used a CNN inspired by the classical networks (AlexNet and VGGNet) but implemented a novel element dubbed as the *inception module*.

5.5.1   Novel features of Inception

Szegedy et al. took a different approach when designing their network architecture. As we've seen in the previous networks, there are some architectural decisions that you need to make for each layer when you are designing a network, such as these:

- *The kernel size of the convolutional layer*—We've seen in previous architectures that the kernel size varies: 1×1, 3×3, 5×5, and, in some cases, 11×11 (as in AlexNet). When designing the convolutional layer, we find ourselves trying to pick and tune the kernel size of each layer that fits our dataset. Recall from chapter 3 that smaller kernels capture finer details of the image, whereas bigger filters will leave out minute details.
- *When to use the pooling layer*—AlexNet uses pooling layers every one or two convolutional layers to downsize spatial features. VGGNet applies pooling after every two, three, or four convolutional layers as the network gets deeper.

Configuring the kernel size and positioning the pool layers are decisions we make mostly by trial and error and experiment with to get the optimal results. Inception says, "Instead of choosing a desired filter size in a convolutional layer and deciding where to place the pooling layers, let's apply all of them all together in one block and call it the *inception module*."

That is, rather than stacking layers on top of each other as in classical architectures, Szegedy and his team suggest that we create an inception module consisting of several convolutional layers with different kernel sizes. The architecture is then developed by stacking the inception modules on top of each other. Figure 5.10 shows how classical convolutional networks are architected versus the Inception network.

---

[4]   Christian Szegedy, Christian, Wei Liu, Yangqing Jia, Pierre Sermanet, Scott Reed, Dragomir Anguelov, Dumitru Erhan, Vincent Vanhoucke, and Andrew Rabinovich, "Going Deeper with Convolutions," in *Proceedings of the IEEE Conference on Computer Vision and Pattern Recognition*, 1–9, 2015, http://mng.bz/YryB.

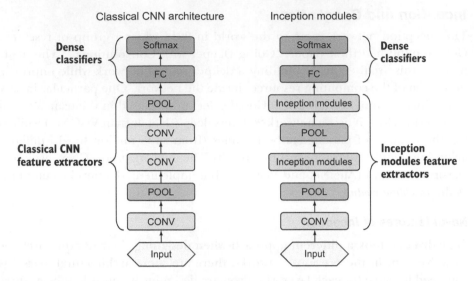

Figure 5.10   Classical convolutional networks vs. the Inception network

From the diagram, you can observe the following:

- In classical architectures like LeNet, AlexNet, and VGGNet, we stack convolutional and pooling layers on top of each other to build the feature extractors. At the end, we add the dense fully connected layers to build the classifier.
- In the Inception architecture, we start with a convolutional layer and a pooling layer, stack the inception modules and pooling layers to build the feature extractors, and then add the regular dense classifier layers.

We've been treating the inception modules as black boxes to understand the bigger picture of the Inception architecture. Now, we will unpack the inception module to understand how it works.

5.5.2   *Inception module: Naive version*

The inception module is a combination of four layers:

- 1×1 convolutional layer
- 3×3 convolutional layer
- 5×5 convolutional layer
- 3×3 max-pooling layer

The outputs of these layers are concatenated into a single output volume forming the input of the next stage. The naive representation of the inception module is shown in figure 5.11.

The diagram may look a little overwhelming, but the idea is simple to understand. Let's follow along with this example:

1 Suppose we have an input dimensional volume from the previous layer of size $32 \times 32 \times 200$.

2 We feed this input to four convolutions simultaneously:
   - 1×1 convolutional layer with `depth` = 64 and `padding` = same. The output of this kernel = $32 \times 32 \times 64$.
   - 3×3 convolutional layer with `depth` = 128 and `padding` = same. Output = $32 \times 32 \times 128$.
   - 5×5 convolutional layer with `depth` = 32 and `padding` = same. Output = $32 \times 32 \times 32$.
   - 3×3 max-pooling layer with `padding` = same and `strides` = 1. Output = $32 \times 32 \times 32$.

3 We concatenate the depth of the four outputs to create one output volume of dimensions $32 \times 32 \times 256$.

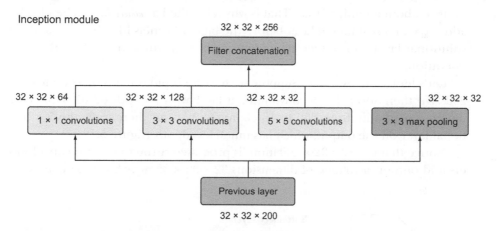

Figure 5.11 Naive representation of an inception module

Now we have an inception module that takes an input volume of $32 \times 32 \times 200$ and outputs a volume of $32 \times 32 \times 256$.

NOTE In the previous example, we use a `padding` value of same. In Keras, `padding` can be set to same or valid, as we saw in chapter 3. The same value results in padding the input such that the output has the same length as the original input. We do that because we want the output to have width and height dimensions similar to the input. And we want to output similar dimensions in the inception module to simplify the depth concatenation process. Now we can just add up the depths of all the outputs to concatenate them into one output volume to be fed to the next layer in our network.

5.5.3   *Inception module with dimensionality reduction*

The naive representation of the inception module that we just saw has a big computational cost problem that comes with processing larger filters like the 5 × 5 convolutional layer. To get a better sense of the compute problem with the naive representation, let's calculate the number of operations that will be performed for the 5 × 5 convolutional layer in the previous example.

The input volume with dimensions of 32 × 32 × 200 will be fed to the 5 × 5 convolutional layer of 32 filters with dimensions = 5 × 5 × 32. This means the total number of multiplications that the computer needs to compute is 32 × 32 × 200 multiplied by 5 × 5 × 32, which is more than 163 million operations. While we can perform this many operations with modern computers, this is still pretty expensive. This is when the dimensionality reduction layers can be very useful.

DIMENSIONALITY REDUCTION LAYER (1 × 1 CONVOLUTIONAL LAYER)

The 1 × 1 convolutional layer can reduce the operational cost of 163 million operations to about a tenth of that. That is why it is called a *reduce layer*. The idea here is to add a 1 × 1 convolutional layer before the bigger kernels like the 3 × 3 and 5 × 5 convolutional layers, to reduce their depth, which in turn will reduce the number of operations.

Let's look at an example. Suppose we have an input dimension volume of 32 × 32 × 200. We then add a 1 × 1 convolutional layer with a depth of 16. This reduces the dimension volume from 200 to 16 channels. We can then apply the 5 × 5 convolutional layer on the output, which has much less depth (figure 5.12).

Notice that the 32 × 32 × 200 input is processed through the two convolutional layers and outputs a volume of dimensions 32 × 32 × 32, which is the same as produced

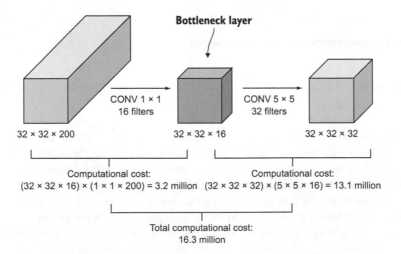

Figure 5.12   Dimensionality reduction is used to reduce the computational cost by reducing the depth of the layer.

without applying the dimensionality reduction layer. But here, instead of processing the 5 × 5 convolutional layer on the entire 200 channels of the input volume, we take this huge volume and shrink its representation to a much smaller intermediate volume that has only 16 channels.

Now, let's look at the computational cost involved in this operation and compare it to the 163 million multiplications that we got before applying the reduce layer:

Computation

= operations in the 1 × 1 convolutional layer + operations in the 5 × 5 convolutional layer

= (32 × 32 × 200) multiplied by (1 × 1 × 16 + 32 × 32 × 16) multiplied by (5 × 5 × 32)

= 3.2 million + 13.1 million

The total number of multiplications in this operation is 16.3 million, which is a tenth of the 163 million multiplications that we calculated without the reduce layers.

The 1 × 1 convolutional layer

The idea of the 1 × 1 convolutional layer is that it preserves the spatial dimensions (height and width) of the input volume but changes the number of channels of the volume (depth):

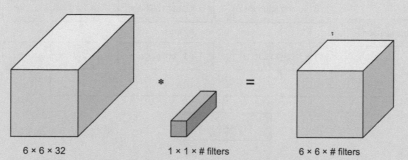

6 × 6 × 32   1 × 1 × # filters   6 × 6 × # filters

1 × 1 conv layers preserve the spatial dimensions but change the depth.

The 1 × 1 convolutional layers are also known as *bottleneck layers* because the bottleneck is the smallest part of the bottle and reduce layers reduce the dimensionality of the network, making it look like a bottleneck:

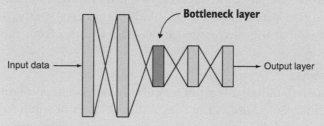

1 × 1 convolutional layers are called *bottleneck layers*.

IMPACT OF DIMENSIONALITY REDUCTION ON NETWORK PERFORMANCE

You might be wondering whether shrinking the representation size so dramatically hurts the performance of the neural network. Szegedy et al. ran experiments and found that as long as you implement the reduce layer in moderation, you can shrink the representation size significantly without hurting performance—and save a lot of computations.

Now, let's put the reduce layers into action and build a new *inception module with dimensionality reduction*. To do that, we will keep the same concept of concatenating the four layers from the naive representation. We will add a 1 × 1 convolutional reduce layer before the 3 × 3 and 5 × 5 convolutional layers to reduce their computational cost. We will also add a 1 × 1 convolutional layer after the 3 × 3 max-pooling layer because pooling layers don't reduce the depth for their inputs. So, we will need to apply the reduce layer to their output before we do the concatenation (figure 5.13).

Inception module with dimensionality reduction

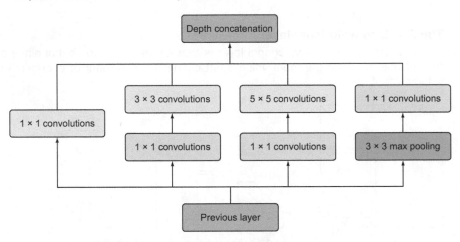

Figure 5.13   Building an inception module with dimensionality reduction

We add dimensionality reduction prior to bigger convolutional layers to allow for increasing the number of units at each stage significantly without an uncontrolled blowup in computational complexity at later stages. Furthermore, the design follows the practical intuition that visual information should be processed at various scales and then aggregated so that the next stage can abstract features from the different scales simultaneously.

RECAP OF INCEPTION MODULES

To summarize, if you are building a layer of a neural network and you don't want to have to decide what filter size to use in the convolutional layers or when to add pooling layers, the inception module lets you use them all and concatenate the depth of all the outputs. This is called the *naive representation* of the inception module.

We then run into the problem of computational cost that comes with using large filters. Here, we use a 1 × 1 convolutional layer called the reduce layer that reduces the computational cost significantly. We add reduce layers before the 3 × 3 and 5 × 5 convolutional layers and after the max-pooling layer to create an inception module with dimensionality reduction.

5.5.4 Inception architecture

Now that we understand the components of the inception module, we are ready to build the Inception network architecture. We use the dimension reduction representation of the inception module, stack inception modules on top of each other, and add a 3 × 3 pooling layer in between for downsampling, as shown in figure 5.14.

We can stack as many inception modules as we want to build a very deep convolutional network. In the original paper, the team built a specific incarnation of the

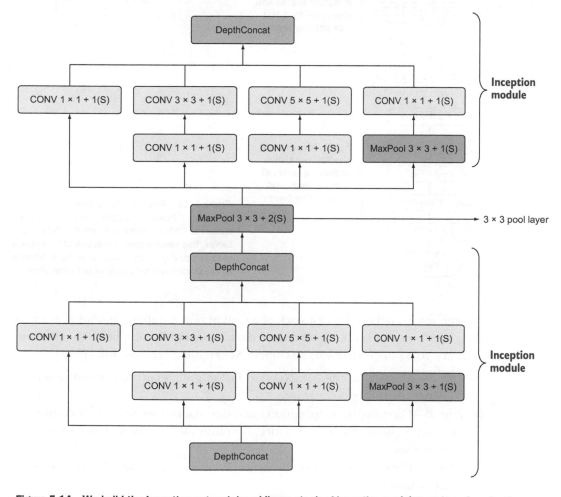

Figure 5.14 We build the Inception network by adding a stack of inception modules on top of each other.

inception module and called it GoogLeNet. They used this network in their submission for the ILSVRC 2014 competition. The GoogLeNet architecture is shown in figure 5.15.

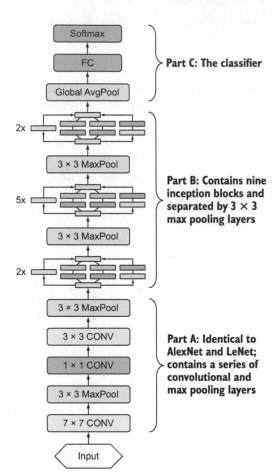

Figure 5.15   **The full GoogLeNet model consists of three parts: the first part has the classical CNN architecture like AlexNet and LeNet, the second part is a stack of inceptions modules and pooling layers, and the third part is the traditional fully connected classifiers.**

As you can see, GoogLeNet uses a stack of a total of nine inception modules and a max pooling layer every several blocks to reduce dimensionality. To simplify this implementation, we are going to break down the GoogLeNet architecture into three parts:

- *Part A*—Identical to the AlexNet and LeNet architectures; contains a series of convolutional and pooling layers.
- *Part B*—Contains nine inception modules stacked as follows: two inception modules + pooling layer + five inception modules + pooling layer + five inception modules.
- *Part C*—The classifier part of the network, consisting of the fully connected and softmax layers.

5.5.5 GoogLeNet in Keras

Now, let's implement the GoogLeNet architecture in Keras (figure 5.16). Notice that the inception module takes the features from the previous module as input, passes them through four routes, concatenates the depth of the output of all four routes, and then passes the concatenated output to the next module. The four routes are as follows:

- 1×1 convolutional layer
- 1×1 convolutional layer + 3×3 convolutional layer
- 1×1 convolutional layer + 5×5 convolutional layer
- 3×3 pooling layer + 1×1 convolutional layer

Inception module with dimensionality reduction

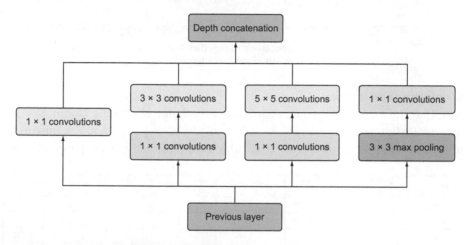

Figure 5.16 The inception module of GoogLeNet

First we'll build the `inception_module` function. It takes the number of filters of each convolutional layer as an argument and returns the concatenated output:

```
def inception_module(x, filters_1 × 1, filters_3x3_reduce, filters_3x3,
    filters_5x5_reduce,
            filters_5x5, filters_pool_proj, name=None):

conv_1x1 = Conv2D(filters_1x1, kernel_size=(1, 1), padding='same',
    activation='relu',
            kernel_initializer=kernel_init, bias_initializer=bias_init)(x)

    # 3 × 3 route = 1 × 1 CONV + 3 × 3 CONV
pre_conv_3x3 = Conv2D(filters_3x3_reduce, kernel_size=(1, 1), padding='same',
            activation='relu', kernel_initializer=kernel_init,
            bias_initializer=bias_init)(x)
conv_3x3 = Conv2D(filters_3x3, kernel_size=(3, 3), padding='same',
    activation='relu',
```

Creates the 1×1 convolutional layer that takes its input directly from the previous layer

```
                    kernel_initializer=kernel_init,
                    bias_initializer=bias_init)(pre_conv_3x3)

      # 5 × 5 route = 1 × 1 CONV + 5 × 5 CONV
pre_conv_5x5 = Conv2D(filters_5x5_reduce, kernel_size=(1, 1), padding='same',
                    activation='relu', kernel_initializer=kernel_init,
                    bias_initializer=bias_init)(x)
conv_5x5 = Conv2D(filters_5x5, kernel_size=(5, 5), padding='same',
      activation='relu',
                    kernel_initializer=kernel_init,
                    bias_initializer=bias_init)(pre_conv_5x5)

      # pool route = POOL + 1 × 1 CONV
pool_proj = MaxPool2D((3, 3), strides=(1, 1), padding='same')(x)
pool_proj = Conv2D(filters_pool_proj, (1, 1), padding='same', activation='relu',
                    kernel_initializer=kernel_init,
      bias_initializer=bias_init)(pool_proj)

output = concatenate([conv_1x1, conv_3x3, conv_5x5, pool_proj], axis=3,
      name=name)

return output
```

Concatenates together the depth of the three filters

GOOGLENET ARCHITECTURE

Now that the inception_module function is ready, let's build the GoogLeNet architecture from figure 5.16. To get the values of the inception_module function's arguments, we will go through figure 5.17, which represents the hyperparameters set up as

type	patch size/ stride	output size	depth	#1 × 1	#3 × 3 reduce	#3 × 3	#5 × 5 reduce	#5 × 5	pool proj	params	ops
convolution	7 × 7/2	112 × 112 × 64	1							2.7K	34M
max pool	3 × 3/2	56 × 56 × 64	0								
convolution	3 × 3/1	56 × 56 × 192	2		2	2	2	2	2	112K	360M
max pool	3 × 3/2	28 × 28 × 192	0								
inception (3a)		28 × 28 × 256	2	64	96	128	16	32	32	159K	128M
inception (3b)		28 × 28 × 480	2	128	128	192	32	96	64	380K	304M
max pool	3 × 3/2	14 × 14 × 480	0								
inception (4a)		14 × 14 × 512	2	192	96	208	16	48	64	364K	73M
inception (4b)		14 × 14 × 512	2	160	112	224	24	64	64	437K	88M
inception (4c)		14 × 14 × 512	2	128	128	256	24	64	64	463K	100M
inception (4d)		14 × 14 × 528	2	112	144	288	32	64	64	580K	119M
inception (4e)		14 × 14 × 832	2	256	160	320	32	128	128	840K	170M
max pool	3 × 3/2	7 × 7 × 832	0								
inception (5a)		7 × 7 × 832	2	256	160	320	32	128	128	1072K	54M
inception (5b)		7 × 7 × 1024	2	384	192	384	48	128	128	1388K	71M
avg pool	7 × 7/1	1 × 1 × 1024	0								
dropout (40%)		1 × 1 × 1024	0								
linear		1 × 1 × 1000	1							1000K	1M
softmax		1 × 1 × 1000	0								

Part A (rows convolution through max pool); Part B (inception 3a through inception 5b); Part C (avg pool through softmax)

Figure 5.17   **Hyperparameters implemented by Szegedy et al. in the original Inception paper**

implemented by Szegedy et al. in the original paper. (Note that "#3 × 3 reduce" and "#5 × 5 reduce" in the figure represent the 1 × 1 filters in the reduction layers that are used before the 3 × 3 and 5 × 5 convolutional layers.)

Now, let's go through the implementations of parts A, B, and C.

PART A: BUILDING THE BOTTOM PART OF THE NETWORK

Let's build the bottom part of the network. This part consists of a 7 × 7 convolutional layer ⇒ 3 × 3 pooling layer ⇒ 1 × 1 convolutional layer ⇒ 3 × 3 convolutional layer ⇒ 3 × 3 pooling layer, as you can see in figure 5.18.

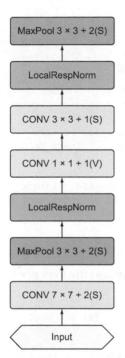

Figure 5.18 The bottom part of the network

In the `LocalResponseNorm` layer, similar to in AlexNet, local response normalization is used to help speed up convergence. Nowadays, batch normalization is used instead.

Here is the Keras code for part A:

```
# input layer with size = 24 × 24 × 3
input_layer = Input(shape=(224, 224, 3))

kernel_init = keras.initializers.glorot_uniform()
bias_init = keras.initializers.Constant(value=0.2)

x = Conv2D(64, (7, 7), padding='same', strides=(2, 2), activation='relu',
    name='conv_1_7x7/2',
kernel_initializer=kernel_init, bias_initializer=bias_init)(input_layer)

x = MaxPool2D((3, 3), padding='same', strides=(2, 2), name='max_pool_1_3x3/2')(x)

x = BatchNormalization()(x)
```

```
x = Conv2D(64, (1, 1), padding='same', strides=(1, 1), activation='relu')(x)
x = Conv2D(192, (3, 3), padding='same', strides=(1, 1), activation='relu')(x)

x = BatchNormalization()(x)

x = MaxPool2D((3, 3), padding='same', strides=(2, 2))(x)
```

PART B: BUILDING THE INCEPTION MODULES AND MAX-POOLING LAYERS

To build inception modules 3a and 3b and the first max-pooling layer, we use table 5.2 to start. The code is as follows:

Table 5.2   Inception modules 3a and 3b

Type	#1 × 1	#3 × 3 reduce	#3 × 3	#5 × 5 reduce	#5 × 5	Pool proj
Inception (3a)	64	96	128	16	32	32
Inception (3b)	128	128	192	32	96	64

```
x = inception_module(x, filters_1x1=64, filters_3x3_reduce=96, filters_3x3=128,
                     filters_5x5_reduce=16, filters_5x5=32, filters_pool_proj=32,
                     name='inception_3a')

x = inception_module(x, filters_1x1=128, filters_3x3_reduce=128, filters_3x3=192,
                     filters_5x5_reduce=32, filters_5x5=96, filters_pool_proj=64,
                     name='inception_3b')

x = MaxPool2D((3, 3), padding='same', strides=(2, 2))(x)
```

Similarly, let's create inception modules 4a, 4b, 4c, 4d, and 4e and the max pooling layer:

```
x = inception_module(x, filters_1x1=192, filters_3x3_reduce=96, filters_3x3=208,
                     filters_5x5_reduce=16, filters_5x5=48, filters_pool_proj=64,
                     name='inception_4a')

x = inception_module(x, filters_1x1=160, filters_3x3_reduce=112, filters_3x3=224,
                     filters_5x5_reduce=24, filters_5x5=64, filters_pool_proj=64,
                     name='inception_4b')

x = inception_module(x, filters_1x1=128, filters_3x3_reduce=128, filters_3x3=256,
                     filters_5x5_reduce=24, filters_5x5=64, filters_pool_proj=64,
                     name='inception_4c')

x = inception_module(x, filters_1x1=112, filters_3x3_reduce=144, filters_3x3=288,
                     filters_5x5_reduce=32, filters_5x5=64, filters_pool_proj=64,
                     name='inception_4d')

x = inception_module(x, filters_1x1=256, filters_3x3_reduce=160, filters_3x3=320,
                     filters_5x5_reduce=32, filters_5x5=128, filters_pool_proj=128,
                     name='inception_4e')

x = MaxPool2D((3, 3), padding='same', strides=(2, 2), name='max_pool_4_3x3/2')(x)
```

Now, let's create modules 5a and 5b:

```
x = inception_module(x, filters_1x1=256, filters_3x3_reduce=160, filters_3x3=320,
                     filters_5x5_reduce=32, filters_5x5=128,
         filters_pool_proj=128,
                     name='inception_5a')

x = inception_module(x, filters_1x1=384, filters_3x3_reduce=192, filters_3x3=384,
                     filters_5x5_reduce=48, filters_5x5=128,
         filters_pool_proj=128,
                     name='inception_5b')
```

PART C: BUILDING THE CLASSIFIER PART

In their experiments, Szegedy et al. found that adding an 7×7 average pooling layer improved the top-1 accuracy by about 0.6%. They then added a dropout layer with 40% probability to reduce overfitting:

```
x = AveragePooling2D(pool_size=(7,7), strides=1, padding='valid')(x)
x = Dropout(0.4)(x)
x = Dense(10, activation='softmax', name='output')(x)
```

5.5.6 Learning hyperparameters

The team used a SGD gradient descent optimizer with 0.9 momentum. They also implemented a fixed learning rate decay schedule of 4% every 8 epochs. An example of how to implement the training specifications similar to the paper is as follows:

```
epochs = 25
initial_lrate = 0.01
```
Implements the learning rate decay function
```
def decay(epoch, steps=100):
    initial_lrate = 0.01
    drop = 0.96
    epochs_drop = 8
    lrate = initial_lrate * math.pow(drop, math.floor((1+epoch)/epochs_drop))
    return lrate

lr_schedule = LearningRateScheduler(decay, verbose=1)

sgd = SGD(lr=initial_lrate, momentum=0.9, nesterov=False)

model.compile(loss='categorical_crossentropy', optimizer=sgd,
    metrics=['accuracy'])

model.fit(X_train, y_train, batch_size=256, epochs=epochs,
    validation_data=(X_test, y_test), callbacks=[lr_schedule], verbose=2,
    shuffle=True)
```

5.5.7 Inception performance on the CIFAR dataset

GoogLeNet was the winner of the ILSVRC 2014 competition. It achieved a top-5 error rate of 6.67%, which was very close to human-level performance and much better than previous CNNs like AlexNet and VGGNet.

5.6   ResNet

The Residual Neural Network (ResNet) was developed in 2015 by a group from the Microsoft Research team.[5] They introduced a novel *residual module* architecture with *skip connections*. The network also features heavy batch normalization for the hidden layers. This technique allowed the team to train very deep neural networks with 50, 101, and 152 weight layers while still having lower complexity than smaller networks like VGGNet (19 layers). ResNet was able to achieve a top-5 error rate of 3.57% in the ILSVRC 2015 competition, which beat the performance of all prior ConvNets.

5.6.1   Novel features of ResNet

Looking at how neural network architectures evolved from LeNet, AlexNet, VGGNet, and Inception, you might have noticed that the deeper the network, the larger its learning capacity, and the better it extracts features from images. This mainly happens because very deep networks are able to represent very complex functions, which allows the network to learn features at many different levels of abstraction, from edges (at the lower layers) to very complex features (at the deeper layers).

Earlier in this chapter, we saw deep neural networks like VGGNet-19 (19 layers) and GoogLeNet (22 layers). Both performed very well in the ImageNet challenge. But can we build even deeper networks? We learned from chapter 4 that one downside of adding too many layers is that doing so makes the network more prone to overfit the training data. This is not a major problem because we can use regularization techniques like dropout, L2 regularization, and batch normalization to avoid overfitting. So, if we can take care of the overfitting problem, wouldn't we want to build networks that are 50, 100, or even 150 layers deep? The answer is yes. We definitely should try to build very deep neural networks. We need to fix just one other problem, to unblock the capability of building super-deep networks: a phenomenon called *vanishing gradients*.

Vanishing and exploding gradients

The problem with very deep networks is that the signal required to change the weights becomes very small at earlier layers. To understand why, let's consider the gradient descent process explained in chapter 2. As the network backpropagates the gradient of the error from the final layer back to the first layer, it is multiplied by the weight matrix at each step; thus the gradient can decrease exponentially quickly to zero, leading to a vanishing gradient phenomenon that prevents the earlier layers from learning. As a result, the network's performance gets saturated or even starts to degrade rapidly.

In other cases, the gradient grows exponentially quickly and "explodes" to take very large values. This phenomenon is called *exploding gradients*.

---

[5]   Kaiming He, Xiangyu Zhang, Shaoqing Ren, and Jian Sun, "Deep Residual Learning for Image Recognition," 2015, http://arxiv.org/abs/1512.03385.

To solve the vanishing gradient problem, He et al. created a shortcut that allows the gradient to be directly backpropagated to earlier layers. These shortcuts are called *skip connections*: they are used to flow information from earlier layers in the network to later layers, creating an alternate shortcut path for the gradient to flow through. Another important benefit of the skip connections is that they allow the model to learn an identity function, which ensures that the layer will perform at least as well as the previous layer (figure 5.19).

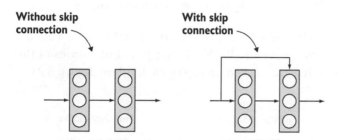

Figure 5.19 **Traditional network without skip connections (left); network with a skip connection (right).**

At left in figure 5.19 is the traditional stacking of convolutional layers one after the other. On the right, we still stack convolutional layers as before, but we also add the original input to the output of the convolutional block. This is a skip connection. We then add both signals: skip connection + main path.

Note that the shortcut arrow points to the end of the second convolutional layer—*not after it*. The reason is that we add both paths before we apply the ReLU activation function of this layer. As you can see in figure 5.20, the X signal is passed along the shortcut path and then added to the main path, $f(x)$. Then, we apply the ReLU activation to $f(x) + x$ to produce the output signal: $\text{relu}(f(x) + x)$.

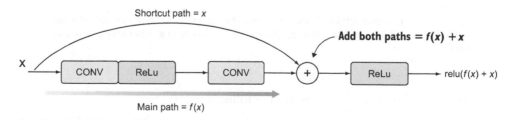

Figure 5.20 **Adding the paths and applying the ReLU activation function to solve the vanishing gradient problem that usually comes with very deep networks**

The code implementation of the skip connection is straightforward:

```
X_shortcut = X                                    Stores the value of the shortcut
                                                  to be equal to the input x            Performs the
                                                                                        main path
X = Conv2D(filters = F1, kernel_size = (3, 3), strides = (1,1))(X)                      operations:
X = Activation('relu')(X)                                                               CONV + ReLU
X = Conv2D(filters = F1, kernel_size = (3, 3), strides = (1,1))(X)                      + CONV

X = Add()([X, X_shortcut])                       Adds both paths together

X = Activation('relu')(X)                        Applies the ReLU activation function
```

This combination of the skip connection and convolutional layers is called a *residual block*. Similar to the Inception network, ResNet is composed of a series of these residual block building blocks that are stacked on top of each other (figure 5.21).

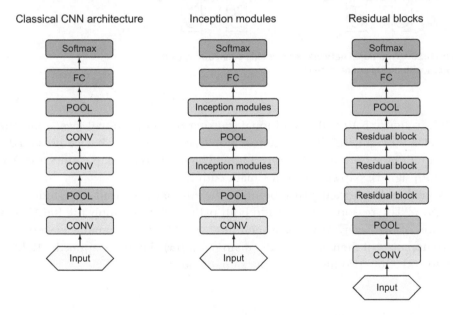

Figure 5.21   Classical CNN architecture (left). The Inception network consists of a set of inception modules (middle). The residual network consists of a set of residual blocks (right).

From the figure, you can observe the following:

- *Feature extractors*—To build the feature extractor part of ResNet, we start with a convolutional layer and a pooling layer and then stack residual blocks on top of each other to build the network. When we are designing our ResNet network, we can add as many residual blocks as we want to build even deeper networks.

- *Classifiers*—The classification part is still the same as we learned for other networks: fully connected layers followed by a softmax.

Now that you know what a skip connection is and you are familiar with the high-level architecture of ResNet, let's unpack residual blocks to understand how they work.

5.6.2 Residual blocks

A residual module consists of two branches:

- *Shortcut path* (figure 5.22)—Connects the input to an addition of the second branch.
- *Main path*—A series of convolutions and activations. The main path consists of three convolutional layers with ReLU activations. We also add batch normalization to each convolutional layer to reduce overfitting and speed up training. The main path architecture looks like this: [CONV $\Rightarrow$ BN $\Rightarrow$ ReLU] $\times$ 3.

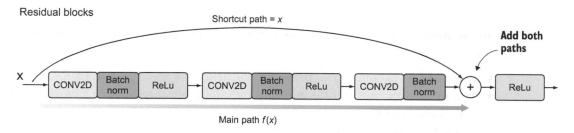

Figure 5.22 The output of the main path is added to the input value through the shortcut before they are fed to the ReLU function.

Similar to what we explained earlier, the shortcut path is added to the main path right before the activation function of the last convolutional layer. Then we apply the ReLU function after adding the two paths.

Notice that there are no pooling layers in the residual block. Instead, He et al. decided to do dimension downsampling using bottleneck 1 × 1 convolutional layers, similar to the Inception network. So, each residual block starts with a 1 × 1 convolutional layer to downsample the input dimension volume, and a 3 × 3 convolutional layer and another 1 × 1 convolutional layer to downsample the output. This is a good technique to keep control of the volume dimensions across many layers. This configuration is called a *bottleneck residual block*.

When we are stacking residual blocks on top of each other, the volume dimensions change from one block to another. And as you might recall from the matrices introduction in chapter 2, to be able to perform matrix addition operations, the matrices should have similar dimensions. To fix this problem, we need to downsample the shortcut path as well, before merging both paths. We do that by adding a bottleneck layer (1 × 1 convolutional layer + batch normalization) to the shortcut path, as shown in figure 5.23. This is called the *reduce shortcut.*

Bottleneck residual block with reduce shortcut

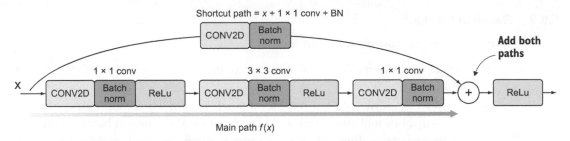

Figure 5.23 **To reduce the input dimensionality, we add a bottleneck layer (1 × 1 convolutional layer + batch normalization) to the shortcut path. This is called the *reduce shortcut.***

Before we jump into the code implementation, let's recap the discussion of residual blocks:

- Residual blocks contain two paths: the shortcut path and the main path.
- The main path consists of three convolutional layers, and we add a batch normalization layer to them:
  - 1 × 1 convolutional layer
  - 3 × 3 convolutional layer
  - 1 × 1 convolutional layer
- There are two ways to implement the shortcut path:
  - *Regular shortcut*—Add the input dimensions to the main path.
  - *Reduce shortcut*—Add a convolutional layer in the shortcut path before merging with the main path.

When we are implementing the ResNet network, we will use both regular and reduce shortcuts. This will be clearer when you see the full implementation. But for now, we will implement `bottleneck_residual_block` function that takes a `reduce` Boolean argument. When `reduce` is `True`, this means we want to use the reduce shortcut; otherwise, it will implement the regular shortcut. The `bottleneck_residual_block` function takes the following arguments:

- `X`—Input tensor of shape (number of samples, height, width, channel)
- `f`—Integer specifying the shape of the middle convolutional layer's window for the main path
- `filters`—Python list of integers defining the number of filters in the convolutional layers of the main path

- reduce—Boolean: `True` identifies the reduction layer
- s—Integer (strides)

The function returns X: the output of the residual block, which is a tensor of shape (height, width, channel).

The function is as follows:

```
def bottleneck_residual_block(X, kernel_size, filters, reduce=False, s=2):
    F1, F2, F3 = filters
```
← *Unpacks the tuple to retrieve the filters of each convolutional layer*

Condition if reduce is True
```
    X_shortcut = X
```
← *Saves the input value to use it later to add back to the main path*

```
    if reduce:
```

To reduce the spatial size, applies a 1 × 1 convolutional layer to the shortcut path. To do that, we need both convolutional layers to have similar strides.
```
        X_shortcut = Conv2D(filters = F3, kernel_size = (1, 1), strides =
        (s,s))(X_shortcut)
        X_shortcut = BatchNormalization(axis = 3)(X_shortcut)

        X = Conv2D(filters = F1, kernel_size = (1, 1), strides = (s,s), padding =
        'valid')(X)
        X = BatchNormalization(axis = 3)(X)
        X = Activation('relu')(X)
```
If reduce, sets the strides of the first convolutional layer to be similar to the shortcut strides.

```
    else:
        # First component of main path
        X = Conv2D(filters = F1, kernel_size = (1, 1), strides = (1,1), padding =
        'valid')(X)
        X = BatchNormalization(axis = 3)(X)
        X = Activation('relu')(X)

    # Second component of main path
    X = Conv2D(filters = F2, kernel_size = kernel_size, strides = (1,1), padding =
    'same')(X)
    X = BatchNormalization(axis = 3)(X)
    X = Activation('relu')(X)

    # Third component of main path
    X = Conv2D(filters = F3, kernel_size = (1, 1), strides = (1,1), padding =
    'valid')(X)
    X = BatchNormalization(axis = 3)(X)

    # Final step
    X = Add()([X, X_shortcut])
    X = Activation('relu')(X)
```
Adds the shortcut value to main path and passes it through a ReLU activation

```
    return X
```

5.6.3 ResNet implementation in Keras

You've learned a lot about residual blocks so far. Let's add these blocks on top of each other to build the full ResNet architecture. Here, we will implement ResNet50: a version of the ResNet architecture that contains 50 weight layers (hence the name). You can use the same approach to develop ResNet with 18, 34, 101, and 152 layers by following the architecture in figure 5.24 from the original paper.

Layer name	Output size	18-layer	34-layer	50-layer	101-layer	152-layer
conv1	112x112	7x7, 64, stride 2				
conv2_x	56x56	3x3, maxpool, stride 2				
		$\begin{bmatrix} 3\text{x}3, 64 \\ 3\text{x}3, 64 \end{bmatrix}$ x2	$\begin{bmatrix} 3\text{x}3, 64 \\ 3\text{x}3, 64 \end{bmatrix}$ x3	$\begin{bmatrix} 1\text{x}1, 64 \\ 3\text{x}3, 64 \\ 1\text{x}1, 256 \end{bmatrix}$ x3	$\begin{bmatrix} 1\text{x}1, 64 \\ 3\text{x}3, 64 \\ 1\text{x}1, 256 \end{bmatrix}$ x3	$\begin{bmatrix} 1\text{x}1, 64 \\ 3\text{x}3, 64 \\ 1\text{x}1, 256 \end{bmatrix}$ x3
conv3_x	28x28	$\begin{bmatrix} 3\text{x}3, 128 \\ 3\text{x}3, 128 \end{bmatrix}$ x2	$\begin{bmatrix} 3\text{x}3, 128 \\ 3\text{x}3, 128 \end{bmatrix}$ x4	$\begin{bmatrix} 1\text{x}1, 128 \\ 3\text{x}3, 128 \\ 1\text{x}1, 512 \end{bmatrix}$ x3	$\begin{bmatrix} 1\text{x}1, 128 \\ 3\text{x}3, 128 \\ 1\text{x}1, 512 \end{bmatrix}$ x4	$\begin{bmatrix} 1\text{x}1, 128 \\ 3\text{x}3, 128 \\ 1\text{x}1, 512 \end{bmatrix}$ x8
conv4_x	14x14	$\begin{bmatrix} 3\text{x}3, 256 \\ 3\text{x}3, 256 \end{bmatrix}$ x2	$\begin{bmatrix} 3\text{x}3, 256 \\ 3\text{x}3, 256 \end{bmatrix}$ x6	$\begin{bmatrix} 1\text{x}1, 256 \\ 3\text{x}3, 256 \\ 1\text{x}1, 1024 \end{bmatrix}$ x3	$\begin{bmatrix} 1\text{x}1, 256 \\ 3\text{x}3, 256 \\ 1\text{x}1, 1024 \end{bmatrix}$ x23	$\begin{bmatrix} 1\text{x}1, 256 \\ 3\text{x}3, 256 \\ 1\text{x}1, 1024 \end{bmatrix}$ x36
conv5_x	7x7	$\begin{bmatrix} 3\text{x}3, 512 \\ 3\text{x}3, 512 \end{bmatrix}$ x2	$\begin{bmatrix} 3\text{x}3, 512 \\ 3\text{x}3, 512 \end{bmatrix}$ x3	$\begin{bmatrix} 1\text{x}1, 512 \\ 3\text{x}3, 512 \\ 1\text{x}1, 2048 \end{bmatrix}$ x3	$\begin{bmatrix} 1\text{x}1, 512 \\ 3\text{x}3, 512 \\ 1\text{x}1, 2048 \end{bmatrix}$ x3	$\begin{bmatrix} 1\text{x}1, 512 \\ 3\text{x}3, 512 \\ 1\text{x}1, 2048 \end{bmatrix}$ x3
	1x1	Average pool, 1000-d fc, softmax				
FLOPs		$1.8\text{x}10^9$	$3.6\text{x}10^9$	$3.8\text{x}10^9$	$7.6\text{x}10^9$	$11.3\text{x}10^9$

Figure 5.24 Architecture of several ResNet variations from the original paper

We know from the previous section that each residual module contains 3×3 convolutional layers, and we now can compute the total number of weight layers inside the ResNet50 network as follows:

- Stage 1: 7×7 convolutional layer
- Stage 2: 3 residual blocks, each containing [1×1 convolutional layer + 3×3 convolutional layer + 1×1 convolutional layer] = 9 convolutional layers
- Stage 3: 4 residual blocks = total of 12 convolutional layers
- Stage 4: 6 residual blocks = total of 18 convolutional layers
- Stage 5: 3 residual blocks = total of 9 convolutional layers
- Fully connected softmax layer

When we sum all these layers together, we get a total of 50 weight layers that describe the architecture of ResNet50. Similarly, you can compute the number of weight layers in the other ResNet versions.

NOTE In the following implementation, we use the residual block with reduce shortcut at the beginning of each stage to reduce the spatial size of the output from the previous layer. Then we use the regular shortcut for the remaining layers of that stage. Recall from our implementation of the `bottleneck_residual_block` function that we will set the argument `reduce` to `True` to apply the reduce shortcut.

Now let's follow the 50-layer architecture from figure 5.24 to build the ResNet50 network. We build a ResNet50 function that takes `input_shape` and `classes` as arguments and outputs the model:

```
def ResNet50(input_shape, classes):
    X_input = Input(input_shape)          <--|  Defines the input as a tensor
                                             |  with shape input_shape

    # Stage 1
    X = Conv2D(64, (7, 7), strides=(2, 2), name='conv1')(X_input)
    X = BatchNormalization(axis=3, name='bn_conv1')(X)
    X = Activation('relu')(X)
    X = MaxPooling2D((3, 3), strides=(2, 2))(X)

    # Stage 2
    X = bottleneck_residual_block(X, 3, [64, 64, 256], reduce=True, s=1)
    X = bottleneck_residual_block(X, 3, [64, 64, 256])
    X = bottleneck_residual_block(X, 3, [64, 64, 256])

    # Stage 3
    X = bottleneck_residual_block(X, 3, [128, 128, 512], reduce=True, s=2)
    X = bottleneck_residual_block(X, 3, [128, 128, 512])
    X = bottleneck_residual_block(X, 3, [128, 128, 512])
    X = bottleneck_residual_block(X, 3, [128, 128, 512])

    # Stage 4
    X = bottleneck_residual_block(X, 3, [256, 256, 1024], reduce=True, s=2)
    X = bottleneck_residual_block(X, 3, [256, 256, 1024])
    X = bottleneck_residual_block(X, 3, [256, 256, 1024])
    X = bottleneck_residual_block(X, 3, [256, 256, 1024])
    X = bottleneck_residual_block(X, 3, [256, 256, 1024])
    X = bottleneck_residual_block(X, 3, [256, 256, 1024])

    # Stage 5
    X = bottleneck_residual_block(X, 3, [512, 512, 2048], reduce=True, s=2)
    X = bottleneck_residual_block(X, 3, [512, 512, 2048])
    X = bottleneck_residual_block(X, 3, [512, 512, 2048])

    # AVGPOOL
    X = AveragePooling2D((1,1))(X)

    # output layer
    X = Flatten()(X)
    X = Dense(classes, activation='softmax', name='fc' + str(classes))(X)

    model = Model(inputs = X_input, outputs = X, name='ResNet50')   <--|
                                                                       |  Creates the model
    return model
```

5.6.4   *Learning hyperparameters*

He et al. followed a training procedure similar to that of AlexNet: the training is carried out using mini-batch GD with momentum of 0.9. The team set the learning rate to start with a value of 0.1 and then decreased it by a factor of 10 when the validation error stopped improving. They also used L2 regularization with a weight decay of 0.0001 (not implemented in this chapter for simplicity). As you saw in the earlier implementation, they used batch normalization right after each convolutional and before activation to speed up training:

```
from keras.callbacks import ReduceLROnPlateau

epochs = 200          Sets the training
batch_size = 256      parameters

reduce_lr= ReduceLROnPlateau(monitor='val_loss',factor=np.sqrt(0.1),
    patience=5, min_lr=0.5e-6)

model.compile(loss='categorical_crossentropy', optimizer=SGD,
    metrics=['accuracy'])

model.fit(X_train, Y_train, batch_size=batch_size, validation_data=(X_test,
    Y_test),
        epochs=epochs, callbacks=[reduce_lr])
```

min_lr is the lower bound on the learning rate, and factor is the factor by which the learning rate will be reduced.

Compiles the model

Trains the model, calling the reduce_lr value using callbacks in the training method

5.6.5   *ResNet performance on the CIFAR dataset*

Similar to the other networks explained in this chapter, the performance of ResNet models is benchmarked based on their results in the ILSVRC competition. ResNet-152 won first place in the 2015 classification competition with a top-5 error rate of 4.49% with a single model and 3.57% using an ensemble of models. This was much better than all the other networks, such as GoogLeNet (Inception), which achieved a top-5 error rate of 6.67%. ResNet also won first place in many object detection and image localization challenges, as we will see in chapter 7. More importantly, the residual blocks concept in ResNet opened the door to new possibilities for efficiently training super-deep neural networks with hundreds of layers.

Using open source implementations

Now that you have learned some of the most popular CNN architectures, I want to share some practical advice on how to use them. It turns out that a lot of these neural networks are difficult or finicky to replicate due to details of tuning hyperparameters such as learning decay and other things that make a difference for performance. DL researchers can even have a hard time replicating someone else's polished work based on reading their paper.

Fortunately, many DL researchers routinely open source their work on the internet. A simple search for the network implementation on GitHub will point you toward implementations in several DL libraries that you can clone and train. If you can locate the author's implementation, you can usually get going much faster than by trying to re-implement a network from scratch—although sometimes, re-implementing from scratch can be a good exercise, like what we did earlier.

Summary

- Classical CNN architectures have the same classical architecture of stacking convolutional and pooling layers on top of each other with different configurations for their layers.
- LeNet consists of five weight layers: three convolutional and two fully connected layers, with a pooling layer after the first and second convolutional layers.
- AlexNet is deeper than LeNet and contains eight weight layers: five convolutional and three fully connected layers.
- VGGNet solved the problem of setting up the hyperparameters of the convolutional and pooling layers by creating a uniform configuration for them to be used across the entire network.
- Inception tried to solve the same problem as VGGNet: instead of having to decide which filter size to use and where to add the pooling layer, Inception says, "Let's use them all."
- ResNet followed the same approach as Inception and created residual blocks that, when stacked on top of each other, form the network architecture. ResNet attempted to solve the vanishing gradient problem that made learning plateau or degrade when training very deep neural networks. The ResNet team introduced skip connections that allow information to flow from earlier layers in the network to later layers, creating an alternate shortcut path for the gradient to flow through. The fundamental breakthrough with ResNet was that it allowed us to train extremely deep neural networks with hundreds of layers.

Transfer learning

6

This chapter covers

- Understanding the transfer learning technique
- Using a pretrained network to solve your problem
- Understanding network fine-tuning
- Exploring open source image datasets for training a model
- Building two end-to-end transfer learning projects

Transfer learning is one of the most important techniques of deep learning. When building a vision system to solve a specific problem, you usually need to collect and label a huge amount of data to train your network. You can build convnets, as you learned in chapter 3, and start the training from scratch; that is an acceptable approach. But what if you could download an existing neural network that someone else has tuned and trained, and use it as a starting point for your new task? Transfer learning allows you to do just that. You can download an open source model that someone else has already trained and tuned and use their optimized parameters (weights) as a starting point to train your model on a smaller dataset for a given task. This way, you can train your network a lot faster and achieve higher results.

DL researchers and practitioners have posted many research papers and open source projects of trained algorithms that they have worked on for weeks and months and trained on GPUs to get state-of-the-art results on an array of problems. Often, the fact that someone else has done this work and gone through the painful high-performance research process means you can download an open source architecture and weights and use them as a good start for your own neural network. This is *transfer learning*: the transfer of knowledge from a pretrained network in one domain to your own problem in a different domain.

In this chapter, I will explain transfer learning and outline reasons why using it is important. I will also detail different transfer learning scenarios and how to use them. Finally, we will see examples of using transfer learning to solve real-world problems. Ready? Let's get started!

6.1 What problems does transfer learning solve?

As the name implies, transfer learning means transferring what a neural network has learned from being trained on a specific dataset to another related problem (figure 6.1). Transfer learning is currently very popular in the field of DL because it enables you to train deep neural networks with comparatively little data in a short training time. The importance of transfer learning comes from the fact that in most real-world problems, we typically do not have millions of labeled images to train such complex models.

Figure 6.1 Transfer learning is the transfer of the knowledge that the network has acquired from one task to a new task. In the context of neural networks, the acquired knowledge is the extracted features.

The idea is pretty straightforward. First we train a deep neural network on a very large amount of data. During the training process, the network extracts a large number of useful features that can be used to detect objects in this dataset. We then transfer these extracted features (*feature maps*) to a new network and train this new network on our new dataset to solve a different problem. Transfer learning is a great way to short-cut the process of collecting and training huge amounts of data simply by reusing the model weights from pretrained models that were developed for standard CV benchmark datasets, such as the ImageNet image-recognition tasks. Top-performing models can be downloaded and used directly, or integrated into a new model for your own CV problems.

The question is, why would we want to use transfer learning? Why don't we just train a neural network directly on our new dataset to solve our problem? To answer this question, we first need to know the main problems that transfer learning solves. We'll discuss those now; then I'll go into the details of how transfer learning works and the different approaches to apply it.

Deep neural networks are immensely data-hungry and rely on huge amounts of labeled data to achieve high performance. In practice, very few people train an entire convolutional network from scratch. This is due to two main problems:

- *Data problem*—Training a network from scratch requires a lot of data in order to get decent results, which is not feasible in most cases. It is relatively rare to have a dataset of sufficient size to solve your problem. It is also very expensive to acquire and label data: this is mostly a manual process done by humans capturing images and labeling them one by one, which makes it a nontrivial task.
- *Computation problem*—Even if you are able to acquire hundreds of thousands of images for your problem, it is computationally very expensive to train a deep neural network on millions of images because doing so usually requires weeks of training on multiple GPUs. Also keep in mind that training a neural network is an iterative process. So, even if you happen to have the computing power required to train a complex neural network, spending weeks experimenting with different hyperparameters in each training iteration until you finally reach satisfactory results will make the project very costly.

Additionally, an important benefit of using transfer learning is that it helps the model generalize its learnings and avoid overfitting. When you apply a DL model in the wild, it is faced with countless conditions it may never have seen before and does not know how to deal with; each client has its own preferences and generates data that is different from the data used for training. The model is asked to perform well on many tasks that are related to but not exactly similar to the task it was trained for.

For example, when you deploy a car classifier model to production, people usually have different camera types, each with its own image quality and resolution. Also, images can be taken during different weather conditions. These image nuances vary from one user to another. To train the model on all these different cases, you either have to account for every case and acquire a lot of images to train the network on, or try to build a more robust model that is better at generalizing to new use cases. This is what transfer learning does. Since it is not realistic to account for all the cases the model may face in the wild, transfer learning can help us deal with novel scenarios. It is necessary for production-scale use of DL that goes beyond tasks and domains where labeled data is plentiful. Transferring features extracted from another network that has seen millions of images will make our model less prone to overfit and help it generalize better when faced with novel scenarios. You will be able to fully grasp this concept when we explain how transfer learning works in the following sections.

6.2 What is transfer learning?

Armed with the understanding of the problems that transfer learning solves, let's look at its formal definition. *Transfer learning* is the transfer of the knowledge (feature maps) that the network has acquired from one task, where we have a large amount of data, to a new task where data is not abundantly available. It is generally used where a neural network model is first trained on a problem similar to the problem that is being solved. One or more layers from the trained model are then used in a new model trained on the problem of interest.

As we discussed earlier, to train an image classifier that will achieve image classification accuracy near to or above the human level, we'll need massive amounts of data, large compute power, and lots of time on our hands. I'm sure most of us don't have all these things. Knowing that this would be a problem for people with little-to-no resources, researchers built state-of-the-art models that were trained on large image datasets like ImageNet, MS COCO, Open Images, and so on, and then shared their models with the general public for reuse. This means you should never have to train an image classifier from scratch again, unless you have an exceptionally large dataset and a very large computation budget to train everything from scratch by yourself. Even if that is the case, you might be better off using transfer learning to fine-tune the pretrained network on your large dataset. Later in this chapter, we will discuss the different transfer learning approaches, and you will understand what fine-tuning means and why it is better to use transfer learning even when you have a large dataset. We will also talk briefly about some of the popular datasets mentioned here.

> **NOTE** When we talk about training a model from scratch, we mean that the model starts with zero knowledge of the world, and the model's structure and parameters begin as random guesses. Practically speaking, this means the weights of the model are randomly initialized, and they need to go through a training process to be optimized.

The intuition behind transfer learning is that if a model is trained on a large and general enough dataset, this model will effectively serve as a generic representation of the visual world. We can then use the feature maps it has learned, without having to train on a large dataset, by transferring what it learned to our model and using that as a base starting model for our own task.

In transfer learning, we first train a base network on a base dataset and task, and then we repurpose the learned features, or transfer them to a second target network to be trained on a target dataset and task. This process will tend to work if the features are general, meaning suitable to both base and target tasks, instead of specific to the base task.

—Jason Yosinski et al.[1]

Let's jump directly to an example to get a better intuition for how to use transfer learning. Suppose we want to train a model that classifies dog and cat images, and we have only two classes in our problem: dog and cat. We need to collect hundreds of thousands of images for each class, label them, and train our network from scratch. Another option is to use transfer knowledge from another pretrained network.

First, we need to find a dataset that has similar features to our problem at hand. This involves spending some time exploring different open source datasets to find the one closest to our problem. For the sake of this example, let's use ImageNet, since we are already familiar with it from the previous chapter and it has a lot of dog and cat images. So the pretrained network is familiar with dog and cat features and will require minimum training. (Later in this chapter, we will explore other datasets.) Next, we need to choose a network that has been trained on Image-Net and achieved good results. In chapter 5, we learned about state-of-the-art architectures like VGGNet, GoogLeNet, and ResNet. Any of them would work fine. For this example, we will go with a VGG16 network that has been trained on Image-Net datasets.

To adapt the VGG16 network to our problem, we are going to download it with the pretrained weights, remove the classifier part, add our own classifier, and then retrain the new network (figure 6.2). This is called *using a pretrained network as a feature extractor*. We will discuss the different types of transfer learning later in this chapter.

DEFINITION   A *pretrained model* is a network that has been previously trained on a large dataset, typically on a large-scale image classification task. We can either use the pretrained model directly as is to run our predictions, or use the pretrained feature extraction part of the network and add our own classifier. The classifier here could be one or more dense layers or even traditional ML algorithms like support vector machines (SVMs).

---

[1]   Jason Yosinski, Jeff Clune, Yoshua Bengio, and Hod Lipson, "How Transferable Are Features in Deep Neural Networks?" *Advances in Neural Information Processing Systems* 27 (Dec. 2014): 3320–3328, https://arxiv.org/abs/1411.1792.

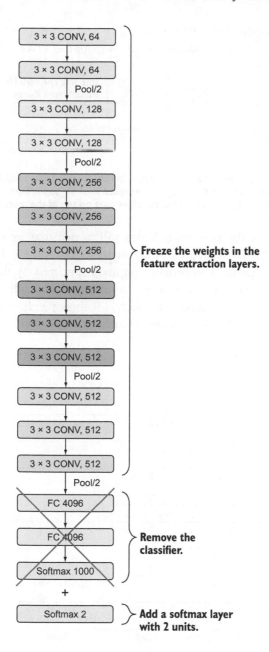

Figure 6.2 Example of applying transfer learning to a VGG16 network. We freeze the feature extraction part of the network and remove the classifier part. Then we add our new classifier softmax layer with two hidden units.

To fully understand how to use transfer learning, let's implement this example in Keras. (Luckily, Keras has a set of pretrained networks that are ready for us to download and use: the complete list of models is at https://keras.io/api/applications.) Here are the steps:

1 Download the open source code of the VGG16 network and its weights to create our base model, and remove the classification layers from the VGG network
(FC_4096 > FC_4096 > Softmax_1000):

```
from keras.applications.vgg16 import VGG16        ⟵┐ Imports the VGG16
                                                     model from Keras

base_model = VGG16(weights = "imagenet", include_top=False,
                   input_shape = (224,224, 3))    ⟵─────────────┐
base_model.summary()
```

**Downloads the model's pretrained weights and saves them in the variable base_model.
We specify that Keras should download the ImageNet weights. include_top is false to
ignore the fully connected classifier part on top of the model.**

2 When you print a summary of the base model, you will notice that we downloaded the exact VGG16 architecture that we implemented in chapter 5. This is
a fast approach to download popular networks that are supported by the DL
library you are using. Alternatively, you can build the network yourself, as we
did in chapter 5, and download the weights separately. I'll show you how in the
project at the end of this chapter. But for now, let's look at the base_model summary that we just downloaded:

```
Layer (type)                   Output Shape              Param #
=================================================================
input_1 (InputLayer)           (None, 224, 224, 3)       0
_____
block1_conv1 (Conv2D)          (None, 224, 224, 64)      1792
_____
block1_conv2 (Conv2D)          (None, 224, 224, 64)      36928
_____
block1_pool (MaxPooling2D)     (None, 112, 112, 64)      0
_____
block2_conv1 (Conv2D)          (None, 112, 112, 128)     73856
_____
block2_conv2 (Conv2D)          (None, 112, 112, 128)     147584
_____
block2_pool (MaxPooling2D)     (None, 56, 56, 128)       0
_____
block3_conv1 (Conv2D)          (None, 56, 56, 256)       295168
_____
block3_conv2 (Conv2D)          (None, 56, 56, 256)       590080
_____
block3_conv3 (Conv2D)          (None, 56, 56, 256)       590080
_____
block3_pool (MaxPooling2D)     (None, 28, 28, 256)       0
_____
block4_conv1 (Conv2D)          (None, 28, 28, 512)       1180160
_____
block4_conv2 (Conv2D)          (None, 28, 28, 512)       2359808
_____
block4_conv3 (Conv2D)          (None, 28, 28, 512)       2359808
_____
```

```
block4_pool (MaxPooling2D)     (None, 14, 14, 512)         0
_____
block5_conv1 (Conv2D)          (None, 14, 14, 512)         2359808
_____
block5_conv2 (Conv2D)          (None, 14, 14, 512)         2359808
_____
block5_conv3 (Conv2D)          (None, 14, 14, 512)         2359808
_____
block5_pool (MaxPooling2D)     (None, 7, 7, 512)           0
======================================================================
Total params: 14,714,688
Trainable params: 14,714,688
Non-trainable params: 0
```

Notice that this downloaded architecture does not contain the classifier part (three fully connected layers) at the top of the network because we set the `include_top` argument to `False`. More importantly, notice the number of trainable and non-trainable parameters in the summary. The downloaded network as it is makes all the network parameters trainable. As you can see, our `base_model` has more than 14 million trainable parameters. Next, we want to freeze all the downloaded layers and add our own classifier.

3 Freeze the feature extraction layers that have been trained on the ImageNet dataset. *Freezing* layers means freezing their trained weights to prevent them from being retrained when we run our training:

```
for layer in base_model.layers:        ←┐ Iterates through layers
    layer.trainable = False              │ and locks them to make them
                                         │ non-trainable with this code
base_model.summary()
```

The model summary is omitted in this case for brevity, as it is similar to the previous one. The difference is that all the weights have been frozen, the trainable parameters are now equal to zero, and all the parameters of the frozen layers are non-trainable:

```
Total params: 14,714,688
Trainable params: 0
Non-trainable params: 14,714,688
```

4 Add our own classification dense layer. Here, we will add a softmax layer with two units because we have only two classes in our problem (see figure 6.3):

```
from keras.layers import Dense, Flatten        ←┐ Imports Keras modules
from keras.models import Model
                                                         Uses the get_layer
                                                         method to save the last
last_layer = base_model.get_layer('block5_pool')    ←┘ layer of the network
last_output = last_layer.output        ←┐ Saves the output of the last layer
                                         │ to be the input of the next layer
```

```
x = Flatten()(last_output)

x = Dense(2, activation='softmax', name='softmax')(x)
```

**Flattens the classifier input, which is the
output of the last layer of the VGG16 model**

**Adds our new softmax layer
with two hidden units**

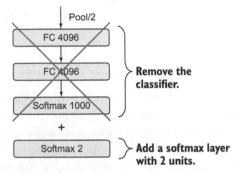

Figure 6.3   Remove the classifier part of
the network, and add a softmax layer with
two hidden nodes.

5   Build a new_model that takes the input of the base model as its input and the
output of the last softmax layer as an output. The new model is composed of all
the feature extraction layers in VGGNet with the pretrained weights, plus our
new, *untrained,* softmax layer. In other words, when we train the model, we are
only going to train the softmax layer in this example to detect the specific features of our new problem (German Shepherd, Beagle, Neither):

**Instantiates a new_model using
Keras's Model class**

```
new_model = Model(inputs=base_model.input, outputs=x)

new_model.summary()
```

Prints the new_model summary

Layer (type)	Output Shape	Param #
input_1 (InputLayer)	(None, 224, 224, 3)	0
block1_conv1 (Conv2D)	(None, 224, 224, 64)	1792
block1_conv2 (Conv2D)	(None, 224, 224, 64)	36928
block1_pool (MaxPooling2D)	(None, 112, 112, 64)	0
block2_conv1 (Conv2D)	(None, 112, 112, 128)	73856
block2_conv2 (Conv2D)	(None, 112, 112, 128)	147584
block2_pool (MaxPooling2D)	(None, 56, 56, 128)	0

block3_conv1 (Conv2D)	(None, 56, 56, 256)	295168
block3_conv2 (Conv2D)	(None, 56, 56, 256)	590080
block3_conv3 (Conv2D)	(None, 56, 56, 256)	590080
block3_pool (MaxPooling2D)	(None, 28, 28, 256)	0
block4_conv1 (Conv2D)	(None, 28, 28, 512)	1180160
block4_conv2 (Conv2D)	(None, 28, 28, 512)	2359808
block4_conv3 (Conv2D)	(None, 28, 28, 512)	2359808
block4_pool (MaxPooling2D)	(None, 14, 14, 512)	0
block5_conv1 (Conv2D)	(None, 14, 14, 512)	2359808
block5_conv2 (Conv2D)	(None, 14, 14, 512)	2359808
block5_conv3 (Conv2D)	(None, 14, 14, 512)	2359808
block5_pool (MaxPooling2D)	(None, 7, 7, 512)	0
flatten_layer (Flatten)	(None, 25088)	0
softmax (Dense)	(None, 2)	50178

```
=====================================================
Total params: 14,789,955
Trainable params: 50,178
Non-trainable params: 14,714,688
```

Training the new model is a lot faster than training the network from scratch. To verify that, look at the number of trainable params in this model (~50,000) compared to the number of non-trainable params in the network (~14 million). These "non-trainable" parameters are already trained on a large dataset, and we froze them to use the extracted features in our problem. With this new model, we don't have to train the entire VGGNet from scratch because we only have to deal with the newly added softmax layer.

Additionally, we get much better performance with transfer learning because the new model has been trained on millions of images (ImageNet dataset + our small dataset). This allows the network to understand the finer details of object nuances, which in turn makes it generalize better on new, previously unseen images.

Note that in this example, we only explored the part where we build the model, to show how transfer learning is used. At the end of this chapter, I'll walk you through two end-to-end projects to demonstrate how to train the new network on your small dataset. But now, let's see how transfer learning works.

6.3   *How transfer learning works*

So far, we learned what the transfer learning technique is and the main problems it solves. We also saw an example of how to take a pretrained network that was trained on ImageNet and transfer its learnings to our specific task. Now, let's see *why transfer learning works*, what is really being transferred from one problem to another, and how a network that is trained on one dataset can perform well on a different, possibly unrelated, dataset.

The following quick questions are reminders from previous chapters to get us to the core of what is happening in transfer learning:

1. What is really being learned by the network during training? The short answer is: *feature maps.*
2. How are these features learned? During the backpropagation process, the weights are updated until we get to the *optimized weights* that minimize the error function.
3. What is the relationship between features and weights? A feature map is the result of passing the weights filter on the input image during the convolution process (figure 6.4).

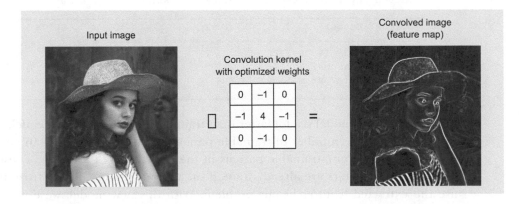

Figure 6.4   Example of generating a feature map by applying a convolutional kernel to the input image

4. What is really being transferred from one network to another? To transfer features, we download the *optimized weights* of the pretrained network. These weights are then reused as the starting point for the training process and retrained to adapt to the new problem.

Okay, let's dive into the details to understand what we mean when we say *pretrained network*. When we're training a convolutional neural network, the network extracts features from an image in the form of feature maps: outputs of each layer in a neural network after applying the weights filter. They are representations of the features that exist in the training set. They are called feature maps because they map where a certain kind of feature is found in the image. CNNs look for features such as straight lines, edges, and even objects. Whenever they spot these features, they report them to the feature map. Each weight filter is looking for something different that is reflected in the feature maps: one filter could be looking for straight lines, another for curves, and so on (figure 6.5).

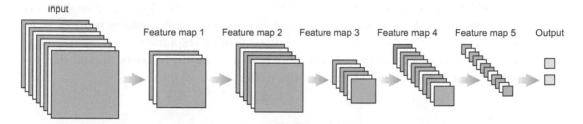

Figure 6.5   The network extracts features from an image in the form of feature maps. They are representations of the features that exist in the training set after applying the weight filters.

Now, recall that neural networks iteratively update their weights during the training cycle of feedforward and backpropagation. We say the network has been *trained* when we go through a series of training iterations and hyperparameter tuning until the network yields satisfactory results. When training is complete, we output two main items: the network architecture and the trained weights. So, when we say that we are going to use a *pretrained network*, we mean that we will download the network architecture together with the weights.

During training, the model learns only the features that exist in this training dataset. But when we download large models (like Inception) that have been trained on huge numbers of datasets (like ImageNet), all the features that have already been extracted from these large datasets are now available for us to use. I find that really exciting because these pretrained models have spotted other features that weren't in our dataset and will help us build better convolutional networks.

In vision problems, there's a huge amount of stuff for neural networks to learn about the training dataset. There are low-level features like edges, corners, round shapes, curvy shapes, and blobs; and then there are mid- and higher-level features like eyes, circles, squares, and wheels. There are many details in the images that CNNs can pick up on—but if we have only 1,000 images or even 25,000 images in our training dataset, this may not be enough data for the model to learn all those things. By using a pretrained network, we can basically download all this knowledge into our neural network to give it a huge and much faster start with even higher performance levels.

6.3.1 *How do neural networks learn features?*

A neural network learns the features in a dataset step by step in increasing levels of complexity, one layer after another. These are called *feature maps*. The deeper you go through the network layers, the more image-specific features are learned. In figure 6.6, the first layer detects low-level features such as edges and curves. The output of the first layer becomes input to the second layer, which produces higher-level features like semicircles and squares. The next layer assembles the output of the previous layer into parts of familiar objects, and a subsequent layer detects the objects. As we go through more layers, the network yields an *activation map* that represents more complex features. As we go deeper into the network, the filters begin to be more responsive to a larger region of the pixel space. Higher-level layers amplify aspects of the received inputs that are important for discrimination and suppress irrelevant variations.

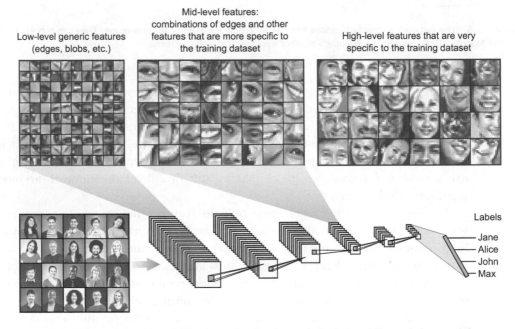

Figure 6.6 An example of how CNNs detect low-level generic features at the early layers of the network. The deeper you go through the network layers, the more image-specific features are learned.

Consider the example in figure 6.6. Suppose we are building a model that detects human faces. We notice that the network learns low-level features like lines, edges, and blobs in the first layer. These low-level features appear not to be specific to a particular dataset or task; they are general features that are applicable to many datasets and tasks. The mid-level layers assemble those lines to be able to recognize shapes, corners, and circles. Notice that the extracted features start to get a little more specific to our task (human faces): mid-level features contain combinations of shapes that form objects in the human face like eyes and noses. As we go deeper through the network, we notice that features eventually transition from general to specific and, by the last layer of the network, form high-level features that are very specific to our task. We start seeing parts of human faces that distinguish one person from another.

Now, let's take this example and compare the feature maps extracted from four models that are trained to classify faces, cars, elephants, and chairs (see figure 6.7). Notice that the earlier layers' features are very similar for all the models. They represent low-level features like edges, lines, and blobs. This means models that are trained on one task capture similar relations in the data types in the earlier layers of the network and can easily be reused for different problems in other domains. The deeper we go into the network, the more specific the features, until the network overfits its training data and it becomes harder to generalize to different tasks. The lower-level features are almost always transferable from one task to another because they contain generic information like the structure and nature of how images look. Transferring information like lines, dots, curves, and small parts of objects is very valuable for the network to learn faster and with less data on the new task.

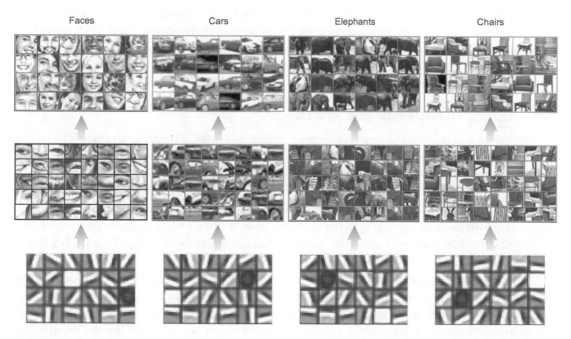

Figure 6.7   Feature maps extracted from four models that are trained to classify faces, cars, elephants, and chairs

6.3.2   *Transferability of features extracted at later layers*

The transferability of features that are extracted at later layers depends on the similarity of the original and new datasets. The idea is that all images must have shapes and edges, so the early layers are usually transferable between different domains. We can only identify differences between objects when we start extracting higher-level features: say, the nose on a face or the tires on a car. Only then can we say, "Okay, this is a person, because it has a nose. And this is a car, because it has tires." Based on the similarity of the source and target domains, we can decide whether to transfer only the low-level features from the source domain, or the high-level features, or somewhere in between. This is motivated by the observation that the later layers of the network become progressively more specific to the details of the classes contained in the original dataset, as we are going to discuss in the next section.

> **DEFINITIONS**   The *source domain* is the original dataset that the pretrained network is trained on. The *target domain* is the new dataset that we want to train the network on.

6.4   *Transfer learning approaches*

There are three major transfer learning approaches: pretrained network as a classifier, pretrained network as a feature extractor, and fine-tuning. Each approach can be effective and save significant time in developing and training a deep CNN model. It may not be clear which use of a pretrained model may yield the best results on your new CV task, so some experimentation may be required. In this section, we will explain these three scenarios and give examples of how to implement them.

6.4.1   *Using a pretrained network as a classifier*

Using a pretrained network as a classifier doesn't involve freezing any layers or doing extra model training. Instead, we just take a network that was trained on a similar problem and deploy it directly to our task. The pretrained model is used directly to classify new images with no changes applied to it and no extra training. All we do is download the network architecture and its pretrained weights and then run the predictions directly on our new data. In this case, we are saying that the domain of our new problem is very similar to the one that the pretrained network was trained on, and it is ready to be deployed.

In the dog breed example, we could have used a VGG16 network that was trained on an ImageNet dataset directly to run predictions. ImageNet already contains a lot of dog images, so a significant portion of the representational power of the pretrained network may be devoted to features that are specific to differentiating between dog breeds.

Let's see how to use a pretrained network as a classifier. In this example, we will use a VGG16 network that was pretrained on the ImageNet dataset to classify the image of the German Shepherd dog in figure 6.8.

Figure 6.8 A sample image of a German Shepherd that we will use to run predictions

The steps are as follows:

1 Import the necessary libraries:

```
from keras.preprocessing.image import load_img
from keras.preprocessing.image import img_to_array
from keras.applications.vgg16 import preprocess_input
from keras.applications.vgg16 import decode_predictions
from keras.applications.vgg16 import VGG16
```

2 Download the pretrained model of VGG16 and its ImageNet weights. We set
   `include_top` to `True` because we want to use the entire network as a classifier:

```
model = VGG16(weights = "imagenet", include_top=True, input_shape =
   (224,224, 3))
```

3 Load and preprocess the input image:

Loads an image from a file

```
image = load_img('path/to/image.jpg', target_size=(224, 224))

image = img_to_array(image)                                   ← Converts the image
                                                                pixels to a NumPy array

image = image.reshape((1, image.shape[0], image.shape[1], image.shape[2]))

image = preprocess_input(image)       ← Prepares the image
                                        for the VGG model
Reshapes the data
for the model
```

4 Now our input image is ready for us to run predictions:

```
yhat = model.predict(image)          ← Predicts the probability
                                        across all output classes
label = decode_predictions(yhat)     ← Converts the probabilities
                                        to class labels
label = label[0][0]                  ← Retrieves the most likely result
                                        with the highest probability
print('%s (%.2f%%)' % (label[1], label[2]*100))   ← Prints the
                                                      classification
```

When you run this code, you will get the following output:

```
>> German_shepherd (99.72%)
```

You can see that the model was already trained to predict the correct dog breed with a high confidence score (99.72%). This is because the ImageNet dataset has more than 20,000 labeled dog images classified into 120 classes. Go to the book's website to play with the code yourself with your own images: www.manning.com/books/deep-learning-for-vision-systems or www.computervisionbook.com. Feel free to explore the classes available in ImageNet and run this experiment on your own images.

6.4.2 *Using a pretrained network as a feature extractor*

This approach is similar to the dog breed example that we implemented earlier in this chapter: we take a pretrained CNN on ImageNet, freeze its feature extraction part, remove the classifier part, and add our own new, dense classifier layers. In figure 6.9, we use a pretrained VGG16 network, freeze the weights in all 13 convolutional layers, and replace the old classifier with a new one to be trained from scratch.

We usually go with this scenario when our new task is similar to the original dataset that the pretrained network was trained on. Since the ImageNet dataset has a lot of dog and cat examples, the feature maps that the network has learned contain a lot of dog and cat features that are very applicable to our new task. This means we can use the high-level features that were extracted from the ImageNet dataset in this new task.

To do that, we freeze all the layers from the pretrained network and only train the classifier part that we just added on the new dataset. This approach is called using a pretrained network as a feature extractor because we freeze the feature extractor part to transfer all the learned feature maps to our new problem. We only add a new classifier, which will be trained from scratch, on top of the pretrained model so that we can repurpose the previously learned feature maps for our dataset.

We remove the classification part of the pretrained network because it is often very specific to the original classification task, and subsequently it is specific to the set of classes on which the model was trained. For example, ImageNet has 1,000

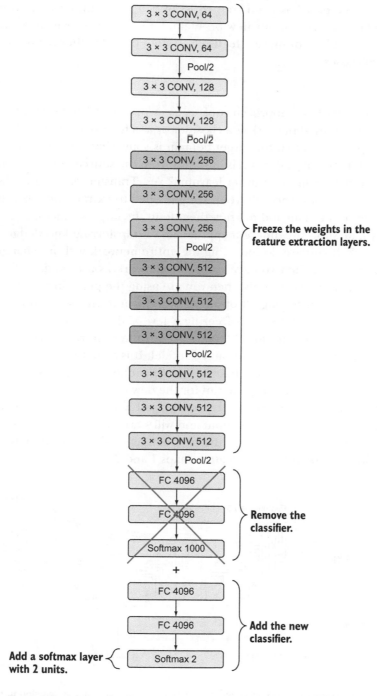

Figure 6.9 Load a pretrained VGG16 network, remove the classifier, and add your own classifier.

classes. The classifier part has been trained to overfit the training data to classify them into 1,000 classes. But in our new problem, let's say cats versus dogs, we have only two classes. So, it is a lot more effective to train a new classifier from scratch to overfit these two classes.

6.4.3   *Fine-tuning*

So far, we've seen two basic approaches of using a pretrained network in transfer learning: using a pretrained network as a classifier or as a feature extractor. We generally use these approaches when the target domain is somewhat similar to the source domain. But what if the target domain is different from the source domain? What if it is *very* different? Can we still use transfer learning? Yes. Transfer learning works great even when the domains are very different. We just need to extract the *correct* feature maps from the source domain and *fine-tune* them to fit the target domain.

In figure 6.10, we show the different approaches of transferring knowledge from a pretrained network. If you are downloading the entire network with no changes and just running predictions, then you are using the network as a classifier. If you are freezing the convolutional layers only, then you are using the pretrained network as a feature extractor and transferring all of its high-level feature maps to your domain. The formal definition of *fine-tuning* is freezing a few of the network layers that are used for feature extraction, and jointly training both the non-frozen layers and the newly added classifier layers of the pretrained model. It is called fine-tuning because when we retrain the feature extraction layers, we fine-tune the higher-order feature representations to make them more relevant for the new task dataset.

In more practical terms, if we freeze features maps 1 and 2 in figure 6.10, the new network will take feature maps 2 as its input and will start learning from this point to adapt the features of the later layers to the new dataset. This saves the network the time that it would have spent learning feature maps 1 and 2.

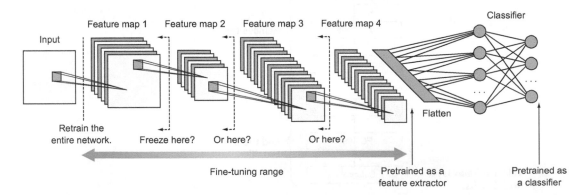

Figure 6.10   The network learns features through its layers. In transfer learning, we make a decision to freeze specific layers of a pretrained network to preserve the learned features. For example, if we freeze the network at feature maps of layer 3, we preserve what it has learned in layers 1, 2, and 3.

As we discussed earlier, feature maps that are extracted early in the network are generic. The feature maps get progressively more specific as we go deeper in the network. This means feature maps 4 in figure 6.10 are very specific to the source domain. Based on the similarity of the two domains, we can decide to freeze the network at the appropriate level of feature maps:

- If the domains are similar, we might want to freeze the network up to the last feature map level (feature maps 4, in the example).
- If the domains are very different, we might decide to freeze the pretrained network after feature maps 1 and retrain all the remaining layers.

Between these two possibilities are a range of fine-tuning options that we can apply. We can retrain the entire network, or freeze the pretrained network at any level of feature maps 1, 2, 3, or 4 and retrain the remainder of the network. We typically decide the appropriate level of fine-tuning by trial and error. But there are guidelines that we can follow to intuitively decide on the fine-tuning level for the pretrained network. The decision is a function of two factors: the amount of data we have and the level of similarity between the source and target domains. We will explain these factors and the four possible scenarios to choose the appropriate level of fine-tuning in section 6.5.

WHY IS FINE-TUNING BETTER THAN TRAINING FROM SCRATCH?

When we train a network from scratch, we usually randomly initialize the weights and apply a gradient descent optimizer to find the best set of weights that optimizes our error function (as discussed in chapter 2). Since these weights start with random values, there is no guarantee that they will begin with values that are close to the desired optimal values. And if the initialized value is far from the optimal value, the optimizer will take a long time to converge. This is when fine-tuning can be very useful. The pretrained network's weights have been already optimized to learn from its dataset. Thus, when we use this network in our problem, we start with the weight values that it ended with. So, the network converges much faster than if it had to randomly initialize the weights. We are basically *fine-tuning* the already-optimized weights to fit our new problem instead of training the entire network from scratch with random weights. Even if we decide to retrain the entire pretrained network, starting with the trained weights will converge faster than having to train the network from scratch with randomly initialized weights.

USING A SMALLER LEARNING RATE WHEN FINE-TUNING

It's common to use a smaller learning rate for ConvNet weights that are being fine-tuned, in comparison to the (randomly initialized) weights for the new linear classifier that computes the class scores of a new dataset. This is because we expect that the ConvNet weights are relatively good, so we don't want to distort them too quickly and too much (especially while the new classifier above them is being trained from random initialization).

6.5   *Choosing the appropriate level of transfer learning*

Recall that early convolutional layers extract generic features and become more specific to the training data the deeper we go through the network. With that said, we can choose the level of detail for feature extraction from an existing pretrained model. For example, if a new task is quite different from the source domain of the pretrained network (for example, different from ImageNet), then perhaps the output of the pretrained model after the first few layers would be appropriate. If a new task is similar to the source domain, then perhaps the output from layers much deeper in the model can be used, or even the output of the fully connected layer prior to the softmax layer.

As mentioned earlier, choosing the appropriate level for transfer learning is a function of two important factors:

- *Size of the target dataset (small or large)*—When we have a small dataset, the network probably won't learn much from training more layers, so it will tend to overfit the new data. In this case, we most likely want to do less fine-tuning and rely more on the source dataset.
- *Domain similarity of the source and target datasets*—How similar is our new problem to the domain of the original dataset? For example, if your problem is to classify cars and boats, ImageNet could be a good option because it contains a lot of images of similar features. On the other hand, if your problem is to classify lung cancer on X-ray images, this is a completely different domain that will likely require a lot of fine-tuning.

These two factors lead to the four major scenarios:

1 The target dataset is *small* and *similar* to the source dataset.
2 The target dataset is *large* and *similar* to the source dataset.
3 The target dataset is *small* and *very different* from the source dataset.
4 The target dataset is *large* and *very different* from the source dataset.

Let's discuss these scenarios one by one to learn the common rules of thumb for navigating our options.

6.5.1   *Scenario 1: Target dataset is small and similar to the source dataset*

Since the original dataset is similar to our new dataset, we can expect that the higher-level features in the pretrained ConvNet are relevant to our dataset as well. Then it might be best to freeze the feature extraction part of the network and only retrain the classifier.

Another reason it might not be a good idea to fine-tune the network is that our new dataset is small. If we fine-tune the feature extraction layers on a small dataset, that will force the network to overfit to our data. This is not good because, by definition, a small dataset doesn't have enough information to cover all possible features of its objects, which makes it fail to generalize to new, previously unseen, data. So in this case, the more fine-tuning we do, the more the network is prone to overfit the new data.

For example, suppose all the images in our new dataset contain dogs in a specific weather environment—snow, for example. If we fine-tuned on this dataset, we would force the new network to pick up features like snow and a white background as dog-specific features and make it fail to classify dogs in other weather conditions. Thus the general rule of thumb is: if you have a small amount of data, be careful of overfitting when you fine-tune your pretrained network.

6.5.2 Scenario 2: Target dataset is large and similar to the source dataset

Since both domains are similar, we can freeze the feature extraction part and retrain the classifier, similar to what we did in scenario 1. But since we have more data in the new domain, we can get a performance boost from fine-tuning through all or part of the pretrained network with more confidence that we won't overfit. Fine-tuning through the entire network is not really needed because the higher-level features are related (since the datasets are similar). So a good start is to freeze approximately 60–80% of the pretrained network and retrain the rest on the new data.

6.5.3 Scenario 3: Target dataset is small and different from the source dataset

Since the dataset is different, it might not be best to freeze the higher-level features of the pretrained network, because they contain more dataset-specific features. Instead, it would work better to retrain layers from somewhere earlier in the network—or to not freeze any layers and fine-tune the entire network. However, since you have a small dataset, fine-tuning the entire network on the dataset might not be a good idea, because doing so will make it prone to overfitting. A midway solution will work better in this case. A good start is to freeze approximately the first third or half of the pretrained network. After all, the early layers contain very generic feature maps that will be useful for your dataset even if it is very different.

6.5.4 Scenario 4: Target dataset is large and different from the source dataset

Since the new dataset is large, you might be tempted to just train the entire network from scratch and not use transfer learning at all. However, in practice, it is often still very beneficial to initialize weights from a pretrained model, as we discussed earlier. Doing so makes the model converge faster. In this case, we have a large dataset that provides us with the confidence to fine-tune through the entire network without having to worry about overfitting.

6.5.5   *Recap of the transfer learning scenarios*

We've explored the two main factors that help us define which transfer learning approach to use (size of our data and similarity between the source and target datasets). These two factors give us the four major scenarios defined in table 6.1. Figure 6.11 summarizes the guidelines for the appropriate fine-tuning level to use in each of the scenarios.

Table 6.1   Transfer learning scenarios

Scenario	Size of the target data	Similarity of the original and new datasets	Approach
1	Small	Similar	Pretrained network as a feature extractor
2	Large	Similar	Fine-tune through the full network
3	Small	Very different	Fine-tune from activations earlier in the network
4	Large	Very different	Fine-tune through the entire network

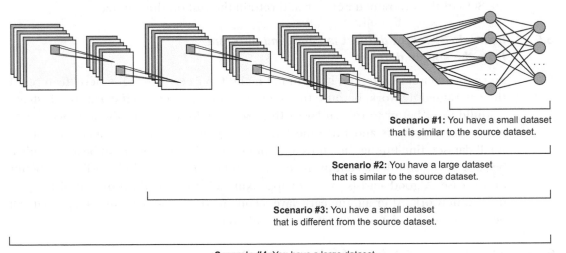

Scenario #1: You have a small dataset that is similar to the source dataset.

Scenario #2: You have a large dataset that is similar to the source dataset.

Scenario #3: You have a small dataset that is different from the source dataset.

Scenario #4: You have a large dataset that is different from the source dataset.

Figure 6.11   Guidelines for the appropriate fine-tuning level to use in each of the four scenarios

6.6   *Open source datasets*

The CV research community has been pretty good about posting datasets on the internet. So, when you hear names like ImageNet, MS COCO, Open Images, MNIST, CIFAR, and many others, these are datasets that people have posted online and that a lot of computer researchers have used as benchmarks to train their algorithms and get state-of-the-art results.

In this section, we will review some of the popular open source datasets to help guide you in your search to find the most suitable dataset for your problem. Keep in mind that the ones listed in this chapter are the most popular datasets used in the CV research community at the time of writing; we do not intend to provide a comprehensive list of all the open source datasets out there. A great many image datasets are available, and the number is growing every day. Before starting your project, I encourage you to do your own research to explore the available datasets.

6.6.1　*MNIST*

MNIST (http://yann.lecun.com/exdb/mnist) stands for Modified National Institute of Standards and Technology. It contains labeled handwritten images of digits from 0 to 9. The goal of this dataset is to classify handwritten digits. MNIST has been popular with the research community for benchmarking classification algorithms. In fact, it is considered the "hello, world!" of image datasets. But nowadays, the MNIST dataset is comparatively pretty simple, and a basic CNN can achieve more than 99% accuracy, so MNIST is no longer considered a benchmark for CNN performance. We implemented a CNN classification project using MNIST dataset in chapter 3; feel free to go back and review it.

MNIST consists of 60,000 training images and 10,000 test images. All are grayscale (one-channel), and each image is 28 pixels high and 28 pixels wide. Figure 6.12 shows some sample images from the MNIST dataset.

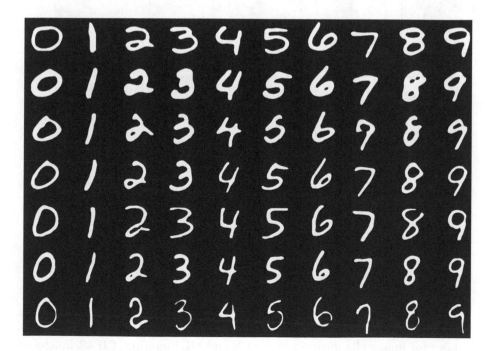

Figure 6.12　Samples from the MNIST dataset

6.6.2   *Fashion-MNIST*

Fashion-MNIST was created with the intention of replacing the original MNIST data-set, which has become too simple for modern convolutional networks. The data is stored in the same format as MNIST, but instead of handwritten digits, it contains 60,000 training images and 10,000 test images of 10 fashion clothing classes: t-shirt/top, trouser, pullover, dress, coat, sandal, shirt, sneaker, bag, and ankle boot. Visit https://github.com/zalandoresearch/fashion-mnist to explore and download the dataset. Figure 6.13 shows a sample of the represented classes.

Figure 6.13   Sample images from the Fashion-MNIST dataset

6.6.3   *CIFAR*

CIFAR-10 (www.cs.toronto.edu/~kriz/cifar.html) is considered another benchmark dataset for image classification in the CV and ML literature. CIFAR images are more complex than those in MNIST in the sense that MNIST images are all grayscale with perfectly centered objects, whereas CIFAR images are color (three channels) with dramatic variation in how the objects appear. The CIFAR-10 dataset consists of 32×32 color images in 10 classes, with 6,000 images per class. There are 50,000 training images and 10,000 test images. Figure 6.14 shows the classes in the dataset.

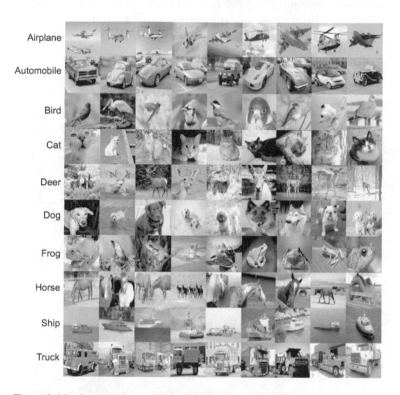

Figure 6.14   Sample images from the CIFAR-10 dataset

CIFAR-100 is the bigger brother of CIFAR-10: it contains 100 classes with 600 images each. These 100 classes are grouped into 20 superclasses. Each image comes with a *fine* label (the class to which it belongs) and a *coarse* label (the superclass to which it belongs).

6.6.4   *ImageNet*

We've discussed the ImageNet dataset several times in the previous chapters and used it extensively in chapter 5 and this chapter. But for completeness of this list, we are discussing it here as well. At the time of writing, ImageNet is considered the current benchmark and is widely used by CV researchers to evaluate their classification algorithms.

ImageNet is a large visual database designed for use in visual object recognition software research. It is aimed at labeling and categorizing images into almost 22,000 categories based on a defined set of words and phrases. The images were collected from the web and labeled by humans via Amazon's Mechanical Turk crowdsourcing tool. At the time of this writing, there are over 14 million images in the ImageNet project. To organize such a massive amount of data, the creators of ImageNet followed the WordNet hierarchy: each meaningful word/phrase in WordNet is called a *synonym set* (*synset* for short). Within the ImageNet project, images are organized according to these synsets, with the goal being to have 1,000+ images per synset. Figure 6.15 shows a collage of ImageNet examples put together by Stanford University.

Figure 6.15   A collage of ImageNet examples compiled by Stanford University

The CV community usually refers to the ImageNet Large Scale Visual Recognition Challenge (ILSVRC) when talking about ImageNet. In this challenge, software programs compete to correctly classify and detect objects and scenes. We will be using the ILSVRC challenge as a benchmark to compare the different networks' performance.

6.6.5   *MS COCO*

MS COCO (http://cocodataset.org) is short for Microsoft Common Objects in Context. It is an open source database that aims to enable future research for object detection, instance segmentation, image captioning, and localizing person keypoints. It contains 328,000 images. More than 200,000 of them are labeled, and they include 1.5 million object instances and 80 object categories that would be easily recognizable by a 4-year-old. The original research paper by the creators of the dataset describes the motivation for and content of this dataset.[2] Figure 6.16 shows a sample of the dataset provided on the MS COCO website.

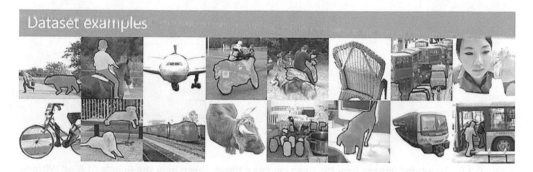

Figure 6.16   A sample of the MS COCO dataset
(Image copyright © 2015, COCO Consortium, used by permission under Creative Commons Attribution 4.0 License.)

6.6.6   *Google Open Images*

Open Images (https://storage.googleapis.com/openimages/web/index.html) is an open source image database created by Google. It contains more than 9 million images as of this writing. What makes it stand out is that these images are mostly of complex scenes that span thousands of classes of objects. Additionally, more than 2 million of these images are hand-annotated with bounding boxes, making Open Images by far the largest existing dataset with object-location annotations (see figure 6.17). In this subset of images, there are ~15.4 million bounding boxes of 600 classes of objects. Similar to ImageNet and ILSVRC, Open Images has a challenge called the Open Images Challenge (http://mng.bz/aRQz).

6.6.7   *Kaggle*

In addition to the datasets listed in this section, Kaggle (www.kaggle.com) is another great source for datasets. Kaggle is a website that hosts ML and DL challenges where people from all around the world can participate and submit algorithms for evaluations.

You are strongly encouraged to explore these datasets and search for the many other open source datasets that come up every day, to gain a better understanding of the classes and use cases they support. We mostly use ImageNet in this chapter's projects; and throughout the book, we will be using MS COCO, especially in chapter 7.

---

[2] Tsung-Yi Lin, Michael Maire, Serge Belongie, et al., "Microsoft COCO: Common Objects in Context" (February 2015), https://arxiv.org/pdf/1405.0312.pdf.

Figure 6.17   Annotated images from the Open Images dataset, taken from the Google AI Blog (Vittorio Ferrari, "An Update to Open Images—Now with Bounding-Boxes," July 2017, http://mng.bz/yyVG).

6.7   Project 1: A pretrained network as a feature extractor

In this project, we use a very small amount of data to train a classifier that detects images of dogs and cats. This is a pretty simple project, but the goal of the exercise is to see how to implement transfer learning when you have a very small amount of data and the target domain is similar to the source domain (scenario 1). As explained in this chapter, in this case, we will use the pretrained convolutional network as a feature extractor. This means we are going to freeze the feature extractor part of the network, add our own classifier, and then retrain the network on our new small dataset.

One other important takeaway from this project is learning how to preprocess custom data and make it ready to train your neural network. In previous projects, we used the CIFAR and MNIST datasets: they are preprocessed by Keras, so all we had to do was download them from the Keras library and use them directly to train the network. This project provides a tutorial of how to structure your data repository and use the Keras library to get your data ready.

Visit the book's website at www.manning.com/books/deep-learning-for-vision-systems or www.computervisionbook.com to download the code notebook and the dataset used for this project. Since we are using transfer learning, the training does not require high computation power, so you can run this notebook on your personal computer; you don't need a GPU.

For this implementation, we'll be using the VGG16. Although it didn't record the lowest error in the ILSVRC, I found that it worked well for the task and was quicker to train than other models. I got an accuracy of about 96%, but you can feel free to use GoogLeNet or ResNet to experiment and compare results.

The process to use a pretrained model as a feature extractor is well established:

1 Import the necessary libraries.

2 Preprocess the data to make it ready for the neural network.

3 Load pretrained weights from the VGG16 network trained on a large dataset.

4 Freeze all the weights in the convolutional layers (feature extraction part). Remember, the layers to freeze are adjusted depending on the similarity of the new task to the original dataset. In our case, we observed that ImageNet has a lot of dog and cat images, so the network has already been trained to extract the detailed features of our target object.

5 Replace the fully connected layers of the network with a custom classifier. You can add as many fully connected layers as you see fit, and each can have as many hidden units as you want. For simple problems like this, we will just add one hidden layer with 64 units. You can observe the results and tune up if the model is underfitting or down if the model is overfitting. For the softmax layer, the number of units must be set equal to the number of classes (two units, in our case).

6 Compile the network, and run the training process on the new data of cats and dogs to optimize the model for the smaller dataset.

7 Evaluate the model.

Now, let's go through these steps and implement this project:

1 Import the necessary libraries:

```
from keras.preprocessing.image import ImageDataGenerator
from keras.preprocessing import image
from keras.applications import imagenet_utils
from keras.applications import vgg16
from keras.applications import mobilenet
from keras.optimizers import Adam, SGD
from keras.metrics import categorical_crossentropy
from keras.layers import Dense, Flatten, Dropout, BatchNormalization
from keras.models import Model
from sklearn.metrics import confusion_matrix
import itertools
import matplotlib.pyplot as plt
%matplotlib inline
```

2 Preprocess the data to make it ready for the neural network. Keras has an ImageDataGenerator class that allows us to easily perform image augmentation on the fly; you can read about it at https://keras.io/api/preprocessing/image. In this example, we use ImageDataGenerator to generate our image tensors, but for simplicity, we will not implement image augmentation.

The ImageDataGenerator class has a method called flow_from_directory() that is used to read images from folders containing images. This method expects your data directory to be structured as in figure 6.18.

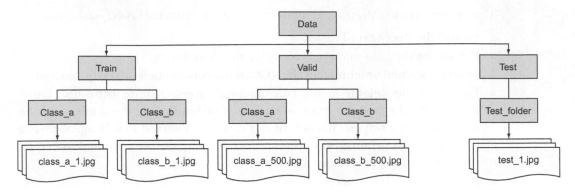

Figure 6.18 **The required directory structure for your dataset to use the** `.flow_from_directory()` **method from Keras**

I have the data structured in the book's code so it's ready for you to use `flow_from_directory()`. Now, load the data into `train_path`, `valid_path`, and `test_path` variables, and then generate the train, valid, and test batches:

> **ImageDataGenerator generates batches of tensor image data with real-time data augmentation. The data will be looped over (in batches). In this example, we won't be doing any image augmentation.**

```
train_path  = 'data/train'
valid_path  = 'data/valid'
test_path   = 'data/test'

train_batches = ImageDataGenerator().flow_from_directory(train_path,
                                        target_size=(224,224),
                                        batch_size=10)

valid_batches = ImageDataGenerator().flow_from_directory(valid_path,
                                        target_size=(224,224),
                                        batch_size=30)

test_batches = ImageDataGenerator().flow_from_directory(test_path,
                                        target_size=(224,224),
                                        batch_size=50,
                                        shuffle=False)
```

3 Load in pretrained weights from the VGG16 network trained on a large dataset. Similar to the examples in this chapter, we download the VGG16 network from Keras and download its weights after they are pretrained on the ImageNet dataset. Remember that we want to remove the classifier part from this network, so we set the parameter `include_top=False`:

```
base_model = vgg16.VGG16(weights = "imagenet", include_top=False,
                         input_shape = (224,224, 3))
```

4 Freeze all the weights in the convolutional layers (feature extraction part). We freeze the convolutional layers from the `base_model` created in the previous

step and use that as a feature extractor, and then add a classifier on top of it in the next step:

```
for layer in base_model.layers:
    layer.trainable = False
```
⟵ Iterates through layers and locks them to make them non-trainable with this code

5   Add the new classifier, and build the new model. We add a few layers on top of the base model. In this example, we add one fully connected layer with 64 hidden units and a softmax with 2 hidden units. We also add batch norm and drop out layers to avoid overfitting:

Uses the get_layer method to save the last layer of the network. Then saves the output of the last layer to be the input of the next layer.

```
last_layer = base_model.get_layer('block5_pool')   ⟵
last_output = last_layer.output

x = Flatten()(last_output)   ⟵ Flattens the classifier input, which is output of the last layer of the VGG16 model

x = Dense(64, activation='relu', name='FC_2')(x)
x = BatchNormalization()(x)
x = Dropout(0.5)(x)
x = Dense(2, activation='softmax', name='softmax')(x)
```
Adds one fully connected layer that has 64 units and batchnorm, dropout, and softmax layers

Instantiates a new_model using Keras's Model class
```
new_model = Model(inputs=base_model.input, outputs=x)
new_model.summary()
```

Layer (type)	Output Shape	Param #
input_1 (InputLayer)	(None, 224, 224, 3)	0
block1_conv1 (Conv2D)	(None, 224, 224, 64)	1792
block1_conv2 (Conv2D)	(None, 224, 224, 64)	36928
block1_pool (MaxPooling2D)	(None, 112, 112, 64)	0
block2_conv1 (Conv2D)	(None, 112, 112, 128)	73856
block2_conv2 (Conv2D)	(None, 112, 112, 128)	147584
block2_pool (MaxPooling2D)	(None, 56, 56, 128)	0
block3_conv1 (Conv2D)	(None, 56, 56, 256)	295168
block3_conv2 (Conv2D)	(None, 56, 56, 256)	590080
block3_conv3 (Conv2D)	(None, 56, 56, 256)	590080
block3_pool (MaxPooling2D)	(None, 28, 28, 256)	0

```
block4_conv1 (Conv2D)        (None, 28, 28, 512)      1180160

block4_conv2 (Conv2D)        (None, 28, 28, 512)      2359808

block4_conv3 (Conv2D)        (None, 28, 28, 512)      2359808

block4_pool (MaxPooling2D)   (None, 14, 14, 512)      0

block5_conv1 (Conv2D)        (None, 14, 14, 512)      2359808

block5_conv2 (Conv2D)        (None, 14, 14, 512)      2359808

block5_conv3 (Conv2D)        (None, 14, 14, 512)      2359808

block5_pool (MaxPooling2D)   (None, 7, 7, 512)        0

flatten_1 (Flatten)          (None, 25088)            0

FC_2 (Dense)                 (None, 64)               1605696

batch_normalization_1 (Batch (None, 64)               256

dropout_1 (Dropout)          (None, 64)               0

softmax (Dense)              (None, 2)                130
=================================================================
Total params: 16,320,770
Trainable params: 1,605,954
Non-trainable params: 14,714,816
```

6 Compile the model and run the training process:

```
new_model.compile(Adam(lr=0.0001), loss='categorical_crossentropy',
                  metrics=['accuracy'])

new_model.fit_generator(train_batches, steps_per_epoch=4,
                        validation_data=valid_batches, validation_steps=2,
                        epochs=20, verbose=2)
```

When you run the previous code snippet, the verbose training is printed after each epoch as follows:

```
Epoch 1/20
 - 28s - loss: 1.0070 - acc: 0.6083 - val_loss: 0.5944 - val_acc: 0.6833
Epoch 2/20
 - 25s - loss: 0.4728 - acc: 0.7754 - val_loss: 0.3313 - val_acc: 0.8605
Epoch 3/20
 - 30s - loss: 0.1177 - acc: 0.9750 - val_loss: 0.2449 - val_acc: 0.8167
Epoch 4/20
 - 25s - loss: 0.1640 - acc: 0.9444 - val_loss: 0.3354 - val_acc: 0.8372
Epoch 5/20
 - 29s - loss: 0.0545 - acc: 1.0000 - val_loss: 0.2392 - val_acc: 0.8333
Epoch 6/20
```

```
 - 25s - loss: 0.0941 - acc: 0.9505 - val_loss: 0.2019 - val_acc: 0.9070
Epoch 7/20
 - 28s - loss: 0.0269 - acc: 1.0000 - val_loss: 0.1707 - val_acc: 0.9000
Epoch 8/20
 - 26s - loss: 0.0349 - acc: 0.9917 - val_loss: 0.2489 - val_acc: 0.8140
Epoch 9/20
 - 28s - loss: 0.0435 - acc: 0.9891 - val_loss: 0.1634 - val_acc: 0.9000
Epoch 10/20
 - 26s - loss: 0.0349 - acc: 0.9833 - val_loss: 0.2375 - val_acc: 0.8140
Epoch 11/20
 - 28s - loss: 0.0288 - acc: 1.0000 - val_loss: 0.1859 - val_acc: 0.9000
Epoch 12/20
 - 29s - loss: 0.0234 - acc: 0.9917 - val_loss: 0.1879 - val_acc: 0.8372
Epoch 13/20
 - 32s - loss: 0.0241 - acc: 1.0000 - val_loss: 0.2513 - val_acc: 0.8500
Epoch 14/20
 - 29s - loss: 0.0120 - acc: 1.0000 - val_loss: 0.0900 - val_acc: 0.9302
Epoch 15/20
 - 36s - loss: 0.0189 - acc: 1.0000 - val_loss: 0.1888 - val_acc: 0.9000
Epoch 16/20
 - 30s - loss: 0.0142 - acc: 1.0000 - val_loss: 0.1672 - val_acc: 0.8605
Epoch 17/20
 - 29s - loss: 0.0160 - acc: 0.9917 - val_loss: 0.1752 - val_acc: 0.8667
Epoch 18/20
 - 25s - loss: 0.0126 - acc: 1.0000 - val_loss: 0.1823 - val_acc: 0.9070
Epoch 19/20
 - 29s - loss: 0.0165 - acc: 1.0000 - val_loss: 0.1789 - val_acc: 0.8833
Epoch 20/20
 - 25s - loss: 0.0112 - acc: 1.0000 - val_loss: 0.1743 - val_acc: 0.8837
```

Notice that the model was trained very quickly using regular CPU computing power. Each epoch took approximately 25 to 29 seconds, which means the model took less than 10 minutes to train for 20 epochs.

7 Evaluate the model. First, let's define the `load_dataset()` method that we will use to convert our dataset into tensors:

```python
from sklearn.datasets import load_files
from keras.utils import np_utils
import numpy as np

def load_dataset(path):
    data = load_files(path)
    paths = np.array(data['filenames'])
    targets = np_utils.to_categorical(np.array(data['target']))
    return paths, targets

test_files, test_targets = load_dataset('small_data/test')
```

Then, we create test_tensors to evaluate the model on them:

```python
from keras.preprocessing import image
from keras.applications.vgg16 import preprocess_input
from tqdm import tqdm
```

```
def path_to_tensor(img_path):
    img = image.load_img(img_path, target_size=(224, 224))
    x = image.img_to_array(img)
    return np.expand_dims(x, axis=0)

def paths_to_tensor(img_paths):
    list_of_tensors = [path_to_tensor(img_path) for img_path in
tqdm(img_paths)]
    return np.vstack(list_of_tensors)

test_tensors = preprocess_input(paths_to_tensor(test_files))
```

Converts the PIL.Image.Image type to a 3D tensor with shape (224, 224, 3)

Converts the 3D tensor to a 4D tensor with shape (1, 224, 224, 3) and returns the 4D tensor

Loads an RGB image as PIL.Image.Image type

Now we can run Keras's `evaluate()` method to calculate the model accuracy:

```
print('\nTesting loss: {:.4f}\nTesting accuracy:
    {:.4f}'.format(*new_model.evaluate(test_tensors, test_targets)))

Testing loss: 0.1042
Testing accuracy: 0.9579
```

The model has achieved an accuracy of 95.79% in less than 10 minutes of training. This is very good, given our very small dataset.

6.8 *Project 2: Fine-tuning*

In this project, we are going to explore scenario 3, discussed earlier in this chapter, where the target dataset is small and very different from the source dataset. The goal of this project is to build a sign language classifier that distinguishes 10 classes: the sign language digits from 0 to 9. Figure 6.19 shows a sample of our dataset.

Figure 6.19   A sample from the sign language dataset

Following are the details of our dataset:

- Number of classes = 10 (digits 0, 1, 2, 3, 4, 5, 6, 7, 8, and 9)
- Image size = 100 × 100
- Color space = RGB
- 1,712 images in the training set
- 300 images in the validation set
- 50 images in the test set

It is very noticeable how small our dataset is. If you try to train a network from scratch on this very small dataset, you will not achieve good results. On the other hand, we were able to achieve an accuracy higher than 98% by using transfer learning, even though the source and target domains were very different.

> **NOTE** Please take this evaluation with a grain of salt, because the network hasn't been thoroughly tested with a lot of data. We only have 50 test images in this dataset. Transfer learning is expected to achieve good results anyway, but I wanted to highlight this fact.

Visit the book's website at www.manning.com/books/deep-learning-for-vision-systems or www.computervisionbook.com to download the source code notebook and the dataset used for this project. Similar to project 1, the training does not require high computation power, so you can run this notebook on your personal computer; you don't need a GPU.

For ease of comparison with the previous project, we will use the VGG16 network trained on the ImageNet dataset. The process to fine-tune a pretrained network is as follows:

1 Import the necessary libraries.
2 Preprocess the data to make it ready for the neural network.
3 Load in pretrained weights from the VGG16 network trained on a large dataset (ImageNet).
4 Freeze *part* of the feature extractor part.
5 Add the new classifier layers.
6 Compile the network, and run the training process to optimize the model for the smaller dataset.
7 Evaluate the model.

Now let's implement this project:

1 Import the necessary libraries:

```
from keras.preprocessing.image import ImageDataGenerator
from keras.preprocessing import image
from keras.applications import imagenet_utils
from keras.applications import vgg16
from keras.optimizers import Adam, SGD
from keras.metrics import categorical_crossentropy
```

```
from keras.layers import Dense, Flatten, Dropout, BatchNormalization
from keras.models import Model
from sklearn.metrics import confusion_matrix
import itertools
import matplotlib.pyplot as plt
%matplotlib inline
```

2   Preprocess the data to make it ready for the neural network. Similar to project 1, we use the `ImageDataGenerator` class from Keras and the `flow_from_directory()` method to preprocess our data. The data is already structured for you to directly create your tensors:

> **ImageDataGenerator generates batches of tensor image data with real-time data augmentation. The data will be looped over (in batches). In this example, we won't be doing any image augmentation.**

```
train_path  = 'dataset/train'
valid_path  = 'dataset/valid'
test_path   = 'dataset/test'

train_batches = ImageDataGenerator().flow_from_directory(train_path,     ◁────┐
                                            target_size=(224,224),
                                            batch_size=10)

valid_batches = ImageDataGenerator().flow_from_directory(valid_path,
                                            target_size=(224,224),
                                            batch_size=30)

test_batches = ImageDataGenerator().flow_from_directory(test_path,
                                            target_size=(224,224),
                                            batch_size=50,
                                            shuffle=False)
```

```
Found 1712 images belonging to 10 classes.
Found 300 images belonging to 10 classes.
Found 50 images belonging to 10 classes.
```

3   Load in pretrained weights from the VGG16 network trained on a large dataset (ImageNet). We download the VGG16 architecture from the Keras library with ImageNet weights. Note that we use the parameter `pooling='avg'` here: this basically means global average pooling will be applied to the output of the last convolutional layer, and thus the output of the model will be a 2D tensor. We use this as an alternative to the `Flatten` layer before adding the fully connected layers:

```
base_model = vgg16.VGG16(weights = "imagenet", include_top=False,
                         input_shape = (224,224, 3), pooling='avg')
```

4   Freeze some of the feature extractor part, and fine-tune the rest on our new training data. The level of fine-tuning is usually determined by trial and error. VGG16 has 13 convolutional layers: you can freeze them all or freeze a few of them, depending on how similar your data is to the source data. In the sign

language case, the new domain is very different from our domain, so we will start with fine-tuning only the last five layers; if we don't get satisfying results, we can fine-tune more. It turns out that after we trained the new model, we got 98% accuracy, so this was a good level of fine-tuning. But in other cases, if you find that your network doesn't converge, try fine-tuning more layers.

```
for layer in base_model.layers[:-5]:          Iterates through layers
    layer.trainable = False                    and locks them, except
                                               for the last five layers
base_model.summary()
```

Layer (type)	Output Shape	Param #
input_1 (InputLayer)	(None, 224, 224, 3)	0
block1_conv1 (Conv2D)	(None, 224, 224, 64)	1792
block1_conv2 (Conv2D)	(None, 224, 224, 64)	36928
block1_pool (MaxPooling2D)	(None, 112, 112, 64)	0
block2_conv1 (Conv2D)	(None, 112, 112, 128)	73856
block2_conv2 (Conv2D)	(None, 112, 112, 128)	147584
block2_pool (MaxPooling2D)	(None, 56, 56, 128)	0
block3_conv1 (Conv2D)	(None, 56, 56, 256)	295168
block3_conv2 (Conv2D)	(None, 56, 56, 256)	590080
block3_conv3 (Conv2D)	(None, 56, 56, 256)	590080
block3_pool (MaxPooling2D)	(None, 28, 28, 256)	0
block4_conv1 (Conv2D)	(None, 28, 28, 512)	1180160
block4_conv2 (Conv2D)	(None, 28, 28, 512)	2359808
block4_conv3 (Conv2D)	(None, 28, 28, 512)	2359808
block4_pool (MaxPooling2D)	(None, 14, 14, 512)	0
block5_conv1 (Conv2D)	(None, 14, 14, 512)	2359808
block5_conv2 (Conv2D)	(None, 14, 14, 512)	2359808
block5_conv3 (Conv2D)	(None, 14, 14, 512)	2359808
block5_pool (MaxPooling2D)	(None, 7, 7, 512)	0
global_average_pooling2d_1 (	(None, 512)	0

```
Total params: 14,714,688
Trainable params: 7,079,424
Non-trainable params: 7,635,264
```

5   Add the new classifier layers, and build the new model:

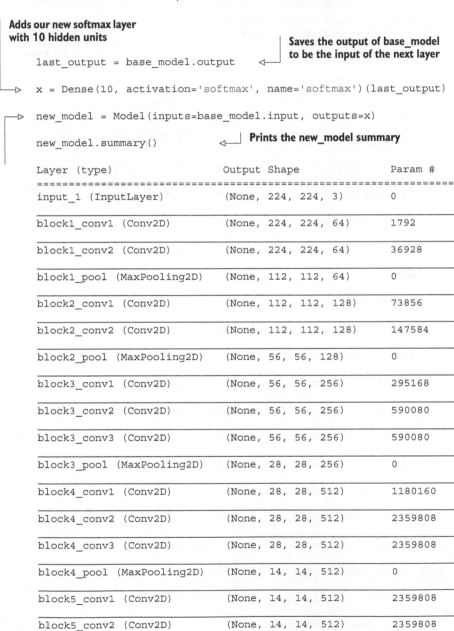

**Adds our new softmax layer
with 10 hidden units**

**Saves the output of base_model
to be the input of the next layer**

```
last_output = base_model.output
```

```
x = Dense(10, activation='softmax', name='softmax')(last_output)
```

**Instantiates
a new_model
using Keras's
Model class**

```
new_model = Model(inputs=base_model.input, outputs=x)
```

```
new_model.summary()
```
   Prints the new_model summary

Layer (type)	Output Shape	Param #
input_1 (InputLayer)	(None, 224, 224, 3)	0
block1_conv1 (Conv2D)	(None, 224, 224, 64)	1792
block1_conv2 (Conv2D)	(None, 224, 224, 64)	36928
block1_pool (MaxPooling2D)	(None, 112, 112, 64)	0
block2_conv1 (Conv2D)	(None, 112, 112, 128)	73856
block2_conv2 (Conv2D)	(None, 112, 112, 128)	147584
block2_pool (MaxPooling2D)	(None, 56, 56, 128)	0
block3_conv1 (Conv2D)	(None, 56, 56, 256)	295168
block3_conv2 (Conv2D)	(None, 56, 56, 256)	590080
block3_conv3 (Conv2D)	(None, 56, 56, 256)	590080
block3_pool (MaxPooling2D)	(None, 28, 28, 256)	0
block4_conv1 (Conv2D)	(None, 28, 28, 512)	1180160
block4_conv2 (Conv2D)	(None, 28, 28, 512)	2359808
block4_conv3 (Conv2D)	(None, 28, 28, 512)	2359808
block4_pool (MaxPooling2D)	(None, 14, 14, 512)	0
block5_conv1 (Conv2D)	(None, 14, 14, 512)	2359808
block5_conv2 (Conv2D)	(None, 14, 14, 512)	2359808

```
block5_conv3 (Conv2D)        (None, 14, 14, 512)      2359808
_____
block5_pool (MaxPooling2D)   (None, 7, 7, 512)        0
_____
global_average_pooling2d_1 ( (None, 512)              0
_____
softmax (Dense)              (None, 10)               5130
=================================================================
Total params: 14,719,818
Trainable params: 7,084,554
Non-trainable params: 7,635,264
```

6 Compile the network, and run the training process to optimize the model for the smaller dataset:

```
new_model.compile(Adam(lr=0.0001), loss='categorical_crossentropy',
                  metrics=['accuracy'])

from keras.callbacks import ModelCheckpoint

checkpointer = ModelCheckpoint(filepath='signlanguage.model.hdf5',
                  save_best_only=True)

history = new_model.fit_generator(train_batches, steps_per_epoch=18,
                  validation_data=valid_batches, validation_steps=3,
                  epochs=20, verbose=1, callbacks=[checkpointer])


Epoch 1/150
18/18 [==============================] - 40s 2s/step - loss: 3.2263 - acc:
   0.1833 - val_loss: 2.0674 - val_acc: 0.1667
Epoch 2/150
18/18 [==============================] - 41s 2s/step - loss: 2.0311 - acc:
   0.1833 - val_loss: 1.7330 - val_acc: 0.3000
Epoch 3/150
18/18 [==============================] - 42s 2s/step - loss: 1.5741 - acc:
   0.4500 - val_loss: 1.5577 - val_acc: 0.4000
Epoch 4/150
18/18 [==============================] - 42s 2s/step - loss: 1.3068 - acc:
   0.5111 - val_loss: 0.9856 - val_acc: 0.7333
Epoch 5/150
18/18 [==============================] - 43s 2s/step - loss: 1.1563 - acc:
   0.6389 - val_loss: 0.7637 - val_acc: 0.7333
Epoch 6/150
18/18 [==============================] - 41s 2s/step - loss: 0.8414 - acc:
   0.6722 - val_loss: 0.7550 - val_acc: 0.8000
Epoch 7/150
18/18 [==============================] - 41s 2s/step - loss: 0.5982 - acc:
   0.8444 - val_loss: 0.7910 - val_acc: 0.6667
Epoch 8/150
18/18 [==============================] - 41s 2s/step - loss: 0.3804 - acc:
   0.8722 - val_loss: 0.7376 - val_acc: 0.8667
Epoch 9/150
18/18 [==============================] - 41s 2s/step - loss: 0.5048 - acc:
   0.8222 - val_loss: 0.2677 - val_acc: 0.9000
```

```
Epoch 10/150
18/18 [==============================] - 39s 2s/step - loss: 0.2383 - acc:
    0.9276 - val_loss: 0.2844 - val_acc: 0.9000
Epoch 11/150
18/18 [==============================] - 41s 2s/step - loss: 0.1163 - acc:
    0.9778 - val_loss: 0.0775 - val_acc: 1.0000
Epoch 12/150
18/18 [==============================] - 41s 2s/step - loss: 0.1377 - acc:
    0.9667 - val_loss: 0.5140 - val_acc: 0.9333
Epoch 13/150
18/18 [==============================] - 41s 2s/step - loss: 0.0955 - acc:
    0.9556 - val_loss: 0.1783 - val_acc: 0.9333
Epoch 14/150
18/18 [==============================] - 41s 2s/step - loss: 0.1785 - acc:
    0.9611 - val_loss: 0.0704 - val_acc: 0.9333
Epoch 15/150
18/18 [==============================] - 41s 2s/step - loss: 0.0533 - acc:
    0.9778 - val_loss: 0.4692 - val_acc: 0.8667
Epoch 16/150
18/18 [==============================] - 41s 2s/step - loss: 0.0809 - acc:
    0.9778 - val_loss: 0.0447 - val_acc: 1.0000
Epoch 17/150
18/18 [==============================] - 41s 2s/step - loss: 0.0834 - acc:
    0.9722 - val_loss: 0.0284 - val_acc: 1.0000
Epoch 18/150
18/18 [==============================] - 41s 2s/step - loss: 0.1022 - acc:
    0.9611 - val_loss: 0.0177 - val_acc: 1.0000
Epoch 19/150
18/18 [==============================] - 41s 2s/step - loss: 0.1134 - acc:
    0.9667 - val_loss: 0.0595 - val_acc: 1.0000
Epoch 20/150
18/18 [==============================] - 39s 2s/step - loss: 0.0676 - acc:
    0.9777 - val_loss: 0.0862 - val_acc: 0.9667
```

Notice the training time of each epoch from the verbose output. The model was trained very quickly using regular CPU computing power. Each epoch took approximately 40 seconds, which means it took the model less than 15 minutes to train for 20 epochs.

7   Evaluate the accuracy of the model. Similar to the previous project, we create a `load_dataset()` method to create `test_targets` and `test_tensors` and then use the `evaluate()` method from Keras to run inferences on the test images and get the model accuracy:

```
print('\nTesting loss: {:.4f}\nTesting accuracy:
    {:.4f}'.format(*new_model.evaluate(test_tensors, test_targets)))

Testing loss: 0.0574
Testing accuracy: 0.9800
```

A deeper level of evaluating your model involves creating a confusion matrix. We explained the confusion matrix in chapter 4: it is a table that is often used to describe the performance of a classification model, to provide a deeper understanding of how the model performed on the test dataset. See chapter 4 for details on the different model evaluation metrics. Now, let's build the confusion matrix for our model (see figure 6.20):

```python
from sklearn.metrics import confusion_matrix
import numpy as np

cm_labels = ['0','1','2','3','4','5','6','7','8','9']

cm = confusion_matrix(np.argmax(test_targets, axis=1),
                      np.argmax(new_model.predict(test_tensors), axis=1))
plt.imshow(cm, cmap=plt.cm.Blues)
plt.colorbar()
indexes = np.arange(len(cm_labels))
for i in indexes:
    for j in indexes:
        plt.text(j, i, cm[i, j])
plt.xticks(indexes, cm_labels, rotation=90)
plt.xlabel('Predicted label')
plt.yticks(indexes, cm_labels)
plt.ylabel('True label')
plt.title('Confusion matrix')
plt.show()
```

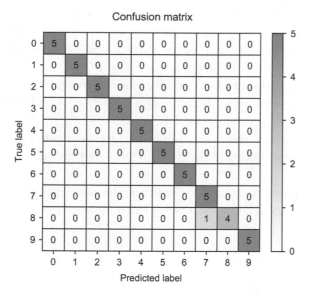

Figure 6.20 Confusion matrix for the sign language classifier

To read this confusion matrix, look at the number on the Predicted Label axis and check whether it was correctly classified on the True Label axis. For example, look at number 0 on the Predicted Label axis: all five images were classified as 0, and no images were mistakenly classified as any other number. Similarly, go through the rest of the numbers on the Predicted Label axis. You will notice that the model successfully made the correct predictions for all the test images except the image with true label = 8. In that case, the model mistakenly classified an image of number 8 as number = 7.

Summary

- Transfer learning is usually the go-to approach when starting a classification and object detection project, especially when you don't have a lot of training data.
- Transfer learning migrates the knowledge learned from the source dataset to the target dataset, to save training time and computational cost.
- The neural network learns the features in your dataset step by step in increasing levels of complexity. The deeper you go through the network layers, the more image-specific the features that are learned.
- Early layers in the network learn low-level features like lines, blobs, and edges. The output of the first layer becomes input to the second layer, which produces higher-level features. The next layer assembles the output of the previous layer into parts of familiar objects, and a subsequent layer detects the objects.
- The three main transfer learning approaches are using a pretrained network as a classifier, using a pretrained network as a feature extractor, and fine-tuning.
- Using a pretrained network as a classifier means using the network directly to classify new images without freezing layers or applying model training.
- Using a pretrained network as a feature extractor means freezing the classifier part of the network and retraining the new classifier.
- Fine-tuning means freezing a few of the network layers that are used for feature extraction, and jointly training both the non-frozen layers and the newly added classifier layers of the pretrained model.
- The transferability of features from one network to another is a function of the size of the target data and the domain similarity between the source and target data.
- Generally, fine-tuning parameters use a smaller learning rate, while training the output layer from scratch can use a larger learning rate.

Object detection with R-CNN, SSD, and YOLO

This chapter covers

- Understanding image classification vs. object detection

- Understanding the general framework of object detection projects

- Using object detection algorithms like R-CNN, SSD, and YOLO

In the previous chapters, we explained how we can use deep neural networks for image classification tasks. In image classification, we assume that there is only one main target object in the image, and the model's sole focus is to identify the target category. However, in many situations, we are interested in multiple targets in the image. We want to not only classify them, but also obtain their specific positions in the image. In computer vision, we refer to such tasks as *object detection*. Figure 7.1 explains the difference between image classification and object detection tasks.

Object detection is a CV task that involves both main tasks: localizing one or more objects within an image and classifying each object in the image (see table 7.1). This is done by drawing a bounding box around the identified object with its predicted class. This means the system doesn't just predict the class of the image, as in image classification tasks; it also predicts the coordinates of the bounding box that

Image classification

Object detection
(classification and localization)

Cat

Cat, Cat, Duck, Dog

Figure 7.1   Image classification vs. object detection tasks. In classification tasks, the classifier outputs the class probability (cat), whereas in object detection tasks, the detector outputs the bounding box coordinates that localize the detected objects (four boxes in this example) and their predicted classes (two cats, one duck, and one dog).

Table 7.1   Image classification vs. object detection

Image classification	Object detection
The goal is to predict the type or class of an object in an image.	The goal is to predict the location of objects in an image via bounding boxes and the classes of the located objects.

■ Input: an image with a single object
■ Output: a class label (cat, dog, etc.)
■ Example output: class probability (for example, 84% cat)
	■ Input: an image with one or more objects
	■ Output: one or more bounding boxes (defined by coordinates) and a class label for each bounding box
	■ Example output for an image with two objects:
	    – box1 coordinates (x, y, w, h) and class probability
	    – box2 coordinates and class probability
	
	Note that the image coordinates (x, y, w, h) are as follows: (x and y) are the coordinates of the bounding-box center point, and (w and h) are the width and height of the box.

fits the detected object. This is a challenging CV task because it requires both successful object localization, in order to locate and draw a bounding box around each object in an image, and object classification to predict the correct class of object that was localized.

Object detection is widely used in many fields. For example, in self-driving technology, we need to plan routes by identifying the locations of vehicles, pedestrians, roads, and obstacles in a captured video image. Robots often perform this type of task to detect targets of interest. And systems in the security field need to detect abnormal targets, such as intruders or bombs.

This chapter's layout is as follows:

1 We will explore the general framework of the object detection algorithms.

2 We will dive deep into three of the most popular detection algorithms: the R-CNN family of networks, SSD, and the YOLO family of networks.

3 We will use what we've learned in a real-world project to train an end-to-end object detector.

By the end of this chapter, we will have gained an understanding of how DL is applied to object detection, and how the different object detection models inspire and diverge from one another. Let's get started!

7.1 *General object detection framework*

Before we jump into the object detection systems like R-CNN, SSD, and YOLO, let's discuss the general framework of these systems to understand the high-level workflow that DL-based systems follow to detect objects and the metrics they use to evaluate their detection performance. Don't worry about the code implementation details of object detectors yet. The goal of this section is to give you an overview of how different object detection systems approach this task and introduce you to a new way of thinking about this problem and a set of new concepts to set you up to understand the DL architectures that we will explain in sections 7.2, 7.3, and 7.4.

Typically, an object detection framework has four components:

1 *Region proposal*—An algorithm or a DL model is used to generate regions of interest (RoIs) to be further processed by the system. These are regions that the network believes might contain an object; the output is a large number of bounding boxes, each of which has an *objectness score*. Boxes with large objectness scores are then passed along the network layers for further processing.

2 *Feature extraction and network predictions*—Visual features are extracted for each of the bounding boxes. They are evaluated, and it is determined whether and which objects are present in the proposals based on visual features (for example, an object classification component).

3 *Non-maximum suppression (NMS)*—In this step, the model has likely found multiple bounding boxes for the same object. NMS helps avoid repeated detection of the same instance by combining overlapping boxes into a single bounding box for each object.

4 *Evaluation metrics*—Similar to accuracy, precision, and recall metrics in image classification tasks (see chapter 4), object detection systems have their own metrics to evaluate their detection performance. In this section, we will explain the most popular metrics, like mean average precision (mAP), precision-recall curve (PR curve), and intersection over union (IoU).

Now, let's dive one level deeper into each one of these components to build an intuition about what their goals are.

7.1.1   *Region proposals*

In this step, the system looks at the image and proposes RoIs for further analysis. RoIs are regions that the system believes have a high likelihood of containing an object, called the *objectness score* (figure 7.2). Regions with high objectness scores are passed to the next steps; regions with low scores are abandoned.

Figure 7.2   Regions of interest (RoIs) proposed by the system. Regions with high objectness score represent areas of high likelihood to contain objects (foreground), and the ones with low objectness score are ignored because they have a low likelihood of containing objects (background).

There are several approaches to generate region proposals. Originally, the *selective search* algorithm was used to generate object proposals; we will talk more about this algorithm when we discuss the R-CNN network. Other approaches use more complex visual features extracted from the image by a deep neural network to generate regions (for example, based on the features from a DL model).

We will talk in more detail about how different object detection systems approach this task. The important thing to note is that this step produces a lot (thousands) of bounding boxes to be further analyzed and classified by the network. During this step, the network analyzes these regions in the image and classifies each region as *foreground* (object) or *background* (no object) based on its objectness score. If the objectness score is above a certain threshold, then this region is considered a foreground and pushed forward in the network. Note that this threshold is configurable based on your problem. If the threshold is too low, your network will exhaustively generate all possible proposals, and you will have a better chance of detecting all objects in the image. On the flip side, this is very computationally expensive and will slow down detection. So, the trade-off with generating region proposals is the number of regions versus computational complexity—and the right approach is to use problem-specific information to reduce the number of RoIs.

7.1.2 Network predictions

This component includes the pretrained CNN network that is used for feature extraction to extract features from the input image that are representative for the task at hand and to use these features to determine the class of the image. In object detection frameworks, people typically use pretrained image classification models to extract visual features, as these tend to generalize fairly well. For example, a model trained on the MS COCO or ImageNet dataset is able to extract fairly generic features.

In this step, the network analyzes all the regions that have been identified as having a high likelihood of containing an object and makes two predictions for each region:

- *Bounding-box prediction*—The coordinates that locate the box surrounding the object. The bounding box coordinates are represented as the tuple (x, y, w, h), where x and y are the coordinates of the center point of the bounding box and w and h are the width and height of the box.
- *Class prediction*: The classic softmax function that predicts the class probability for each object.

Since thousands of regions are proposed, each object will always have multiple bounding boxes surrounding it with the correct classification. For example, take a look at the image of the dog in figure 7.3. The network was clearly able to find the object (dog) and successfully classify it. But the detection fired a total of five times because

Figure 7.3 The bounding-box detector produces more than one bounding box for an object. We want to consolidate these boxes into one bounding box that fits the object the most.

the dog was present in the five RoIs produced in the previous step: hence the five bounding boxes around the dog in the figure. Although the detector was able to successfully locate the dog in the image and classify it correctly, this is not exactly what we need. We need just one bounding box for each object for most problems. In some problems, we only want the one box that fits the object the most. What if we are building a system to count dogs in an image? Our current system will count five dogs. We don't want that. This is when the non-maximum suppression technique comes in handy.

7.1.3   *Non-maximum suppression (NMS)*

As you can see in figure 7.4, one of the problems of an object detection algorithm is that it may find multiple detections of the same object. So, instead of creating only one bounding box around the object, it draws multiple boxes for the same object. NMS is a technique that makes sure the detection algorithm detects each object only once. As the name implies, NMS looks at all the boxes surrounding an object to find the box that has the *maximum* prediction probability, and it *suppresses* or eliminates the other boxes (hence the name).

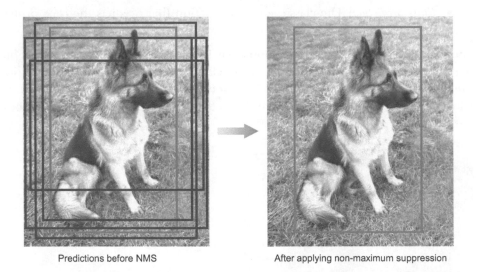

Predictions before NMS   After applying non-maximum suppression

Figure 7.4   Multiple regions are proposed for the same object. After NMS, only the box that fits the object the best remains; the rest are ignored, as they have large overlaps with the selected box.

The general idea of NMS is to reduce the number of candidate boxes to only one bounding box for each object. For example, if the object in the frame is fairly large and more than 2,000 object proposals have been generated, it is quite likely that some of them will have significant overlap with each other and the object.

Let's see the steps of how the NMS algorithm works:

1 Discard all bounding boxes that have predictions that are less than a certain threshold, called the *confidence threshold*. This threshold is tunable, which means a box will be suppressed if the prediction probability is less than the set threshold.

2 Look at all the remaining boxes, and select the bounding box with the highest probability.

3 Calculate the overlap of the remaining boxes that have the same class prediction. Bounding boxes that have high overlap with each other and that predict the same class are averaged together. This overlap metric is called *intersection over union (IoU)*. IoU is explained in detail in the next section.

4 Suppress any box that has an IoU value smaller than a certain threshold (called the *NMS threshold*). Usually the NMS threshold is equal to 0.5, but it is tunable as well if you want to output fewer or more bounding boxes.

NMS techniques are typically standard across the different detection frameworks, but it is an important step that may require tweaking hyperparameters such as the confidence threshold and the NMS threshold based on the scenario.

7.1.4   *Object-detector evaluation metrics*

When evaluating the performance of an object detector, we use two main evaluation metrics: frames per second and mean average precision.

FRAMES PER SECOND (FPS) TO MEASURE DETECTION SPEED

The most common metric used to measure detection speed is the number of frames per second (FPS). For example, Faster R-CNN operates at only 7 FPS, whereas SSD operates at 59 FPS. In benchmarking experiments, you will see the authors of a paper state their network results as: "Network X achieves mAP of Y% at Z FPS," where X is the network name, Y is the mAP percentage, and Z is the FPS.

MEAN AVERAGE PRECISION (MAP) TO MEASURE NETWORK PRECISION

The most common evaluation metric used in object recognition tasks is *mean average precision (mAP)*. It is a percentage from 0 to 100, and higher values are typically better, but its value is different from the accuracy metric used in classification.

To understand how mAP is calculated, you first need to understand intersection over union (IoU) and the precision-recall curve (PR curve). Let's explain IoU and the PR curve and then come back to mAP.

INTERSECTION OVER UNION (IOU)

This measure evaluates the overlap between two bounding boxes: the ground truth bounding box ($B_{\text{ground truth}}$) and the predicted bounding box ($B_{\text{predicted}}$). By applying the IoU, we can tell whether a detection is valid (True Positive) or not (False Positive). Figure 7.5 illustrates the IoU between a ground truth bounding box and a predicted bounding box.

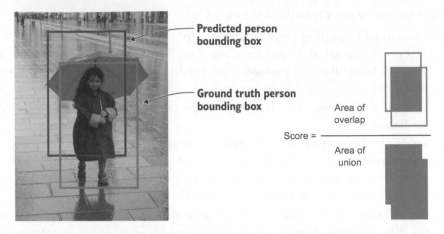

Figure 7.5   The IoU score is the overlap between the ground truth bounding box and the predicted bounding box.

The intersection over the union value ranges from 0 (no overlap at all) to 1 (the two bounding boxes overlap each other 100%). The higher the overlap between the two bounding boxes (IoU value), the better (figure 7.6).

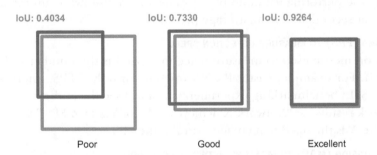

Figure 7.6   IoU scores range from 0 (no overlap) to 1 (100% overlap). The higher the overlap (IoU) between the two bounding boxes, the better.

To calculate the IoU of a prediction, we need the following:

- The ground truth bounding box ($B_{\text{ground truth}}$): the hand-labeled bounding box created during the labeling process
- The predicted bounding box ($B_{\text{predicted}}$) from our model

We calculate IoU by dividing the area of overlap by the area of the union, as in the following equation:

$$\text{IoU} = \frac{B_{\text{ground truth}} \cap B_{\text{predicted}}}{B_{\text{ground truth}} \cup B_{\text{predicted}}}$$

IoU is used to define a *correct prediction*, meaning a prediction (True Positive) that has an IoU greater than some threshold. This threshold is a tunable value depending on the challenge, but 0.5 is a standard value. For example, some challenges, like Microsoft COCO, use mAP@0.5 (IoU threshold of 0.5) or mAP@0.75 (IoU threshold of 0.75). If the IoU value is above this threshold, the prediction is considered a True Positive (TP); and if it is below the threshold, it is considered a False Positive (FP).

PRECISION-RECALL CURVE (PR CURVE)

With the TP and FP defined, we can now calculate the precision and recall of our detection for a given class across the testing dataset. As explained in chapter 4, we calculate the precision and recall as follows (recall that FN stands for False Negative):

$$\text{Recall} = \frac{TP}{TP + FN}$$

$$\text{Precision} = \frac{TP}{TP + FP}$$

After calculating the precision and recall for all classes, the PR curve is then plotted as shown in figure 7.7.

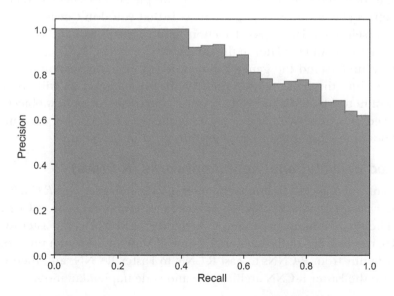

Figure 7.7 A precision-recall curve is used to evaluate the performance of an object detector.

The PR curve is a good way to evaluate the performance of an object detector, as the confidence is changed by plotting a curve for each object class. A detector is considered good if its precision stays high as recall increases, which means if you vary the confidence threshold, the precision and recall will still be high. On the other hand, a poor detector needs to increase the number of FPs (lower precision) in order to achieve a high recall. That's why the PR curve usually starts with high precision values, decreasing as recall increases.

Now that we have the PR curve, we can calculate the average precision (AP) by calculating the area under the curve (AUC). Finally, the mAP for object detection is the average of the AP calculated for all the classes. It is also important to note that some research papers use AP and mAP interchangeably.

RECAP

To recap, the mAP is calculated as follows:

1 Get each bounding box's associated objectness score (probability of the box containing an object).
2 Calculate precision and recall.
3 Compute the PR curve for each class by varying the score threshold.
4 Calculate the AP: the area under the PR curve. In this step, the AP is computed for each class.
5 Calculate the mAP: the average AP over all the different classes.

The last thing to note about mAP is that it is more complicated to calculate than other traditional metrics like accuracy. The good news is that you don't need to compute mAP values yourself: most DL object detection implementations handle computing the mAP for you, as you will see later in this chapter.

Now that we understand the general framework of object detection algorithms, let's dive deeper into three of the most popular. In this chapter, we will discuss the R-CNN family of networks, SSD, and YOLO networks in detail to see how object detectors have evolved over time. We will also examine the pros and cons of each network so you can choose the most appropriate algorithm for your problem.

7.2 *Region-based convolutional neural networks (R-CNNs)*

The R-CNN family of object detection techniques usually referred to as *R-CNNs*, which is short for *region-based convolutional neural networks*, was developed by Ross Girshick et al. in 2014.[1] The R-CNN family expanded to include Fast-RCNN[2] and Faster-RCN[3] in 2015 and 2016, respectively. In this section, I'll quickly walk you through the evolution of the R-CNN family from R-CNNs to Fast R-CNN to Faster R-CNN, and then we will dive deeper into the Faster R-CNN architecture and code implementation.

---

[1] Ross Girshick, Jeff Donahue, Trevor Darrell, and Jitendra Malik, "Rich Feature Hierarchies for Accurate Object Detection and Semantic Segmentation," 2014, http://arxiv.org/abs/1311.2524.

[2] Ross Girshick, "Fast R-CNN," 2015, http://arxiv.org/abs/1504.08083.

[3] Shaoqing Ren, Kaiming He, Ross Girshick, and Jian Sun, "Faster R-CNN: Towards Real-Time Object Detection with Region Proposal Networks," 2016, http://arxiv.org/abs/1506.01497.

7.2.1   R-CNN

R-CNN is the least sophisticated region-based architecture in its family, but it is the basis for understanding how multiple object-recognition algorithms work for all of them. It was one of the first large, successful applications of convolutional neural networks to the problem of object detection and localization, and it paved the way for the other advanced detection algorithms. The approach was demonstrated on benchmark datasets, achieving then-state-of-the-art results on the PASCAL VOC-2012 dataset and the ILSVRC 2013 object detection challenge. Figure 7.8 shows a summary of the R-CNN model architecture.

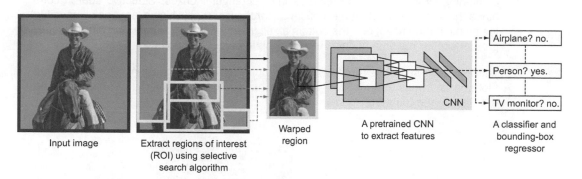

Figure 7.8   Summary of the R-CNN model architecture. (Modified from Girshick et al., "Rich Feature Hierarchies for Accurate Object Detection and Semantic Segmentation.")

The R-CNN model consists of four components:

- *Extract regions of interest*—Also known as *extracting region proposals*. These regions have a high probability of containing an object. An algorithm called *selective search* scans the input image to find regions that contain blobs, and proposes them as RoIs to be processed by the next modules in the pipeline. The proposed RoIs are then warped to have a fixed size; they usually vary in size, but as we learned in previous chapters, CNNs require a fixed input image size.
- *Feature extraction module*—We run a pretrained convolutional network on top of the region proposals to extract features from each candidate region. This is the typical CNN feature extractor that we learned about in previous chapters.
- *Classification module*—We train a classifier like a support vector machine (SVM), a traditional machine learning algorithm, to classify candidate detections based on the extracted features from the previous step.
- *Localization module*—Also known as a *bounding-box regressor*. Let's take a step back to understand regression. ML problems are categorized as classification or regression problems. Classification algorithms output discrete, predefined classes (dog, cat, elephant), whereas regression algorithms output continuous value predictions. In this module, we want to predict the location and size of the bounding

box that surrounds the object. The bounding box is represented by identifying four values: the x and y coordinates of the box's origin (x, y), the width, and the height of the box (w, h). Putting this together, the regressor predicts the four real-valued numbers that define the bounding box as the following tuple: (x, y, w, h).

Selective search

Selective search is a greedy search algorithm that is used to provide region proposals that potentially contain objects. It tries to find areas that might contain an object by combining similar pixels and textures into rectangular boxes. Selective search combines the strength of both the *exhaustive search algorithm* (which examines all possible locations in the image) and the *bottom-up segmentation algorithm* (which hierarchically groups similar regions) to capture all possible object locations.

The selective search algorithm works by applying a segmentation algorithm to find blobs in an image, in order to figure out what could be an object (see the image on the right in the following figure).

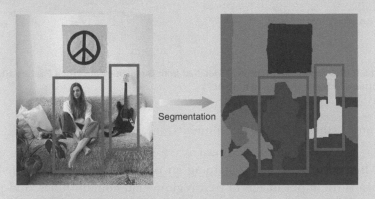

Segmentation

The selective search algorithm looks for blob-like areas in the image to extract regions. At right, the segmentation algorithm defines blobs that could be objects. Then the selective search algorithm selects these areas to be passed along for further investigation.

Bottom-up segmentation recursively combines these groups of regions together into larger ones to create about 2,000 areas to be investigated, as follows:

1 The similarities between all neighboring regions are calculated.
2 The two most similar regions are grouped together, and new similarities are calculated between the resulting region and its neighbors.
3 This process is repeated until the entire object is covered in a single region.

Note that a review of the selective search algorithm and how it calculates regions' similarity is outside the scope of this book. If you are interested in learning more

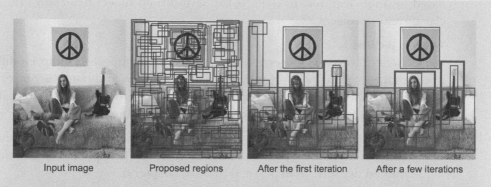

| Input image | Proposed regions | After the first iteration | After a few iterations |

An example of bottom-up segmentation using the selective search algorithm. It combines similar regions in every iteration until the entire object is covered in a single region.

about this technique, you can refer to the original paper.[a] For the purpose of understanding R-CNNs, you can treat the selective search algorithm as a black box that intelligently scans the image and proposes RoI locations for us to use.

[a] J.R.R. Uijlings, K.E.A. van de Sande, T. Gevers, and A.W.M. Smeulders, "Selective Search for Object Recognition," 2012, www.huppelen.nl/publications/selectiveSearchDraft.pdf.

Figure 7.9 illustrates the R-CNN architecture in an intuitive way. As you can see, the network first proposes RoIs, then extracts features, and then classifies those regions

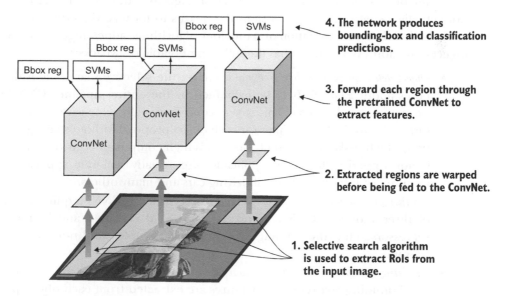

Figure 7.9 Illustration of the R-CNN architecture. Each proposed RoI is passed through the CNN to extract features, followed by a bounding-box regressor and an SVM classifier to produce the network output prediction.

based on their features. In essence, we have turned object detection into an image classification problem.

TRAINING R-CNNs

We learned in the previous section that R-CNNs are composed of four modules: selective search region proposal, feature extractor, classifier, and bounding-box regressor. All of the R-CNN modules need to be trained except the selective search algorithm. So, in order to train R-CNNs, we need to do the following:

1 Train the feature extractor CNN. This is a typical CNN training process. We either train a network from scratch, which rarely happens, or fine-tune a pretrained network, as we learned to do in chapter 6.

2 Train the SVM classifier. The SVM algorithm is not covered in this book, but it is a traditional ML classifier that is no different from DL classifiers in the sense that it needs to be trained on labeled data.

3 Train the bounding-box regressors. This model outputs four real-valued numbers for each of the K object classes to tighten the region bounding boxes.

Looking through the R-CNN learning steps, you could easily find out that training an R-CNN model is expensive and slow. The training process involves training three separate modules without much shared computation. This multistage pipeline training is one of the disadvantages of R-CNNs, as we will see next.

DISADVANTAGES OF R-CNN

R-CNN is very simple to understand, and it achieved state-of-the-art results when it first came out, especially when using deep ConvNets to extract features. However, it is not actually a single end-to-end system that learns to localize via a deep neural network. Rather, it is a combination of standalone algorithms, added together to perform object detection. As a result, it has the following notable drawbacks:

- *Object detection is very slow.* For each image, the selective search algorithm proposes about 2,000 RoIs to be examined by the entire pipeline (CNN feature extractor and classifier). This is very computationally expensive because it performs a ConvNet forward pass for each object proposal without sharing computation, which makes it incredibly slow. This high computation need means R-CNN is not a good fit for many applications, especially real-time applications that require fast inferences like self-driving cars and many others.

- *Training is a multi-stage pipeline.* As discussed earlier, R-CNNs require the training of three modules: CNN feature extractor, SVM classifier, and bounding-box regressors. Thus the training process is very complex and not an end-to-end training.

- *Training is expensive in terms of space and time.* When training the SVM classifier and bounding-box regressor, features are extracted from each object proposal in each image and written to disk. With very deep networks, such as VGG16, the training process for a few thousand images takes days using GPUs. The training process is expensive in space as well, because the extracted features require hundreds of gigabytes of storage.

What we need is an end-to-end DL system that fixes the disadvantages of R-CNN while improving its speed and accuracy.

7.2.2 Fast R-CNN

Fast R-CNN was an immediate descendant of R-CNN, developed in 2015 by Ross Girshick. Fast R-CNN resembled the R-CNN technique in many ways but improved on its detection speed while also increasing detection accuracy through two main changes:

- Instead of starting with the regions proposal module and then using the feature extraction module, like R-CNN, Fast-RCNN proposes that we apply the CNN feature extractor first to the entire input image and then propose regions. This way, we run only one ConvNet over the entire image instead of 2,000 ConvNets over 2,000 overlapping regions.
- It extends the ConvNet's job to do the classification part as well, by replacing the traditional SVM machine learning algorithm with a softmax layer. This way, we have a single model to perform both tasks: feature extraction and object classification.

FAST R-CNN ARCHITECTURE

As shown in figure 7.10, Fast R-CNN generates region proposals based on the last feature map of the network, not from the original image like R-CNN. As a result, we can train just one ConvNet for the entire image. In addition, instead of training many different SVM algorithms to classify each object class, a single softmax layer outputs the class probabilities directly. Now we only have one neural net to train, as opposed to one neural net and many SVMs.

The architecture of Fast R-CNN consists of the following modules:

1 *Feature extractor module*—The network starts with a ConvNet to extract features from the full image.

2 *RoI extractor*—The selective search algorithm proposes about 2,000 region candidates per image.

3 *RoI pooling layer*—This is a new component that was introduced to extract a fixed-size window from the feature map before feeding the RoIs to the fully connected layers. It uses max pooling to convert the features inside any valid RoI into a small feature map with a fixed spatial extent of height × width ($H \times W$). The RoI pooling layer will be explained in more detail in the Faster R-CNN section; for now, understand that it is applied on the last feature map layer extracted from the CNN, and its goal is to extract fixed-size RoIs to feed to the fully connected layers and then the output layers.

4 *Two-head output layer*—The model branches into two heads:
  – A softmax classifier layer that outputs a discrete probability distribution per RoI
  – A bounding-box regressor layer to predict offsets relative to the original RoI

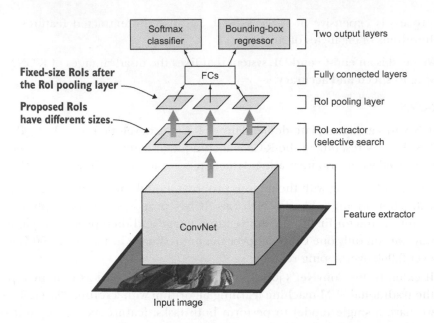

Figure 7.10   The Fast R-CNN architecture consists of a feature extractor ConvNet, RoI extractor, RoI pooling layers, fully connected layers, and a two-head output layer. Note that, unlike R-CNNs, Fast R-CNNs apply the feature extractor to the entire input image before applying the regions proposal module.

MULTI-TASK LOSS FUNCTION IN FAST R-CNNS

Since Fast R-CNN is an end-to-end learning architecture to learn the class of an object as well as the associated bounding box position and size, the loss is *multi-task loss*. With multi-task loss, the output has the softmax classifier and bounding-box regressor, as shown in figure 7.10.

In any optimization problem, we need to define a loss function that our optimizer algorithm is trying to minimize. (Chapter 2 gives more details about optimization and loss functions.) In object detection problems, our goal is to optimize for two goals: object classification and object localization. Therefore, we have two loss functions in this problem: L_{cls} for the classification loss and L_{loc} for the bounding box prediction defining the object location.

A Fast R-CNN network has two sibling output layers with two loss functions:

- *Classification*—The first outputs a discrete probability distribution (per RoI) over $K+1$ categories (we add one class for the background). The probability P is computed by a softmax over the $K+1$ outputs of a fully connected layer. The classification loss function is a log loss for the true class u

$$L_{cls}(p,u) = -\log p_u$$

where u is the true label, $u \in 0, 1, 2, \ldots (K+1)$; where u = 0 is the background; and p is the discrete probability distribution per RoI over $K+1$ classes.

- *Regression*—The second sibling layer outputs bounding box regression offsets $v = (x, y, w, h)$ for each of the K object classes. The loss function is the loss for bounding box for class u

$$L_{loc}(t^u, u) = \sum L1_{\text{smooth}}(t_i^u - v_i)$$

where:

- v is the true bounding box, $v = (x, y, w, h)$.
- t^u is the prediction bounding box correction:

$$t^u = (t_x^u, t_y^u, t_w^u, t_h^u)$$

- $L1_{\text{smooth}}$ is the bounding box loss that measures the difference between t_i^u and v_i using the smooth L1 loss function. It is a robust function and is claimed to be less sensitive to outliers than other regression losses like L2.

The overall loss function is

$$L = L_{cls} + L_{loc}$$

$$L(p, u, t^u, v) = L_{cls}(p, u) + [u \geq 1] l_{\text{box}}(t^u, v)$$

Note that $[u \geq 1]$ is added before the regression loss to indicate 0 when the region inspected doesn't contain any object and contains a background. It is a way of ignoring the bounding box regression when the classifier labels the region as a background. The indicator function $[u \geq 1]$ is defined as

$$[u \geq 1] = \begin{cases} 1 & \text{if } u \geq 1 \\ 0 & \text{otherwise} \end{cases}$$

DISADVANTAGES OF FAST R-CNN

Fast R-CNN is much faster in terms of testing time, because we don't have to feed 2,000 region proposals to the convolutional neural network for every image. Instead, a convolution operation is done only once per image, and a feature map is generated from it. Training is also faster because all the components are in one CNN network: feature extractor, object classifier, and bounding-box regressor. However, there is a big bottleneck remaining: the selective search algorithm for generating region proposals is very slow and is generated separately by another model. The last step to achieve a complete end-to-end object detection system using DL is to find a way to combine the region proposal algorithm into our end-to-end DL network. This is what Faster R-CNN does, as we will see next.

7.2.3 *Faster R-CNN*

Faster R-CNN is the third iteration of the R-CNN family, developed in 2016 by Shaoqing Ren et al. Similar to Fast R-CNN, the image is provided as an input to a convolutional network that provides a convolutional feature map. Instead of using a selective search algorithm on the feature map to identify the region proposals, a *region proposal network (RPN)* is used to predict the region proposals as part of the training process. The predicted region proposals are then reshaped using an RoI pooling layer and used to classify the image within the proposed region and predict the offset values for the bounding boxes. These improvements both reduce the number of region proposals and accelerate the test-time operation of the model to near real-time with then-state-of-the-art performance.

FASTER R-CNN ARCHITECTURE

The architecture of Faster R-CNN can be described using two main networks:

- *Region proposal network (RPN)*—Selective search is replaced by a ConvNet that proposes RoIs from the last feature maps of the feature extractor to be considered for investigation. The RPN has two outputs: the objectness score (object or no object) and the box location.
- *Fast R-CNN*—It consists of the typical components of Fast R-CNN:
  - Base network for the feature extractor: a typical pretrained CNN model to extract features from the input image
  - RoI pooling layer to extract fixed-size RoIs
  - Output layer that contains two fully connected layers: a softmax classifier to output the class probability and a bounding box regression CNN for the bounding box predictions

As you can see in figure 7.11, the input image is presented to the network, and its features are extracted via a pretrained CNN. These features, in parallel, are sent to two different components of the Faster R-CNN architecture:

- The RPN to determine where in the image a potential object could be. At this point, we do not know what the object is, just that there is potentially an object at a certain location in the image.
- RoI pooling to extract fixed-size windows of features.

The output is then passed into two fully connected layers: one for the object classifier and one for the bounding box coordinate predictions to obtain our final localizations.

This architecture achieves an end-to-end trainable, complete object detection pipeline where all of the required components are inside the network:

- Base network feature extractor
- Regions proposal
- RoI pooling
- Object classification
- Bounding-box regressor

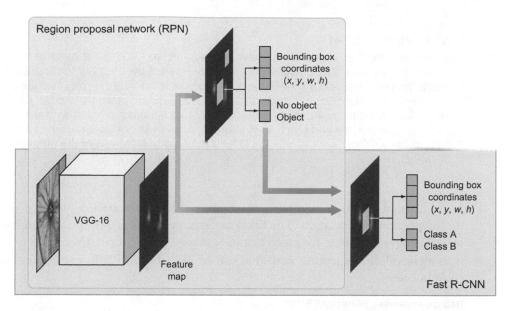

Figure 7.11 The Faster R-CNN architecture has two main components: an RPN that identifies regions that may contain objects of interest and their approximate location, and a Fast R-CNN network that classifies objects and refines their location defined using bounding boxes. The two components share the convolutional layers of the pretrained VGG16.

BASE NETWORK TO EXTRACT FEATURES

Similar to Fast R-CNN, the first step is to use a pretrained CNN and slice off its classification part. The base network is used to extract features from the input image. We covered how this works in detail in chapter 6. In this component, you can use any of the popular CNN architectures based on the problem you are trying to solve. The original Faster R-CNN paper used ZF[4] and VGG[5] pretrained networks on ImageNet; but since then, there have been lots of different networks with a varying number of weights. For example, MobileNet,[6] a smaller and efficient network architecture optimized for speed, has approximately 3.3 million parameters, whereas ResNet-152 (152 layers)—once the state of the art in the ImageNet classification competition—has around 60 million. Most recently, new architectures like DenseNet[7] are both improving results and reducing the number of parameters.

---

[4] Matthew D. Zeiler and Rob Fergus, "Visualizing and Understanding Convolutional Networks," 2013, http://arxiv.org/abs/1311.2901.

[5] Karen Simonyan and Andrew Zisserman, "Very Deep Convolutional Networks for Large-Scale Image Recognition," 2014, http://arxiv.org/abs/1409.1556.

[6] Andrew G. Howard, Menglong Zhu, Bo Chen, Dmitry Kalenichenko, Weijun Wang, Tobias Weyand, Marco Andreetto, and Hartwig Adam, "MobileNets: Efficient Convolutional Neural Networks for Mobile Vision Applications," 2017, http://arxiv.org/abs/1704.04861.

[7] Gao Huang, Zhuang Liu, Laurens van der Maaten, and Kilian Q. Weinberger, "Densely Connected Convolutional Networks," 2016, http://arxiv.org/abs/1608.06993.

VGGNet vs. ResNet

Nowadays, ResNet architectures have mostly replaced VGG as a base network for extracting features. The obvious advantage of ResNet over VGG is that it has many more layers (is deeper), giving it more capacity to learn very complex features. This is true for the classification task and should be equally true in the case of object detection. In addition, ResNet makes it easy to train deep models with the use of residual connections and batch normalization, which was not invented when VGG was first released. Please revisit chapter 5 for a more detailed review of the different CNN architectures.

As we learned in earlier chapters, each convolutional layer creates abstractions based on the previous information. The first layer usually learns edges, the second finds patterns in edges to activate for more complex shapes, and so forth. Eventually we end up with a convolutional feature map that can be fed to the RPN to extract regions that contain objects.

REGION PROPOSAL NETWORK (RPN)

The RPN identifies regions that could potentially contain objects of interest, based on the last feature map of the pretrained convolutional neural network. An RPN is also known as an *attention network* because it guides the network's attention to interesting regions in the image. Faster R-CNN uses an RPN to bake the region proposal directly into the R-CNN architecture instead of running a selective search algorithm to extract RoIs.

The architecture of the RPN is composed of two layers (figure 7.12):

- A 3 × 3 fully convolutional layer with 512 channels
- Two parallel 1 × 1 convolutional layers: a classification layer that is used to predict whether the region contains an object (the score of it being background or foreground), and a layer for regression or bounding box prediction.

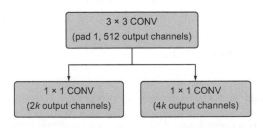

Figure 7.12 Convolutional implementation of an RPN architecture, where *k* is the number of anchors

Fully convolutional networks (FCNs)

One important aspect of object detection networks is that they should be fully convolutional. A fully convolutional neural network means that the network does not contain any fully connected layers, typically found at the end of a network prior to making output predictions.

In the context of image classification, removing the fully connected layers is normally accomplished by applying average pooling across the entire volume prior to using a single dense softmax classifier to output the final predictions. An FCN has two main benefits:

- It is faster because it contains only convolution operations and no fully connected layers.
- It can accept images of any spatial resolution (width and height), provided the image and network can fit into the available memory.

Being an FCN makes the network invariant to the size of the input image. However, in practice, we might want to stick to a constant input size due to issues that only become apparent when we are implementing the algorithm. A significant such problem is that if we want to process images in batches (because images in batches can be processed in parallel by the GPU, leading to speed boosts), all of the images must have a fixed height and width.

The 3 × 3 convolutional layer is applied on the last feature map of the base network where a sliding window of size 3 × 3 is passed over the feature map. The output is then passed to two 1 × 1 convolutional layers: a classifier and a bounding-box regressor. Note that the classifier and the regressor of the RPN are not trying to predict the class of the object and its bounding box; this comes later, after the RPN. Remember, the goal of the RPN is to determine whether the region has an object to be investigated afterward by the fully connected layers. In the RPN, we use a binary classifier to predict the objectness score of the region, to determine the probability of this region being a foreground (contains an object) or a background (doesn't contain an object). It basically looks at the region and asks, "Does this region contain an object?" If the answer is yes, then the region is passed along for further investigation by RoI pooling and the final output layers (see figure 7.13).

How does the regressor predict the bounding box?

To answer this question, let's first define the bounding box. It is the box that surrounds the object and is identified by the tuple (x, y, w, h), where x and y are the coordinates in the image that describes the center of the bounding box and h and w are the height and width of the bounding box. Researchers have found that defining the (x, y) coordinates of the center point can be challenging because we have to enforce some rules to make sure the network predicts values *inside* the boundaries of the image. Instead, we can create reference boxes called *anchor boxes* in the image and make the regression layer predict offsets from these boxes called

Figure 7.13 The RPN classifier predicts the objectness score, which is the probability of an image containing an object (foreground) or a background.

Low objectness score (background)

High objectness score (foreground)

deltas (Δ_x, Δ_y, Δ_w, Δ_h) to adjust the anchor boxes to better fit the object to get final proposals (figure 7.14).

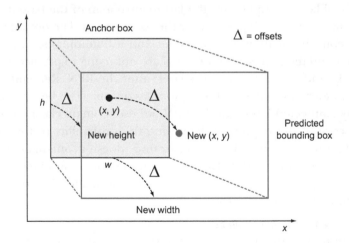

Figure 7.14 Illustration of predicting the delta shift from the anchor boxes and the bounding box coordinates

Anchor boxes

Using a sliding window approach, the RPN generates k regions for each location in the feature map. These regions are represented as *anchor boxes*. The anchors are centered in the middle of their corresponding sliding window and differ in terms of scale and aspect ratio to cover a wide variety of objects. They are fixed bounding boxes that are placed throughout the image to be used for reference when first predicting object locations. In their paper, Ren et. al. generated nine anchor boxes that all had the same center but that had three different aspect ratios and three different scales.

Figure 7.15 shows an example of how anchor boxes are applied. Anchors are at the center of the sliding windows; each window has k anchor boxes with the anchor at their center.

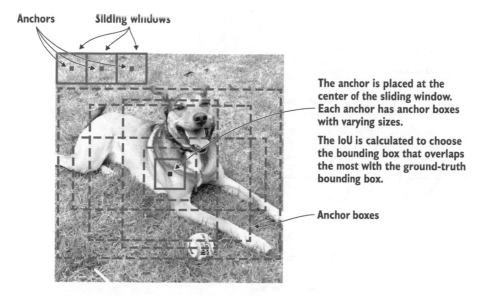

Figure 7.15 Anchors are at the center of each sliding window. IoU is calculated to select the bounding box that overlaps the most with the ground truth.

Training the RPN

The RPN is trained to classify an anchor box to output an objectness score and to approximate the four coordinates of the object (location parameters). It is trained using human annotators to label the bounding boxes. A labeled box is called the *ground truth*.

For each anchor box, the overlap probability value (p) is computed, which indicates how much these anchors overlap with the ground-truth bounding boxes:

$$p = \begin{cases} 1 & \text{if} \quad \text{IoU} > 0.7 \\ -1 & \text{if} \quad \text{IoU} < 0.3 \\ 0 & \text{otherwise} \end{cases}$$

If an anchor has high overlap with a ground-truth bounding box, then it is likely that the anchor box includes an object of interest, and it is labeled as positive with respect to the *object versus no object* classification task. Similarly, if an anchor has small overlap with a ground-truth bounding box, it is labeled as negative. During the training process, the positive and negative anchors are passed as input to two fully connected layers corresponding to the classification of anchors as containing an object or no object, and to the regression of location parameters (four coordinates), respectively. Corresponding to the k number of anchors from a location, the RPN network outputs $2k$ scores and $4k$ coordinates. Thus, for example, if the number of anchors per sliding window (k) is 9, then the RPN outputs 18 objectness scores and 36 location coordinates (figure 7.16).

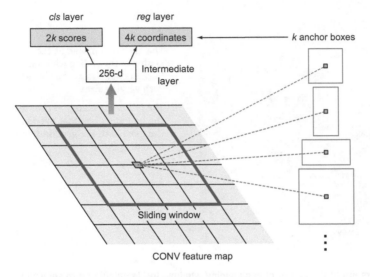

Figure 7.16   Region proposal network

RPN as a standalone application

An RPN can be used as a standalone application. For example, in problems with a single class of objects, the objectness probability can be used as the final class probability. This is because in such a case, *foreground* means *single class*, and *background* means *not a single class*.

The reason you would want to use RPN for cases like single-class detection is the gain in speed in both training and prediction. Since the RPN is a very simple network that only uses convolutional layers, the prediction time can be faster than using the classification base network.

FULLY CONNECTED LAYER

The output fully connected layer takes two inputs: the feature maps coming from the base ConvNet and the RoIs coming from the RPN. It then classifies the selected regions and outputs their prediction class and the bounding box parameters. The object classification layer in Faster R-CNN uses softmax activation, while the location regression layer uses linear regression over the coordinates defining the location as a bounding box. All of the network parameters are trained together using multi-task loss.

MULTI-TASK LOSS FUNCTION

Similar to Fast R-CNN, Faster R-CNN is optimized for a multi-task loss function that combines the losses of classification and bounding box regression:

$$L = L_{cls} + L_{loc}$$

$$L(\{p_i\},\{t_i\}) = \frac{1}{N_{cls}} \sum L_{cls}(p_i, p_i^*) + \frac{\lambda}{N_{loc}} \sum p_i^* \cdot L1_{\text{smooth}}(t_i - t_i^*)$$

The loss equation might look a little overwhelming at first, but it is simpler than it appears. Understanding it is not necessary to be able to run and train Faster R-CNNs, so feel free to skip this section. But I encourage you to power through this explanation, because it will add a lot of depth to your understanding of how the optimization process works under the hood. Let's go through the symbols first; see table 7.2.

Table 7.2 Multi-task loss function symbols

Symbol	Explanation
p_i and p_i^*	p_i is the predicted probability of the anchor (i) being an object and the ground, and p_i^* is the binary ground truth (0 or 1) of the anchor being an object.
t_i and t_i^*	t_i is the predicted four parameters that define the bounding box, and t_i^* is the ground-truth parameters.
N_{cls}	Normalization term for the classification loss. Ren et al. set it to be a mini-batch size of ~256.
N_{loc}	Normalization term for the bounding box regression. Ren et al. set it to the number of anchor locations, ~2400.
$L_{cls}(p_i, p_i^*)$	The log loss function over two classes. We can easily translate a multi-class classification into a binary classification by predicting whether a sample is a target object: $L_{cls}(p_i, p_i^*) = -p_i^* \log p_i - (1 - p_i^*) \log (1 - p_i)$
$L1_{\text{smooth}}$	As described in section 7.2.2, the bounding box loss measures the difference between the predicted and true location parameters (t_i, t_i^*) using the smooth L1 loss function. It is a robust function and is claimed to be less sensitive to outliers than other regression losses like L2.
λ	A balancing parameter, set to be ~10 in Ren et al. (so the L_{cls} and L_{loc} terms are roughly equally weighted).

Now that you know the definitions of the symbols, let's try to read the multi-task loss function again. To help understand this equation, just for a moment, ignore the normalization terms and the (i) terms. Here's the simplified loss function for each instance (i):

$$\text{Loss} = L_{cls}(p, p^*) + p^* \cdot L1_{\text{smooth}}(t - t^*)$$

This simplified function is the summation of two loss functions: the classification loss and the location loss (bounding box). Let's look at them one at a time:

- The idea of any loss function is that it subtracts the predicted value from the true value to find the amount of error. The *classification loss* is the cross-entropy function explained in chapter 2. Nothing new. It is a log loss function that calculates the error between the prediction probability (p) and the ground truth (p^*):

$$L_{cls}(p_i, p_i^*) = -p_i^* \log p_i - (1 - p_i^*) \log (1 - p_i)$$

- The *location loss* is the difference between the predicted and true location parameters (t_i, t_i^*) using the smooth L1 loss function. The difference is then multiplied by the ground truth probability of the region containing an object p^*. If it is not an object, p^* is 0 to eliminate the entire location loss for non-object regions.

Finally, we add the values of both losses to create the multi-loss function:

$$L = L_{cls} + L_{loc}$$

There you have it: the multi-loss function for each instance (i). Put back the (i) and Σ symbols to calculate the summation of losses for each instance.

7.2.4 *Recap of the R-CNN family*

Table 7.3 recaps the evolution of the R-CNN architecture:

- *R-CNN*—Bounding boxes are proposed by the selective search algorithm. Each is warped, and features are extracted via a deep convolutional neural network such as AlexNet, before a final set of object classifications and bounding box predictions is made with linear SVMs and linear regressors.
- *Fast R-CNN*—A simplified design with a single model. An RoI pooling layer is used *after* the CNN to consolidate regions. The model predicts both class labels and RoIs directly.
- *Faster R-CNN*—A fully end-to-end DL object detector. It replaces the selective search algorithm to propose RoIs with a region proposal network that interprets features extracted from the deep CNN and learns to propose RoIs directly.

Table 7.3 The evolution of the CNN family of networks from R-CNN to Fast R-CNN to Faster R-CNN

	R-CNN	Fast R-CNN	Faster R-CNN
mAP on the PASCAL Visual Object Classes Challenge 2007	66.0%	66.9%	66.9%
Features	1 Applies selective search to extract RoIs (~2,000) from each image. 2 A ConvNet is used to extract features from each of the ~2,000 regions extracted. 3 Uses classification and bounding box predictions.	Each image is passed only once to the CNN, and feature maps are extracted. 1 A ConvNet is used to extract feature maps from the input image. 2 Selective search is used on these maps to generate predictions. This way, we run only one ConvNet over the entire image instead of ~2,000 ConvNets over 2000 overlapping regions.	Replaces the selective search method with a region proposal network, which makes the algorithm much faster. An end-to-end DL network.
Limitations	High computation time, as each region is passed to the CNN separately. Also, uses three different models for making predictions.	Selective search is slow and, hence, computation time is still high.	Object proposal takes time. And as there are different systems working one after the other, the performance of systems depends on how the previous system performed.
Test time per image	50 seconds	2 seconds	0.2 seconds
Speed-up from R-CNN	1x	25x	250x

R-CNN LIMITATIONS

As you might have noticed, each paper proposes improvements to the seminal work done in R-CNN to develop a faster network, with the goal of achieving real-time object detection. The achievements displayed through this set of work is truly amazing, yet none of these architectures manages to create a real-time object detector. Without going into too much detail, the following problems have been identified with these networks:

- Training the data is unwieldy and takes too long.
- Training happens in multiple phases (such as the training region proposal versus a classifier).
- The network is too slow at inference time.

Fortunately, in the last few years, new architectures have been created to address the bottlenecks of R-CNN and its successors, enabling real-time object detection. The most famous are the single-shot detector (SSD) and you only look once (YOLO), which we will explain in sections 7.3 and 7.4.

MULTI-STAGE VS. SINGLE-STAGE DETECTOR

Models in the R-CNN family are all region-based. Detection happens in two stages, and thus these models are called two-stage detectors:

1 The model proposes a set of RoIs using selective search or an RPN. The proposed regions are sparse because the potential bounding-box candidates can be infinite.

2 A classifier only processes the region candidates.

One-stage detectors take a different approach. They skip the region proposal stage and run detection directly over a dense sampling of possible locations. This approach is faster and simpler but can potentially drag down performance a bit. In the next two sections, we will examine the SSD and YOLO one-stage object detectors. In general, single-stage detectors tend to be less accurate than two-stage detectors but are significantly faster.

7.3   *Single-shot detector (SSD)*

The SSD paper was released in 2016 by Wei Liu et al.[8] The SSD network reached new records in terms of performance and precision for object detection tasks, scoring over 74% mAP at 59 FPS on standard datasets such as the PASCAL VOC and Microsoft COCO.

---

[8] Wei Liu, Dragomir Anguelov, Dumitru Erhan, Christian Szegedy, Scott Reed, Cheng-Yang Fu, and Alexander C. Berg, "SSD: Single Shot MultiBox Detector," 2016, http://arxiv.org/abs/1512.02325.

Measuring detector speed (FPS: Frames per second)

As discussed at the beginning of this chapter, the most common metric for measuring detection speed is the number of frames per second. For example, Faster R-CNN operates at only 7 frames per second (FPS). There have been many attempts to build faster detectors by attacking each stage of the detection pipeline, but so far, significantly increased speed has come only at the cost of significantly decreased detection accuracy. In this section, you will see why single-stage networks like SSD can achieve faster detections that are more suitable for real-time detection.

For benchmarking, SSD300 achieves 74.3% mAP at 59 FPS, while SSD512 achieves 76.8% mAP at 22 FPS, which outperforms Faster R-CNN (73.2% mAP at 7 FPS). SSD300 refers to an input image of size 300 × 300, and SSD512 refers to an input image of size 512 × 512.

We learned earlier that the R-CNN family are multi-stage detectors: the network first predicts the objectness score of the bounding box and then passes this box through a classifier to predict the class probability. In single-stage detectors like SSD and YOLO (discussed in section 7.4), the convolutional layers make both predictions directly in one shot: hence the name single-shot detector. The image is passed once through the network, and the objectness score for each bounding box is predicted using logistic regression to indicate the level of overlap with the ground truth. If the bounding box overlaps 100% with the ground truth, the objectness score is 1; and if there is no overlap, the objectness score is 0. We then set a threshold value (0.5) that says, "If the objectness score is above 50%, this bounding box likely has an object of interest, and we get predictions. If it is less than 50%, we ignore the predictions."

7.3.1 *High-level SSD architecture*

The SSD approach is based on a feed-forward convolutional network that produces a fixed-size collection of bounding boxes and scores for the presence of object class instances in those boxes, followed by a NMS step to produce the final detections. The architecture of the SSD model is composed of three main parts:

- *Base network to extract feature maps*—A standard pretrained network used for high-quality image classification, which is truncated before any classification layers. In their paper, Liu et al. used a VGG16 network. Other networks like VGG19 and ResNet can be used and should produce good results.
- *Multi-scale feature layers*—A series of convolution filters are added after the base network. These layers decrease in size progressively to allow predictions of detections at multiple scales.
- *Non-maximum suppression*—NMS is used to eliminate overlapping boxes and keep only one box for each object detected.

As you can see in figure 7.17, layers 4_3, 7, 8_2, 9_2, 10_2, and 11_2 make predictions directly to the NMS layer. We will talk about why these layers progressively decrease in

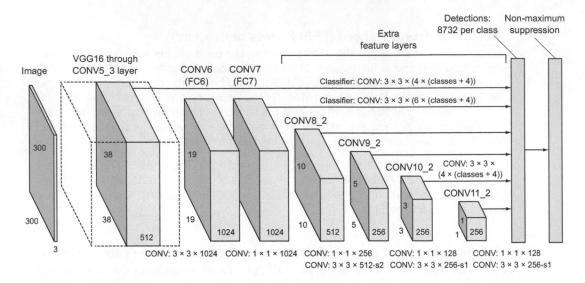

Figure 7.17 The SSD architecture is composed of a base network (VGG16), extra convolutional layers for object detection, and a non-maximum suppression (NMS) layer for final detections. Note that convolution layers 7, 8, 9, 10, and 11 make predictions that are directly fed to the NMS layer. (*Source:* Liu et al., 2016.)

size in section 7.3.3. For now, let's follow along to understand the end-to-end flow of data in SSD.

You can see in figure 7.17, that the network makes a total of 8,732 detections per class that are then fed to an NMS layer to reduce down to one detection per object. Where did the number 8,732 come from?

To have more accurate detection, different layers of feature maps also go through a small 3 × 3 convolution for object detection. For example, Conv4_3 is of size 38 × 38 × 512, and a 3 × 3 convolutional is applied. There are four bounding boxes, each of which has (*number of classes* + 4 box values) outputs. Suppose there are 20 object classes plus 1 background class; then the output number of bounding boxes is 38 × 38 × 4 = 5,776 bounding boxes. Similarly, we calculate the number of bounding boxes for the other convolutional layers:

- Conv7: 19 × 19 × 6 = 2,166 boxes (6 boxes for each location)
- Conv8_2: 10 × 10 × 6 = 600 boxes (6 boxes for each location)
- Conv9_2: 5 × 5 × 6 = 150 boxes (6 boxes for each location)
- Conv10_2: 3 × 3 × 4 = 36 boxes (4 boxes for each location)
- Conv11_2: 1 × 1 × 4 = 4 boxes (4 boxes for each location)

If we sum them up, we get 5,776 + 2,166 + 600 + 150 + 36 + 4 = 8,732 boxes produced. This is a huge number of boxes to show for our detector. That's why we apply NMS to reduce the number of the output boxes. As you will see in section 7.4, in YOLO there are 7 × 7 locations at the end with two bounding boxes for each location: 7 × 7 × 2 = 98 boxes.

What does the output prediction look like?

For each feature, the network predicts the following:

- 4 values that describe the bounding box (x, y, w, h)
- 1 value for the objectness score
- C values that represent the probability of each class

That's a total of $5 + C$ prediction values. Suppose there are four object classes in our problem. Then each prediction will be a vector that looks like this: [x, y, w, h, *objectness score*, C_1, C_2, C_3, C_4].

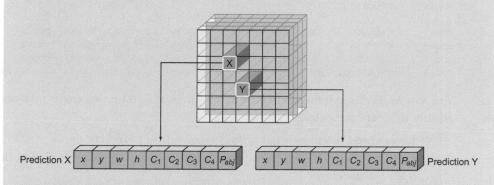

An example visualization of the output prediction when we have four classes in our problem. The convolutional layer predicts the bounding box coordinates, objectness score, and four class probabilities: C_1, C_2, C_3, and C_4.

Now, let's dive a little deeper into each component of the SSD architecture.

7.3.2 Base network

As you can see in figure 7.17, the SSD architecture builds on the VGG16 architecture after slicing off the fully connected classification layers (VGG16 is explained in detail in chapter 5). VGG16 was used as the base network because of its strong performance in high-quality image classification tasks and its popularity for problems where transfer learning helps to improve results. Instead of the original VGG fully connected layers, a set of supporting convolutional layers (from Conv6 onward) was added to enable us to extract features at multiple scales and progressively decrease the size of the input to each subsequent layer.

Following is a simplified code implementation of the VGG16 network used in SSD using Keras. You will not need to implement this from scratch; my goal in including this code snippet is to show you that this is a typical VGG16 network like the one implemented in chapter 5:

```
conv1_1 = Conv2D(64, (3, 3), activation='relu', padding='same')
conv1_2 = Conv2D(64, (3, 3), activation='relu', padding='same')(conv1_1)
pool1 = MaxPooling2D(pool_size=(2, 2), strides=(2, 2), padding='same')(conv1_2)
```

```
conv2_1 = Conv2D(128, (3, 3), activation='relu', padding='same')(pool1)
conv2_2 = Conv2D(128, (3, 3), activation='relu', padding='same')(conv2_1)
pool2 = MaxPooling2D(pool_size=(2, 2), strides=(2, 2), padding='same')(conv2_2)

conv3_1 = Conv2D(256, (3, 3), activation='relu', padding='same')(pool2)
conv3_2 = Conv2D(256, (3, 3), activation='relu', padding='same')(conv3_1)
conv3_3 = Conv2D(256, (3, 3), activation='relu', padding='same')(conv3_2)
pool3 = MaxPooling2D(pool_size=(2, 2), strides=(2, 2), padding='same')(conv3_3)

conv4_1 = Conv2D(512, (3, 3), activation='relu', padding='same')(pool3)
conv4_2 = Conv2D(512, (3, 3), activation='relu', padding='same')(conv4_1)
conv4_3 = Conv2D(512, (3, 3), activation='relu', padding='same')(conv4_2)
pool4 = MaxPooling2D(pool_size=(2, 2), strides=(2, 2), padding='same')(conv4_3)

conv5_1 = Conv2D(512, (3, 3), activation='relu', padding='same')(pool4)
conv5_2 = Conv2D(512, (3, 3), activation='relu', padding='same')(conv5_1)
conv5_3 = Conv2D(512, (3, 3), activation='relu', padding='same')(conv5_2)
pool5 = MaxPooling2D(pool_size=(3, 3), strides=(1, 1), padding='same')(conv5_3)
```

You saw VGG16 implemented in Keras in chapter 5. The two main takeaways from adding this here are as follows:

- Layer conv4_3 will be used again to make direct predictions.
- Layer pool5 will be fed to the next layer (conv6), which is the first of the multi-scale features layers.

HOW THE BASE NETWORK MAKES PREDICTIONS

Consider the following example. Suppose you have the image in figure 7.18, and the network's job is to draw bounding boxes around all the boats in the image. The process goes as follows:

1 Similar to the anchors concept in R-CNN, SSD overlays a grid of anchors around the image. For each anchor, the network creates a set of bounding boxes at its center. In SSD, anchors are called *priors*.

2 The base network looks at each bounding box as a separate image. For each bounding box, the network asks, "Is there a boat in this box?" Or in other words, "Did I extract any features of a boat in this box?"

3 When the network finds a bounding box that contains boat features, it sends its coordinates prediction and object classification to the NMS layer.

4 NMS eliminates all the boxes except the one that overlaps the most with the ground-truth bounding box.

NOTE Liu et al. used VGG16 because of its strong performance in complex image classification tasks. You can use other networks like the deeper VGG19 or ResNet for the base network, and it should perform as well if not better in accuracy; but it could be slower if you chose to implement a deeper network. MobileNet is a good choice if you want a balance between a complex, high-performing deep network and being fast.

Now, on to the next component of the SSD architecture: multi-scale feature layers.

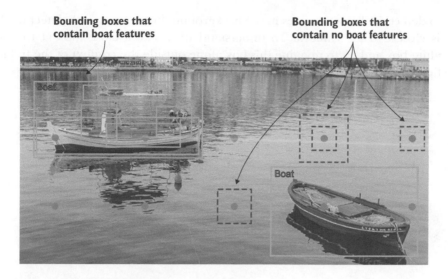

Bounding boxes that contain boat features

Bounding boxes that contain no boat features

Figure 7.18 The SSD base network looks at the anchor boxes to find features of a boat. Solid boxes indicate that the network has found boat features. Dotted boxes indicate no boat features.

7.3.3 Multi-scale feature layers

These are convolutional feature layers that are added to the end of the truncated base network. These layers decrease in size progressively to allow predictions of detections at multiple scales.

MULTI-SCALE DETECTIONS

To understand the goal of the multi-scale feature layers and why they vary in size, let's look at the image of horses in figure 7.19. As you can see, the base network may be

Figure 7.19 Horses at different scales in an image. The horses that are far from the camera are easier to detect because they are small in size and can fit inside the priors (anchor boxes). The base network might fail to detect the horse closest to the camera because it needs a different scale of anchors to be able to create priors that cover more identifiable features.

able to detect the horse features in the background, but it may fail to detect the horse that is closest to the camera. To understand why, take a close look at the dotted bounding box and try to imagine this box alone outside the context of the full image (see figure 7.20).

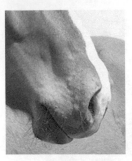

Figure 7.20   **An isolated horse feature**

Can you see horse features in the bounding box in figure 7.20? No. To deal with objects of different scales in an image, some methods suggest preprocessing the image at different sizes and combining the results afterward (figure 7.21). However, by using different convolution layers that vary in size, we can use feature maps from several different layers in a single network; for prediction we can mimic the same effect, while also sharing parameters across all object scales. As CNN reduces the spatial dimension gradually, the resolution of the feature maps also decreases. SSD uses lower-resolution layers to detect larger-scale objects. For example, 4 × 4 feature maps are used for larger scale objects.

To visualize this, imagine that the network reduces the image dimensions to be able to fit all of the horses inside its bounding boxes (figure 7.22). The multi-scale feature layers resize the image dimensions and keep the bounding-box sizes so that they

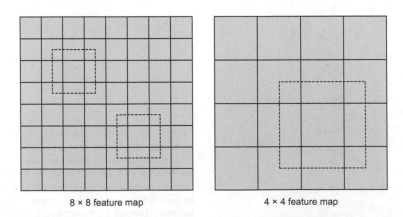

8 × 8 feature map   4 × 4 feature map

Figure 7.21   **Lower-resolution feature maps detect larger-scale objects (right); higher-resolution feature maps detect smaller-scale objects (left).**

Figure 7.22 Multi-scale feature layers reduce the spatial dimensions of the input image to detect objects with different scales. In this image, you can see that the new priors are kind of zoomed out to cover more identifiable features of the horse close to the camera.

can fit the larger horse. In reality, convolutional layers do not literally reduce the size of the image; this is just for illustration to help us intuitively understand the concept. The image is not just resized, it actually goes through the convolutional process and thus won't look anything like itself anymore. It will be a completely random-looking image, but it will preserve its features. The convolutional process is explained in detail in chapter 3.

Using multi-scale feature maps improves network accuracy significantly. Liu et al. ran an experiment to measure the advantage gained by adding the multi-scale feature layers. Figure 7.23 shows a decrease in accuracy with fewer layers; you can see the accuracy with different numbers of feature map layers used for object detection.

Prediction source layers from:						mAP use boundary boxes?		# boxes
conv4_3	conv7	conv8_2	conv9_2	conv10_2	conv11_2	Yes	No	
✔	✔	✔	✔	✔	✔	74.3	63.4	8,732
✔	✔	✔	✔	✔		**74.6**	63.1	8,764
✔	✔	✔	✔			73.8	68.4	8,942
✔	✔	✔				70.7	69.2	9,864
✔	✔					64.2	64.4	9,025
	✔					62.4	64.0	8,664

Figure 7.23 Effects of using multiple output layers from the original paper. The detector's accuracy (mAP) increases when the authors add multi-scale features. (*Source:* Liu et al., 2016.)

Notice that network accuracy drops from 74.3% when having the prediction source from all six layers to 62.4% for one source layer. When using only the conv7 layer for prediction, performance is the worst, reinforcing the message that it is critical to spread boxes of different scales over different layers.

ARCHITECTURE OF THE MULTI-SCALE LAYERS

Liu et al. decided to add six convolutional layers that decrease in size. They did this with a lot of tuning and trial and error until they produced the best results. As you saw in figure 7.17, convolutional layers 6 and 7 are pretty straightforward. Conv6 has a kernel size of 3 × 3, and conv7 has a kernel size of 1 × 1. Layers 8 through 11, on the other hand, are treated more like blocks, where each block consists of two convolutional layers of kernel sizes 1 × 1 and 3 × 3.

Here is the code implementation in Keras for layers 6 through 11 (you can see the full implementation in the book's downloadable code):

```
# conv6 and conv7
conv6 = Conv2D(1024, (3, 3), dilation_rate=(6, 6), activation='relu',
    padding='same')(pool5)
conv7 = Conv2D(1024, (1, 1), activation='relu', padding='same')(conv6)

# conv8 block
conv8_1 = Conv2D(256, (1, 1), activation='relu', padding='same')(conv7)
conv8_2 = Conv2D(512, (3, 3), strides=(2, 2), activation='relu',
    padding='valid')(conv8_1)

# conv9 block
conv9_1 = Conv2D(128, (1, 1), activation='relu', padding='same')(conv8_2)
conv9_2 = Conv2D(256, (3, 3), strides=(2, 2), activation='relu',
    padding='valid')(conv9_1)

# conv10 block
conv10_1 = Conv2D(128, (1, 1), activation='relu', padding='same')(conv9_2)
conv10_2 = Conv2D(256, (3, 3), strides=(1, 1), activation='relu',
    padding='valid')(conv10_1)

# conv11 block
conv11_1 = Conv2D(128, (1, 1), activation='relu', padding='same')(conv10_2)
conv11_2 = Conv2D(256, (3, 3), strides=(1, 1), activation='relu',
    padding='valid')(conv11_1)
```

As mentioned before, if you are not working in research or academia, you most probably won't need to implement object detection architectures yourself. In most cases, you will download an open source implementation and build on it to work on your problem. I just added these code snippets to help you internalize the information discussed about different layer architectures.

Atrous (or dilated) convolutions

Dilated convolutions introduce another parameter to convolutional layers: the *dilation rate*. This defines the spacing between the values in a kernel. A 3 × 3 kernel with a dilation rate of 2 has the same field of view as a 5 × 5 kernel while only using nine parameters. Imagine taking a 5 × 5 kernel and deleting every second column and row.

This delivers a wider field of view at the same computational cost.

A 3 × 3 kernel with a dilation rate of 2 has the same field of view as a 5 × 5 kernel while only using nine parameters.

Dilated convolutions are particularly popular in the field of real-time segmentation. Use them if you need a wide field of view and cannot afford multiple convolutions or larger kernels.

The following code builds a dilated 3 × 3 convolution layer with a dilation rate of 2 using Keras:

```
Conv2D(1024, (3, 3), dilation_rate=(2,2), activation='relu', padding='same')
```

Next, we discuss the third and last component of the SSD architecture: NMS.

7.3.4   *Non-maximum suppression*

Given the large number of boxes generated by the detection layer per class during a forward pass of SSD at inference time, it is essential to prune most of the bounding box by applying the NMS technique (explained earlier in this chapter). Boxes with a confidence loss and IoU less than a certain threshold are discarded, and only the top *N* predictions are kept (figure 7.24). This ensures that only the most likely predictions are retained by the network, while the noisier ones are removed.

How does SSD use NMS to prune the bounding boxes? SSD sorts the predicted boxes by their confidence scores. Starting from the top confidence prediction, SSD evaluates whether there are any previously predicted boundary boxes for the same class that overlap with each other above a certain threshold by calculating their IoU. (The IoU threshold value is tunable. Liu et al. chose 0.45 in their paper.) Boxes with IoU above the threshold are ignored because they overlap too much with another box that has a higher confidence score, so they are most likely detecting the same object. At most, we keep the top 200 predictions per image.

Figure 7.24   Non-maximum suppression reduces the number of bounding boxes to only one box for each object.

7.4   *You only look once (YOLO)*

Similar to the R-CNN family, YOLO is a family of object detection networks developed by Joseph Redmon et al. and improved over the years through the following versions:

- *YOLOv1*, published in 2016[9]—Called "unified, real-time object detection" because it is a single-detection network that unifies the two components of a detector: object detector and class predictor.
- *YOLOv2* (also known as YOLO9000), published later in 2016[10]—Capable of detecting over 9,000 objects; hence the name. It has been trained on ImageNet and COCO datasets and has achieved 16% mAP, which is not good; but it was very fast during test time.
- *YOLOv3*, published in 2018[11]—Significantly larger than previous models and has achieved a mAP of 57.9%, which is the best result yet out of the YOLO family of object detectors.

The YOLO family is a series of end-to-end DL models designed for fast object detection, and it was among the first attempts to build a fast real-time object detector. It is one of the faster object detection algorithms out there. Although the accuracy of the models is close but not as good as R-CNNs, they are popular for object detection because of their detection speed, often demonstrated in real-time video or camera feed input.

---

9   Joseph Redmon, Santosh Divvala, Ross Girshick, and Ali Farhadi, "You Only Look Once: Unified, Real-Time Object Detection," 2016, http://arxiv.org/abs/1506.02640.

10 Joseph Redmon and Ali Farhadi, "YOLO9000: Better, Faster, Stronger," 2016, http://arxiv.org/abs/1612.08242.

11 Joseph Redmon and Ali Farhadi, "YOLOv3: An Incremental Improvement," 2018, http://arxiv.org/abs/1804.02767.

The creators of YOLO took a different approach than the previous networks. YOLO does not undergo the region proposal step like R-CNNs. Instead, it only predicts over a limited number of bounding boxes by splitting the input into a grid of cells; each cell directly predicts a bounding box and object classification. The result is a large number of candidate bounding boxes that are consolidated into a final prediction using NMS (figure 7.25).

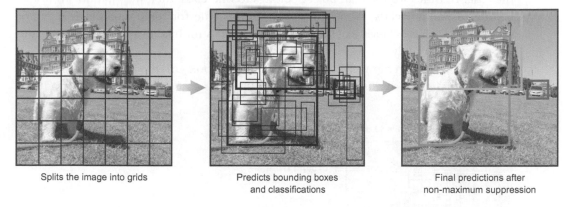

Splits the image into grids   Predicts bounding boxes   Final predictions after
and classifications   non-maximum suppression

Figure 7.25 YOLO splits the image into grids, predicts objects for each grid, and then uses NMS to finalize predictions.

YOLOv1 proposed the general architecture, YOLOv2 refined the design and made use of predefined anchor boxes to improve bounding-box proposals, and YOLOv3 further refined the model architecture and training process. In this section, we are going to focus on YOLOv3 because it is currently the state-of-the-art architecture in the YOLO family.

7.4.1 How YOLOv3 works

The YOLO network splits the input image into a grid of $S \times S$ cells. If the center of the ground-truth box falls into a cell, that cell is responsible for detecting the existence of that object. Each grid cell predicts B number of bounding boxes and their objectness score along with their class predictions, as follows:

- *Coordinates of B bounding boxes*—Similar to previous detectors, YOLO predicts four coordinates for each bounding box (b_x, b_y, b_w, b_h), where x and y are set to be offsets of a cell location.
- *Objectness score* (P_0)—indicates the probability that the cell contains an object. The objectness score is passed through a sigmoid function to be treated as a probability with a value range between 0 and 1. The objectness score is calculated as follows:

$$P_0 = \text{Pr (containing an object)} \times \text{IoU (pred, truth)}$$

- *Class prediction*—If the bounding box contains an object, the network predicts the probability of *K* number of classes, where *K* is the total number of classes in your problem.

It is important to note that before v3, YOLO used a softmax function for the class scores. In v3, Redmon et al. decided to use sigmoid instead. The reason is that softmax imposes the assumption that each box has exactly one class, which is often not the case. In other words, if an object belongs to one class, then it's guaranteed not to belong to another class. While this assumption is true for some datasets, it may not work when we have classes like Women and Person. A multilabel approach models the data more accurately.

As you can see in figure 7.26, for each bounding box (*B*), the prediction looks like this: [(*bounding box coordinates*), (*objectness score*), (*class predictions*)]. We've learned that

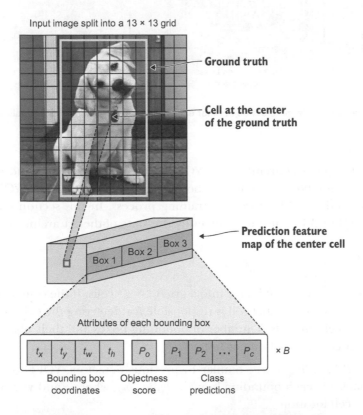

Figure 7.26   Example of a YOLOv3 workflow when applying a 13 × 13 grid to the input image. The input image is split into 169 cells. Each cell predicts *B* number of bounding boxes and their objectness score along with their class predictions. In this example, we show the cell at the center of the ground-truth making predictions for 3 boxes (*B* = 3). Each prediction has the following attributes: bounding box coordinates, objectness score, and class predictions.

the bounding box coordinates are four values plus one value for the objectness score and K values for class predictions. Then the total number of values predicted for all bounding boxes is $5B + K$ multiplied by the number of cells in the grid $S \times S$:

$$\text{Total predicted values} = S \times S \times (5B + K)$$

PREDICTIONS ACROSS DIFFERENT SCALES

Look closely at figure 7.26. Notice that the prediction feature map has three boxes. You might have wondered why there are three boxes. Similar to the anchors concept in SSD, YOLOv3 has nine anchors to allow for prediction at three different scales per cell. The detection layer makes detections at feature maps of three different sizes having strides 32, 16, and 8, respectively. This means that with an input image of size 416×416, we make detections on scales 13×13, 26×26, and 52×52 (figure 7.27). The 13×13 layer is responsible for detecting large objects, the 26×26 layer is for detecting medium objects, and the 52×52 layer detects smaller objects.

| 13 × 13 | 26 × 26 | 52× 52 |

Figure 7.27   Prediction feature maps at different scales

This results in the prediction of three bounding boxes for each cell ($B = 3$). That's why in figure 7.26, the prediction feature map is predicting Box 1, Box 2, and Box 3. The bounding box responsible for detecting the dog will be the one whose anchor has the highest IoU with the ground-truth box.

> **NOTE** Detections at different layers help address the issue of detecting small objects, which was a frequent complaint with YOLOv2. The upsampling layers can help the network preserve and learn fine-grained features, which are instrumental for detecting small objects.

The network does this by downsampling the input image until the first detection layer, where a detection is made using feature maps of a layer with stride 32. Further, layers are upsampled by a factor of 2 and concatenated with feature maps of previous layers having identical feature-map sizes. Another detection is now made at layer with stride 16. The same upsampling procedure is repeated, and a final detection is made at the layer of stride 8.

YOLOv3 OUTPUT BOUNDING BOXES

For an input image of size 416×416, YOLO predicts $((52 \times 52) + (26 \times 26) + 13 \times 13))$ $\times 3 = 10{,}647$ bounding boxes. That is a huge number of boxes for an output. In our dog example, we have only one object. We want only one bounding box around this object. How do we reduce the boxes from 10,647 down to 1?

First, we filter the boxes based on their objectness score. Generally, boxes having scores below a threshold are ignored. Second, we use NMS to cure the problem of multiple detections of the same image. For example, all three bounding boxes of the outlined grid cell at the center of the image may detect a box, or the adjacent cells may detect the same object.

7.4.2 *YOLOv3 architecture*

Now that you understand how YOLO works, going through the architecture will be very simple and straightforward. YOLO is a single neural network that unifies object detection and classifications into one end-to-end network. The neural network architecture was inspired by the GoogLeNet model (Inception) for feature extraction. Instead of the Inception modules, YOLO uses 1×1 reduction layers followed by 3×3 convolutional layers. Redmon and Farhadi called this *DarkNet* (figure 7.28).

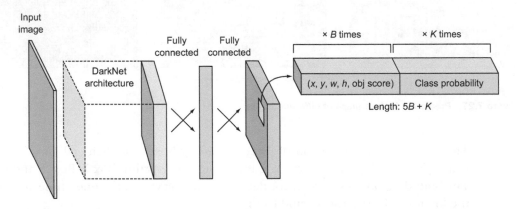

Figure 7.28   High-level architecture of YOLO

YOLOv2 used a custom deep architecture darknet-19, an originally 19-layer network supplemented with 11 more layers for object detection. With a 30-layer architecture, YOLOv2 often struggled with small object detections. This was attributed to loss of fine-grained features as the layers downsampled the input. However, YOLOv2's architecture was still lacking some of the most important elements that are now stable in most state-of-the art algorithms: no residual blocks, no skip connections, and no upsampling. YOLOv3 incorporates all of these updates.

YOLOv3 uses a variant of DarkNet called Darknet-53 (figure 7.29). It has a 53-layer network that is trained on ImageNet. For the task of detection, 53 more layers are stacked onto it, giving us a 106-layer fully convolutional underlying architecture for YOLOv3. This is the reason behind the slowness of YOLOv3 compared to YOLOv2— but this comes with a great boost in detection accuracy.

	Type	Filters	Size	Output
	Convolutional	32	3 × 3	256 × 256
	Convolutional	64	3 × 3 / 2	128 × 128
1×	Convolutional	32	1 × 1	
	Convolutional	34	3 × 3	
	Residual			128 × 128
	Convolutional	128	3 × 3 / 2	64 × 64
2×	Convolutional	64	1 × 1	
	Convolutional	128	3 × 3	
	Residual			64 × 64
	Convolutional	256	3 × 3 / 2	32 × 32
8×	Convolutional	128	1 × 1	
	Convolutional	256	3 × 3	
	Residual			32 × 32
	Convolutional	512	3 × 3 / 2	16 × 16
8×	Convolutional	256	1 × 1	
	Convolutional	512	3 × 3	
	Residual			16 × 16
	Convolutional	1024	3 × 3 / 2	8 × 8
4×	Convolutional	512	1 × 1	
	Convolutional	1024	3 × 3	
	Residual			8 × 8
	Avgpool		Global	
	Connected		1000	
	Softmax			

Figure 7.29   DarkNet-53 feature extractor architecture. (*Source:* Redmon and Farhadi, 2018.)

FULL ARCHITECTURE OF YOLOv3

We just learned that YOLOv3 makes predictions across three different scales. This becomes a lot clearer when you see the full architecture, shown in figure 7.30.

The input image goes through the DarkNet-53 feature extractor, and then the image is downsampled by the network until layer 79. The network branches out and continues to downsample the image until it makes its first prediction at layer 82. This detection is made on a grid scale of 13 × 13 that is responsible for detecting large objects, as we explained before.

Next the feature map from layer 79 is *upsampled* by 2x to dimensions 26 × 26 and *concatenated* with the feature map from layer 61. Then the second detection is made by layer 94 on a grid scale of 26 × 26 that is responsible for detecting medium objects.

Finally, a similar procedure is followed again, and the feature map from layer 91 is subjected to few upsampling convolutional layers before being depth concatenated with a feature map from layer 36. A third prediction is made by layer 106 on a grid scale of 52 × 52, which is responsible for detecting small objects.

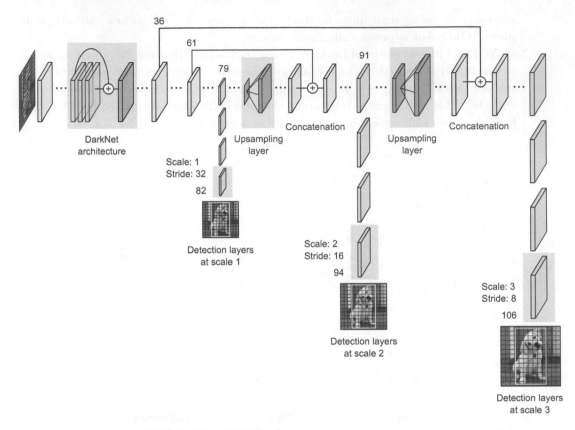

Figure 7.30   YOLOv3 network architecture. (Inspired by the diagram in Ayoosh Kathuria's post "What's new in YOLO v3?" *Medium,* **2018, http://mng.bz/lGN2.)**

7.5   *Project: Train an SSD network in a self-driving car application*

The code for this project was created by Pierluigi Ferrari in his GitHub repository (https://github.com/pierluigiferrari/ssd_keras). The project was adapted for this chapter; you can find this implementation with the book's downloadable code.

Note that for this project, we are going to build a smaller SSD network called SSD7. SSD7 is a seven-layer version of the SSD300 network. It is important to note that while an SSD7 network would yield some acceptable results, this is not an optimized network architecture. The goal is just to build a low-complexity network that is fast enough for you to train on your personal computer. It took me around 20 hours to train this network on the road traffic dataset; training could take a lot less time on a GPU.

NOTE   The original repository created by Pierluigi Ferrari comes with implementation tutorials for SSD7, SSD300, and SSD512 networks. I encourage you to check it out.

In this project, we will use a toy dataset created by Udacity. You can visit Udacity's GitHub repository for more information on the dataset (https://github.com/udacity/self-driving-car/tree/master/annotations). It has more than 22,000 labeled images and 5 object classes: car, truck, pedestrian, bicyclist, and traffic light. All of the images have been resized to a height of 300 pixels and a width of 480 pixels. You can download the dataset as part of the book's code.

> **NOTE** The GitHub data repository is owned by Udacity, and it may be updated after this writing. To avoid any confusion, I downloaded the dataset that I used to create this project and provided it with the book's code to allow you to replicate the results in this project.

What makes this dataset very interesting is that these are real-time images taken while driving in Mountain View, California, and neighboring cities during daylight conditions. No image cleanup was done. Take a look at the image examples in figure 7.31.

Figure 7.31 Example images from the Udacity self-driving dataset
(Image copyright © 2016 Udacity and published under MIT License.)

As stated on Udacity's page, the dataset was labeled by CrowdAI and Autti. You can find the labels in CSV format in the folder, split into three files: training, validation, and test datasets. The labeling format is straightforward, as follows:

frame	xmin	xmax	ymin	ymax	class_id
1478019952686311006.jpg	237	251	143	155	1

Xmin, xmax, ymin, and ymax are the bounding box coordinates. Class_id is the correct label, and frame is the image name.

Data annotation using Labellmg

If you are annotating your own data, there are several open source labeling applications that you can use, like Labellmg (https://pypi.org/project/labellmg). They are very easy to set up and use.

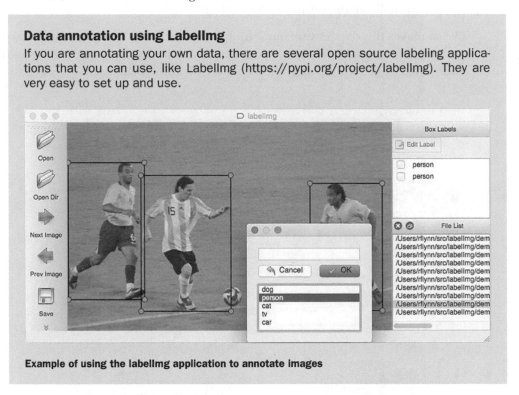

Example of using the labellmg application to annotate images

7.5.1   *Step 1: Build the model*

Before jumping into the model training, take a close look at the `build_model` method in the `keras_ssd7.py` file. This file builds a Keras model with the SSD architecture. As we learned earlier in this chapter, the model consists of convolutional feature layers and a number of convolutional predictor layers that make their input from different feature layers.

Here is what the `build_model` method looks like. Please read the comments in the keras_ssd7.py file to understand the arguments passed:

```
def build_model(image_size,
                mode='training',
```

```
                          l2_regularization=0.0,
                          min_scale=0.1,
                          max_scale=0.9,
                          scales=None,
                          aspect_ratios_global=[0.5, 1.0, 2.0],
                          aspect_ratios_per_layer=None,
                          two_boxes_for_ar1=True,
                          clip_boxes=False,
                          variances=[1.0, 1.0, 1.0, 1.0],
                          coords='centroids',
                          normalize_coords=False,
                          subtract_mean=None,
                          divide_by_stddev=None,
                          swap_channels=False,
                          confidence_thresh=0.01,
                          iou_threshold=0.45,
                          top_k=200,
                          nms_max_output_size=400,
                          return_predictor_sizes=False)
```

7.5.2 Step 2: Model configuration

In this section, we set the model configuration parameters. First we set the height, width, and number of color channels to whatever we want the model to accept as image input. If your input images have a different size than defined here, or if your images have non-uniform size, you must use the data generator's image transformations (resizing and/or cropping) so that your images end up having the required input size before they are fed to the model:

```
img_height = 300       │ Height, width,
img_width = 480        │ and channels of
img_channels = 3       │ the input images

intensity_mean = 127.5     │ Set to your preference (maybe None).
intensity_range = 127.5    │ The current settings transform the input
                           │ pixel values to the interval [–1,1].
```

The number of classes is the number of positive classes in your dataset: for example, 20 for PASCAL VOC or 80 for COCO. Class ID 0 must always be reserved for the background class:

In case you'd like to set the step sizes for the anchor box grids manually; not recommended

```
n_classes = 5                                ← Number of classes
                                               in our dataset

scales = [0.08, 0.16, 0.32, 0.64, 0.96]      ← An explicit list of anchor box
                                               scaling factors. If this is passed,
                                               it overrides the min_scale and
                                               max_scale arguments.

aspect_ratios = [0.5, 1.0, 2.0]      ← List of aspect ratios
steps = None                           for the anchor boxes
offsets = None       ←

                        In case you'd like to set the offsets for the anchor
                        box grids manually; not recommended
```

```
        two_boxes_for_ar1 = True          ◁──┐  Specifies whether to generate two
                                              │  anchor boxes for aspect ratio 1
  ┌─▷  clip_boxes = False
  │
  │     variances = [1.0, 1.0, 1.0, 1.0]   ◁──┤  List of variances by which the encoded
  │                                            │  target coordinates are scaled
  │     normalize_coords = True            ◁──┐  Specifies whether the model is supposed to
  │                                            │  use coordinates relative to the image size
  └  Specifies whether to clip the anchor
     boxes to lie entirely within the image
     boundaries
```

7.5.3 *Step 3: Create the model*

Now we call the `build_model()` function to build our model:

```
model = build_model(image_size=(img_height, img_width, img_channels),
                    n_classes=n_classes,
                    mode='training',
                    l2_regularization=0.0005,
                    scales=scales,
                    aspect_ratios_global=aspect_ratios,
                    aspect_ratios_per_layer=None,
                    two_boxes_for_ar1=two_boxes_for_ar1,
                    steps=steps,
                    offsets=offsets,
                    clip_boxes=clip_boxes,
                    variances=variances,
                    normalize_coords=normalize_coords,
                    subtract_mean=intensity_mean,
                    divide_by_stddev=intensity_range)
```

You can optionally load saved weights. If you don't want to load weights, skip the following code snippet:

```
model.load_weights('<path/to/model.h5>', by_name=True)
```

Instantiate an Adam optimizer and the SSD loss function, and compile the model. Here, we will use a custom Keras function called `SSDLoss`. It implements the multitask log loss for classification and smooth L1 loss for localization. `neg_pos_ratio` and `alpha` are set as in the SSD paper (Liu et al., 2016):

```
adam = Adam(lr=0.001, beta_1=0.9, beta_2=0.999, epsilon=1e-08, decay=0.0)

ssd_loss = SSDLoss(neg_pos_ratio=3, alpha=1.0)

model.compile(optimizer=adam, loss=ssd_loss.compute_loss)
```

7.5.4   *Step 4: Load the data*

To load the data, follow these steps:

1 Instantiate two `DataGenerator` objects—one for training and one for validation:

```
train_dataset = DataGenerator(load_images_into_memory=False,
    hdf5_dataset_path=None)
val_dataset = DataGenerator(load_images_into_memory=False,
    hdf5_dataset_path=None)
```

2 Parse the image and label lists for the training and validation datasets:

```
images_dir = 'path_to_downloaded_directory'

train_labels_filename = 'path_to_dataset/labels_train.csv'      ◁─┐ Ground
val_labels_filename   = 'path_to_dataset/labels_val.csv'          │ truth

train_dataset.parse_csv(images_dir=images_dir,
                labels_filename=train_labels_filename,
                input_format=['image_name', 'xmin', 'xmax', 'ymin',
                                'ymax', 'class_id'],
                include_classes='all')

val_dataset.parse_csv(images_dir=images_dir,
                labels_filename=val_labels_filename,
                input_format=['image_name', 'xmin', 'xmax', 'ymin',
                                'ymax', 'class_id'],
                include_classes='all')
```

```
                                                        Gets the number
                                                        of samples in the
train_dataset_size = train_dataset.get_dataset_size()   training and
val_dataset_size   = val_dataset.get_dataset_size()     validation datasets
print("Number of images in the training
    dataset:\t{:>6}".format(train_dataset_size))
print("Number of images in the validation
    dataset:\t{:>6}".format(val_dataset_size))
```

This cell should print out the size of your training and validation datasets as follows:

```
Number of images in the training dataset:      18000
Number of images in the validation dataset:     4241
```

3 Set the batch size:

```
batch_size = 16
```

As you learned in chapter 4, you can increase the batch size to get a boost in the computing speed based on the hardware that you are using for this training.

4 Define the data augmentation process:

```
data_augmentation_chain = DataAugmentationConstantInputSize(
                              random_brightness=(-48, 48, 0.5),
                              random_contrast=(0.5, 1.8, 0.5),
                              random_saturation=(0.5, 1.8, 0.5),
                              random_hue=(18, 0.5),
                              random_flip=0.5,
                              random_translate=((0.03,0.5),
                                                (0.03,0.5), 0.5),
                              random_scale=(0.5, 2.0, 0.5),
                              n_trials_max=3,
                              clip_boxes=True,
                              overlap_criterion='area',
                              bounds_box_filter=(0.3, 1.0),
                              bounds_validator=(0.5, 1.0),
                              n_boxes_min=1,
                              background=(0,0,0))
```

5 Instantiate an encoder that can encode ground-truth labels into the format
   needed by the SSD loss function. Here, the encoder constructor needs the
   spatial dimensions of the model's predictor layers to create the anchor boxes:

```
predictor_sizes = [model.get_layer('classes4').output_shape[1:3],
                   model.get_layer('classes5').output_shape[1:3],
                   model.get_layer('classes6').output_shape[1:3],
                   model.get_layer('classes7').output_shape[1:3]]

ssd_input_encoder = SSDInputEncoder(img_height=img_height,
                                    img_width=img_width,
                                    n_classes=n_classes,
                                    predictor_sizes=predictor_sizes,
                                    scales=scales,
                                    aspect_ratios_global=aspect_ratios,
                                    two_boxes_for_ar1=two_boxes_for_ar1,
                                    steps=steps,
                                    offsets=offsets,
                                    clip_boxes=clip_boxes,
                                    variances=variances,
                                    matching_type='multi',
                                    pos_iou_threshold=0.5,
                                    neg_iou_limit=0.3,
                                    normalize_coords=normalize_coords)
```

6 Create the generator handles that will be passed to Keras's `fit_generator()`
   function:

```
train_generator = train_dataset.generate(batch_size=batch_size,
                                          shuffle=True,
                                          transformations=[
                                              data_augmentation_chain],
                                          label_encoder=ssd_input_encoder,
```

```
                                         returns={'processed_images',
                                                  'encoded_labels'},
                                keep_images_without_gt=False)

    val_generator = val_dataset.generate(batch_size=batch_size,
                                         shuffle=False,
                                         transformations=[],
                                         label_encoder=ssd_input_encoder,
                                         returns={'processed_images',
                                                  'encoded_labels'},
                                         keep_images_without_gt=False)
```

7.5.5   *Step 5: Train the model*

Everything is set, and we are ready to train our SSD7 network. We've already chosen an optimizer and a learning rate and set the batch size; now let's set the remaining training parameters and train the network. There are no new parameters here that you haven't learned already. We will set the model checkpoint, early stopping, and learning rate reduction rate:

```
model_checkpoint =
ModelCheckpoint(filepath='ssd7_epoch-{epoch:02d}_loss-{loss:.4f}_val_loss-
    {val_loss:.4f}.h5',
                               monitor='val_loss',
                               verbose=1,
                               save_best_only=True,
                               save_weights_only=False,
                               mode='auto',
                               period=1)

csv_logger = CSVLogger(filename='ssd7_training_log.csv',
                       separator=',',
                       append=True)

early_stopping = EarlyStopping(monitor='val_loss',
                               min_delta=0.0,
                               patience=10,
                               verbose=1)

reduce_learning_rate = ReduceLROnPlateau(monitor='val_loss',
                                         factor=0.2,
                                         patience=8,
                                         verbose=1,
                                         epsilon=0.001,
                                         cooldown=0,
                                         min_lr=0.00001)

callbacks = [model_checkpoint, csv_logger, early_stopping, reduce_learning_rate]
```

Early stopping if val_loss did not improve for 10 consecutive epochs

Learning rate reduction rate when it plateaus

Set one epoch to consist of 1,000 training steps. I've arbitrarily set the number of epochs to 20 here. This does not necessarily mean that 20,000 training steps is the optimum number. Depending on the model, dataset, learning rate, and so on, you might have to train much longer (or less) to achieve convergence:

```
initial_epoch   = 0          If you're resuming previous training, set
final_epoch     = 20         initial_epoch and final_epoch accordingly.
steps_per_epoch = 1000

history = model.fit_generator(generator=train_generator,          ←── Starts
                              steps_per_epoch=steps_per_epoch,          training
                              epochs=final_epoch,
                              callbacks=callbacks,
                              validation_data=val_generator,
                              validation_steps=ceil(
                                          val_dataset_size/batch_size),
                              initial_epoch=initial_epoch)
```

7.5.6   *Step 6: Visualize the loss*

Let's visualize the `loss` and `val_loss` values to look at how the training and validation loss evolved and check whether our training is going in the right direction (figure 7.32):

```
plt.figure(figsize=(20,12))
plt.plot(history.history['loss'], label='loss')
plt.plot(history.history['val_loss'], label='val_loss')
plt.legend(loc='upper right', prop={'size': 24})
```

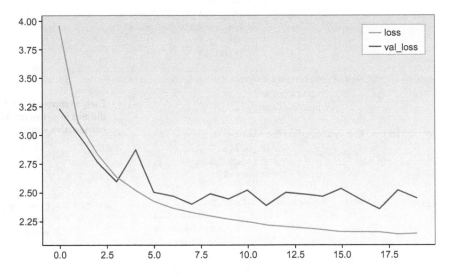

Figure 7.32   Visualized `loss` and `val_loss` values during SSD7 training for 20 epochs

7.5.7 Step 7: Make predictions

Now let's make some predictions on the validation dataset with the trained model. For convenience, we'll use the validation generator that we've already set up. Feel free to change the batch size:

```
predict_generator = val_dataset.generate(batch_size=1,
                                          shuffle=True,
                                          transformations=[],
                                          label_encoder=None,
                                          returns={'processed_images',
                                                   'processed_labels',
                                                   'filenames'},
                                          keep_images_without_gt=False)

batch_images, batch_labels, batch_filenames = next(predict_generator)

y_pred = model.predict(batch_images)

y_pred_decoded = decode_detections(y_pred,
                                   confidence_thresh=0.5,
                                   iou_threshold=0.45,
                                   top_k=200,
                                   normalize_coords=normalize_coords,
                                   img_height=img_height,
                                   img_width=img_width)

np.set_printoptions(precision=2, suppress=True, linewidth=90)
print("Predicted boxes:\n")
print('   class   conf xmin   ymin   xmax   ymax')
print(y_pred_decoded[i])
```

1. Set the generator for the predictions.

2. Generate samples.

3. Make a prediction.

4. Decode the raw prediction y_pred.

This code snippet prints the predicted bounding boxes along with their class and the level of confidence for each one, as shown in figure 7.33.

```
   class   conf xmin   ymin   xmax   ymax
[[ 1.    0.93 131.96 152.12 159.29 172.3 ]
 [ 1.    0.88  52.39 151.89  87.44 179.34]
 [ 1.    0.88 262.65 140.26 286.45 164.05]
 [ 1.    0.6  234.53 148.43 267.19 170.34]
 [ 1.    0.58  73.2  153.51  91.79 175.64]
 [ 1.    0.5  225.06 130.93 274.15 169.79]
 [ 2.    0.6  266.38 116.4  282.23 173.16]]
```

Figure 7.33 Predicted bounding boxes, confidence level, and class

When we draw these predicted boxes onto the image, as shown in figure 7.34, each predicted box has its confidence next to the category name. The ground-truth boxes are also drawn onto the image for comparison.

Figure 7.34   Predicted boxes drawn onto the image

Summary

- Image classification is the task of predicting the type or class of an object in an image.
- Object detection is the task of predicting the location of objects in an image via bounding boxes and the classes of the located objects.
- The general framework of object detection systems consists of four main components: region proposals, feature extraction and predictions, non-maximum suppression, and evaluation metrics.
- Object detection algorithms are evaluated using two main metrics: frame per second (FPS) to measure the network's speed, and mean average precision (mAP) to measure the network's precision.
- The three most popular object detection systems are the R-CNN family of networks, SSD, and the YOLO family of networks.
- The R-CNN family of networks has three main variations: R-CNN, Fast R-CNN, and Faster R-CNN. R-CNN and Fast R-CNN use a selective search algorithm to propose RoIs, whereas Faster R-CNN is an end-to-end DL system that uses a region proposal network to propose RoIs.
- The YOLO family of networks include YOLOv1, YOLOv2 (or YOLO9000), and YOLOv3.

- R-CNN is a multi-stage detector: it separates the process to predict the object-ness score of the bounding box and the object class into two different stages.
- SSD and YOLO are single-stage detectors: the image is passed once through the network to predict the objectness score and the object class.
- In general, single-stage detectors tend to be less accurate than two-stage detectors but are significantly faster.

Part 3

Generative models and visual embeddings

At this point, we've covered a lot of ground about how deep neural networks can help us understand image features and perform deterministic tasks on them, like object classification and detection. Now it's time to turn our focus to a different, slightly more advanced area of computer vision and deep learning: generative models. These neural network models actually create new content that didn't exist before—new people, new objects, a new reality, like magic! We train these models on a dataset from a specific domain, and then they create new images with objects from the same domain that look close to the real data. In this part of the book, we'll cover both training and image generation, as well as look at neural transfer and the cutting edge of what's happening in visual embeddings.

Generative adversarial networks (GANs)

This chapter covers

- Understanding the basic components of GANs: generative and discriminative models
- Evaluating generative models
- Learning about popular vision applications of GANs
- Building a GAN model

Generative adversarial networks (GANs) are a new type of neural architecture introduced by Ian Goodfellow and other researchers at the University of Montreal, including Yoshua Bengio, in 2014.[1] GANs have been called "the most interesting idea in the last 10 years in ML" by Yann LeCun, Facebook's AI research director. The excitement is well justified. The most notable feature of GANs is their capacity to create hyperrealistic images, videos, music, and text. For example, except for the far-right column, none of the faces shown on the right side of figure 8.1 belong to real humans; they are all fake. The same is true for the handwritten digits on the

---

[1] Ian J. Goodfellow, Jean Pouget-Abadie, Mehdi Mirza, Bing Xu, David Warde-Farley, Sherjil Ozair, Aaron Courville, and Yoshua Bengio, "Generative Adversarial Networks," 2014, http://arxiv.org/abs/1406.2661.

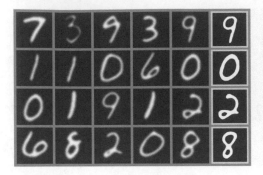

Figure 8.1 Illustration of GANs' abilities by Goodfellow and co-authors. These are samples generated by GANs after training on two datasets: MNIST and the Toronto Faces Dataset (TFD). In both cases, the right-most column contains true data. This shows that the produced data is really generated and not only memorized by the network. (*Source:* Goodfellow et al., 2014.)

left side of the figure. This shows a GAN's ability to learn features from the training images and imagine its own new images using the patterns it has learned.

We've learned in the past chapters how deep neural networks can be used to understand image features and perform deterministic tasks on them like object classification and detection. In this part of the book, we will talk about a different type of application for deep learning in the computer vision world: *generative models*. These are neural network models that are able to imagine and produce new content that hasn't been created before. They can imagine new worlds, new people, and new realities in a seemingly magical way. We train generative models by providing a training dataset in a specific domain; their job is to create images that have new objects from the same domain that look like the real data.

For a long time, humans have had an advantage over computers: the ability to imagine and create. Computers have excelled in solving problems like regression, classification, and clustering. But with the introduction of generative networks, researchers can make computers generate content of the same or higher quality compared to that created by their human counterparts. By learning to mimic any distribution of data, computers can be taught to create worlds that are similar to our own in any domain: images, music, speech, prose. They are robot artists, in a sense, and their output is impressive. GANs are also seen as an important stepping stone toward achieving artificial general intelligence (AGI), an artificial system capable of matching human cognitive capacity to acquire expertise in virtually any domain—from images, to language, to creative skills needed to compose sonnets.

Naturally, this ability to generate new content makes GANs look a little bit like magic, at least at first sight. In this chapter, we will only attempt to scratch the surface of what is possible with GANs. We will overcome the apparent magic of GANs in order to dive into the architectural ideas and math behind these models in order to provide the necessary theoretical knowledge and practical skills to continue exploring any facet of this field that you find most interesting. Not only will we discuss the fundamental notions that GANs rely on, but we will also implement and train an end-to-end GAN and go through it step by step. Let's get started!

8.1 GAN architecture

GANs are based on the idea of *adversarial training*. The GAN architecture basically consists of two neural networks that compete against each other:

- The *generator* tries to convert random noise into observations that look as if they have been sampled from the original dataset.
- The *discriminator* tries to predict whether an observation comes from the original dataset or is one of the generator's forgeries.

This competitiveness helps them to mimic any distribution of data. I like to think of the GAN architecture as two boxers fighting (figure 8.2): in their quest to win the bout, both are learning each others' moves and techniques. They start with less knowledge about their opponent, and as the match goes on, they *learn* and become better.

Figure 8.2   A fight between two adversarial networks: generative and discriminative

Another analogy will help drive home the idea: think of a GAN as the opposition of a counterfeiter and a cop in a game of cat and mouse, where the counterfeiter is learning to pass false notes, and the cop is learning to detect them (figure 8.3). Both are dynamic: as the counterfeiter learns to perfect creating false notes, the cop is in training and getting better at detecting the fakes. Each side learns the other's methods in a constant escalation.

Figure 8.3   The GAN's generator and discriminator models are like a counterfeiter and a police officer.

As you can see in the architecture diagram in figure 8.4, a GAN takes the following steps:

1 The generator takes in random numbers and returns an image.
2 This generated image is fed into the discriminator alongside a stream of images taken from the actual, ground-truth dataset.
3 The discriminator takes in both real and fake images and returns probabilities: numbers between 0 and 1, with 1 representing a prediction of authenticity and 0 representing a prediction of fake.

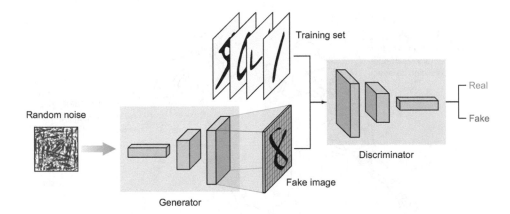

Figure 8.4   The GAN architecture is composed of generator and discriminator networks. Note that the discriminator network is a typical CNN where the convolutional layers reduce in size until they get to the flattened layer. The generator network, on the other hand, is an inverted CNN that starts with the flattened vector: the convolutional layers increase in size until they form the dimension of the input images.

If you take a close look at the generator and discriminator networks, you will notice that the generator network is an inverted ConvNet that starts with the flattened vector. The images are upscaled until they are similar in size to the images in the training dataset. We will dive deeper into the generator architecture later in this chapter—I just wanted you to notice this phenomenon now.

8.1.1 Deep convolutional GANs (DCGANs)

In the original GAN paper in 2014, multi-layer perceptron (MLP) networks were used to build the generator and discriminator networks. However, since then, it has been proven that convolutional layers give greater predictive power to the discriminator, which in turn enhances the accuracy of the generator and the overall model. This type of GAN is called a deep convolutional GAN (DCGAN) and was developed by Alec Radford et al. in 2016.[2] Now, all GAN architectures contain convolutional layers, so the "DC" is implied when we talk about GANs; so, for the rest of this chapter, we refer to DCGANs as both GANs and DCGANs. You can also go back to chapters 2 and 3 to learn more about the differences between MLP and CNN networks and why CNN is preferred for image problems. Next, let's dive deeper into the architecture of the discriminator and generator networks.

8.1.2 The discriminator model

As explained earlier, the goal of the discriminator is to predict whether an image is real or fake. This is a typical supervised classification problem, so we can use the traditional classifier network that we learned about in the previous chapters. The network consists of stacked convolutional layers, followed by a dense output layer with a sigmoid activation function. We use a sigmoid activation function because this is a binary classification problem: the goal of the network is to output prediction probabilities values that range between 0 and 1, where 0 means the image generated by the generator is fake and 1 means it is 100% real.

The discriminator is a normal, well understood classification model. As you can see in figure 8.5, training the discriminator is pretty straightforward. We feed the discriminator

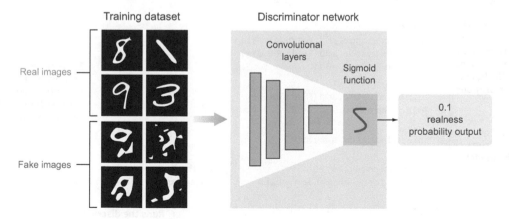

Figure 8.5   The discriminator for the GAN

---

2   Alec Radford, Luke Metz, and Soumith Chintala, "Unsupervised Representation Learning with Deep Convolutional Generative Adversarial Networks," 2016, http://arxiv.org/abs/1511.06434.

labeled images: fake (or generated) and real images. The real images come from the training dataset, and the fake images are the output of the generator model.

Now, let's implement the discriminator network in Keras. At the end of this chapter, we will compile all the code snippets together to build an end-to-end GAN. We will first implement a `discriminator_model` function. In this code snippet, the shape of the image input is 28 × 28; you can change it as needed for your problem:

```python
def discriminator_model():
    discriminator = Sequential()

    discriminator.add(Conv2D(32, kernel_size=3, strides=2,
                      input_shape=(28,28,1),padding="same"))

    discriminator.add(LeakyReLU(alpha=0.2))

    discriminator.add(Dropout(0.25))

    discriminator.add(Conv2D(64, kernel_size=3, strides=2, padding="same"))
    discriminator.add(ZeroPadding2D(padding=((0,1),(0,1))))

    discriminator.add(BatchNormalization(momentum=0.8))
    discriminator.add(LeakyReLU(alpha=0.2))
    discriminator.add(Dropout(0.25))

    discriminator.add(Conv2D(128, kernel_size=3, strides=2, padding="same"))
    discriminator.add(BatchNormalization(momentum=0.8))
    discriminator.add(LeakyReLU(alpha=0.2))
    discriminator.add(Dropout(0.25))

    discriminator.add(Conv2D(256, kernel_size=3, strides=1, padding="same"))
    discriminator.add(BatchNormalization(momentum=0.8))
    discriminator.add(LeakyReLU(alpha=0.2))
    discriminator.add(Dropout(0.25))

    discriminator.add(Flatten())
    discriminator.add(Dense(1, activation='sigmoid'))

    discriminator.summary()

    img_shape = (28,28,1)
    img = Input(shape=img_shape)

    probability = discriminator(img)

    return Model(img, probability)
```

Annotations:
- Instantiates a sequential model and names it discriminator
- Adds a convolutional layer to the discriminator model
- Adds a leaky ReLU activation function
- Adds a dropout layer with a 25% dropout probability
- Adds a second convolutional layer with zero padding
- Adds a batch normalization layer for faster learning and higher accuracy
- Adds a third convolutional layer with batch normalization, leaky ReLU, and a dropout
- Adds the fourth convolutional layer with batch normalization, leaky ReLU, and a dropout
- Flattens the network and adds the output dense layer with sigmoid activation function
- Prints the model summary
- Sets the input image shape
- Runs the discriminator model to get the output probability
- Returns a model that takes the image as input and produces the probability output

The output summary of the discriminator model is shown in figure 8.6. As you might have noticed, there is nothing new: the discriminator model follows the regular pattern of the traditional CNN networks that we learned about in chapters 3, 4, and 5. We stack convolutional, batch normalization, activation, and dropout layers to create our model. All of these layers have hyperparameters that we tune when we are training the network. For your own implementation, you can tune these hyperparameters and add or remove layers as you see fit. Tuning CNN hyperparameters is explained in detail in chapters 3 and 4.

Layer (type)	Output Shape	Param #
conv2d_1 (Conv2D)	(None, 14, 14, 32)	320
leaky_re_lu_1 (LeakyReLU)	(None, 14, 14, 32)	0
dropout_1 (Dropout)	(None, 14, 14, 32)	0
conv2d_2 (Conv2D)	(None, 7, 7, 64)	18496
zero_padding2d_1 (ZeroPaddin	(None, 8, 8, 64)	0
batch_normalization_1 (Batch	(None, 8, 8, 64)	250
leaky_re_lu_2 (LeakyReLU)	(None, 8, 8, 64)	0
dropout_2 (Dropout)	(None, 8, 8, 64)	0
conv2d_3 (Conv2D)	(None, 4, 4, 128)	73856
batch_normalization_2 (Batch	(None, 4, 4, 128)	512
leaky_re_lu_3 (LeakyReLU)	(None, 4, 4, 128)	0
dropout_3 (Dropout)	(None, 4, 4, 128)	0
conv2d_4 (Conv2D)	(None, 4, 4, 256)	295168
batch_normalization_3 (Batch	(None, 4, 4, 256)	1024
leaky_re_lu_4 (LeakyReLU)	(None, 4, 4, 256)	0
dropout_4 (Dropout)	(None, 4, 4, 256)	0
flatten_1 (Flatten)	(None, 4096	0
dense_1 (Dense)	(None, 1)	4097

Total params: 393,729
Trainable params: 392,833
Non-trainable params: 896

Figure 8.6 The output summary for the discriminator model

In the output summary in figure 8.6, note that the width and height of the output feature maps decrease in size, whereas the depth increases in size. This is the expected behavior for traditional CNN networks as we've seen in previous chapters. Let's see what happens to the feature maps' size in the generator network in the next section.

8.1.3   *The generator model*

The generator takes in some random data and tries to mimic the training dataset to generate fake images. Its goal is to trick the discriminator by trying to generate images that are perfect replicas of the training dataset. As it is trained, it gets better and better after each iteration. But the discriminator is being trained at the same time, so the generator has to keep improving as the discriminator learns its tricks.

As you can see in figure 8.7, the generator model looks like an inverted ConvNet. The generator takes a vector input with some random noise data and reshapes it into a cube volume that has a width, height, and depth. This volume is meant to be treated as a feature map that will be fed to several convolutional layers that will create the final image.

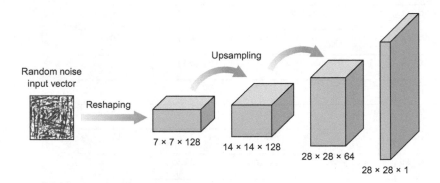

Figure 8.7   The generator model of the GAN

UPSAMPLING TO SCALE FEATURE MAPS

Traditional convolutional neural networks use pooling layers to downsample input images. In order to scale the feature maps, we use upsampling layers that scale the image dimensions by repeating each row and column of the input pixels.

Keras has an upsampling layer (`Upsampling2D`) that scales the image dimensions by taking a scaling factor (`size`) as an argument:

```
keras.layers.UpSampling2D(size=(2, 2))
```

This line of code repeats every row and column of the image matrix two times, because the size of the scaling factor is set to $(2, 2)$; see figure 8.8. If the scaling factor is $(3, 3)$, the upsampling layer repeats each row and column of the input matrix three times, as shown in figure 8.9.

```
Input = 1, 2
        3, 4

Output = 1, 1, 2, 2
         1, 1, 2, 2
         3, 3, 4, 4
         3, 3, 4, 4
```

```
[[1. 1. 1. 2. 2. 2.]
 [1. 1. 1. 2. 2. 2.]
 [1. 1. 1. 2. 2. 2.]
 [3. 3. 3. 4. 4. 4.]
 [3. 3. 3. 4. 4. 4.]
 [3. 3. 3. 4. 4. 4.]]
```

Figure 8.8 Upsampling example when the scaling size is (2, 2)

Figure 8.9 Upsampling example when scaling size is (3, 3)

When we build the generator model, we keep adding upsampling layers until the size of the feature maps is similar to the training dataset. You will see how this is implemented in Keras in the next section.

Now, let's build the generator_model function that builds the generator network:

Reshapes the image dimensions to 7 × 7 × 128

Instantiates a sequential model and names it generator

Adds a dense layer that has a number of neurons = 128 × 7 × 7

Upsampling layer to double the size of the image dimensions to 14 × 14

Adds a convolutional layer to run the convolutional process and batch normalization

```python
def generator_model():
    generator = Sequential()
    generator.add(Dense(128 * 7 * 7, activation="relu", input_dim=100))
    generator.add(Reshape((7, 7, 128)))
    generator.add(UpSampling2D(size=(2,2)))

    generator.add(Conv2D(128, kernel_size=3, padding="same"))
    generator.add(BatchNormalization(momentum=0.8))
    generator.add(Activation("relu"))
    generator.add(UpSampling2D(size=(2,2)))

    # convolutional + batch normalization layers
    generator.add(Conv2D(64, kernel_size=3, padding="same"))
    generator.add(BatchNormalization(momentum=0.8))
    generator.add(Activation("relu"))

    # convolutional layer with filters = 1
    generator.add(Conv2D(1, kernel_size=3, padding="same"))
    generator.add(Activation("tanh"))
    generator.summary()

    noise = Input(shape=(100,))
    fake_image = generator(noise)
    return Model(noise, fake_image)
```

Upsamples the image dimensions to 28 × 28

Prints the model summary

Generates the input noise vector of length = 100. We use 100 here to create a simple network.

We don't add upsampling here because the image size of 28 × 28 is equal to the image size in the MNIST dataset. You can adjust this for your own problem.

Returns a model that takes the noise vector as input and outputs the fake image

Runs the generator model to create the fake image

The output summary of the generator model is shown in figure 8.10. In the code snippet, the only new component is the Upsampling layer to double its input dimensions by repeating pixels. Similar to the discriminator, we stack convolutional layers on top of each other and add other optimization layers like BatchNormalization. The key difference in the generator model is that it starts with the flattened vector; images are upsampled until they have dimensions similar to the training dataset. All of these layers have hyperparameters that we tune when we are training the network. For your own implementation, you can tune these hyperparameters and add or remove layers as you see fit.

```
Layer (type)                      Output Shape              Param #
==================================================================
dense_2 (Dense)                   (None, 6272               633472

reshape_1 (Reshape)               (None, 7, 7, 128)         0

up_sampling2d_1 (UpSampling2      (None, 14, 14, 128)       0

conv2d_5 (Conv2D)                 (None, 14, 14, 128)       147584

batch_normalization_4 (Batch      (None, 14, 14, 128)       512

activation_1 (Activation)         (None, 14, 14, 128)       0

up_sampling2d_2 (UpSampling2      (None, 28, 28, 128)       0

conv2d_6 (Conv2D)                 (None, 28, 28, 64)        73792

batch_normalization_5 (Batch      (None, 28, 28, 64)        256

activation_2 (Activation)         (None, 28, 28, 64)        0

conv2d_7 (Conv2D)                 (None, 28, 28, 1)         577

activation_3 (Activation)         (None, 28, 28, 1)         0
==================================================================
Total params: 856,193
Trainable params: 855,809
Non-trainable params: 384
```

Figure 8.10   The output summary of the generator model

Notice the change in the output shape after each layer. It starts from a 1D vector of 6,272 neurons. We reshaped it to a $7 \times 7 \times 128$ volume, and then the width and height were upsampled twice to 14×14 followed by 28×28. The depth decreased from 128 to 64 to 1 because this network is built to deal with the grayscale MNIST dataset project that we will implement later in this chapter. If you are building a generator model to generate color images, then you should set the filters in the last convolutional layer to 3.

8.1.4 *Training the GAN*

Now that we've learned the discriminator and generator models separately, let's put them together to train an end-to-end generative adversarial network. The discriminator is being trained to become a better classifier to maximize the probability of assigning the correct label to both training examples (real) and images generated by the generator (fake): for example, the police officer becomes better at differentiating between fakes and real currency. The generator, on the other hand, is being trained to become a better forger, to maximize its chances of fooling the discriminator. Both networks are getting better at what they do.

The process of training GAN models involves two processes:

1. *Train the discriminator.* This is a straightforward supervised training process. The network is given labeled images coming from the generator (fake) and the training data (real), and it learns to classify between real and fake images with a sigmoid prediction output. Nothing new here.

2. *Train the generator.* This process is a little tricky. The generator model cannot be trained alone like the discriminator. It needs the discriminator model to tell it whether it did a good job of faking images. So, we create a *combined network* to train the generator, composed of both discriminator and generator models.

Think of the training processes as two parallel lanes. One lane trains the discriminator alone, and the other lane is the combined model that trains the generator. The GAN training process is illustrated in figure 8.11.

As you can see in figure 8.11, when training the combined model, we freeze the weights of the discriminator because this model focuses only on training the generator.

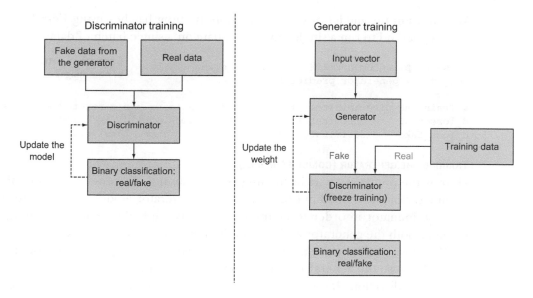

Figure 8.11   The process flow to train GANs

We will discuss the intuition behind this idea when we explain the generator training proces. For now, just know that we need to build and train two models: one for the discriminator alone and the other for both discriminator and generator models.

Both processes follow the traditional neural network training process explained in chapter 2. It starts with the feedforward process and then makes predictions and calculates and backpropagates the error. When training the discriminator, the error is backpropagated back to the discriminator model to update its weights; in the combined model, the error is backpropagated back to the generator to update its weights.

During the training iterations, we follow the same neural network training procedure to observe the network's performance and tune its hyperparameters until we see that the generator is achieving satisfying results for our problem. This is when we can stop the training and deploy the generator model. Now, let's see how we compile the discriminator and the combined networks to train the GAN model.

TRAINING THE DISCRIMINATOR

As we said before, this is a straightforward process. First, we build the model from the `discriminator_model` method that we created earlier in this chapter. Then we compile the model and use the `binary_crossentropy` loss function and an `optimizer` of your choice (we use `Adam` in this example).

Let's see the Keras implementation that builds and compiles the generator. Please note that this code snippet is not meant to be compilable on its own—it is here for illustration. At the end of this chapter, you can find the full code of this project:

```
discriminator = discriminator_model()
discriminator.compile(loss='binary_crossentropy',optimizer='adam',
    metrics=['accuracy'])
```

We can train the model by creating random training batches using Keras' `train_on _batch` method to run a single gradient update on a single batch of data:

Sample noise →
```
noise = np.random.normal(0, 1, (batch_size, 100))
gen_imgs = generator.predict(noise)
```
← **Generates a batch of new images**

```
# Train the discriminator (real classified as ones and generated as zeros)
d_loss_real = discriminator.train_on_batch(imgs, valid)
d_loss_fake = discriminator.train_on_batch(gen_imgs, fake)
```

TRAINING THE GENERATOR (COMBINED MODEL)

Here is the one tricky part in training GANs: training the generator. While the discriminator can be trained in isolation from the generator model, the generator needs the discriminator in order to be trained. For this, we build a combined model that contains both the generator and the discriminator, as shown in figure 8.12.

When we want to train the generator, we freeze the weights of the discriminator model because the generator and discriminator have different loss functions pulling in different directions. If we don't freeze the discriminator weights, it will be pulled in the same direction the generator is learning so it will be more likely to predict generated

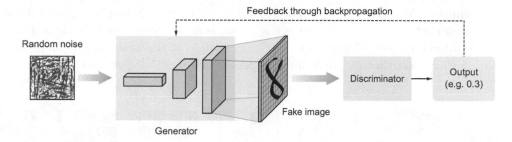

Feedback through backpropagation

Random noise

Generator

Fake image

Discriminator

Output
(e.g. 0.3)

Figure 8.12 Illustration of the combined model that contains both the generator and discriminator models

images as real, which is not the desired outcome. Freezing the weights of the discriminator model doesn't affect the existing discriminator model that we compiled earlier when we were training the discriminator. Think of it as having two discriminator models—this is not the case, but it is easier to imagine.

Now, let's build the combined model:

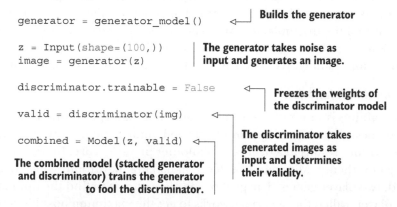

```
generator = generator_model()            ⊲┘ Builds the generator

z = Input(shape=(100,))       │ The generator takes noise as
image = generator(z)          │ input and generates an image.

discriminator.trainable = False   ⊲┐ Freezes the weights of
                                   │ the discriminator model
valid = discriminator(img)    ⊲┐
                              ┌┘  The discriminator takes
combined = Model(z, valid) ⊲┘    generated images as
                                 input and determines
   The combined model (stacked generator    their validity.
   and discriminator) trains the generator
   to fool the discriminator.
```

Now that we have built the combined model, we can proceed with the training process as normal. We compile the combined model with a `binary_crossentropy` loss function and an Adam optimizer:

```
combined.compile(loss='binary_crossentropy', optimizer=optimizer)
g_loss = self.combined.train_on_batch(noise, valid)          ⊲┐
                                                              │
         Trains the generator (wants the discriminator       │
         to mistake images for being real)                   │
```

TRAINING EPOCHS

In the project at the end of the chapter, you will see that the previous code snippet is put inside a loop function to perform the training for a certain number of epochs. For each epoch, the two compiled models (discriminator and combined) are trained simultaneously. During the training process, both the generator and discriminator improve. You can observe the performance of your GAN by printing out the results after each epoch (or a set of epochs) to see how the generator is doing at generating synthetic images. Figure 8.13 shows an example of the evolution of the generator's performance throughout its training process on the MNIST dataset.

Epoch: 0   Epoch: 1,500   Epoch: 2,500   Epoch: 3,500   Epoch: 5,500   Epoch: 7,500   Epoch: 9,500

Figure 8.13   The generator gets better at mimicking the handwritten digits of the MNIST dataset throughout its training from epoch 0 to epoch 9,500.

In the example, epoch 0 starts with random noise data that doesn't yet represent the features in the training dataset. As the GAN model goes through the training, its generator gets better and better at creating high-quality imitations of the training dataset that can fool the discriminator. Manually observing the generator's performance is a good way to evaluate system performance to decide on the number of epochs and when to stop training. We'll look more at GAN evaluation techniques in section 8.2.

8.1.5   GAN minimax function

GAN training is more of a zero-sum game than an optimization problem. In zero-sum games, the total utility score is divided among the players. An increase in one player's score results in a decrease in another player's score. In AI, this is called *minimax* game theory. Minimax is a decision-making algorithm, typically used in turn-based, two-player games. The goal of the algorithm is to find the optimal next move. One player, called the *maximizer*, works to get the maximum possible score; the other player, called the *minimizer*, tries to get the lowest score by counter-moving against the maximizer.

GANs play a minimax game where the entire network attempts to optimize the function $V(D,G)$ in the following equation:

$$\underset{G}{\text{Min}}\ \underset{D}{\text{Max}}\ V(D,G) = E_{x \sim p_{data}} \underbrace{[\log D(x)]}_{} + E_{z \sim P_{z(z)}} \underbrace{[\log (1 - D(G(z)))]}_{}$$

Discriminator output   **Discriminator output**
for real data x   **for generated fake data G(z)**

The goal of the discriminator (D) is to *maximize* the probability of getting the correct label of the image. The generator's (G) goal, on the other hand, is to *minimize* the chances of getting caught. So, we train D to maximize the probability of assigning the correct label to both training examples and samples from G. We simultaneously train G to minimize $\log(1 - D(G(z)))$. In other words, D and G play a two-player minimax game with the value function $V(D,G)$.

Minimax game theory

In a two-person, zero-sum game, a person can win only if the other player loses. No cooperation is possible. This game theory is widely used in games such as tic-tac-toe, backgammon, mancala, chess, and so on. The maximizer player tries to get the highest score possible, while the minimizer player tries to do the opposite and get the lowest score possible.

In a given game state, if the maximizer has the upper hand, then the score will tend to be a positive value. If the minimizer has the upper hand in that state, then the score will tend to be a negative value. The values are calculated by heuristics that are unique for every type of game.

Like any other mathematical equation, the preceding one looks terrifying to anyone who isn't well versed in the math behind it, but the idea it represents is simple yet powerful. It's just a mathematical representation of the two competing objectives of the discriminator and the generator models. Let's go through the symbols first (table 8.1) and then explain it.

Table 8.1 Symbols used in the minimax equation

Symbol	Explanation
G	Generator.
D	Discriminator.
z	Random noise fed to the generator (G).
$G(z)$	The generator takes the random noise data (z) and tries to reconstruct the real images.
$D(G(z))$	The discriminator (D) output from the generator.
$\log D(x)$	The discriminator's probability output for real data.

The discriminator takes its input from two sources:

- *Data from the generator, $G(z)$*—This is fake data (z). The discriminator output from the generator is denoted as $D(G(z))$.
- *Real input from the real training data (x)*—The discriminator output from the real data is denoted as $\log D(x)$.

To simplify the minimax equation, the best way to look at it is to break it down into two components: the discriminator training function and the generator training (combined model) function. During the training process, we created two training flows, and each has its own error function:

- One for the discriminator alone, represented by the following function that aims to maximize the minimax function by making the predictions as close as possible to 1:

$$E_{x \sim p_{data}} \left[\log D(x) \right]$$

- One for the combined model to train the generator represented by the following function, which aims to minimize the minimax function by making the predictions as close as possible to 0:

$$E_{z \sim Pz(z)} \left[\log(1 - D(G(z))) \right]$$

Now that we understand the equation symbols and have a better understanding of how the minimax function works, let's look at the function again:

$$\underset{G}{\text{Min}} \, \underset{D}{\text{Max}} \, V(D,G) = \underbrace{E_{x \sim p_{data}} \left[\log D(x) \right]}_{\substack{\textbf{Error from the} \\ \textbf{discriminator} \\ \textbf{model training}}} + \underbrace{E_{z \sim Pz(z)} \left[\log(1 - D(G(z))) \right]}_{\substack{\textbf{Error from the combined} \\ \textbf{model training}}}$$

The goal of the minimax objective function $V(D, G)$ is to maximize $D(x)$ from the true data distribution and minimize $D(G(z))$ from the fake data distribution. To achieve this, we use the log-likelihood of $D(x)$ and $1 - D(z)$ in the objective function. The log of a value just makes sure that the closer we are to an incorrect value, the more we are penalized.

Early in the GAN training process, the discriminator will reject fake data from the generator with high confidence, because the fake images are very different from the real training data—the generator hasn't learned yet. As we train the discriminator to maximize the probability of assigning the correct labels to both real examples and fake images from the generator, we simultaneously train the generator to minimize the discriminator classification error for the generated fake data. The discriminator wants to maximize objectives such that $D(x)$ is close to 1 for real data and $D(G(z))$ is close to 0 for fake data. On the other hand, the generator wants to minimize objectives such that $D(G(z))$ is close to 1 so that the discriminator is fooled into thinking the generated $G(z)$ is real. We stop the training when the fake data generated by the generator is recognized as real data.

8.2   Evaluating GAN models

Deep learning neural network models that are used for classification and detection problems are trained with a loss function until convergence. A GAN generator model, on the other hand, is trained using a discriminator that learns to classify images as real or generated. As we learned in the previous section, both the generator and discriminator models are trained together to maintain an equilibrium. As such, no objective loss function is used to train the GAN generator models, and there is no way to objectively assess the progress of the training and the relative or absolute quality of the model from loss alone. This means models must be evaluated using the quality of the generated synthetic images and by manually inspecting the generated images.

A good way to identify evaluation techniques is to review research papers and the techniques the authors used to evaluate their GANs. Tim Salimans et al. (2016) evaluated their GAN performance by having human annotators manually judge the visual quality of the synthesized samples.[3] They created a web interface and hired annotators on Amazon Mechanical Turk (MTurk) to distinguish between generated data and real data.

One downside of using human annotators is that the metric varies depending on the setup of the task and the motivation of the annotators. The team also found that results changed drastically when they gave annotators feedback about their mistakes: by learning from such feedback, annotators are better able to point out the flaws in generated images, giving a more pessimistic quality assessment.

Other non-manual approaches were used by Salimans et al. and by other researchers we will discuss in this section. In general, there is no consensus about a correct way to evaluate a given GAN generator model. This makes it challenging for researchers and practitioners to do the following:

- Select the best GAN generator model during a training run—in other words, decide when to stop training.
- Choose generated images to demonstrate the capability of a GAN generator model.
- Compare and benchmark GAN model architectures.
- Tune the model hyperparameters and configuration and compare results.

Finding quantifiable ways to understand a GAN's progress and output quality is still an active area of research. A suite of qualitative and quantitative techniques has been developed to assess the performance of a GAN model based on the quality and diversity of the generated synthetic images. Two commonly used evaluation metrics for image quality and diversity are the *inception score* and the *Fréchet inception distance* (*FID*). In this section, you will discover techniques for evaluating GAN models based on generated synthetic images.

---

[3]   Tim Salimans, Ian Goodfellow, Wojciech Zaremba, Vicki Cheung, Alec Radford, and Xi Chen. "Improved Techniques for Training GANs," 2016, http://arxiv.org/abs/1606.03498.

8.2.1   Inception score

The inception score is based on a heuristic that realistic samples should be able to be classified when passed through a pretrained network such as Inception on Image-Net (hence the name *inception score*). The idea is really simple. The heuristic relies on two values:

- *High predictability of the generated image*—We apply a pretrained inception classifier model to every generated image and get its softmax prediction. If the generated image is good enough, then it should give us a high predictability score.
- *Diverse generated samples*—No classes should dominate the distribution of the generated images.

A large number of generated images are classified using the model. Specifically, the probability of the image belonging to each class is predicted. The probabilities are then summarized in the score to capture both how much each image looks like a known class and how diverse the set of images is across the known classes. If both these traits are satisfied, there should be a large inception score. A higher inception score indicates better-quality generated images.

8.2.2   Fréchet inception distance (FID)

The FID score was proposed and used by Martin Heusel et al. in 2017.[4] The score was proposed as an improvement over the existing inception score.

Like the inception score, the FID score uses the Inception model to capture specific features of an input image. These activations are calculated for a collection of real and generated images. The activations for each real and generated image are summarized as a multivariate Gaussian, and the distance between these two distributions is then calculated using the Fréchet distance, also called the Wasserstein-2 distance.

An important note is that the FID needs a decent sample size to give good results (the suggested size is 50,000 samples). If you use too few samples, you will end up overestimating your actual FID, and the estimates will have a large variance. A lower FID score indicates more realistic images that match the statistical properties of real images.

8.2.3   Which evaluation scheme to use

Both measures (inception score and FID) are easy to implement and calculate on batches of generated images. As such, the practice of systematically generating images and saving models during training can and should continue to be used to allow post hoc model selection. Diving deep into the inception score and FID is out of the scope of this book. As mentioned earlier, this is an active area of research, and there is no consensus in the industry as of the time of writing about the one best

---

[4]   Martin Heusel, Hubert Ramsauer, Thomas Unterthiner, Bernhard Nessler, and Sepp Hochreiter, "GANs Trained by a Two Time-Scale Update Rule Converge to a Local Nash Equilibrium," 2017, http://arxiv.org/abs/1706.08500.

approach to evaluate GAN performance. Different scores assess various aspects of the image-generation process, and it is unlikely that a single score can cover all aspects. The goal of this section is to expose you to some techniques that have been developed in recent years to automate the GAN evaluation process, but manual evaluation is still widely used.

When you are getting started, it is a good idea to begin with manual inspection of generated images in order to evaluate and select generator models. Developing GAN models is complex enough for both beginners and experts; manual inspection can get you a long way while refining your model implementation and testing model configurations.

Other researchers are taking different approaches by using domain-specific evaluation metrics. For example, Konstantin Shmelkov and his team (2018) used two measures based on image classification, GAN-train and GAN-test, which approximated the recall (diversity) and precision (quality of the image) of GANs, respectively.[5]

8.3 Popular GAN applications

Generative modeling has come a long way in the last five years. The field has developed to the point where it is expected that the next generation of generative models will be more comfortable creating art than humans. GANs now have the power to solve the problems of industries like healthcare, automotive, fine arts, and many others. In this section, we will learn about some of the use cases of adversarial networks and which GAN architecture is used for that application. The goal of this section is not to implement the variations of the GAN network, but to provide some exposure to potential applications of GAN models and resources for further reading.

8.3.1 Text-to-photo synthesis

Synthesis of high-quality images from text descriptions is a challenging problem in CV. Samples generated by existing text-to-image approaches can roughly reflect the meaning of the given descriptions, but they fail to contain necessary details and vivid object parts.

The GAN network that was built for this application is the stacked generative adversarial network (StackGAN).[6] Zhang et al. were able to generate 256 × 256 photo-realistic images conditioned on text descriptions.

StackGANs work in two stages (figure 8.14):

- *Stage-I*: StackGAN sketches the primitive shape and colors of the object based on the given text description, yielding low-resolution images.

---

[5] Konstantin Shmelkov, Cordelia Schmid, and Karteek Alahari, "How Good Is My GAN?" 2018, http://arxiv .org/abs/1807.09499.

[6] Han Zhang, Tao Xu, Hongsheng Li, Shaoting Zhang, Xiaogang Wang, Xiaolei Huang, and Dimitris Metaxas, "StackGAN: Text to Photo-Realistic Image Synthesis with Stacked Generative Adversarial Networks," 2016, http://arxiv.org/abs/1612.03242.

This bird is white with some black on its head and wings, and has a long orange beak.

This bird has a yellow belly and tarsus, gray back, wings, and brown throat, nape with a black face.

This flower has overlapping pink pointed petals surrounding a ring of short yellow filaments.

a) StackGAN Stage-I
   64 × 64 images

b) StackGAN Stage-II
   256 × 256 images

Figure 8.14   (a) Stage-I: Given text descriptions, StackGAN sketches rough shapes and basic colors of objects, yielding low-resolution images. (b) Stage-II takes Stage-I results and text descriptions as inputs, and generates high-resolution images with photorealistic details. (*Source:* Zhang et al., 2016.)

- *Stage-II*: StackGAN takes the output of stage-I and a text description as input and generates high-resolution images with photorealistic details. It is able to rectify defects in the images created in stage-I and add compelling details with the refinement process.

8.3.2   *Image-to-image translation (Pix2Pix GAN)*

Image-to-image translation is defined as translating one representation of a scene into another, given sufficient training data. It is inspired by the language translation analogy: just as an idea can be expressed by many different languages, a scene may be rendered by a grayscale image, RGB image, semantic label maps, edge sketches, and so on. In figure 8.15, image-to-image translation tasks are demonstrated on a range of applications such as converting street scene segmentation labels to real images, grayscale to color images, sketches of products to product photographs, and day photographs to night ones.

Pix2Pix is a member of the GAN family designed by Phillip Isola et al. in 2016 for general-purpose image-to-image translation.[7] The Pix2Pix network architecture is similar to the GAN concept: it consists of a generator model for outputting new synthetic images that look realistic, and a discriminator model that classifies images as

---

[7]   Phillip Isola, Jun-Yan Zhu, Tinghui Zhou, and Alexei A. Efros, "Image-to-Image Translation with Conditional Adversarial Networks," 2016, http://arxiv.org/abs/1611.07004.

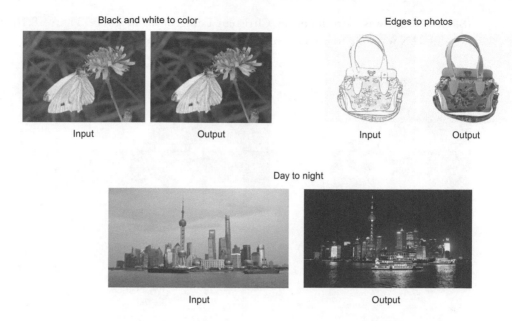

Figure 8.15   Examples of Pix2Pix applications taken from the original paper.

real (from the dataset) or fake (generated). The training process is also similar to that used for GANs: the discriminator model is updated directly, whereas the generator model is updated via the discriminator model. As such, the two models are trained simultaneously in an adversarial process where the generator seeks to better fool the discriminator and the discriminator seeks to better identify the counterfeit images.

The novel idea of Pix2Pix networks is that they learn a loss function adapted to the task and data at hand, which makes them applicable in a wide variety of settings. They are a type of conditional GAN (cGAN) where the generation of the output image is *conditional* on an input source image. The discriminator is provided with both a source image and the target image and must determine whether the target is a plausible transformation of the source image.

The results of the Pix2Pix network are really promising for many image-to-image translation tasks. Visit https://affinelayer.com/pixsrv to play more with the Pix2Pix network; this site has an interactive demo created by Isola and team in which you can convert sketch edges of cats or products to photos and façades to real images.

8.3.3   *Image super-resolution GAN (SRGAN)*

A certain type of GAN models can be used to convert low-resolution images into high-resolution images. This type is called a super-resolution generative adversarial networks

(SRGAN) and was introduced by Christian Ledig et al. in 2016.[8] Figure 8.16 shows how SRGAN was able to create a very high-resolution image.

Original   SRGAN

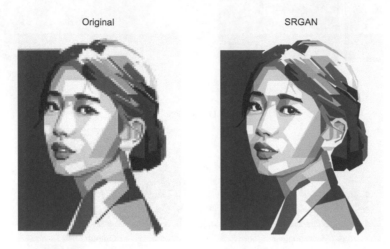

Figure 8.16   SRGAN converting a low-resolution image to a high-resolution image. (*Source:* Ledig et al., 2016.)

8.3.4   *Ready to get your hands dirty?*

GAN models have huge potential for creating and imagining new realities that have never existed before. The applications mentioned in this chapter are just a few examples to give you an idea of what GANs can do today. Such applications come out every few weeks and are worth trying. If you are interested in getting your hands dirty with more GAN applications, visit the amazing Keras-GAN repository at https://github.com/eriklindernoren/Keras-GAN, maintained by Erik Linder-Norén. It includes many GAN models created using Keras and is an excellent resource for Keras examples. Much of the code in this chapter was inspired by and adapted from this repository.

8.4   *Project: Building your own GAN*

In this project, you'll build a GAN using convolutional layers in the generator and discriminator. This is called a deep convolutional GAN (DCGAN) for short. The DCGAN architecture was first explored by Alec Radford et al. (2016), as discussed in section 8.1.1, and has seen impressive results in generating new images. You can follow along with the implementation in this chapter or run code in the project notebook available with this book's downloadable code.

---

[8] Christian Ledig, Lucas Theis, Ferenc Huszar, Jose Caballero, Andrew Cunningham, Alejandro Acosta, Andrew Aitken, et al., "Photo-Realistic Single Image Super-Resolution Using a Generative Adversarial Network," 2016, http://arxiv.org/abs/1609.04802.

In this project, you'll be training DCGAN on the Fashion-MNIST dataset (https://github.com/zalandoresearch/fashion-mnist). Fashion-MNIST consists of 60,000 grayscale images for training and a test set of 10,000 images (figure 8.17). Each 28 × 28 grayscale image is associated with a label from 10 classes. Fashion-MNIST is intended to serve as a direct replacement for the original MNIST dataset for benchmarking machine learning algorithms. I chose grayscale images for this project because it requires less computational power to train convolutional networks on one-channel grayscale images compared to three-channel colored images, which makes it easier for you to train on a personal computer without a GPU.

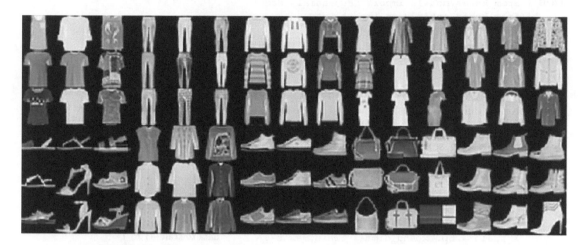

Figure 8.17   Fashion-MNIST dataset examples

The dataset is broken into 10 fashion categories. The class labels are as follows:

Label	Description
0	T-shirt/top
1	Trouser
2	Pullover
3	Dress
4	Coat
5	Sandal
6	Shirt
7	Sneaker
8	Bag
9	Ankle boot

STEP 1: IMPORT LIBRARIES

As always, the first thing to do is to import all the libraries we use in this project:

```
from __future__ import print_function, division

from keras.datasets import fashion_mnist
```
> Imports the fashion_mnist dataset from Keras

Imports Keras layers and models
```
from keras.layers import Input, Dense, Reshape, Flatten, Dropout
from keras.layers import BatchNormalization, Activation, ZeroPadding2D
from keras.layers.advanced_activations import LeakyReLU
from keras.layers.convolutional import UpSampling2D, Conv2D
from keras.models import Sequential, Model
from keras.optimizers import Adam
```

```
import numpy as np
import matplotlib.pyplot as plt
```
> Imports numpy and matplotlib

STEP 2: DOWNLOAD AND VISUALIZE THE DATASET

Keras makes the Fashion-MNIST dataset available for us to download with just one command: `fashion_mnist.load_data()`. Here, we download the dataset and rescale the training set to the range –1 to 1 to allow the model to converge faster (see the "Data normalization" section in chapter 4 for more details on image scaling):

```
(training_data, _), (_, _) = fashion_mnist.load_data()
```
> Loads the dataset

```
X_train = training_data / 127.5 - 1.
X_train = np.expand_dims(X_train, axis=3)
```
> Rescales the training data to scale –1 to 1

Just for the fun of it, let's visualize the image matrix (figure 8.18):

```
def visualize_input(img, ax):
    ax.imshow(img, cmap='gray')
    width, height = img.shape
    thresh = img.max()/2.5
    for x in range(width):
        for y in range(height):
            ax.annotate(str(round(img[x][y],2)), xy=(y,x),
                        horizontalalignment='center',
                        verticalalignment='center',
                        color='white' if img[x][y]<thresh else 'black')

fig = plt.figure(figsize = (12,12))
ax = fig.add_subplot(111)
visualize_input(training_data[3343], ax)
```

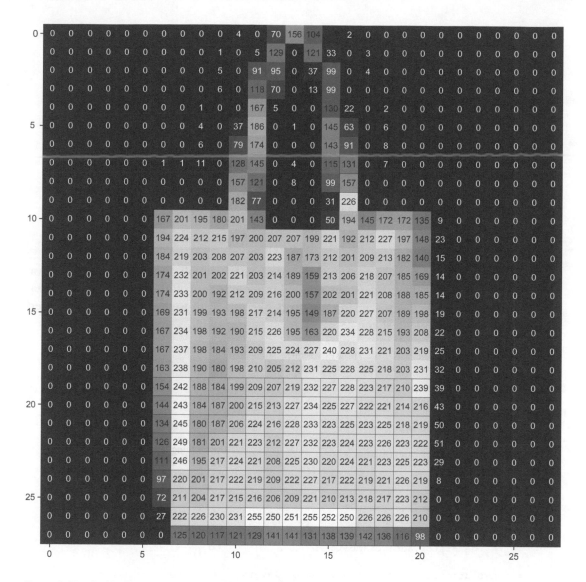

Figure 8.18 A visualized example of the Fashion-MNIST dataset

STEP 3: BUILD THE GENERATOR

Now, let's build the generator model. The input will be our noise vector (z) as explained in section 8.1.5. The generator architecture is shown in figure 8.19.

The first layer is a fully connected layer that is then reshaped into a deep, narrow layer, something like $7 \times 7 \times 128$ (in the original DCGAN paper, the team reshaped the input to $4 \times 4 \times 1024$). Then we use the upsampling layer to double the feature map dimensions from 7×7 to 14×14 and then again to 28×28. In this network, we

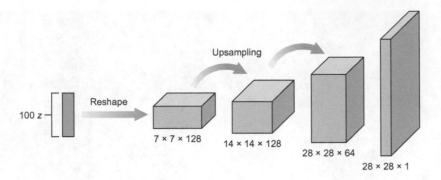

Figure 8.19   Architecture of the generator model

use three convolutional layers. We also use batch normalization and a ReLU activation. For each of these layers, the general scheme is convolution ⇒ batch normalization ⇒ ReLU. We keep stacking up layers like this until we get the final transposed convolution layer with shape 28 × 28 × 1:

Instantiates a sequential model and names it generator

Adds the dense layer that has a number of neurons = 128 × 7 × 7

Reshapes the image dimensions to 7 × 7 × 128

Upsampling layer to double the size of the image dimensions to 14 × 14

Upsamples the image dimensions to 28 × 28

Adds a convolutional layer to run the convolutional process and batch normalization

Prints the model summary

We don't add upsampling here because the image size of 28 × 28 is equal to the image size in the MNIST dataset. You can adjust this for your own problem.

```python
def build_generator():
    generator = Sequential()
    generator.add(Dense(128 * 7 * 7, activation="relu", input_dim=100))
    generator.add(Reshape((7, 7, 128)))
    generator.add(UpSampling2D())
    generator.add(Conv2D(128, kernel_size=3, padding="same",
                    activation="relu"))
    generator.add(BatchNormalization(momentum=0.8))
    generator.add(UpSampling2D())

    # convolutional + batch normalization layers
    generator.add(Conv2D(64, kernel_size=3, padding="same",
                    activation="relu"))
    generator.add(BatchNormalization(momentum=0.8))

    # convolutional layer with filters = 1
    generator.add(Conv2D(1, kernel_size=3, padding="same",
                    activation="relu"))

    generator.summary()
```

```
noise = Input(shape=(100,))

fake_image = generator(noise)

return Model(inputs=noise, outputs=fake_image)
```

Runs the generator model to create the fake image

Returns a model that takes the noise vector as an input and outputs the fake image

Generates the input noise vector of length = 100. We chose 100 here to create a simple network.

STEP 4. BUILD THE DISCRIMINATOR

The discriminator is just a convolutional classifier like what we have built before (figure 8.20). The inputs to the discriminator are 28 × 28 × 1 images. We want a few convolutional layers and then a fully connected layer for the output. As before, we want a sigmoid output, and we need to return the logits as well. For the depths of the convolutional layers, I suggest starting with 32 or 64 filters in the first layer, and then double the depth as you add layers. In this implementation, we start with 64 layers, then 128, and then 256. For downsampling, we do not use pooling layers. Instead, we use only strided convolutional layers for downsampling, similar to Radford et al.'s implementation.

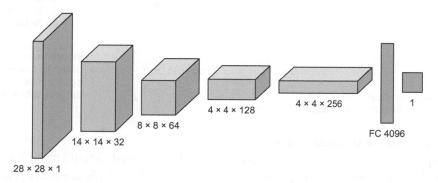

Figure 8.20 **Architecture of the discriminator model**

We also use batch normalization and dropout to optimize training, as we learned in chapter 4. For each of the four convolutional layers, the general scheme is convolution ⇒ batch normalization ⇒ leaky ReLU. Now, let's build the build_discriminator function:

```
def build_discriminator():
    discriminator = Sequential()

    discriminator.add(Conv2D(32, kernel_size=3, strides=2,
                      input_shape=(28,28,1), padding="same"))

    discriminator.add(LeakyReLU(alpha=0.2))

    discriminator.add(Dropout(0.25))
```

Instantiates a sequential model and names it discriminator

Adds a convolutional layer to the discriminator model

Adds a leaky ReLU activation function

Adds a dropout layer with a 25% dropout probability

Adds a second convolutional layer with zero padding

```
discriminator.add(Conv2D(64, kernel_size=3, strides=2,
                        padding="same"))

discriminator.add(ZeroPadding2D(padding=((0,1),(0,1))))
```

Adds a zero-padding layer to change the dimension from 7 × 7 to 8 × 8

Adds a batch normalization layer for faster learning and higher accuracy

```
discriminator.add(BatchNormalization(momentum=0.8))

discriminator.add(LeakyReLU(alpha=0.2))
discriminator.add(Dropout(0.25))

discriminator.add(Conv2D(128, kernel_size=3, strides=2, padding="same"))
discriminator.add(BatchNormalization(momentum=0.8))
discriminator.add(LeakyReLU(alpha=0.2))
discriminator.add(Dropout(0.25))
```

Adds a third convolutional layer with batch normalization, leaky ReLU, and a dropout

Flattens the network and adds the output dense layer with sigmoid activation function

```
discriminator.add(Conv2D(256, kernel_size=3, strides=1, padding="same"))
discriminator.add(BatchNormalization(momentum=0.8))
discriminator.add(LeakyReLU(alpha=0.2))
discriminator.add(Dropout(0.25))

discriminator.add(Flatten())
discriminator.add(Dense(1, activation='sigmoid'))
```

Adds the fourth convolutional layer with batch normalization, leaky ReLU, and a dropout

Sets the input image shape

```
img = Input(shape=(28,28,1))
probability = discriminator(img)

return Model(inputs=img, outputs=probability)
```

Returns a model that takes the image as input and produces the probability output

Runs the discriminator model to get the output probability

STEP 5: BUILD THE COMBINED MODEL

As explained in section 8.1.3, to train the generator, we need to build a combined network that contains both the generator and the discriminator (figure 8.21). The combined model takes the noise signal as input (*z*) and outputs the discriminator's prediction output as fake or real.

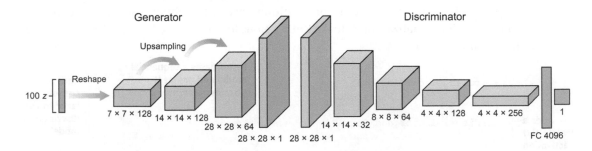

Figure 8.21   Architecture of the combined model

Remember that we want to disable discriminator training for the combined model, as explained in detail in section 8.1.3. When training the generator, we don't want the discriminator to update weights as well, but we still want to include the discriminator model in the generator training. So, we create a combined network that includes both models but freeze the weights of the discriminator model in the combined network:

Defines the optimizer ⟶

```
optimizer = Adam(learning_rate=0.0002, beta_1=0.5)
```
Builds and compiles the discriminator
```
discriminator = build_discriminator()
discriminator.compile(loss='binary_crossentropy', optimizer=optimizer,
    metrics=['accuracy'])
```
Freezes the discriminator weights because we don't want to train it during generator training
```
discriminator.trainable = False
```

Builds the generator ⟶

```
# Build the generator
generator = build_generator()
```
The generator takes noise as input with latent_dim = 100 and generates images.
```
z = Input(shape=(100,))
img = generator(z)
```
The discriminator takes generated images as input and determines their validity.
```
valid = discriminator(img)

combined = Model(inputs=z, outputs=valid)
combined.compile(loss='binary_crossentropy', optimizer=optimizer)
```
The combined model (stacked generator and discriminator) trains the generator to fool the discriminator.

STEP 6: BUILD THE TRAINING FUNCTION

When training the GAN model, we train two networks: the discriminator and the combined network that we created in the previous section. Let's build the `train` function, which takes the following arguments:

- The number of epochs
- The batch size
- `save_interval` to state how often we want to save the results

```
def train(epochs, batch_size=128, save_interval=50):

    valid = np.ones((batch_size, 1))      | Adversarial
    fake = np.zeros((batch_size, 1))      | ground truths

    for epoch in range(epochs):

        ## Train Discriminator network
```
Selects a random half of images
```
        idx = np.random.randint(0, X_train.shape[0], batch_size)
        imgs = X_train[idx]
```

<table>
<tr><td>**Sample noise, and generates a batch of new images**</td><td>

```
noise = np.random.normal(0, 1, (batch_size, 100))
gen_imgs = generator.predict(noise)
```
</td></tr>
</table>

```
d_loss_real = discriminator.train_on_batch(imgs, valid)
d_loss_fake = discriminator.train_on_batch(gen_imgs, fake)
d_loss = 0.5 * np.add(d_loss_real, d_loss_fake)
```

Trains the discriminator (real classified as 1s and generated as 0s)

```
## Train the combined network (Generator)

g_loss = combined.train_on_batch(noise, valid)
```

Trains the generator (wants the discriminator to mistake images for real ones)

```
print("%d [D loss: %f, acc.: %.2f%%] [G loss: %f]" %
      (epoch, d_loss[0], 100*d_loss[1], g_loss))
```

Prints progress

Saves generated image samples if at save_interval

```
    if epoch % save_interval == 0:
        plot_generated_images(epoch, generator)
```

Before you run the train() function, you need to define the following plot_generated _images() function:

```
def plot_generated_images(epoch, generator, examples=100, dim=(10, 10),
                          figsize=(10, 10)):
    noise = np.random.normal(0, 1, size=[examples, latent_dim])
    generated_images = generator.predict(noise)
    generated_images = generated_images.reshape(examples, 28, 28)

    plt.figure(figsize=figsize)
    for i in range(generated_images.shape[0]):
        plt.subplot(dim[0], dim[1], i+1)
        plt.imshow(generated_images[i], interpolation='nearest',
   cmap='gray_r')
        plt.axis('off')
    plt.tight_layout()
    plt.savefig('gan_generated_image_epoch_%d.png' % epoch)
```

STEP 7: TRAIN AND OBSERVE RESULTS

Now that the code implementation is complete, we are ready to start the DCGAN training. To train the model, run the following code snippet:

```
train(epochs=1000, batch_size=32, save_interval=50)
```

This will run the training for 1,000 epochs and saves images every 50 epochs. When you run the train() function, the training progress prints as shown in figure 8.22.

I ran this training myself for 10,000 epochs. Figure 8.23 shows my results after 0, 50, 1,000, and 10,000 epochs.

As you can see in figure 8.23, at epoch 0, the images are just random noise—no patterns or meaningful data. At epoch 50, patterns have started to form. One very apparent pattern is the bright pixels beginning to form at the center of the image, and the surroundings' darker pixels. This happens because in the training data, all of the shapes are located at the center of the image. Later in the training process, at

```
 0 [D loss: 0.963556, acc.: 42.19%] [G loss: 0.726341]
 1 [D loss: 0.707453, acc.: 65.62%] [G loss: 1.239887]
 2 [D loss: 0.478705, acc.: 76.56%] [G loss: 1.666347]
 3 [D loss: 0.721997, acc.: 60.94%] [G loss: 2.243804]
 4 [D loss: 0.937356, acc.: 45.31%] [G loss: 1.459240]
 5 [D loss: 0.881121, acc.: 50.00%] [G loss: 1.417385]
 6 [D loss: 0.558153, acc.: 73.44%] [G loss: 1.393961]
 7 [D loss: 0.404117, acc.: 78.12%] [G loss: 1.141378]
 8 [D loss: 0.452483, acc.: 82.81%] [G loss: 0.802813]
 9 [D loss: 0.591792, acc.: 76.56%] [G loss: 0.690274]
10 [D loss: 0.753802, acc.: 67.19%] [G loss: 0.934047]
11 [D loss: 0.957626, acc.: 50.00%] [G loss: 1.140045]
12 [D loss: 0.919308, acc.: 51.56%] [G loss: 1.311618]
13 [D loss: 0.776363, acc.: 56.25%] [G loss: 1.041264]
14 [D loss: 0.763993, acc.: 56.25%] [G loss: 1.090716]
15 [D loss: 0.754735, acc.: 56.25%] [G loss: 1.530865]
16 [D loss: 0.739731, acc.: 68.75%] [G loss: 1.887644]
```

Figure 8.22   Training progress for the first 16 epochs

epoch 1,000, you can see clear shapes and can probably guess the type of training data fed to the GAN model. Fast-forward to epoch 10,000, and you can see that the generator has become very good at re-creating new images not present in the training

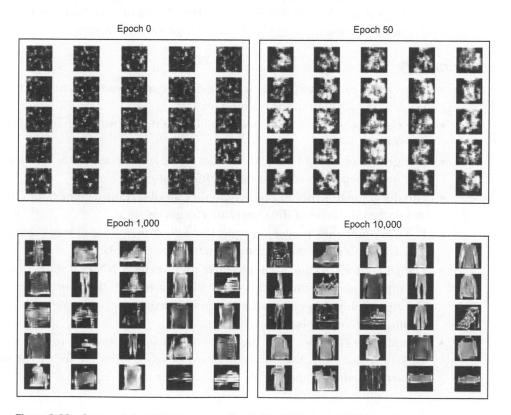

Figure 8.23   Output of the GAN generator after 0, 50, 1,000, and 10,000 epochs

dataset. For example, pick any of the objects created at this epoch: let's say the top-left image (dress). This is a totally new dress design that is not present in the training dataset. The GAN model created a completely new dress design after learning the dress patterns from the training set. You can run the training longer or make the generator network even deeper to get more refined results.

IN CLOSING

For this project, I used the Fashion-MNIST dataset because the images are very small and are in grayscale (one-channel), which makes it computationally inexpensive for you to train on your local computer with no GPU. Fashion-MNIST is also very clean data: all of the images are centered and have less noise so they don't require much preprocessing before you kick off your GAN training. This makes it a good toy dataset to jumpstart your first GAN project.

If you are excited to get your hands dirty with more advanced datasets, you can try CIFAR as your next step (https://www.cs.toronto.edu/~kriz/cifar.html) or Google's Quick, Draw! dataset (https://quickdraw.withgoogle.com), which is considered the world's largest doodle dataset at the time of writing. Another, more serious, dataset is Stanford's Cars Dataset (https://ai.stanford.edu/~jkrause/cars/car_dataset.html), which contains more than 16,000 images of 196 classes of cars. You can try to train your GAN model to design a completely new design for your dream car!

Summary

- GANs learn patterns from the training dataset and create new images that have a similar distribution of the training set.
- The GAN architecture consists of two deep neural networks that compete with each other.
- The generator tries to convert random noise into observations that look as if they have been sampled from the original dataset.
- The discriminator tries to predict whether an observation comes from the original dataset or is one of the generator's forgeries.
- The discriminator's model is a typical classification neural network that aims to classify images generated by the generator as real or fake.
- The generator's architecture looks like an inverted CNN that starts with a narrow input and is upsampled a few times until it reaches the desired size.
- The upsampling layer scales the image dimensions by repeating each row and column of its input pixels.
- To train the GAN, we train the network in batches through two parallel networks: the discriminator and a combined network where we freeze the weights of the discriminator and update only the generator's weights.

- To evaluate the GAN, we mostly rely on our observation of the quality of images created by the generator. Other evaluation metrics are the inception score and Fréchet inception distance (FID).

- In addition to generating new images, GANs can be used in applications such as text-to-photo synthesis, image-to-image translation, image super-resolution, and many other applications.

DeepDream and
neural style transfer

9

This chapter covers

- Visualizing CNN feature maps
- Understanding the DeepDream algorithm and implementing your own dream
- Using the neural style transfer algorithm to create artistic images

In fine art, especially painting, humans have mastered the skill of creating unique visual experiences through composing a complex interplay between the content and style of an image. So far, the algorithmic basis of this process is unknown, and there exists no artificial system with similar capabilities. Nowadays, deep neural networks have demonstrated great promise in many areas of visual perception such as object classification and detection. Why not try using deep neural networks to create art? In this chapter, we introduce an artificial system based on a deep neural network that creates artistic images of high perceptual quality. The system uses neural representations to separate and recombine content and style of arbitrary images, providing a neural algorithm for the creation of artistic images.

In this chapter, we explore two new techniques to create artistic images using neural networks: DeepDream and neural style transfer. First, we examine how convolutional neural networks see the world. We've learned how CNNs are used to extract features in object classification and detection problems; here, we learn how to visualize the extracted feature maps. One reason is that we need this visualization technique in order to understand the DeepDream algorithm. Additionally, this will help us gain a better understanding of what our network learned during training; we can use that to improve the network's performance when solving classification and detection problems.

Next, we discuss the DeepDream algorithm. The key idea of this technique is to print the features we visualize in a certain layer onto our input image, to create a dream-like hallucinogenic image. Finally, we explore the neural style transfer technique, which takes two images as inputs—a style image and a content image—and creates a new combined image that contains the layout from the content image and the texture, colors, and patterns from the style image.

Why is this discussion important? Because these techniques help us understand and visualize how neural networks are able to carry out difficult classification and detection tasks and check what the network has learned during training. Being able to see what the network thinks is an important feature to use when distinguishing objects will help you understand what is missing from your training set and thus improve the network's performance.

These techniques also make us wonder whether neural networks could become tools for artists, give us a new way to combine visual concepts, or perhaps even shed a little light on the roots of the creative process in general. Moreover, these algorithms offer a path forward to an algorithmic understanding of how humans create and perceive artistic imagery.

9.1 *How convolutional neural networks see the world*

We have talked a lot in this book about all the amazing things deep neural networks can do. But despite all the exciting news about deep learning, the exact way neural networks see and interpret the world remains a black box. Yes, we have tried to explain how the training process works, and we explained intuitively and mathematically the backpropagation process that the network applies to update weights through many iterations to optimize the loss function. This all sounds good and makes sense on the scientific side of things. But how do CNNs see the world? How do they see the extracted features between all the layers?

A better understanding of exactly how they recognize specific patterns or objects and why they work so well might allow us to improve their performance even further. Additionally, on the business side, this would also solve the "AI explainability" problem. In many cases, business leaders feel unable to make decisions based on model predictions because nobody really understands what is happening inside the black box. This is what we do in this section: we open the black box and visualize what the network sees through its layers, to help make neural network decisions interpretable by humans.

In computer vision problems, we can visualize the feature maps inside the convolutional network to understand how they see the world and what features they think are distinctive in an object for differentiating between classes. The idea of visualizing convolutional layers was proposed by Erhan et al. in 2009.[1] In this section, we will explain this concept and implement it in Keras.

9.1.1   *Revisiting how neural networks work*

Before we jump into the explanation of how we can visualize the activation maps (or feature maps) in a CNN, let's revisit how neural networks work. We train a deep neural network by showing it millions of training examples. The network then gradually updates its parameters until it gives the classifications we want. The network typically consists of 10–30 stacked layers of artificial neurons. Each image is fed into the input layer, which then talks to the next layer, until eventually the "output" layer is reached. The network's prediction is then produced by its final output layer.

One of the challenges of neural networks is understanding what exactly goes on at each layer. We know that after training, each layer progressively extracts image features at higher and higher levels, until the final layer essentially makes a decision about what the image contains. For example, the first layer may look for edges or corners, intermediate layers interpret the basic features to look for overall shapes or components, and the final few layers assemble those into complete interpretations. These neurons activate in response to very complex images such as a car or a bike.

To understand what the network has learned through its training, we want to open this black box and visualize its feature maps. One way to visualize the extracted features is to turn the network upside down and ask it to enhance an input image in such a way as to elicit a particular interpretation. Say you want to know what sort of image would result in the output "Bird." Start with an image full of random noise, and then gradually tweak the image toward what the neural net considers an important feature of a bird (figure 9.1).

Input: random noise   Output: visualized filter

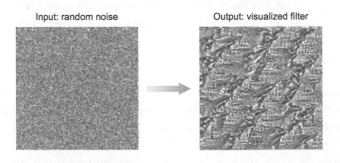

Figure 9.1   Start with an image consisting of random noise, and tweak it until we visualize what the network considers important features of a bird.

[1]   Dumitru Erhan, Yoshua Bengio, Aaron Courville, and Pascal Vincent. "Visualizing Higher-Layer Features of a Deep Network." University of Montreal 1341 (3): 1. 2009. http://mng.bz/yyMq.

We will dive deeper into the bird example and see how to visualize the network filters. The takeaway from this introduction is that neural networks are smart enough to understand which are the important features to pass along through its layers to be classified by its fully connected layers. Non-important features are discarded along the way. To put it simply, neural networks learn the features of the objects in the training dataset. If we are able to *visualize* these feature maps at the deeper layers of the network, we can find out where the neural network is paying attention and see the exact features that it uses to make its predictions.

> **NOTE** This process is described best in François Chollet's book, *Deep Learning with Python* (Manning, 2017; www.manning.com/books/deep-learning-with-python): "You can think of a deep network as a multistage information-distillation operation, where information goes through successive filters and comes out increasingly purified."

9.1.2 *Visualizing CNN features*

An easy way to visualize the features learned by convolutional networks is to display the visual pattern that each filter is meant to respond to. This can be done with *gradient ascent* in input space. By applying gradient ascent to the value of the input image of a ConvNet, we can maximize the response of a specific filter, starting from a blank input image. The resulting input image will be one that the chosen filter is maximally responsive to.

Gradient ascent vs. gradient descent

As a reminder, the general definition of a *gradient* is that it is the function that defines the slope or rate of change of the line tangent to a curve at any given point. In simpler words, the gradient is the slope of the line at that point. Here are some example gradients at certain points on a curve.

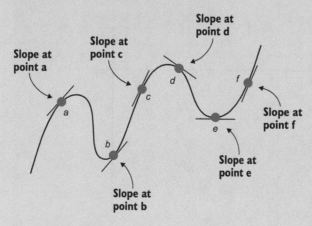

The gradient at different points on the curve

(continued)

Whether we want to descend or ascend the curve is based on our project. We learned in chapter 2 that GD is the algorithm that *descends* the error function to find the local minimum (for example, minimize the loss function) by taking steps toward the negative of the gradient.

To visualize feature maps, we want to maximize these features to make them show on the output image. In order to maximize the loss function, we want to reverse the GD process by using a *gradient ascent algorithm*. It takes steps proportional to the *positive* of the gradient to approach a local maximum of that function.

Now comes the fun part of this section. In this exercise, we will see the visualized feature maps of a few examples at the beginning, middle, and end of a VGG16 network. The implementation is straightforward, and we will get to it soon. Before we go to the code implementation, let's take a look at what these visualized filters look like.

From the VGG16 diagram we saw in figure 9.1, let's visualize the output feature maps of the first, middle, and deep layers as follows: `block1_conv1`, `block3_conv2`, and `block5_conv3`. Figures 9.2, 9.3, and 9.4 show how the features evolve throughout the network layers.

As you can see in figure 9.2, the early layers basically just encode low-level, generic features like direction and color. These direction and color filters then get combined

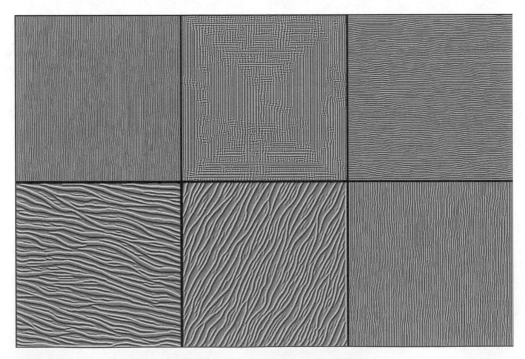

Figure 9.2   **Visualizing feature maps produced by** `block1_conv1` **filters**

into basic grid and spot textures in later layers. These textures are gradually combined into increasingly complex patterns (figure 9.3): the network starts to see some patterns that create basic shapes. These shapes are not very identifiable yet, but they are much clearer than the earlier ones.

Figure 9.3   Visualizing feature maps produced by `block3_conv2` **filters**

Now this is the most exciting part. In figure 9.4, you see that the network was able to find patterns in patterns. These features contain identifiable shapes. While the network relies on more than one feature map to make its prediction, we can look at these maps and make a close guess about the content of these images. In the left image, I can see eyes and maybe a beak, and I would guess that this is a type of bird or fish. Even if our guess is not correct, we can easily eliminate most other classes like car, boat, building, bike, and so on, because we can clearly see eyes and none of those classes have eyes. Similarly, looking at the middle image, we can guess from the patterns that this is some kind of a chain. The right image feels more like food or fruit.

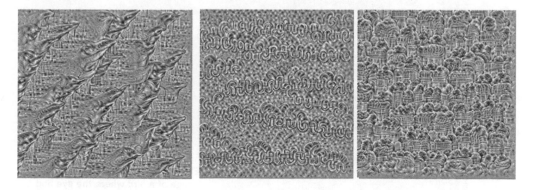

Figure 9.4   Visualizing feature maps produced by `block5_conv3` **filters**

How is this helpful in classification and detection problems? Let's take the left feature map in figure 9.4 as an example. Looking at the visible features like eyes and beaks, I can interpret that the network relies on these two features to identify a bird. With this knowledge about what the network learned about birds, I will guess that it can detect the bird in figure 9.5, because the bird's eye and beak are visible.

Figure 9.5   Example of a bird image with visible eye and beak features

Now, let's consider a more adversarial case where we can see the bird's body but the eye and beak are covered by leaves (figure 9.6). Given that the network adds high weights

Figure 9.6   Example of an adversarial image of a bird where the eye and beak are not visible but the body is recognizable by a human

on the eye and beak features to recognize a bird, there is a good chance that it might miss this bird because the bird's main features are hidden. On the other hand, an average human can easily detect the bird in the image. The solution to this problem is using one of several data-augmentation techniques and collecting more adversarial cases in your training dataset to force the network to add higher weights on other features of a bird, like shape and color.

9.1.3 *Implementing a feature visualizer*

Now that you've seen the visualized examples, it is time to get your hands dirty and develop the code to visualize these activation filters yourself. This section walks through the CNN visualization code implementation from the official Keras documentation, with minor tweaking.[2] You will learn how to generate patterns that maximize the mean activation of a chosen feature map. You can see the full code in Keras's Github repository (http://mng.bz/Md8n).

> **NOTE** You will run into errors if you try to run the code snippets in this section. These snippets are just meant to illustrate the topic. You are encouraged to check out the full executable code that is downloadable with the book.

First, we load the VGG16 model from the Keras library. To do that, we first import VGG16 from Keras and then load the model, which is pretrained on the ImageNet dataset, without including the classification fully connected layers (top part) of the network:

```
from keras.applications.vgg16 import VGG16          ◁──┐ Imports the VGG
model = VGG16(weights='imagenet', include_top=False) ◁──┘ model from Keras
                                                      ◁──┐ Loads the model
```

Now, let's view the names and output shape of all the VGG16 layers. We do that to pick the specific layer whose filters we want to visualize:

```
for layer in model.layers:          ◁──┘ Loops through the
    if 'conv' not in layer.name:    ◁──     model layers
        continue                           Checks for a
    filters, biases = layer.get_weights()  ◁──┐ convolutional layer
    print(layer.name, layer.output.shape)    Gets the filter weights
```

When you run this code cell, you will get the output shown in figure 9.7. These are all the convolutional layers contained in the VGG16 network. You can visualize any of their outputs simply by referring to each layer by name, as you will see in the next code snippet.

Let's say we want to visualize the first conv layer: `block1_conv1`. Note that this layer has 64 filters, each of which has an index from 0 to 63 called `filter_index`. Now let's

---

[2] François Chollet, "How convolutional neural networks see the world," The Keras Blog, 2016, https://blog .keras.io/category/demo.html.

```
block1_conv1       (None, None, None, 64)
block1_conv2       (None, None, None, 64)
block2_conv1       (None, None, None, 128)
block2_conv2       (None, None, None, 128)
block3_conv1       (None, None, None, 256)
block3_conv2       (None, None, None, 256)
block3_conv3       (None, None, None, 256)
block4_conv1       (None, None, None, 512)
block4_conv2       (None, None, None, 512)
block4_conv3       (None, None, None, 512)
block5_conv1       (None, None, None, 512)
block5_conv2       (None, None, None, 512)
block5_conv3       (None, None, None, 512)
```

Figure 9.7   Output showing convolution layers in the downloaded VGG16 network

define a loss function that seeks to maximize the activation of a specific filter (`filter _index`) in a specific layer (`layer_name`). We also want to compute the gradient using Keras's backend function `gradients` and normalize the gradient to avoid very small and very large values, to ensure a smooth gradient ascent process.

In this code snippet, we set the stage for gradient ascent. We define a loss function, compute the gradients, and normalize the gradients:

```
from keras import backend as K

layer_name = 'block1_conv1'
filter_index = 0

layer_dict = dict([(layer.name, layer) for layer in model.layers[1:]])

layer_output = layer_dict[layer_name].output
loss = K.mean(layer_output[:, :, :, filter_index])

grads = K.gradients(loss, input_img)[0]

grads /= (K.sqrt(K.mean(K.square(grads))) + 1e-5)

iterate = K.function([input_img], [loss, grads])
```

Identifies the filter that we want to visualize. This can be any integer from 0 to 63, as there are 64 filters in that layer.

Gets the symbolic outputs of each key layer (we gave them unique names).

Builds a loss function that maximizes the activation of the nth filter of the layer considered

Computes the gradient of the input picture with respect to this loss

Normalizes the gradient

This function returns the loss and grads given the input picture.

We can use the Keras function that we just defined to do gradient ascent to our filter activation loss:

```
import numpy as np

input_img_data = np.random.random((1, 3, img_width, img_height)) * 20 + 128
for i in range(20):
    loss_value, grads_value = iterate([input_img_data])
    input_img_data += grads_value * step
```

Starts from a gray image with some noise

Runs gradient ascent for 20 steps

Now that we have implemented the gradient ascent, we need to build a function that converts the tensor into a valid image. We will call it `deprocess_image(x)`. Then we save the image on disk to view it:

```python
from keras.preprocessing.image import save_img

def deprocess_image(x):
    x -= x.mean()
    x /= (x.std() + 1e-5)       Normalizes the tensor:
    x *= 0.1                    centers on 0. and ensures
                                that std is 0.1

    x += 0.5
    x = np.clip(x, 0, 1)        Clips to [0, 1]

    x *= 255
    x = x.transpose((1, 2, 0))                          Converts to an
    x = np.clip(x, 0, 255).astype('uint8')              RGB array
    return x

img = input_img_data[0]
img = deprocess_image(img)
imsave('%s_filter_%d.png' % (layer_name, filter_index), img)
```

The result should be something like figure 9.8.

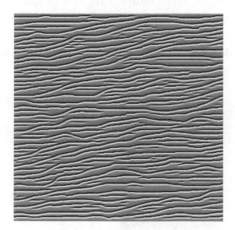

Figure 9.8   VGG16 layer `block1_conv1` visualized

You can try to change the visualized filters to deeper layers in later blocks like `block2` and `block3` to see more defined features extracted as a result of the network recognizing patterns within patterns through its layers. In the highest layers (`block5_conv2`, `block5_conv3`) you will start to recognize textures similar to those found in the objects the network was trained to classify, such as feathers, eyes, and so on.

9.2   *DeepDream*

DeepDream was developed by Google researchers Alexander Mordvintsev et al. in 2015.[3] It is an artistic image modification technique that creates dream-like, hallucinogenic images using CNNs, as shown in the example in figure 9.9).

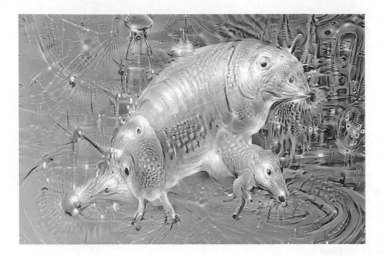

Figure 9.9   DeepDream output image

For comparison, the original input image is shown in figure 9.10. The original is a scenic image from the ocean, containing two dolphins and other creatures. DeepDream merged both dolphins into one object and replaced one of the faces with what looks like a dog face. Other objects were also deformed in an artistic way, and the sea background has an edge-like texture.

Figure 9.10   DeepDream input image

---

[3] Alexander Mordvintsev, Christopher Olah, and Mike Tyka, "Deepdream—A Code Example for Visualizing Neural Networks," Google AI Blog, 2015, http://mng.bz/aROB.

DeepDream quickly became an internet sensation, thanks to the trippy pictures it generates, full of algorithmic artifacts, bird feathers, dog faces, and eyes. These artifacts are byproducts of the fact that the DeepDream ConvNet was trained on ImageNet, where dog breeds and bird species are vastly overrepresented. If you tried another network that was pretrained on a dataset with a majority distribution of other objects, such as cars, you would see car features in your output image.

The project started as a fun experiment to run a CNN in reverse and visualize its activation maps using the same convolutional filter-visualization techniques explained in section 9.1: run a ConvNet in reverse, doing gradient ascent on the input in order to maximize the activation of a specific filter in an upper layer of the ConvNet. Deep-Dream uses this same idea, with a few alterations:

- *Input image*—In filter visualization, we don't use an input image. We start from a blank image (or a slightly noisy one) and then maximize the filter activations of the convolutional layers to view their features. In DeepDream, we use an input image to the network because the goal is to print these visualized features on an image.
- *Maximizing filters versus layers*—In filter visualization, as the name implies, we only maximize activations of specific filters within the layer. But in DeepDream, we aim to maximize the activation of the entire layer to mix together a large number of features at once.
- *Octaves*—In DeepDream, the input images are processed at different scales called *octaves* to improve the quality of the visualized features. This process will be explained next.

9.2.1 How the DeepDream algorithm works

Similar to the filter-visualization technique, DeepDream uses a pretrained network on a large dataset. The Keras library has many pretrained ConvNets available to use: VGG16, VGG19, Inception, ResNet, and so on. We can use any of these networks in the DeepDream implementation; we can even train a custom network on our own dataset and use it in the DeepDream algorithm. Intuitively, the choice of network and the data it is pretrained on will affect our visualizations because different ConvNet architectures result in different learned features; and, of course, different training datasets will create different features as well.

The creators of DeepDream used an Inception model because they found that in practice, it produces nice-looking dreams. So in this chapter, we will use the Inception v3 model. You are encouraged to try different models to observe the difference.

The overall idea with DeepDream is that we pass an input image through a pretrained neural network such as the Inception v3 model. At some layer, we calculate the gradient, which tells us how we should change the input image to maximize the value at this layer. We continue doing this for 10, 20, or 40 iterations until eventually, patterns start to emerge in the input image (figure 9.11).

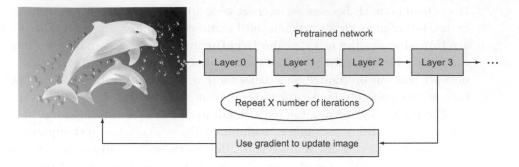

Figure 9.11   DeepDream algorithm

This works fine, except that if the pretrained network has been trained on fairly small image sizes, like ImageNet, then when our input image is large (say, 1000 × 1000), the DeepDream algorithm will print a lot of small patterns in the image that look noisy rather than artistic. This happens because all the extracted features are small in size. To solve this problem, the DeepDream algorithm processes the input image at different scales called octaves.

Octave is just a fancy word for an interval. The idea is to apply the DeepDream algorithm on the input image through intervals. We first downscale the image several times into different scales. The number of scales is configurable, as you will see soon. For each interval, we do the following:

1 Inject details: to avoid losing a lot of image details after each successive scale-up, we re-inject the lost details back into the image after each upscale process to create a blended image.
2 Apply the DeepDream algorithm: send the blended image through the Deep-Dream algorithm.
3 Upscale to the next interval.

As you can see in figure 9.12, we start with the large input image and then downscale two times to get a small image in octave 3. For the first interval of applying Deep-Dream, we don't need to do detail injection because the input image is the source image that hasn't been upscaled before. We pass it through the DeepDream algorithm and then upscale the output. After upscaling, details are lost, which results in an increasingly blurry or pixelated image. This is why it is valuable to re-inject the image details from the input image in octave 2 and then pass the blended image through the DeepDream algorithm. We apply the same process of upscale, detail injection, and DeepDream one more time to get the final result image. This process is run recursively for an identified number of iterations until we are satisfied with the output art.

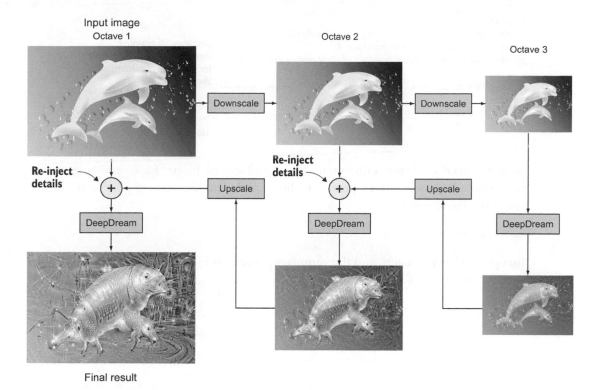

Figure 9.12 The DeepDream process: successive image downscales called octaves, detail re-injection, and then upscaling to the next octave

We set the DeepDream parameters as follows:

```
num_octave = 3          ⟵┐ Number of scales

octave_scale = 1.4      ⟵┤ Size ratio between scales. Each successive
                            scale is larger than the previous one by a
                            factor of 1.4 (40% larger).

iterations = 20         ⟵┐ Number of iterations
```

Now that you understand how the DeepDream algorithm works, let's take a look at DeepDream in action using Keras.

9.2.2 DeepDream implementation in Keras

The DeepDream implementation that we are going to implement is based on François Chollet's code from the official Keras documentation (https://keras.io/examples/generative/deep_dream/) and his book, *Deep Learning with Python*. We'll explain this code after adapting it to work on Jupyter Notebooks:

```
import numpy as np
from keras.applications import inception_v3
from keras import backend as K
from keras.preprocessing.image import save_img

K.set_learning_phase(0)

model = inception_v3.InceptionV3(weights='imagenet', include_top=False)
```

Disables all training operations since we won't be doing any training with the model

Downloads the pretrained Inception v3 model without its top part

Now, we need to define a dictionary that specifies which layers are used to generate the dream. To do that, let's print out the model summary to view all the layers and select the layers names:

```
model.summary()
```

Inception v3 is very deep, and the summary printout is long. For simplicity, figure 9.13 shows a few layers of the network.

Layer (type)	Output Shape	Param #
activation_20 (Activation)	(None, None, None, 60	batch_normalization_20[0][0]
activation_22 (Activation)	(None, None, None, 60	batch_normalization_22[0][0]
activation_25 (Activation)	(None, None, None, 90	batch_normalization_25[0][0]
activation_26 (Activation)	(None, None, None, 60	batch_normalization_26[0][0]
mixed2 (Concatenate)	(None, None, None, 20	activation_20[0][0] activation_22[0][0] activation_25[0][0] activation_26[0][0]

Figure 9.13 Part of the Inception v3 model summary

The exact layers you choose and their contribution to the final loss have an important influence on the visuals you can produce in the dream image, so you want to make these parameters easily configurable. To define the layers that we want to contribute to the dream creation, we create a dictionary with the layer names and their respective weights. The larger the weight of the layer, the higher its level of contribution to the dream:

```
layer_contributions = {
                        'mixed2': 0.4,
                        'mixed3': 2.,
                        'mixed4': 1.5,
                        'mixed5': 2.3,
                      }
```

These are the names of the layers for which we try to maximize activations. Note that when you change the layers in this dictionary, you will produce different dreams, so you are encouraged to experiment with different layers and their corresponding weights. For this project, we will start with a somewhat arbitrary configuration by adding four layers to our dictionary and their weights: mixed2, mixed3, mixed4, and mixed5. As a guide, remember from earlier in this chapter that lower layers can be used to generate edges and geometric patterns, while high layers result in the injection of trippy visual patterns, including hallucinations of dogs, cats, and birds.

Now, let's define a tensor that contains the loss: the weighted sum of the L2 norm of the activations of the layers:

```
layer_dict = dict([(layer.name, layer) for layer in model.layers])    ←   Dictionary that maps layer
                                                                           names to layer instances

loss = K.variable(0.)                          ←   Defines the loss by adding
                                                   layer contributions to this
for layer_name in layer_contributions:             scalar variable
    coeff = layer_contributions[layer_name]
    activation = layer_dict[layer_name].output
    scaling = K.prod(K.cast(K.shape(activation), 'float32'))

    loss = loss + coeff *
        K.sum(K.square(activation[:, 2: -2, 2: -2, :])) / scaling    ←
```

Dictionary that maps layer names to layer instances

Defines the loss by adding layer contributions to this scalar variable

Adds the L2 norm of the features of a layer to the loss. We avoid border artifacts by only involving non-border pixels in the loss.

Next, we compute the loss, which is the quantity we will try to maximize during the gradient ascent process. In filter visualization, we wanted to maximize the value of a specific filter in a specific layer. Here, we will simultaneously maximize the activation of all filters in a number of layers. Specifically, we will maximize a weighted sum of the L2 norm of the activations of a set of high-level layers:

```
dream = model.input         ←   Tensors that holds the
                                 generated image

grads = K.gradients(loss, dream)[0]    ←   Computes the gradients of
                                           the dream image with
                                           regard to the loss

grads /= K.maximum(K.mean(K.abs(grads)), 1e-7)    ←   Normalizes the gradients

outputs = [loss, grads]
fetch_loss_and_grads = K.function([dream], outputs)    ←   Sets up a Keras function to
                                                           retrieve the value of the
def eval_loss_and_grads(x):                                loss and gradients given an
    outs = fetch_loss_and_grads([x])                       input image
    loss_value = outs[0]
    grad_values = outs[1]
    return loss_value, grad_values
                                                       Runs the gradient
def gradient_ascent(x, iterations, step, max_loss=None):  ←  ascent process for a
    for i in range(iterations):                              number of iterations
```

Tensors that holds the generated image

Computes the gradients of the dream image with regard to the loss

Normalizes the gradients

Sets up a Keras function to retrieve the value of the loss and gradients given an input image

Runs the gradient ascent process for a number of iterations

```
    loss_value, grad_values = eval_loss_and_grads(x)
    if max_loss is not None and loss_value > max_loss:
        break
    print('...Loss value at', i, ':', loss_value)
    x += step * grad_values
return x
```

Now we are ready to develop our DeepDream algorithm. The process is as follows:

1. Load the input image.
2. Define the number of scales, from smallest to largest.
3. Resize the input image to the smallest scale.
4. For each scale, start with the smallest and apply the following:
   - Gradient ascent function
   - Upscaling to the next scale
   - Re-injecting details that were lost during the upscale process
5. Stop the process when we are back to the original size.

First, we set the algorithm parameters:

Gradient ascent step size

```
step = 0.01
num_octave = 3
octave_scale = 1.4
iterations = 20
max_loss = 10.
```

Number of scales at which we run gradient ascent

Size ratio between scales

Number of iterations

Note that playing with these hyperparameters will allow you to achieve new effects.

Let's define the input image that we want to use to create our dream. For this example, I downloaded an image of the Golden Gate Bridge in San Francisco (see figure 9.14); feel free to use an image of your own. Figure 9.15 shows the DeepDream output image.

Figure 9.14   Example input image

Figure 9.15   DeepDream output

Here's the Keras code:

```
base_image_path = 'input.jpg'
img = preprocess_image(base_image_path)          Defines the path to
original_shape = img.shape[1:3]                  the input image

successive_shapes = [original_shape]

for i in range(1, num_octave):
    shape = tuple([int(dim / (octave_scale ** i)) for dim in original_shape])

    successive_shapes.append(shape)

successive_shapes = successive_shapes[::-1]

original_img = np.copy(img)

shrunk_original_img = resize_img(img, successive_shapes[0])

for shape in successive_shapes:

    print('Processing image shape', shape)

    img = resize_img(img, shape)
    img = gradient_ascent(img, iterations=iterations, step=step,
                          max_loss=max_loss)
    upscaled_shrunk_original_img = resize_img(shrunk_original_img, shape)
    same_size_original = resize_img(original_img, shape)
    lost_detail = same_size_original - upscaled_shrunk_original_img
    img += lost_detail
    shrunk_original_img = resize_img(original_img, shape)

    phil_img = deprocess_image(np.copy(img))
    save_img('deepdream_output/dream_at_scale_' + str(shape) + '.png', phil_img)

final_img = deprocess_image(np.copy(img))          Saves the
save_img('final_dream.png', final_img)             result to disk
```

9.3   *Neural style transfer*

So far, we have learned how to visualize specific filters in a network. We also learned how to manipulate features of an input image to create dream-like hallucinogenic images using the DeepDream algorithm. In this section, we explore a new type of artistic image that ConvNets can create using *neural style transfer*: the technique of transferring the style from one image to another.

The goal of the neural style transfer algorithm is to take the style of an image (style image) and apply it to the content of another image (content image). *Style* in this context means texture, colors, and other visual patterns in the image. And *content* is the higher-level macrostructure of the image. The result is a combined image that contains both the content of the content image and the style of the style image.

For example, let's look at figure 9.16. The objects in the content image (like dolphins, fish, and plants) are kept in the combined image but with the specific texture of the style image (blue and yellow brushstrokes).

Figure 9.16   Example of neural style transfer

The idea of neural style transfer was introduced by Leon A. Gatys et al. in 2015.[4] The concept of style transfer, which is tightly related to texture generation, had a long history in the image-processing community prior to that; but as it turns out, the DL-based implementations of style transfer offer results unparalleled by what had been previously achieved with traditional CV techniques, and they triggered an amazing renaissance in creative CV applications.

Among the different neural network techniques that create art (like DeepDream), style transfer is the closest to my heart. DeepDream can create cool hallucination-like images, but it can be disturbing sometimes. Plus, as a DL engineer, it is not easy to intentionally create a specific piece of art that you have in your mind. Style transfer, on the other hand, can use an artistic engineer to mix the content that you want from an image with your favorite painting to create something that you have imagined. It is

---

[4]   Leon A. Gatys, Alexander S. Ecker, and Matthias Bethge, "A Neural Algorithm of Artistic Style," 2015, http://arxiv.org/abs/1508.06576.

a really cool technique that, if used by an artist engineer, can be used to create beautiful art on par with that produced by professional painters.

The main idea behind implementing style transfer is the same as the one central to all DL algorithms, as explained in chapter 2: we first define a loss function to define what we aim to achieve, and then we work on optimizing this function. In style-transfer problems, we know what we want to achieve: conserving the *content* of the original image while adopting the *style* of the reference image. Now all we need to do is to define both content and style in a mathematical representation, and then define an appropriate loss function to minimize.

The key notion in defining the loss function is to remember that we want to preserve content from one image and style from another:

- *Content loss*—Calculate the loss between the content image and the combined image. Minimizing this loss means the combined image will have more content from the original image.
- *Style loss*—Calculate the loss in style between the style image and the combined image. Minimizing this loss means the combined image will have style similar to the style image.
- *Noise loss*—This is called the *total variation loss*. It measures the noise in the combined image. Minimizing this loss creates an image with a higher spatial smoothness.

Here is the equation of the total loss:

```
total_loss = [style(style_image) - style(combined_image)] +
    [content(original_image) - content(combined_image)] + total_variation_loss
```

> **NOTE** Gatys et al. (2015) on transfer learning does not include the total variation loss. After experimentation, the researchers found that the network generated better, more aesthetically-pleasing style transfers when they encouraged spatial smoothness across the output image.

Now that we have a big-picture idea of how the neural style transfer algorithm works, we are going to dive deeper into each type of loss to see how it is derived and coded in Keras. We will then understand how to train a neural style transfer network to minimize the `total_loss` function that we just defined.

9.3.1 Content loss

The content loss measures how different two images are in terms of subject matter and the overall placement of content. In other words, two images that contain similar scenes should have a smaller loss value than two images that contain completely different scenes. Image subject matter and content placement are measured by scoring images based on higher-level feature representations in the ConvNet, such as *dolphins*, *plants*, and *water*. Identifying these features is the whole premise behind deep neural networks: these networks are trained to extract the content of an image and learn the higher-level features at the deeper layers by recognizing patterns in simpler features from the previous layers. With that said, we need a deep neural network that has been trained to extract the features of the content image so that we can tap into a deep layer of the network to extract high-level features.

To calculate the content loss, we measure the mean squared error between the output for the content image and the combined image. By trying to minimize this error, the network tries to add more content to the combined image to make it more and more similar to the original content image:

$$\text{Content loss} = \frac{1}{2} \sum [\text{content(original\_image)} - \text{content(combined\_image)}]^2$$

Minimizing the content loss function ensures that we preserve the content of the original image and create it in the combined image.

To calculate the content loss, we feed both the content and style images into a pretrained network and select a deep layer from which to extract high-level features. We then calculate the mean squared error between both images. Let's see how we calculate the content loss between two images in Keras.

> **NOTE** The code snippets in this section are adapted from the neural style transfer example in the official Keras documentation (https://keras.io/examples/generative/neural_style_transfer/). If you want to re-create this project and experiment with different parameters, I suggest that you work from Keras' Github repository as a starting point (http://mng.bz/GVzv) or run the adapted code available for download with this book.

First, we define two Keras variables to hold the content image and style image. And we create a placeholder tensor that will contain the generated combined image:

```
content_image_path = '/path_to_images/content_image.jpg'
style_image_path = '/path_to_images/style_image.jpg'
```
Paths to the content and style images

```
content_image = K.variable(preprocess_image(content_image_path))
style_image = K.variable(preprocess_image(style_image_path))
combined_image = K.placeholder((1, img_nrows, img_ncols, 3))
```
Gets tensor representations of our images

Now, we concatenate the three images into one input tensor and feed it to the VGG19 neural network. Note that when we load the VGG19 model, we set the `include_top` parameter to `False` because we don't need to include the classification fully connected layers for this task. This is because we are only interested in the feature-extraction part of the network:

Combines the three images into a single Keras tensor

```
input_tensor = K.concatenate([content_image, style_image,
                        combined_image], axis=0)
```

```
model = vgg19.VGG19(input_tensor=input_tensor,
                weights='imagenet', include_top=False)
```

Builds the VGG19 network with our three images as input. The model will be loaded with pretrained ImageNet weights.

Similar to what we did in section 9.1, we now select the network layer we want to use to calculate the content loss. We wanted to choose a deep layer to make sure it contains higher-level features of the content image. If you choose an earlier layer of the network (like block 1 or block 2), the network won't be able to transfer the full content from the original image because the earlier layers extract low-level features like lines, edges, and blobs. In this example, we choose the second convolutional layer in block 5 (block5_conv2):

```
outputs_dict = dict([(layer.name, layer.output) for layer in model.layers])
layer_features = outputs_dict['block5_conv2']
```

Gets the symbolic outputs of each key layer (we gave them unique names)

Now we can extract the features from the layer that we chose from the input tensor:

```
content_image_features = layer_features[0, :, :, :]
combined_features = layer_features[2, :, :, :]
```

Finally, we create the content_loss function that calculates the mean squared error between the content image and the combined image. We create an auxiliary loss function designed to preserve the features of the content_image and transfer it to the combined-image:

```
def content_loss(content_image, combined_image):
    return K.sum(K.square(combined - base))
```

Mean square error function between the content image output and the combined image

```
content_loss = content_weight * content_loss(content_image_features,
                                             combined_features)
```

content_loss is scaled by a weighting parameter.

Weighting parameters

In this code implementation, you will see the following weighting parameters: content _weight, style_weight, and total_variation_weight. These are scaling parameters set by us as an input to the network as follows:

```
content_weight = content_weight
total_variation_weight = tv_weight
style_weight = style_weight
```

These weight parameters describe the importance of content, style, and noise in our output image. For example, if we set style_weight = 100 and content_weight = 1, we are implying that we are willing to sacrifice a bit of the content for a more artistic style transfer. Also, a higher total_variation_weight implies higher spatial smoothness.

9.3.2 *Style loss*

As we mentioned before, *style* in this context means texture, colors, and other visual patterns in the image.

MULTIPLE LAYERS TO REPRESENT STYLE FEATURES

Defining the style loss is a little more challenging than what we did with the content loss. In the content loss, we cared only about the higher-level features that are extracted at the deeper levels, so we only needed to choose *one* layer from the VGG19 network to preserve its features. In style loss, on the other hand, we want to choose *multiple* layers because we want to obtain a multi-scale representation of the image style. We want to capture the image style at lower-level layers, mid-level layers, and higher-level layers. This allows us to capture the texture and style of our style image and exclude the global arrangement of objects in the content image.

GRAM MATRIX TO MEASURE JOINTLY ACTIVATED FEATURE MAPS

The *gram matrix* is a method that is used to numerically measure how much two feature maps are jointly activated. Our goal is to build a loss function that captures the style and texture of multiple layers in a CNN. To do that, we need to compute the correlations between the activation layers in our CNN. This correlation can be captured by computing the gram matrix—the feature-wise outer product—between the activations.

To calculate the gram matrix of the feature map, we flatten the feature map and calculate the dot product:

```
def gram_matrix(x):
    features = K.batch_flatten(K.permute_dimensions(x, (2, 0, 1)))
    gram = K.dot(features, K.transpose(features))
    return gram
```

Let's build the style_loss function. It calculates the gram matrix for a set of layers throughout the network for both the style and combined images. It then compares the similarities of style and texture between them by calculating the sum of squared errors:

```
def style_loss(style, combined):
    S = gram_matrix(style)
    C = gram_matrix(combined)
    channels = 3
    size = img_nrows * img_ncols
    return K.sum(K.square(S - C)) / (4.0 * (channels ** 2) * (size ** 2))
```

In this example, we are going to calculate the style loss over five layers: the first convolutional layer in each of the five blocks of the VGG19 network (note that if you change the feature layers, the network will preserve different styles):

```
feature_layers = ['block1_conv1', 'block2_conv1',
                  'block3_conv1', 'block4_conv1',
                  'Block5_conv1']
```

Finally, we loop through these `feature_layers` to calculate the style loss:

```
for layer_name in feature_layers:
    layer_features = outputs_dict[layer_name]
    style_reference_features = layer_features[1, :, :, :]
    combination_features = layer_features[2, :, :, :]
    sl = style_loss(style_reference_features, combination_features)
    style_loss += (style_weight / len(feature_layers)) * sl
```

> Scales the style loss by a weighting parameter and the number of layers over which the style loss is calculated

During training, the network works on minimizing the loss between the style of the output image (combined image) and the style of the input style image. This forces the style of the combined image to correlate with the style image.

9.3.3 Total variance loss

The total variance loss is the measure of noise in the combined image. The network's goal is to minimize this loss function in order to minimize the noise in the output image.

Let's create the `total_variation_loss` function that calculates how noisy an image is. This is what we are going to do:

1 Shift the image one pixel to the right, and calculate the sum of the squared error between the transferred image and the original.
2 Repeat step 1, this time shifting the image one pixel down.

The sum of these two terms (a and b) is the total variance loss:

```
def total_variation_loss(x):
    a = K.square(
        x[:, :img_nrows - 1, :img_ncols - 1, :] - x[:, 1:, :img_ncols - 1, :])
    b = K.square(
        x[:, :img_nrows - 1, :img_ncols - 1, :] - x[:, :img_nrows - 1, 1:, :])

    return K.sum(K.pow(a + b, 1.25))

tv_loss = total_variation_weight * total_variation_loss(combined_image)
```

> Scales the total variance loss by the weighting parameter

Finally, we calculate the overall loss of our problem, which is the sum of the content, style, and total variance losses:

```
total_loss = content_loss + style_loss + tv_loss
```

9.3.4 Network training

Now that we have defined the total loss function for our problem, we can run the GD optimizer to minimize this loss function. First we create an object class `Evaluator` that contains methods that calculate the overall loss, as described previously, and gradients of the loss with respect to the input image:

```
class Evaluator(object):
    def __init__(self):
        self.loss_value = None
        self.grads_values = None

    def loss(self, x):
        assert self.loss_value is None
        loss_value, grad_values = eval_loss_and_grads(x)
        self.loss_value = loss_value
        self.grad_values = grad_values
        return self.loss_value

    def grads(self, x):
        assert self.loss_value is not None
        grad_values = np.copy(self.grad_values)
        self.loss_value = None
        self.grad_values = None
        return grad_values


evaluator = Evaluator()
```

Next, we use the methods in our evaluator class in the training process. To minimize the total loss function, we use the SciPy (https://scipy.org/scipylib) based optimization method scipy.optimize.fmin_l_bfgs_b:

```
from scipy.optimize import fmin_l_bfgs_b

Iterations = 1000          ◁─┘ Trains for 1,000 iterations

x = preprocess_image(content_image_path)   ◁─
```

The training process is initialized with content_image as the first iteration of the combined image.

```
for i in range(iterations):
    x, min_val, info = fmin_l_bfgs_b(evaluator.loss, x.flatten(),
                                     fprime=evaluator.grads, maxfun=20)
    img = deprocess_image(x.copy())
    fname = result_prefix + '_at_iteration_%d.png' % i
    save_img(fname, img)
```

Saves the current generated image

Runs scipy-based optimization (L-BFGS) over the pixels of the generated image to minimize total_loss.

TIP When training your own neural style transfer network, keep in mind that content images that do not require high levels of detail work better and are known to create visually appealing or recognizable artistic images. In addition, style images that contain a lot of textures are better than flat style images: flat images (like a white background) will not produce aesthetically appealing results because there is not much texture to transfer.

Summary

- CNNs learn the information in the training set through successive filters. Each layer of the network deals with features at a different level of abstraction, so the complexity of the features generated depends on the layer's location in the network. Earlier layers learn low-level features; the deeper the layer is in the network, the more identifiable the extracted features are.

- Once a network is trained, we can run it in reverse to adjust the original image slightly so that a given output neuron (such as the one for faces or certain animals) yields a higher confidence score. This technique can be used for visualizations to better understand the emergent structure of the neural network and is the basis for the DeepDream concept.

- DeepDream processes the input image at different scales called octaves. We pass each scale, re-inject image details, pass it through the DeepDream algorithm, and then upscale the image for the next octave.

- The DeepDream algorithm is similar to the filter-visualization algorithm. It runs the ConvNet in reverse to generate output based on the representations extracted by the network.

- DeepDream differs from filter-visualization in that it needs an input image and maximizes the entire layer, not specific filters within the layer. This allows Deep-Dream to mix together a large number of features at once.

- DeepDream is not specific to images—it can be used for speech, music, and more.

- Neural style transfer is a technique that trains the network to preserve the style (texture, color, patterns) of the style image and preserve the content of the content image. The network then creates a new combined image that combines the style of the style image and the content from the content image.

- Intuitively, if we minimize the content, style, and variation losses, we get a new image that contains low variance in content and style from the content and style images, respectively, and low noise.

- Different values for content weight, style weight, and total variation weight will give you different results.

Visual embeddings

10

BY RATNESH KUMAR

> **This chapter covers**
> - Expressing similarity between images via loss functions
> - Training CNNs to achieve a desired embedding function with high accuracy
> - Using visual embeddings in real-world applications

Obtaining meaningful relationships between images is a vital building block for many applications that touch our lives every day, such as face recognition and image search algorithms. To tackle such problems, we need to build an algorithm

---

Ratnesh Kumar obtained his PhD from the STARS team at Inria, France, in 2014. While working on his PhD, he focused on problems in video understanding: video segmentation and multiple object tracking. He also has a Bachelor of Engineering from Manipal University, India, and a Master of Science from the University of Florida at Gainesville. He has co-authored several scientific publications on learning visual embedding for re-identifying objects in camera networks.

that can extract relevant features from images and subsequently compare them using their corresponding features.

In the previous chapters, we learned that we can use convolutional neural networks (CNNs) to extract meaningful features for an image. This chapter will use our understanding of CNNs to train (jointly) a *visual embedding layer*. In this chapter's context, *visual embedding* refers to the last fully connected layer (prior to a loss layer) appended to a CNN. *Joint training* refers to training both the embedding layer and the CNN parameters jointly.

This chapter explores the nuts and bolts of training and using visual embeddings for large-scale, image-based query-retrieval systems such as applications of visual embeddings (see figure 10.1). To perform this task, we first need to project (*embed*) our database of images onto a *vector space* (*embedding*). This way, comparisons between images can be performed by measuring their pairwise distances in this embedding space. This is the high-level idea of visual embedding systems.

Figure 10.1 Example applications we encounter in everyday life when working with images: a machine comparing two images (left); querying the database to find images similar to the input image (right). Comparing two images is a non-trivial task and is key to many applications relating to meaningful image search.

> **DEFINITION** An *embedding* is a vector space, typically of lower dimension than the input space, which preserves relative dissimilarity (in the input space). We use the terms *vector space* and *embedding space* interchangeably. In the context of this chapter, the last fully connected layer of a trained CNN is this vector (embedding) space. As an example, a fully connected layer of 128 neurons corresponds to a vector space of 128 dimensions.

For a reliable comparison among images, the embedding function needs to capture a desired input similarity measure. This embedding function can be learned using various approaches; one of the popular ways is to use a deep CNN. Figure 10.2 illustrates a high-level process of using CNNs to create an embedding.

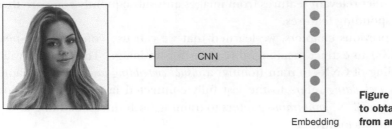

Figure 10.2 Using CNNs to obtain an embedding from an input image

In the following section, we explore some example applications of using visual embeddings for large-scale query-retrieval systems. Then we will dive deeper into the different components of the visual embedding systems: loss functions, mining informative data, and training and testing the embedding network. Subsequently, we will use these concepts to solve our chapter project on building visual embedding–based query-retrieval systems. Thereafter, we will explore approaches to push the boundaries of the project's network accuracy. By the end of this chapter, you will be able to train a CNN to obtain a reliable and meaningful embedding and use it in real-world applications.

10.1 Applications of visual embeddings

Let's look at some practical day-to-day information-retrieval algorithms that use the concept of visual embeddings. Some of the prominent applications for retrieving similar images given an input query include face recognition (FR), image recommendation, and object re-identification systems.

10.1.1 Face recognition

FR is about automatically identifying or tagging an image with the exact identities of persons in the image. Day-to-day applications include searching for celebrities on the web, auto-tagging friends and family in images, and many more. Recognition is a form of fine-grained classification. *The Handbook of Face Recognition* [1] categorizes two modes of a FR system (figure 10.3 compares them):

- *Face identification*—One-to-many matches that compare a query face image against all the template images in the database to determine the identity of the query face. For example, city authorities can check a watch list to match a query to a list of suspects (one-to-few matches). Another fun example is automatically tagging users to photos they appear in, a feature implemented by major social network platforms.
- *Face verification*—One-to-one match that compares a query face image against a template face image whose identity is being claimed.

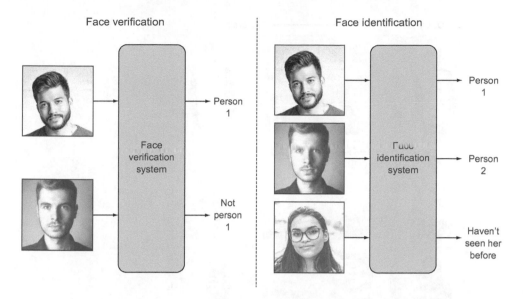

Figure 10.3 Face-verification and face-recognition systems: an example of a face-verification system comparing one-on-one matches to identify whether or not the image is Sundar (left); an example of a face-identification system comparing one-to-many matches to identify all images (right). Despite the objective-level difference between recognition and identification, they both rely on a good embedding function that captures meaningful differences between faces. (The figure was inspired by [2].)

10.1.2 *Image recommendation systems*

In this task, the user seeks to find similar images with respect to a given query image. Shopping websites provide product suggestions (via images) based on the selection of a particular product, such as showing all kinds of shoes that are similar to the ones a user selected. Figure 10.4 shows an example in the context of apparel search.

Note that the similarity between two images varies depending on the context of choosing the similarity measure. The embedding of an image differs based on the type of similarity measure chosen. Some examples of similarity measures are *color similarity* and *semantic similarity*:

- *Color similarity*—The retrieved images have similar colors, as shown in figure 10.5. This measure is used in applications like retrieving similarly colored paintings, similarly colored shoes (not necessarily determining style), and many more.
- *Semantic similarity*—The retrieved image has the same semantic properties, as shown in figure 10.6. In our earlier example of shoe retrieval, the user expects to see suggestions of shoes having the same semantics as high-heeled shoes. You can be creative and decide to incorporate color similarity with semantics for more meaningful suggestions.

Query ————————→ Retrievals

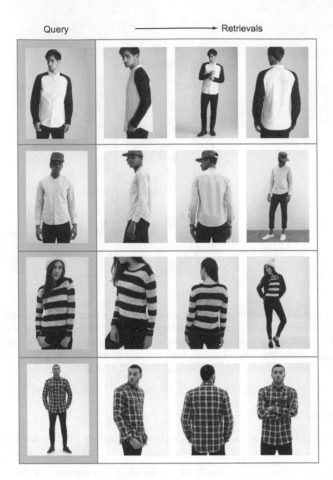

Figure 10.4 Apparel search. The leftmost image in each row is the query image, and the subsequent columns show various apparel that look similar to it. (Images in this figure are taken from [3].)

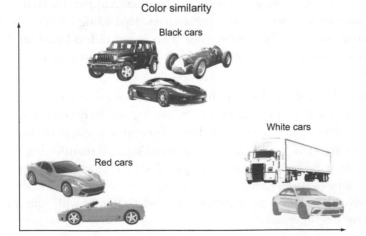

Figure 10.5 Similarity example where cars are differentiated by their color. Notice that the similarly colored cars are closer in this illustrative two-dimensional embedding space.

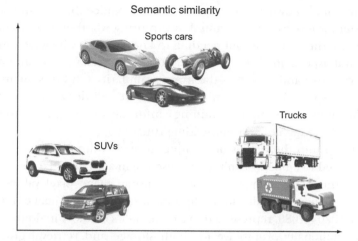

Figure 10.6 **Example of identity embeddings. Cars with similar features are projected closer to each other in the embedding space.**

10.1.3 *Object re-identification*

An example of object re-identification is security camera networks (CCTV monitoring), as depicted in figure 10.7. The security operator may be interested in querying a particular person and finding out their location in all the cameras. The system is required to identify a moving object in one camera and then *re-identify* the object across cameras to establish consistent identity.

Figure 10.7 **Multi-camera dataset showing the presence of a person (queried) across cameras. (*Source:* [4].)**

This problem is commonly known as *person re-identification*. Notice that it is similar to a face-verification system where we are interested in capturing whether any two people in separate cameras are the same, without needing to know exactly who a person is.

One of the central aspects in all these applications is the reliance on an embedding function that captures and preserves the input's similarity (and dissimilarity) to the output embedding space. In the following sections, we will delve into designing appropriate loss functions and sampling (mining) informative data points to guide the training of a CNN for a high-quality embedding function.

But before we jump into the details of creating an embedding, let's answer this question: why do we need to embed—can't we just use the images directly? Let's review the bottlenecks with this naive approach of directly using image pixel values as an embedding. Embedding dimensionality in this approach (assuming all images are high definition) would be 1920×1080, represented in a computer's memory in double precision, which is computationally prohibitive for both storage and retrieval given any meaningful time requirements. Moreover, most embeddings need to be learned in a supervised setting, as *a priori* semantics for comparison are not known (that is when we unleash the power of CNNs to extract meaningful and relevant semantics). Any learning algorithm on such a high-dimensional embedding space will suffer from the curse of dimensionality: as the dimensionality increases, the volume of the space increases so fast that the available data becomes sparse.

The geometry and data distribution of natural data are non-uniform and concatenate around low-dimensional structures. Hence, using an image size as data dimensions is overkill (let alone the exorbitant computational complexity and redundancy). Therefore, our goal in learning embedding is twofold: learning the required semantics for comparison, and achieving a low(er) dimensionality of the embedding space.

10.2   *Learning embedding*

Learning an embedding function involves defining a desired criterion to measure a similarity; it can be based on color, semantics of the objects present in an image, or purely data-driven in a supervised form. Since *a priori* knowing the right semantics (for comparing images) is difficult, supervised learning is more popular. Instead of hand-crafting similarity criteria features, in this chapter we will focus on the supervised data-driven learning of embeddings wherein we assume we are given a training set. Figure 10.8 depicts a high-level architecture to learn an embedding using a deep CNN.

The process to learn an embedding is straightforward:

1 Choose a CNN architecture. Any suitable CNN architecture can be used. In practice, the last fully connected layer is used to determine the embedding. Hence the size of this fully connected layer determines the dimension of the embedding vector space. Depending on the size of the training dataset, it may be prudent to use pretraining with, for example, the ImageNet dataset.

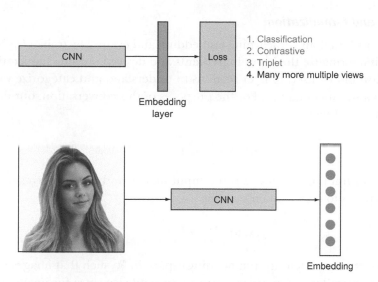

Figure 10.8   An illustration of learning machinery (top); the (test) process outline (bottom).

2 Choose a loss function. Popular loss functions are contrastive and triplet loss. (These are explained in section 10.3.)

3 Choose a dataset sampling (mining) method. Naively feeding all possible samples from the dataset is wasteful and prohibitive. Hence we need to resort to sampling (mining) informative data points to train our CNN. We will learn various sampling techniques in section 10.4.

4 During test time, the last fully connected layer acts as the embedding of the corresponding image.

Now that we have reviewed the big picture of the training and inference process for learning embedding, we will delve into defining useful loss functions to express our desired embedding objectives.

10.3   Loss functions

We learned in chapter 2 that optimization problems require the definition of a loss function to minimize. Learning embedding is not different from any other DL problem: we first define a loss function that we need to minimize, and then we train a neural network to choose the parameter (weights) values that yield the minimum error value. In this section, we will look more deeply at key embedding loss functions: *cross-entropy*, *contrastive*, and *triplet*.

First we will formalize the problem setup. Then we will explore the different loss functions and their mathematical formulas.

10.3.1 Problem setup and formalization

To understand loss functions for learning embedding and eventually train a CNN (for this loss), let's first formalize the input ingredients and desired output characteristics. This formalization will be used in later sections to understand and categorize various loss functions in a succinct manner. For the purposes of this conversation, our dataset can be represented as follows:

$$\chi = \{(x_i, y_i)\}_{i=1}^{N}$$

N is the number of training images, x_i is the input image, and y_i is its corresponding label. Our objective is to create an embedding

$$f(x; \theta): \mathbb{R}^D \rightarrow \mathbb{R}^F$$

to map images in $\mathbb{R}^D$ onto a feature (embedding) space in $\mathbb{R}^F$ such that images of similar identity are metrically close in this feature space (and vice versa for images of dissimilar identities)

$$\theta^* = \arg\min_{\theta} \mathcal{L}(f(\theta; \chi))$$

where θ is the parameter set of the learning function.

Let

$$D(x_i, x_j) : \mathbb{R}^F X \mathbb{R}^F \rightarrow \mathbb{R}$$

be the metric measuring distance of images x_i and x_j in the embedding space. For simplicity, we drop the input labels and denote $D(x_i, x_j)$ as $D_{ij} \cdot y_{ij} = 1$. Both samples (i) and (j) belong to the same class, and the value $y_{ij} = 0$ indicates samples of different classes.

Once we train an embedding network for its optimal parameters, we desire the learned function to have the following characteristics:

- An embedding should be invariant to viewpoints, illumination, and shape changes in the object.
- From a practical application deployment, computation of embedding and ranking should be efficient. This calls for a low-dimension vector space (embedding). The bigger this space is, the more computation is required to compare any two images, which in turn affects the time complexity.

Popular choices for learning an embedding are cross-entropy loss, contrastive loss, and triplet loss. The subsequent sections will introduce and formalize these losses.

10.3.2 *Cross-entropy loss*

Learning an embedding can also be formulated as a fine-grained classification problem, and the corresponding CNN can be trained using the popular cross-entropy loss (explained in detail in chapter 2). The following equation expresses cross-entropy loss, where $p(y_{ij}|f(x; \theta))$ represents the posterior class probability. In CNN literature, softmax loss implies a softmax layer trained in a discriminative regime using cross-entropy loss:

$$\mathcal{L}(\mathcal{X}) = -\sum_{i=1}^{N} \sum_{k=1}^{C} y_{ij} \log p(y_{ij}|f(x; \theta))$$

During training, a fully connected (embedding) layer is added prior to the loss layer. Each identity is considered a separate category, and the number of categories is equal to the number of identities in the training set. Once the network is trained using classification loss, the final classification layer is stripped off and an embedding is obtained from the new final layer of the network (figure 10.9).

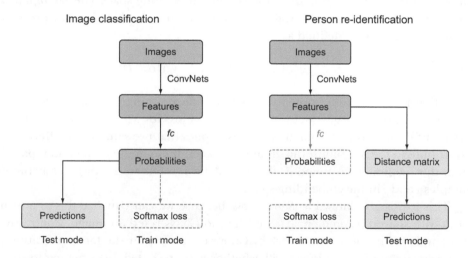

Figure 10.9 An illustration of how cross-entropy loss is used to train an embedding layer (fully connected). The right side demonstrates the inference process and outlines the disconnect in training and inference in straightforward usage of cross-entropy loss for learning an embedding. (This figure is adapted from [5].)

By minimizing the cross-entropy loss, the parameters (θ) of the CNN are chosen such that the estimated probability is close to 1 for the correct class and close to 0 for all other classes. Since the target of the cross-entropy loss is to categorize features into predefined classes, usually the performance of such a network is poor when compared to losses incorporating similarity (and dissimilarity) constraints directly in the embedding space during training. Furthermore, learning becomes computationally prohibitive when considering datasets of, for example, 1 million identities. (Imagine a loss layer with 1 million neurons!) Nevertheless, pretraining a network with cross-entropy loss (on a viable subset of the dataset, such as a subset of 1,000 identities) is a popular strategy used to pretrain the CNN, which in turn makes embedding losses converge faster. We will explore this further while mining informative samples during training in section 10.4.

> **NOTE** One of the disadvantages of the cross-entropy loss is the disconnect between training and inference. Hence, it generally performs poorly when compared with embedding learning losses (contrastive and triplet). These losses explicitly try to incorporate the relative distance preservation from the input image space to the embedding space.

10.3.3 *Contrastive loss*

Contrastive loss optimizes the training objective by encouraging all similar class instances to come infinitesimally closer to each other, while forcing instances from other classes to move far apart in the output embedding space (we say *infinitesimally* here because a CNN can't be trained with exactly zero loss). Using our problem formalization, this loss is defined as

$$l_{\text{contrastive}}(i, j) = y_{ij} D_{ij}^2 + (1 - y_{ij})[\alpha - D_{ij}^2]_+$$

Note that $[.]_+ = \max(0,.)$ in the loss function indicates hinge loss, and α is a predetermined threshold (margin) determining the max loss for when the two samples i and j are in different classes. Geometrically, this implies that two samples of different classes contribute to the loss only if the distance between them in the embedding space is less than this margin. D_{ij}, as noted in the formulation, refers to the distance between two samples i and j in the embedding space.

This loss is also known as *Siamese loss*, because we can visualize this as a twin network with shared parameters; each of the two CNNs is fed an image. Contrastive loss was employed in the seminal work by Chopra et al. [6] for the face-verification problem, where the objective is to verify whether two presented faces belong to the same identity. An illustration of this loss is provided in the context of face recognition in figure 10.10.

Notice that the choice of the margin α is the same for all dissimilar classes. Manmatha et al. [7] analyze the impact: this choice of α implies that for dissimilar identities, visually diverse classes are embedded in the same feature space as the visually similar ones. This assumption is stricter when compared to triplet loss (explained next) and restricts the structure of the embedding manifold, which subsequently makes learning tougher. The training complexity per epoch is $O(N^2)$ for a dataset of N samples, as this loss requires traversing a pair of samples to compute the contrastive loss.

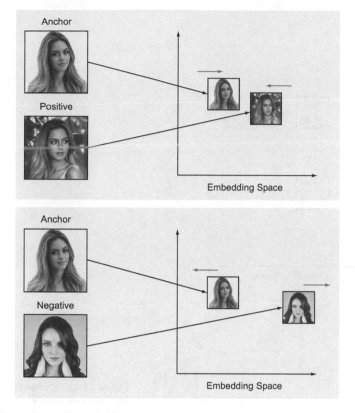

Figure 10.10 Computing contrastive loss requires two images. When the two images are of the same class, the optimization tries to put them closer in the embedding space, and vice versa when the images belong to different classes.

10.3.4 *Triplet loss*

Inspired by the seminal work on metric learning for nearest neighbor classification by Weinberger et al. [8], FaceNet (Schroff et al. [9]) proposed a modification suited for query-retrieval tasks called *triplet loss*. Triplet loss forces data points from the same class to be closer to each other than they are to a data point from another class. Unlike contrastive loss, triplet loss adds context to the loss function by considering both positive and negative pair distances from the same point. Mathematically, with respect to our problem formalization from earlier, triplet loss can be formulated as follows:

$$l_{\text{triplet}}(a, p, n) = [D_{ap} - D_{an} + \alpha]_+$$

Note that D_{ap} represents the distance between the anchor and a positive sample, while D_{an} is the distance between the anchor and a negative sample. Figure 10.11 illustrates the computation of the loss term using an anchor, a positive sample, and a negative sample. Upon successful training, the hope is that we will get all the same class pairs closer than pairs from different classes.

Because computing triplet loss requires three terms, the training complexity per epoch is $O(N^3)$, which is computationally prohibitive on practical datasets. High

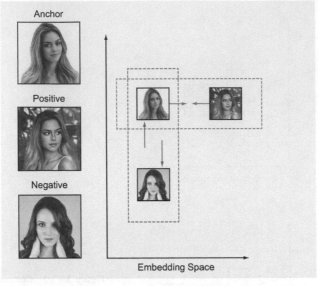

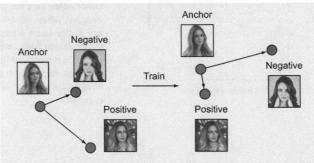

Figure 10.11   Computing triplet loss requires three samples. The goal of learning is to embed the samples of the same class closer than samples belonging to different classes.

computational complexity in triplet and contrastive losses have motivated a host of sampling approaches for efficient optimization and convergence. Let's review the complexity of implementing these losses in a naive and straightforward manner.

10.3.5   *Naive implementation and runtime analysis of losses*

Consider a toy example with the following specifications:

- Number of identities (N): 100
- Number of samples per identity (S): 10

If we implement the losses in a naive manner (see figure 10.12), it leads to per-epoch (inner `for` loop,[1] in figure 10.12) training complexity:

- *Cross-entropy loss*—This is a relatively straightforward loss. In an epoch, it just needs to traverse all samples. Hence our complexity here is $O(N \times S) = O(10^3)$.

---

[1] In practice, this step gets unwound into two `for` loops due to host memory limitations.

Algorithm 1: Naive implementation of training for learning an embedding.

Result: A trained CNN with a desirable embedding size.
Initialization: Dataset, a CNN, a loss function, embedding dimension;
while *numEpochs* > 0 **do**

> **for** *all dataset samples* **do**
>> Compute any one of the losses (from *cross-entropy, contrastive, triplet*) over all possible data samples.
>
> **end**
> *numEpochs* − = 1

end

Figure 10.12 Algorithm 1, for a naive implementation

- *Contrastive loss*—This loss visits all pairwise distances, so complexity is quadratic in terms of number of samples ($N \times S$): that is, $O(100 \times 10 \times 100 \times 10) = O(10^6)$.
- *Triplet loss*—For every loss computation, we need to visit three samples, so the worst-case complexity is cubic. In terms of total number of samples, that is $O(10^9)$.

Despite the ease of computing cross-entropy loss, its performance is relatively low when compared to other embedding losses. Some intuitive explanations are pointed out in section 10.3.2. In recent academic works (such as [10, 11, 13]), triplet loss has generally given better results than contrastive loss when provided with appropriate hard data mining, which we will explain in the next section.

> **NOTE** In the following sections, we refer to triplet loss, owing to its high performance over contrastive loss in several academic works.

One important point to notice is that not many of the triplets of the $O(10^9)$ contribute to the loss in a strong manner. In practice, during a training epoch, most of the triplets are trivial: that is, the current network is already at a low loss on these, and hence anchor-positive pairs of these trivial triplets are much closer (in the embedding space) than anchor-negative pairs. These trivial triplets do not add meaningful information to update the network parameters, thereby stagnating convergence. Furthermore, there are far fewer informative triplets than trivial triplets, which in turn leads to washing out the contribution of informative triplets.

To improve the computational complexity of triplet enumeration and convergence, we need to come up with an efficient strategy for enumerating triplets and feed the CNN (during training) *informative* triplet samples (without trivial triplets). This process of selecting informative triplets is called *mining*. Informative data points is the essence of this chapter and is discussed in the following sections.

A popular strategy to tackle this cubic complexity is to enumerate triplets in the following manner:

1. Construct a triplet set using *only* the current batch constructed by the dataloader.
2. Mine an informative triplet subset from this set.

The next section looks at this strategy in detail.

10.4 *Mining informative data*

So far, we have looked at how triplet and contrastive losses are computationally prohibitive for practical dataset sizes. In this section, we take a deep dive into understanding the key steps during training a CNN for triplet loss and learn how to improve the training convergence and computational complexity.

The straightforward implementation in figure 10.12 is classified under *offline* training, as the selection of a triplet must consider the full dataset and therefore cannot be done on the fly while training a CNN. As we noted earlier, this approach of computing valid triplets is inefficient and is computationally infeasible for DL datasets.

To deal with this complexity, FaceNet [9] proposes using online batch-based triplet mining. The authors construct a batch on the fly and perform mining of triplets for this batch, ignoring the rest of the dataset outside this batch. This strategy proved effective and led to state-of-the-art accuracy in face recognition.

Let's summarize this information flow during a training epoch (see figure 10.13). During training, mini-batches are constructed from the dataset, and valid triplets are subsequently identified for each sample in the mini-batch. These triplets are then used to update the loss, and the process iterates until all the batches are exhausted, thereby completing an epoch.

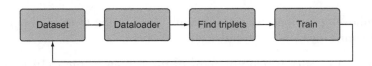

Figure 10.13   Information flow during an *online* training process. The dataloader samples a random subset of training data to the GPU. Subsequently, triplets are computed to update the loss.

Similar to FaceNet, OpenFace [37] proposed a training scheme wherein the dataloader constructs a training batch of predefined statistics, and embeddings for the batch are computed on the GPU. Subsequently, valid triplets are generated on the CPU to compute the loss.

In the next subsection, we look into an improved dataloader that can give us good batch statistics to mine triplets. Subsequently, we will explore how we can efficiently mine good, informative triplets to improve training convergence.

10.4.1 *Dataloader*

Let's examine the dataloader's setup and its role in training with triplet loss. The dataloader selects a random subset from the dataset and is crucial to mining informative triplets. If we resort to a trivial dataloader to choose a random subset (mini-batch) of the dataset, it may not result in good class diversity for finding many triplets. For example, randomly selecting a batch with only one category will not have any valid triplets and thus will result in a wasteful batch iteration. We must take care at the data-loader level to have well distributed batches to mine triplets.

> **NOTE** The requirement for better convergence at the dataloader level is to form a batch with enough class diversity to facilitate the triplet mining step in figure 10.11.

A general and effective approach to training is to first mine a set of triplets of size B, so that B terms contribute to the triplet loss. Once set B is chosen, their images are stacked to form a batch size of $3B$ images (B anchors, B positives, and B negatives), and subsequently $3B$ embeddings are computed to update the loss.

Hermans et al. [11], in their impressive work on revisiting triplet loss, realize the under-utilization of valid triplets in online generation presented in the previous section. In a set of $3B$ images (B anchors, B positives, B negatives), we have a total of $6B^2 - 4B$ valid triplets, so using only B triplets is under-utilization.

Computing the number of valid triplets in stacked 3B images of B triplets

To understand the computation of the number of valid triplets in a stack of $3B$ images (that is, B anchors, B positives, B negatives), let's assume we have exactly one pair of the same class. This implies we could choose $3B - 2$ negatives for an (anchor, positive) pair. There are $2B$ possible anchor-positive pairs in this set, leading to a total of $2B(3B - 2)$ valid triplets. The following figure shows an example.

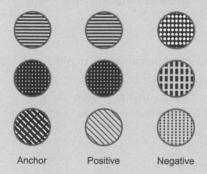

Anchor   Positive   Negative

An example with $B = 3$. Circles with the same pattern are of the same class. Since only the first two columns have a possible positive sample, there are a total of $2B$ (six) anchors. After selecting an anchor, we are left with $3B - 2$ (seven) negatives, implying a sum total of $2B(3B - 2)$ triplets.

In light of the previous discussion, to use the triplets more efficiently, Hermans et al. propose a key organizational modification at the dataloader level: construct a batch by randomly sampling P identities from dataset X and subsequently sampling K images (randomly) for each identity, thus resulting in a batch size of PK images. Using this dataloader (with appropriate triplet mining), the authors demonstrate state-of-the-art accuracy on the task of person re-identification. We look more at the mining techniques introduced in [11] in the following subsections. Using this organizational modification, Kumar et al. [10, 12] demonstrate state-of-the-art results for the task of vehicle re-identification across many diverse datasets.

Owing to the superior results on re-identification tasks, [11] has become one of the mainstays in recognition literature, and the batch construction (dataloader) is now a standard in practice. The default recommendation for the batch size is $P = 18$, $K = 4$, leading to 42 samples.

Computing the number of valid triplets

Let's make this concept clearer with a working example of computing the number of valid triplets in a batch. Assuming we have selected a random batch of size PK:

- $P = 10$ different classes
- $K = 4$ samples per class

Using these values, we have the following batch statistics:

- Total number of anchors = 40 = (PK)
- Number of positive samples per anchor = 3 = $(K - 1)$
- Number of negative samples per anchor = $9 \times 4 = (K(P - 1))$
- Total number of valid triplets = products of the previous results = $40 \times 3 \times (9 \times 4)$

Taking a peek at upcoming concepts on mining informative triplets, notice that for each anchor, we have a set of positive samples and a set of negative samples. We argued earlier that many triplets are non-informative, and hence in the subsequent sections we look at various ways to filter out important triplets. More precisely, we examine techniques that help filter out informative subsets of positive and negative samples (for an anchor).

Now that we have built an efficient dataloader for mining triplets, we are ready to explore various techniques for mining informative triplets while training a CNN. In the following sections, we first look at hard data mining in general and subsequently focus on online generation (mining) of informative triplets following the batch construction approach in [11].

10.4.2 *Informative data mining: Finding useful triplets*

Mining informative samples while training a machine learning model is an important problem, and many solutions exist in academic literature. We take a quick peek at them here.

A popular sampling approach to find informative samples *is hard data mining*, which is used in many CV applications such as object detection and action localization. Hard data mining is a bootstrapping technique used in iterative training of a model: at every iteration, the current model is applied on a validation set to mine hard data on which this model performs poorly. Only this hard data is then presented to the optimizer, which increases the ability of the model to learn effectively and converge faster to an optimum. On the flip side, if a model is only presented with hard data, which could consist of outliers, its ability to discriminate outliers with respect to normal data suffers, stalling the training progress. An outlier in a dataset could be a result of mislabeling or a sample captured with poor image quality.

In the context of triplet loss, a *hard negative* sample is one that is closer to the anchor (as this sample would incur a high loss). Similarly, a *hard positive* sample is one that is far from an anchor in embedding space.

To deal with outliers during hard data sampling, FaceNet [9] proposed semi-hard sampling that mines moderate triplets that are neither too hard nor too trivial for getting meaningful gradients during training. This is done by using the margin parameter: only negatives that lie in the margin and are farther from the selected positive for an anchor are considered (see figure 10.14), thereby ignoring negatives that are too easy and too hard. However, this in turn adds additional burden on training for tuning an additional hyperparameter. This ad hoc strategy of semi-hard negatives is put into practice in a large batch size of 1,800 images, thereby enumerating triplets on the CPU. Notice that with the default batch size (42 images) in [11], it is possible to enumerate the set of valid triplets efficiently on the GPU.

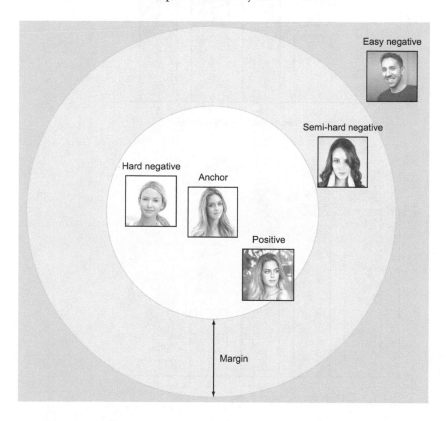

Figure 10.14 **Margin: grading triplets into hard, semi-hard, and easy. This illustration (in the context of face recognition) is for an anchor and a corresponding negative sample. Therefore, negative samples that are closer to the anchor are hard.**

Figure 10.15 illustrates the hardness of a triplet. Remember that a positive sample is harder if the network (at a training epoch) puts this sample far from its anchor in the embedding space. Similarly, in a plot of distances from the anchor to negative data, the samples closer (less distant) to the anchor are harder. As a reminder, here is the triplet loss function for an anchor (a), positive (p), and negative (n):

$$l_{\text{triplet}}(a, p, n) = [D_{ap} - D_{an} + \alpha]_{+}$$

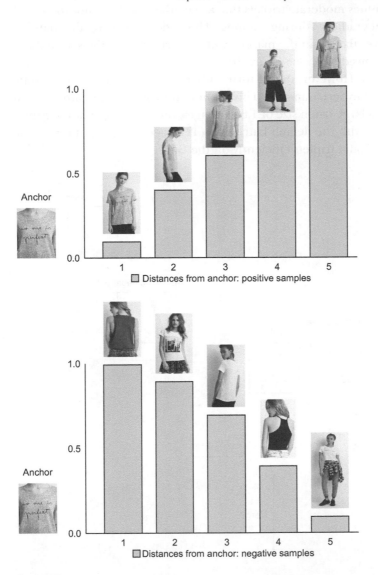

Figure 10.15   Hard-positive and hard-negative data. The plot shows the distances of positive samples (top) and negative samples (bottom) with respect to an anchor (at a particular epoch). The hardness of samples increases as we move from left to right on both plots.

Having explored the concept of hard data and its pitfalls, we will now explore various online triplet mining techniques for our batch. Once a batch (of size *PK*) is constructed by the dataloader, there are *PK* possible anchors. How to find positive and negative data for these anchors is the crux of mining techniques. First we look at two simple and effective online triplet mining techniques: *batch all* (*BA*) and *batch hard* (*BH*).

10.4.3 *Batch all (BA)*

In the context of a batch, *batch all* (*BA*) refers to using all possible and valid triplets; that is, we are not performing any ranking or selection of triplets. In implementation terms, for an anchor, this loss is computed by summing across *all* possible valid triplets. For a batch size of *PK* images, since BA selects all triplets, the number of terms updating the triplet loss is $PK(K-1)(K(P-1))$.

Using this approach, all samples (triplets) are equally important; hence this is straightforward to implement. On the other hand, BA can potentially lead to information averaging out. In general, many valid triplets are trivial (at a low loss or non-informative), and only a few are informative. Summing across all valid triplets with equal weights leads to averaging out the contribution of the informative triplets. Hermans et al. [11] experienced this averaging out and reported it in the context of person re-identification.

10.4.4 *Batch hard (BH)*

As opposed to BA, *batch hard* (*BH*) considers only the hardest data for an anchor. For each possible anchor in a batch, BH computes the loss with exactly one hardest positive data item and one hardest negative data item. Notice that here, the *hardness* of a datapoint is relative to the anchor. For a batch size of *PK* images, since BH selects only one positive and one negative per anchor, the number of terms updating the triplet loss is *PK* (total number of possible anchors).

BH is robust to information averaging out, because trivial (easier) samples are ignored. However, it is potentially difficult to disambiguate with respect to outliers: outliers can creep in due to incorrect annotations, and the model tries hard to converge on them, thereby jeopardizing training quality. In addition, when a not-pretrained network is used prior to using BH, the hardness of a sample (with respect to an anchor) cannot be determined reliably. There is no way to gain this information during training, because the hardest sample is now any random sample, and this can lead to a stall in training. This is reported in [9] and when BH is applied to train a network from scratch in the context of vehicle re-identification in [10].

To visually understand BA and BH, let's look again at our figure illustrating the distances of the anchor to all positive and negative data (figure 10.16). BA performs no selection and uses all five samples to compute a final loss, whereas BH uses only the hardest available data (ignoring all the rest). Figure 10.17 shows the algorithm outline for computing BH and BA.

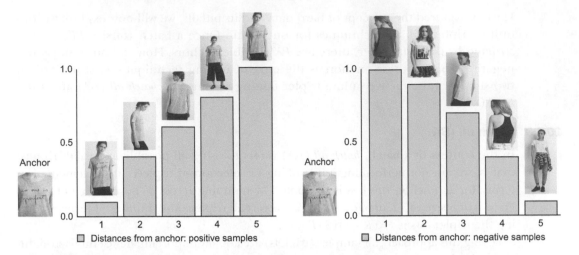

Figure 10.16   Illustration of hard data: distances of positive samples from an anchor (at a particular epoch) (left); distances of negative samples from an anchor (right). BA takes all samples into account, whereas BH takes samples only at the far-right bar (the hardest-positive data for this mini-batch).

Algorithm 2: Algorithm outline for sampling information data points.

Result: A trained CNN with a desirable embedding size.

Initialization: Dataset, a CNN, a loss function, embedding dimension, batch size (*PK*);

while *A valid batch* **do**

    numAnchors = PK

    while *numAnchors > 0* **do**

        Select an anchor in [0 . . . **PK**], without replacement;

        BA: Compute loss over all possible valid triplets for this anchor;

        OR

        BH: Compute loss over all possible valid *hard* triplets for this anchor;

        numAnchors – –

    end

end

Figure 10.17   Algorithm for computing BA and BH

An alternative formalization of triplet loss

Ristani et al., in their famous paper on features for multi-camera re-identification [13], unify various batch-sampling techniques under one expression. In a batch, let *a* be an anchor sample and $N(a)$ and $P(a)$ represent a subset of negative and positive samples for the corresponding anchor *a*. The triplet loss can then be written as

$$l_{\text{triplet}}(a) = [\alpha + \sum_{p \in P(a)} w_p D_{ap} - \sum_{n \in N(a)} w_n D_{an}]_+$$

For an anchor sample *a*, w_p represents the weight (importance) of a positive sample *p*; similarly, w_n signifies the importance of a negative sample *n*. The total loss in an epoch is then obtained by

$$\mathcal{L}(\theta; \mathcal{X}) = - \sum_{\text{all batches}} \sum_{a \in B} l_{\text{triplet}}(a)$$

In this formulation, BA and BH could be integrated as shown in the following figure (see also table 10.1 in the following section). The Y-axis in this figure represents selection weight-age.

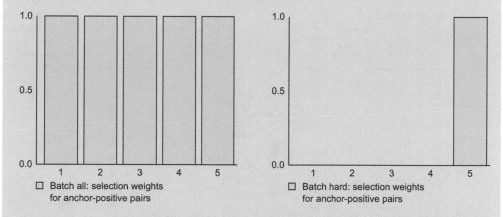

Plot showing selection weights for positive samples with respect to an anchor. For BA, all samples are equally important, while BH gives importance to only the hardest samples (the rest are ignored).

10.4.5 *Batch weighted (BW)*

BA is a straightforward sampling that weights all samples uniformly. This uniform weight distribution can ignore the contribution of important tough samples, as these samples are typically outnumbered by trivial, easy samples. To mitigate this issue with BA, Ristani et al. [13] employ a *batch weighted* (*BW*) weighting scheme: a sample is weighted based on its distance from the corresponding anchor, thereby giving more importance to informative (harder) samples than trivial samples. Corresponding weights for positive and negative data are shown in table 10.1. Figure 10.18 demonstrates the weighting of samples in this technique.

10.4.6 *Batch sample (BS)*

Another sampling technique is *batch sample* (*BS*); it is actively discussed in the implementation page of Hermans el al. [11] and has been used for state-of-the-art vehicle re-identification by Kumar et al. [10]. BS uses the distribution of anchor-to-sample

Table 10.1   Snapshot of various ways to mine good positive x_p and negative x_n [10]. BS and BW are explored in the upcoming section with examples.

Mining	Positive weight: w_p	Negative weight: w_n	Comments
All (BA)	1	1	All samples are weighted uniformly.
Hard (BH)	$[x_p == \underset{x \in P(a)}{\arg\max}\ D_{ax}]$	$[x_n == \underset{x \in N(a)}{\arg\min}\ D_{ax}]$	Pick one hardest sample.
Sample (BS)	$[x_p == \underset{x \in P(a)}{\text{multinomial}\{D_{ax}\}}]$	$[x_n == \underset{x \in N(a)}{\text{multinomial}\{-D_{ax}\}}]$	Pick one from the multinomial distribution.
Weighted (BW)	$\dfrac{e^{D_{ap}}}{\sum\limits_{x \in P(a)} e^{D_{ax}}}$	$\dfrac{e^{-D_{an}}}{\sum\limits_{x \in N(a)} e^{-D_{ax}}}$	Weights are sampled based on their distance from the anchor.

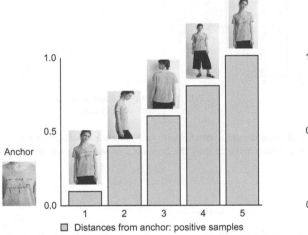

Anchor

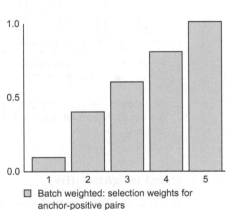

☐ Distances from anchor: positive samples

☐ Batch weighted: selection weights for anchor-positive pairs

Figure 10.18   BW illustration of selecting positive data for the anchor in the left plot. In this case, all five positive samples are used (as in BA), but a weight-age is assigned to each sample. Unlike BA, which weighs every sample equally, the plot at right weighs each sample in proportion to the corresponding distance from the anchor. This effectively means we are paying more attention to a positive sample that is farther from the anchor (and thus is harder and more informative). Negative data for this anchor is chosen in the same manner, but with reverse weight-age.

distances to mine[2] positive and negative data for an anchor (see figure 10.19). This technique thereby avoids sampling outliers when compared with BH, and it also hopes to determine the most relevant sample as the sampling is done using a distances-to-anchor distribution.

---

[2]   Categorically. For an example in Tensorflow, see http://mng.bz/zjvQ.

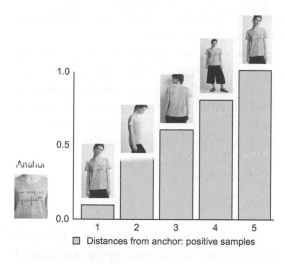
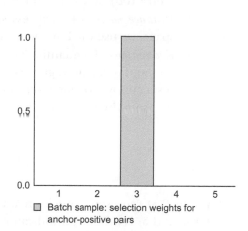

Figure 10.19 BS illustration of selecting a positive data for an anchor. Similarly to BH, the aim is to find one positive data item (for the anchor in the left plot) that is informative and not an outlier. BH would take the hardest data item, which could lead to finding outliers. BS uses the distances as a distribution to mine a sample in a categorical fashion, thereby selecting a sample that is informative and that may not be an outlier. (Note that this is a random multinomial selection; we chose the third sample here just to illustrate the concept.)

Now, let's unpack these ideas by working through a project and diving deeper into the machinery required for training and testing a CNN for an embedding.

10.5 Project: Train an embedding network

In this project, we put our concepts into practice by building an image-based query retrieval system. We chose two problems that are popular in the visual embedding literature and have been actively studied to find better solutions:

- *Shopping dilemma*—Find me apparel that is similar to a query item.
- *Re-identification*—Find similar cars in a database; that is, identify a car from different viewpoints (cameras).

Regardless of the tasks, the training, inference, and evaluation processes are the same. Here are some of the ingredients for successfully training an embedding network:

- *Training set*—We follow a supervised learning approach with annotations underlining the inherent similarity measure. The dataset can be organized into a set of folders where each folder determines the identity/category of the images. The objective is that images belonging to the same category are kept closer to one another in the embedding space, and vice versa for images in separate categories.
- *Testing set*—The test set is usually split into two sets: *query* and *gallery* (often, academic papers refer to the gallery set as the *test set*). The query set consists of images that are used as queries. Each image in the gallery set is ranked (retrieved) against

every query image. If the embedding is learned perfectly, the top-ranked (retrieved) items for a query all belong to the same class.

- *Distance metric*—To express similarity between two images in an embedding space, we use the Euclidean (L_2) distance between the respective embeddings.
- *Evaluation*—To quantitatively evaluate a trained model, we use the top-k accuracy and mean average precision (mAP) metrics explained in chapters 4 and 7, respectively. For each object in a query set, the aim is to retrieve a similar identity from the test set (gallery set). $AP(q)$ for a query image q is defined as

$$AP(q) = \frac{\sum_k P(k) \times \delta_k}{N_{gt}(q)}$$

where $P(k)$ represents precision at rank k, $N_{gt}(q)$ is the total number of true retrievals for q, and δ_k is a Boolean indicator function. So, its value is 1 when the matching of query image q to a test image is *correct* at rank $\leq k$. Correct retrieval means the ground-truth label for both query and test is the same.

The mAP is then computed as an average over all query images

$$mAP = \frac{\sum_q AP(q)}{Q}$$

where Q is the total number of query images. The following sections look at both tasks in more detail.

10.5.1 *Fashion: Get me items similar to this*

The first task is to determine whether two images taken in a shop belong to the same clothing item. Shopping objects (clothes, shoes) related to fashion are key areas of visual search in industrial applications such as image-recommendation engines that recommend products similar to what a shopper is looking for. Liu et al. [3] introduced one of the largest datasets (DeepFashion) for shopping image-retrieval tasks. This benchmark contains 54,642 images of 11,735 clothing items from the popular Forever 21 catalog. The dataset comprises 25,000 training images and about 26,000 test images, split across query and gallery sets; figure 10.20 shows sample images.

10.5.2 *Vehicle re-identification*

Re-identification is the task of matching the appearance of objects in and across camera networks. A usual pipeline here involves a user seeking all instances of a query object's presence in all cameras within a network. For example, a traffic regulator may be looking for a particular car across a city-wide camera network. Other examples are person and face re-identification, which are mainstays in security and biometrics.

This task uses the famous VeRi dataset from Liu et al. [14, 36]. This dataset encompasses 40,000 bounding-box annotations of 776 cars (identities) across 20 cameras in

Figure 10.20 Each row indicates a particular category and corresponding similar images. A perfectly learned embedding would make embeddings of images in each row closer to each other than any two images across columns (which belong to different apparel categories). (Images in this figure are taken from the DeepFashion dataset [3].)

traffic surveillance scenes; figure 10.21 shows sample images. Each vehicle is captured by 2 to 18 cameras in various viewpoints and varying illuminations. Notably, the viewpoints are not restricted to only front/rear but also include side views, thereby

Figure 10.21 Each row indicates a vehicle class. Similar to the apparel task, the goal (training an embedding CNN) here is to push the embeddings of the same class closer than the embeddings of different classes. (Images in this figure are from the VeRi dataset [14].)

making this a challenging dataset. The annotations include make and model of vehicles, color, and inter-camera relations and trajectory information.

We will use only category (or identity) level annotations; we will not use attributes like make, model, and spatio-temporal location. Incorporating more information during training could help gain accuracy, but this is beyond the scope of this chapter. However, the last part of the chapter references some cool new developments in incorporating multi-source information for learning embeddings.

10.5.3 *Implementation*

This project uses the GitHub codebase of triplet learning (https://github.com/VisualComputingInstitute/triplet-reid/tree/sampling) attached to [11]. Dataset preprocessing and a summary of steps are available with the book's downloadable code; go to the project's Jupyter notebook to follow along with a step-by-step tutorial of the project implementation. TensorFlow users are encouraged to look at the blog post "Triplet Loss and Online Triplet Mining in TensorFlow" by Olivier Moindrot (https://omoindrot.github.io/triplet-loss) to understand various ways of implementing triplet loss.

Training a deep CNN involves several key hyperparameters, and we briefly discuss them here. Following is a summary of the hyperparameters we set for this project:

- *Pre-training* is performed on the ImageNet dataset [15].
- *Input image size* is 224×224.
- *Meta-architecture*: We use Mobilenet-v1 [16], which has 569 million MACs and measures the number of fused multiplication and addition operations. This architecture has 4.24 million parameters and achieves a top-1 accuracy of 70.9% on ImageNet's image classification benchmark, with input image size of 224×224.
- *Optimizer*: We use the Adam optimizer [17] with default hyperparameters ($\varepsilon = 10^{-3}$, $\beta_1 = 0.9$, $\beta_2 = 0.999$). Initial learning rate is set to 0.0003.
- *Data augmentation* is performed in an online fashion using a standard image-flip operation.
- *Batch size* is 18 (P) randomly sampled identities, with 4 (K) samples per identity, for a total of 18×4 samples in a batch.
- *Margin*: The authors replaced the hinge loss $[.]_+$ with a smooth variation called *softplus*: $ln(1 + .)$. Our experiments also apply softplus instead of using a hard margin.
- *Embedding dimension* corresponds to the dimension of the last fully connected layer. We fix this to 128 units for all experiments. Using a lower embedding size is helpful for computational efficiency.

DEFINITION In computing, the *multiply–accumulate operation* is a common step that computes the product of two numbers and adds that product to an accumulator. The hardware unit that performs the operation is known as a *multiplier–accumulator* (*MAC,* or *MAC unit*); the operation itself is also often referred to as *MAC* or a *MAC operation.*

A note on comparisons to state-of-the-art approaches

Before diving into comparisons, remember that training a deep neural network requires tuning several hyperparameters. This may in turn lead to pitfalls while comparing several algorithms: for example, an approach could perform better if the underlying CNN performs favorably on the same pretrained dataset(s). Other similar hyperparameters are the training algorithm choice (such as vanilla SGD or a more sophisticated Adam) and many other parameters that we have seen throughout this book. You must delve deeper into an algorithm's machinery to see the complete picture.

10.5.4 *Testing a trained model*

To test a trained model, each dataset presents two files: a query set and a gallery set. These sets can be used to compute the evaluation metrics mentioned earlier: mAP and top-k accuracy. While evaluation metrics are a good summary, we also look at the results visually. To this end, we take random images in a query set and find (plot) the top-k retrievals from the gallery set. The following subsections show quantitative and qualitative results of using various mining techniques from this chapter.

TASK 1: IN-SHOP RETRIEVAL

Let's look at sample retrievals from the learned embeddings in figure 10.22. The results look visually pleasing: the top retrievals are from the same class as the query. The network does reasonably well at inferring different views of the same query in the top ranks.

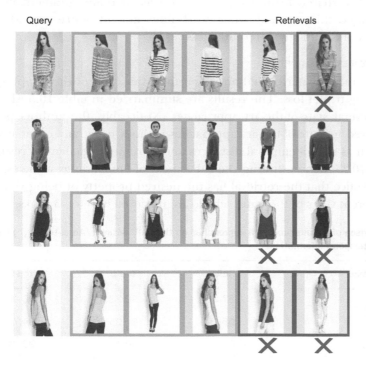

Figure 10.22 Sample retrievals from the fashion dataset using various embedding approaches. Each row indicates the query image and top-5 retrievals for this query image. An X indicates an incorrect retrieval.

Table 10.2 outlines the performance of triplet loss under various sampling scenarios. BW outperforms all other sampling approaches. Top-1 accuracy is quite good in this case: we were able to retrieve the same class of fashion object in the very first retrieval, with accuracy over 87%. Notice that with the evaluation setup, the top-k accuracy for $k > 1$ is higher (monotonically).

Table 10.2   Performance of various sampling approaches on the in-shop retrieval task

Method	top-1	top-2	top-5	top-10	top-20
Batch all	83.79	89.81	94.40	96.38	97.55
Batch hard	86.40	91.22	95.43	96.85	97.83
Batch sample	86.62	91.36	95.36	96.72	97.84
Batch weighted	87.70	92.26	95.77	97.22	98.09
Capsule embeddings	33.90	–	–	75.20	84.60
ABE [18]	87.30	–	–	96.70	97.90
BIER [19]	76.90	–	–	92.80	95.20

Our results compare favorably with the state-of-the-art results. Using attention-based ensemble (ABE) [18], a diverse set of ensembles are trained that attend to parts of the image. Boosting independent embeddings robustly (BIER) [19] trains an ensemble of metric CNNs with a shared feature representation as an online gradient boosting problem. Noticeably, this ensemble framework does not introduce any additional parameters (and works with any differential loss).

TASK 2: VEHICLE RE-IDENTIFICATION

Kumar et al. [12] recently performed an exhaustive evaluation of the sampling variants for optimizing triplet loss. The results are summarized in table 10.3 with comparisons from several state-of-the-art approaches. Noticeably, the authors perform favorably compared to state-of-the-art approaches without using any other information sources, such as spatio-temporal distances and attributes. Qualitative results are shown in figure 10.23, demonstrating the robustness of embeddings with respect to the viewpoints. Notice that the retrieval has the desired property of being viewpoint-invariant, as different views of the same vehicle are retrieved into top-5 ranks.

Table 10.3   Comparison of various proposed approaches on the VeRi dataset. An asterisk (*) indicates the usage of spatio-temporal information.

Method	mAP	top-1	top-5
Batch sample	67.55	90.23	96.42
Batch hard	65.10	87.25	94.76
Batch all	66.91	90.11	96.01

Table 10.3   Comparison of various proposed approaches on the VeRi dataset. An asterisk (*) indicates the usage of spatio-temporal information. *(continued)*

Method	mAP	top-1	top-5
Batch weighted	67.02	89.99	96.54
GSTE [20]	59.47	96.24	98.97
VAMI [21]	50.13	77.03	90.82
VAMI+ST * [21]	61.32	85.92	91.84
Path-LSTM * [22]	58.27	83.49	90.04
PAMTRI (RS) [23]	63.76	90.70	94.40
PAMTRI (All) [23]	71.88	92.86	96.97
MSVR [24]	49.30	88.56	–
AAVER [25]	61.18	88.97	94.70

Figure 10.23   Sample retrievals on the VeRi dataset using various embedding approaches. Each row indicates a query image and the top-5 retrievals for it. An X indicates an incorrect retrieval.

To gauge the pros and cons of various approaches in the literature, let's conceptually examine the competing approaches in vehicle re-identification:

- Kanaci et al. [26] proposed *cross-level vehicle re-identification* (*CLVR*) on the basis of using classification loss with model labels (see figure 10.24) to train a fine-grained vehicle categorization network. This setup is similar to the one we saw in section 10.3.2 and figure 10.9. The authors did not perform an evaluation on the VeRi dataset. You are encouraged to refer to this paper to understand the performance on other vehicle re-identification datasets.

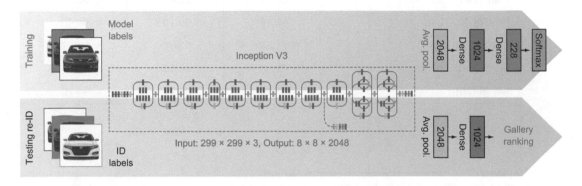

Figure 10.24   Cross-level vehicle re-identification (CLVR). (*Source:* [24].)

- *Group-sensitive triplet embedding* (*GSTE*) by Bai et al. [20] is a novel training process that clusters intra-class variations using K-Means. This helps with more guided training at the expense of an additional parameter, K-Means clustering.
- *Pose aware multi-task learning* (*PAMTRI*) by Zheng et al. [23] trains a network for embedding in a multi-task regime using keypoint annotations in conjunction with synthetic data (thereby tackling keypoint annotation requirements). PAMTRI (All) achieves the best results on this dataset. PAMTRI (RS) uses a mix of real and synthetic data for learning embedding, and PAMTRI (All) additionally uses vehicle keypoints and attributes in a multi-task learning framework.
- *Adaptive attention for vehicle re-identification* (*AAVER*) by Khorramshahi et al. [25] is a recent work wherein the authors construct a dual-path network for extracting global and local features. These are then concatenated to form a final embedding. The proposed embedding loss is minimized using identity and keypoint orientation annotations.
- A training procedure for *viewpoint attentive multi-view inference* (*VAMI*) by Zhou et al. [21] includes a generative adversarial network (GAN) and multi-view attention learning. The authors' conjecture that being able to synthesize (generate using GAN) multiple viewpoint views would help learn a better final embedding.

- With *Path-LSTM*, Shen et al. [22] employ a generation of several path proposals for their spatio-temporal regularization and require an additional LSTM to rank these proposals.
- Kanaci et al. [24] proposed *multi-scale vehicle representation* (*MSVR*) for re-identification by exploiting a pyramid-based DL method. MSVR learns vehicle re-identification sensitive feature representations from an image pyramid with a network architecture of multiple branches, all of which are optimized concurrently.

A snapshot summary of these approaches with respect to the key hyperparameters is summarized in table 10.4.

Table 10.4 Summary of some important hyperparameters and labeling used during training

Method	ED	Annotations
Ours	128	ID
GSTE [20]	1024	ID
VAMI [21]	2048	ID + A
PAMTRI (All) [23]	1024	ID + K + A
MSVR [24]	2048	ID
AAVER [25]	2048	ID + K

Note: ED = embedding dimension; *K* = keypoints; *A* = attributes.

Usually, license plates are a global unique identifier. However, with the standard installation of traffic cameras, license plates are difficult to extract; hence, visual-based features are required for vehicle re-identification. If two cars are of the same make, model, and color, then visual features cannot disambiguate them (unless there are some distinctive marks such as text or scratches). In these tough scenarios, only spatio-temporal information (like GPS information) can help. To learn more, you are encouraged to look into recent proposed datasets by Tang et al. [27].

10.6 *Pushing the boundaries of current accuracy*

Deep learning is an evolving field, and novel approaches to training are being introduced every day. This section provides ideas for improving the current level of embeddings and some recently introduced tips and tricks to train a deep CNN:

- *Re-ranking*—After obtaining an initial ranking of gallery images (to an input query image), re-ranking uses a post-processing step with the aim of improving the ranking of relevant images. This is a powerful, widely used step in many re-identification and information-retrieval systems.

  A popular approach in re-identification is by Zhong et al. [28] (see figure 10.25). Given a probe *p* and a gallery set, the appearance feature (embedding)

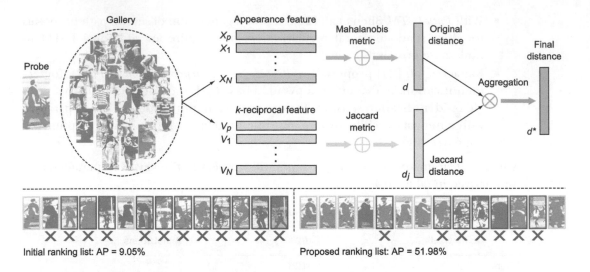

Figure 10.25   Re-ranking proposal by Zhong et al. (*Source*: [28].) An X indicates an incorrect retrieval.

and k-reciprocal feature are extracted for each person. The original distance d and Jaccard distance J_d are calculated for each pair of a probe person and a gallery person. The final distance is then computed as the combination of d and J_d and used to obtain the proposed ranking list.

A recent work in vehicle re-identification, AAVER [25] boosts mAP accuracy by 5% by post-processing using re-ranking.

DEFINITION   The *Jaccard distance* is computed among two sets of data and expresses the intersection over the union of the two sets.

- *Tips and tricks*—Luo et al. [29] demonstrated powerful baseline performance on the task of person re-identification. The authors follow the same batch construction from Hermans et al. [11] (studied in this chapter) and use tricks for data augmentation, warm-up learning rate, and label smoothing, to name a few. Noticeably, the authors perform favorably compared to many state-of-the-art methods. You are encouraged to apply these general tricks for training a CNN for any recognition-related tasks.

DEFINITIONS   The *warm-up learning rate* refers to a strategy with a learning rate scheduler that modulates the learning rate linearly with respect to a predefined number of initial training epochs. *Label smoothing* modulates the cross-entropy loss so the resulting loss is less overconfident on the training set, thereby helping with model generalization and preventing overfitting. This is particularly useful in small-scale datasets.

- *Attention*—In this chapter, we focused on learning embedding in a global fashion: that is, we did not explicitly guide the network to attend to, for example, discriminative parts of an object. Some of the prominent works employing attention are Liu et al. [30] and Chen et al. [31]. Employing attention could also help improve the cross-domain performance of a re-identification network, as demonstrated in [32].

- *Guiding training with more information*—The state-of-the-art comparisons in table 10.3 briefly touched on works incorporating information from multiple sources: identity, attributes (such as the make and model of a vehicle), and spatio-temporal information (GPS location of each query and gallery image). Ideally, including more information helps obtain higher accuracy. However, this comes at the expense of labeling data with annotations. A reasonable approach for training with a multi-attribute setup is to use multi-task learning (MTL). Often, the loss becomes conflicting; this is resolved by weighting the tasks appropriately (using cross validation). A MTL framework to resolve this conflicting loss scenario using multi-objective optimization is by Sener al. [32].

Some popular works of MTL in the context of face, person, and vehicle categorization are by Ranjan et al. [34], Ling et al. [35], and Tang [23].

Summary

- Image-retrieval systems require the learning of visual embeddings (a vector space). Any pair of images can be compared using their geometric distance in this embedding space.
- To learn embeddings using a CNN, there are three popular loss functions: cross-entropy, triplet, and contrastive.
- Naive training of triplet loss is computationally prohibitive. Hence we use batch-based informative data minings: batch all, batch hard, batch sample, and batch weighted.

References

1 S.Z. Li and A.K. Jain. 2011. *Handbook of Face Recognition.* Springer Science & Business Media. https://www.springer.com/gp/book/9780857299314.

2 V. Gupta and S. Mallick. 2019. "Face Recognition: An Introduction for Beginners." Learn OpenCV. April 16, 2019. https://www.learnopencv.com/face-recognition-an-introduction-for-beginners.

3 Z. Liu, P. Luo, S. Qiu, X. Wang, and X. Tang. 2016. "Deepfashion: Powering robust clothes recognition and retrieval with rich annotations." IEEE Conference on Computer Vision and Pattern Recognition (CVPR). http://mmlab.ie.cuhk.edu.hk/projects/DeepFashion.html.

4 T. Xiao, S. Li, B. Wang, L. Lin, and X. Wang. 2016. "Joint Detection and Identification Feature Learning for Person Search." http://arxiv.org/abs/1604.01850.

5   Y. Zhai, X. Guo, Y. Lu, and H. Li. 2018. "In Defense of the Classification Loss for Person Re-Identification." http://arxiv.org/abs/1809.05864.

6   S. Chopra, R. Hadsell, and Y. LeCun. 2005. "Learning a Similarity Metric Discriminatively, with Application to Face Verification." In *2005 IEEE Computer Society Conference on Computer Vision and Pattern Recognition (CVPR'05)*, 1: 539–46 vol. 1. https://doi.org/10.1109/CVPR.2005.202.

7   C-Y. Wu, R. Manmatha, A.J. Smola, and P. Krähenbühl. 2017. "Sampling Matters in Deep Embedding Learning." http://arxiv.org/abs/1706.07567.

8   Q. Weinberger and L.K. Saul. 2009. "Distance Metric Learning for Large Margin Nearest Neighbor Classification." *The Journal of Machine Learning Research* 10: 207–244. https://papers.nips.cc/paper/2795-distance-metric-learning-for-large-margin-nearest-neighbor-classification.pdf.

9   F. Schroff, D. Kalenichenko, and J. Philbin. 2015. "FaceNet: A Unified Embedding for Face Recognition and Clustering." In *2015 IEEE Conference on Computer Vision and Pattern Recognition (CVPR)*, 815–23. https://ieeexplore.ieee.org/document/7298682.

10 R. Kumar, E. Weill, F. Aghdasi, and P. Sriram. 2019. "Vehicle Re-Identification: An Efficient Baseline Using Triplet Embedding." https://arxiv.org/pdf/1901.01015.pdf.

11 A. Hermans, L. Beyer, and B. Leibe. 2017. "In Defense of the Triplet Loss for Person Re-Identification." http://arxiv.org/abs/1703.07737.

12 R. Kumar, E. Weill, F. Aghdasi, and P. Sriram. 2020. "A Strong and Efficient Baseline for Vehicle Re-Identification Using Deep Triplet Embedding." *Journal of Artificial Intelligence and Soft Computing Research* 10 (1): 27–45. https://content.sciendo.com/view/journals/jaiscr/10/1/article-p27.xml.

13 E. Ristani and C. Tomasi. 2018. "Features for Multi-Target Multi-Camera Tracking and Re-Identification." http://arxiv.org/abs/1803.10859.

14 X. Liu, W. Liu, T. Mei, and H. Ma. 2018. "PROVID: Progressive and Multimodal Vehicle Reidentification for Large-Scale Urban Surveillance." *IEEE Transactions on Multimedia* 20 (3): 645–58. https://doi.org/10.1109/TMM.2017.2751966.

15 J. Deng, W. Dong, R. Socher, L. Li, Kai Li, and Li Fei-Fei. 2009. "ImageNet: A Large-Scale Hierarchical Image Database." In *2009 IEEE Conference on Computer Vision and Pattern Recognition*, 248–55. http://ieeexplore.ieee.org/lpdocs/epic03/wrapper.htm?arnumber=5206848.

16 A.G. Howard, M. Zhu, B. Chen, D. Kalenichenko, W. Wang, T. Weyand, M. Andreetto, and H. Adam. 2017. "MobileNets: Efficient Convolutional Neural Networks for Mobile Vision Applications." http://arxiv.org/abs/1704.04861.

17 D.P. Kingma and J. Ba. 2014. "Adam: A Method for Stochastic Optimization." http://arxiv.org/abs/1412.6980.

18 W. Kim, B. Goyal, K. Chawla, J. Lee, and K. Kwon. 2018. "Attention-based ensemble for deep metric learning." In *2018 IEEE Conference on Computer Vision and Pattern Recognition (CVPR)*, 760–777, https://arxiv.org/abs/1804.00382.

19 M. Opitz, G. Waltner, H. Possegger, and H. Bischof. 2017. "BIER—Boosting Independent Embeddings Robustly." In *2017 IEEE International Conference on Computer Vision (ICCV)*, 5199–5208. https://ieeexplore.ieee.org/document/8237817.

20 Y. Bai, Y. Lou, F. Gao, S. Wang, Y. Wu, and L. Duan. 2018. "Group-Sensitive Triplet Embedding for Vehicle Reidentification." *IEEE Transactions on Multimedia* 20 (9): 2385–99. https://ieeexplore.ieee.org/document/8265213.

21 Y. Zhouy and L. Shao. 2018. "Viewpoint-Aware Attentive Multi-View Inference for Vehicle Re-Identification." In *2018 IEEE/CVF Conference on Computer Vision and Pattern Recognition*, 6489–98. https://ieeexplore.ieee.org/document/8578777.

22 Y. Shen, T. Xiao, H. Li, S. Yi, and X. Wang. 2017. "Learning Deep Neural Networks for Vehicle Re-ID with Visual-Spatio-Temporal Path Proposals." In *2017 IEEE International Conference on Computer Vision (ICCV)*, 1918–27. https://ieeexplore .ieee.org/document/8237472.

23 Z. Tang, M. Naphade, S. Birchfield, J. Tremblay, W. Hodge, R. Kumar, S. Wang, and X. Yang. 2019. "PAMTRI: Pose-Aware Multi-Task Learning for Vehicle Re-Identification Using Highly Randomized Synthetic Data." In *Proceedings of the IEEE International Conference on Computer Vision*, 211–20. http://openaccess.thecvf .com/content_ICCV_2019/html/Tang_PAMTRI_Pose-Aware_Multi-Task_Learning _for_Vehicle_Re-Identification_Using_Highly_Randomized_ICCV_2019_paper .html.

24 A. Kanacı, X. Zhu, and S. Gong. 2017. "Vehicle Reidentification by Fine-Grained Cross-Level Deep Learning." In *BMVC AMMDS Workshop*, 2:772–88. https://arxiv.org/abs/1809.09409.

25 P. Khorramshahi, A. Kumar, N. Peri, S.S. Rambhatla, J.-C. Chen, and R. Chellappa. 2019. "A Dual-Path Model With Adaptive Attention For Vehicle Re-Identification." http://arxiv.org/abs/1905.03397.

26 A. Kanacı, X. Zhu, and S. Gong. 2017. "Vehicle Reidentification by Fine-Grained Cross-Level Deep Learning." In *BMVC AMMDS Workshop*, 2:772–88. http://www .eecs.qmul.ac.uk/~xiatian/papers.

27 Z. Tang, M. Naphade, M.-Y. Liu, X. Yang, S. Birchfield, S. Wang, R. Kumar, D. Anastasiu, and J.-N. Hwang. 2019. "CityFlow: A City-Scale Benchmark for Multi-Target Multi-Camera Vehicle Tracking and Re-Identification." In *2019 IEEE Conference on Computer Vision and Pattern Recognition (CVPR)*. http://arxiv.org/ abs/1903.09254.

28 Z. Zhong, L. Zheng, D. Cao, and S. Li. 2017. "Re-Ranking Person Re-Identification with K-Reciprocal Encoding." In 2017 *IEEE Conference on Computer Vision and Pattern Recognition (CVPR)*, 3652–3661, https://arxiv.org/abs/1701.08398.

29 H. Luo, Y. Gu, X. Liao, S. Lai, and W. Jiang. 2019. "Bag of Tricks and A Strong Baseline for Deep Person Re-Identification." In *2019 IEEE Conference on Computer Vision and Pattern Recognition (CVPR) Workshops*. https://arxiv.org/abs/ 1903.07071.

30 H. Liu, J. Feng, M. Qi, J. Jiang, and S. Yan. 2016. "End-to-End Comparative Attention Networks for Person Re-Identification." *IEEE Transactions on Image Processing* 26 (7): 3492–3506. https://arxiv.org/abs/1606.04404.

31 G. Chen, C. Lin, L. Ren, J. Lu, and J. Zhou. 2019. "Self-Critical Attention Learning for Person Re-Identification." In *Proceedings of the IEEE International Conference on Computer Vision*, 9637–46. http://openaccess.thecvf.com/content_ICCV_2019/html/Chen_Self-Critical_Attention_Learning_for_Person_Re-Identification_ICCV_2019_paper.html.

32 H. Liu, J. Cheng, S. Wang, and W. Wang. 2019. "Attention: A Big Surprise for Cross-Domain Person Re-Identification." http://arxiv.org/abs/1905.12830.

33 O. Sener and V. Koltun. 2018. "Multi-Task Learning as Multi-Objective Optimization." In *Proceedings of the 32nd International Conference on Neural Information Processing Systems*, 525–36. http://dl.acm.org/citation.cfm?id=3326943.3326992.

34 R. Ranjan, S. Sankaranarayanan, C. D. Castillo, and R. Chellappa. 2017. "An All-In-One Convolutional Neural Network for Face Analysis." In *2017 12th IEEE International Conference on Automatic Face Gesture Recognition* (*FG 2017*), 17–24. https://arxiv.org/abs/1611.00851.

35 H. Ling, Z. Wang, P. Li, Y. Shi, J. Chen, and F. Zou. 2019. "Improving Person Re-Identification by Multi-Task Learning." *Neurocomputing* 347: 109–118. https://doi.org/10.1016/j.neucom.2019.01.027.

36 X. Liu, W. Liu, T. Mei, and H. Ma. 2016. "A Deep Learning-Based Approach to Progressive Vehicle Re-Identification for Urban Surveillance." In *Computer Vision – ECCV 2016*, 869–84. https://doi.org/10.1007/978-3-319-46475-6_53.

37 B. Amos, B. Ludwiczuk, M. Satyanarayanan, et al. 2016. "Openface: A General-Purpose Face Recognition Library with Mobile Applications." *CMU School of Computer Science* 6: 2. http://elijah.cs.cmu.edu/DOCS/CMU-CS-16-118.pdf.

appendix A
Getting set up

All of the code in this book is written in Python 3, Open CV, Keras, and TensorFlow. The process of setting up a DL environment on your computer is fairly involved and consists of the following steps, which this appendix covers in detail:

1 Download the code repository.
2 Install Anaconda.
3 Set up your DL environment: install all the packages that you need for projects in this book (NumPy, OpenCV, Keras, TensorFlow, and others).
4 [Optional] Set up the AWS EC2 environment. This step is optional if you want to train your networks on GPUs.

A.1 Downloading the code repository

All the code shown in this book can be downloaded from the book's website (www.manning.com/books/deep-learning-for-vision-systems) and also from GitHub (https://github.com/moelgendy/deep_learning_for_vision_systems) in the form of a Git repo. The GitHub repo contains a directory for each chapter. If you're unfamiliar with version control using Git and GitHub, you can review the boot-camp articles (https://help.github.com/categories/bootcamp) and/or beginning resources (https://help.github.com/articles/good-resources-for-learning-git-and-github) for learning these tools.

A.2   *Installing Anaconda*

Anaconda (https://anaconda.org) is a distribution of packages built for data science and ML projects. It comes with conda, a package and environment manager. You'll be using conda to create isolated environments for your projects that use different versions of your libraries. You'll also use it to install, uninstall, and update packages in your environments.

Note that Anaconda is a fairly large download (~600 MB) because it comes with the most common ML packages in Python. If you don't need all the packages or need to conserve bandwidth or storage space, there is also Miniconda, a smaller distribution that includes only conda and Python. You can still install any of the available packages with conda; it just doesn't come with them.

Follow these steps to install Anaconda on your computer:

1 Anaconda is available for Windows, macOS, and Linux. You can find the installers and installation instructions at www.anaconda.com/distribution. Choose the Python 3 version, because Python 2 has been deprecated as of January 2020. Choose the 64-bit installer if you have a 64-bit operating system; otherwise, go with the 32-bit installer. Go ahead and download the appropriate version.

2 Follow the installation through the graphical interface installer shown in figure A.1.

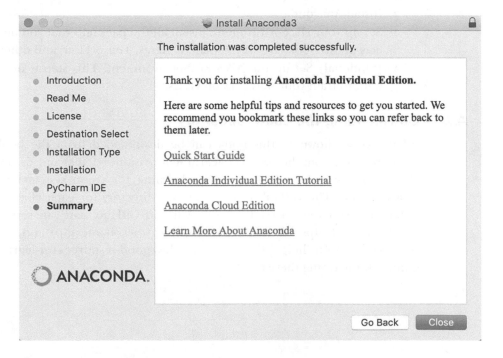

Figure A.1   Anaconda installer on macOS

3 After installation is complete, you're automatically in the default conda environment with all packages installed. You can check out your own install by entering `conda list` into your terminal to see your conda environments.

A.3 Setting up your DL environment

Now you will create a new environment and install the packages that you will use for your projects. You will use conda as a package manager to install libraries that you need. You are probably already familiar with pip; it's the default package manager for Python libraries. Conda is similar to pip, except that the available packages are focused around data science, while pip is for general use.

Conda is also a virtual environment manager. It's similar to other popular environment managers like virtualenv (https://virtualenv.pypa.io/en/stable) and pyenv (https://github.com/pyenv/pyenv). However, conda is not Python-specific like pip is: it can also install non-Python packages. It is a package manager for any software stack. That being said, not all Python libraries are available from the Anaconda distribution and conda. You can (and will) still use pip alongside conda to install packages.

A.3.1 Setting up your development environment manually

Follow these steps to manually install all the libraries needed for the projects in this book. Otherwise, skip to the next section to install the environment created for you in the book's GitHub repo.

1 On your terminal, create a new conda environment with Python 3 and call it `deep_learning_for_vision_systems`:

```
conda create -n deep_learning_for_vision_systems python=3
```

Note that to remove a conda environment, you use `conda env remove -n <env_name>`.

2 Activate your environment. You must activate the environment before installing your packages. This way, all packages are installed only for this environment:

```
conda activate deep_learning_for_vision_systems
```

Note that to deactivate an environment, you use `conda deactivate <env_name>`.

Now you are inside your new environment. To see the default packages installed in this environment, type the following command: `conda list`. Next, you will install the packages used for the projects in this book.

3 Install NumPy, pandas, and Matplotlib. These are very common ML packages that you will almost always use in your projects for math operations, data manipulation, and visualization tasks:

```
conda install numpy pandas matplotlib
```

Note that throughout these installs, you will be prompted to confirm to proceed (Proceed ([y]/n)?). Type Y and press Enter to continue the installation.

4   Install the Jupyter notebooks. We use Jupyter notebooks in this book for easier development:

```
conda install jupyter notebook
```

5   Install OpenCV (the most popular open source CV library):

```
conda install -c conda-forge opencv
```

6   Install Keras:

```
pip install keras
```

7   Install TensorFlow:

```
pip install tensorflow
```

Now everything is complete and your environment is ready to start developing. If you want to view all the libraries installed in your environment, type the following command:

```
conda list
```

These packages are separate from your other environments. This way, you can avoid any version-conflict issues.

A.3.2   *Using the conda environment in the book's repo*

1   Clone the book's GitHub repository from https://github.com/moelgendy/ deep_learning_for_vision_systems. The environment is located in the installer/ application.yaml file:

```
cd installer
```

2   Create the conda deep_learning environment:

```
conda env create -f my_environment.yaml
```

3   Activate the conda environment:

```
conda activate deep_learning
```

4   Launch your Jupyter notebook (make sure you are located in the root of the deep_learning_for_vision_systems repository):

```
jupyter notebook
```

Now you are ready to run the notebooks associated with the book.

A.3.3　Saving and loading environments

It is best practice to save your environment if you want to share it with others so that they can install all the packages used in your code with the correct version. To do that, you can save the packages to a YAML (https://yaml.org) file with this command:

```
conda env export > my_environment.yaml
```

This way, others can use this YAML file to replicate your environment on their machine using the following command:

```
conda env create -f my_environment.yaml
```

You can also export the list of packages in an environment to a .txt file and then include that file with your code. This allows other people to easily load all the dependencies for your code. Pip has similar functionality with this command:

```
pip freeze > requirements.txt
```

You can find the environment details used for this book's projects in the downloaded code in the installer directory. You can use it to replicate my environment in your machine.

A.4　Setting up your AWS EC2 environment

Training and evaluating deep neural networks is a computationally intensive task depending on your dataset size and the size of the neural network. All projects in this book are specifically designed to have modes-sized problems and datasets to allow you to train networks on the CPU in your local machine. But some of these projects could take up to 20 hours to train—or even more, depending on your computer specifications and other parameters like the number of epochs, neural network size, and other factors.

A faster alternative is to train on a graphics processing unit (GPU), which is a type of processor that supports greater parallelism. You can either build your own DL rig or use cloud services like Amazon AWS EC2. Many cloud service providers offer equivalent functionality, but EC2 is a reasonable default that is available to most beginners. In the next few sections, we'll go over the steps from nothing to running a neural network on an Amazon server.

A.4.1　Creating an AWS account

Follow these steps:

1 Visit aws.amazon.com, and click the Create an AWS Account button. You will also need to choose a support plan. You can choose the free Basic Support Plan. You might be asked to provide credit card information, but you won't be charged for anything yet.

2 Launch an EC2 instance:

a Go to the EC2 Management Console (https://console.aws.amazon.com/ec2/v2/home), and click the Launch Instance button.

b Click AWS Marketplace.

c Search for *Deep Learning AMI*, and select the AMI that is suitable for your environment. Amazon Machine Images (AMI) contains all the environment files and drivers for you to train on a GPU. It has cuDNN and many other packages required for projects in this book. Any additional packages required for specific projects are detailed in the appropriate project instructions.

d Choose an instance type:
   – Filter the instance list to only show GPU instances.
   – Select the p2.xlarge instance type. This instance is powerful enough for our projects and not very expensive. Feel free to choose more powerful instances if you are interested in trying them out.
   – Click the Review and Launch button.

e Edit the security group. You will be running Jupyter notebooks in this book, which default to port 8888. To access this port, you need to open it on AWS by editing the security group:
   – Select Create a New Security Group.
   – Set Security Group Name to *Jupyter*.
   – Click Add Rule, and set a Custom TCP Rule.
   – Set Port Range to 8888.
   – Select Anywhere as the Source.
   – Click Review and Launch.

f Click the Launch button to launch your GPU instance. You'll need to specify an authentication key pair to be able to access your instance. So, when you are launching the instance, make sure to select Create a New Key Pair and click the Download Key Pair button. This will download a .pem file, which you'll need to be able to access your instance. Move the .pem file to a secure and easily remembered location on your computer; you'll need to access your instance through the location you select. After the .pem file has been downloaded, click the Launch Instances button.

WARNING From this point on, AWS will charge you for running this EC2 instance. You can find the details on the EC2 On-Demand Pricing page (https://aws.amazon.com/ec2/pricing/on-demand). Most important, *always* remember to stop your instances when you are not using them. Otherwise, they might keep running, and you'll wind up with a large bill! AWS charges primarily for running instances, so most of the charges will cease once you stop the instance. However, smaller storage charges continue to accrue until you terminate (delete) the instance.

A.4.2 *Connecting remotely to your instance*

Now that you have created your EC2 instance, go to your EC2 dashboard, select the instance, and start it, as shown in figure A.2. Allow a minute or two for the EC2 instance to launch. You will know it is ready when the instance Status Check shows "checks passed." Scroll to the Description section, and make a note of the IPv4 Public IP address (in the format X.X.X.X) on the EC2 Dashboard; you will need it in the next step to access your instance remotely.

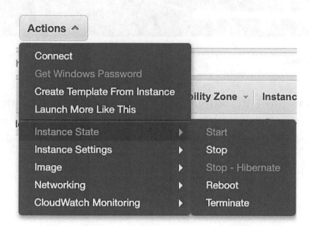

Figure A.2   How to remotely connect to your instance

On your terminal, follow these steps to connect to your EC2 server:

1 Navigate to the location where you stored your .pem file from the previous section.
2 Type the following:

```
ssh -i YourKeyName.pem user@X.X.X.X
```

user could be ubuntu@ or ec2-user@. X.X.X.X is the IPv4 Public IP that you just saved from the EC2 instance description. And YourKeyName.pem is the name of your .pem file.

TIP If you see a "bad permissions" or "permission denied" error message regarding your .pem file, try executing chmod 400 path/to/YourKeyName.pem and then running the ssh command again.

A.4.3 *Running your Jupyter notebook*

The final step is to run your Jupyter notebook on the EC2 server. After you have accessed the instance remotely from your terminal, follow these steps:

1 Type the following command on your terminal:

```
jupyter notebook --ip=0.0.0.0 --no-browser
```

When you press Enter, you will get an access token, as shown in figure A.3. Copy this token value, because you will use it in the next step.

Figure A.3   Copy the token to run the notebook.

2 On your browser, go to this URL: http://<IPv4 Public IP>:8888. Note that the IPv4 public IP is the one you saved from the EC2 instance description. For example, if the public IP was 25.153.17.47, then the URL would be http://25.153.17.47:8888.

3 Enter the token key that you copied in step 1 into the token field, and click Log In (figure A.4).

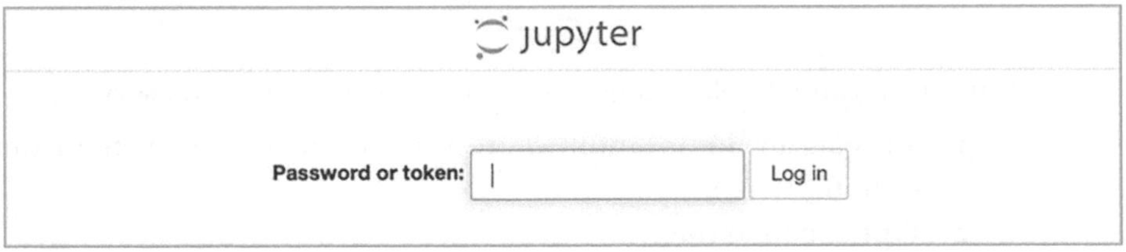

Figure A.4   Logging in

4 Install the libraries that you will need for your projects, similarly to what you did in section A.3.1. But this time, use `pip install` instead of `conda install`. For example, to install Keras, you need to type `pip install keras`.

That's it. You are now ready to start coding!

index

visual embeddings *(continued)*
  mining informative data 414–423
    BA 419
    BH 419
    BS 421–423
    BW 421
    dataloader 414–416
    finding useful triplets 416–419
  training embedding networks 423–431
    finding similar items 424
    implementation 426
    object re-identification 424–426
    testing trained models 427–431
visual perception 5
visualizing
  datasets 364
  features 377–381
  loss 334
VUIs (voice user interfaces) 4

W

warm-up learning rate 432
weight connections 46
weight decay 178
weight layers 199
weight regularization 207
weighted sum 38

weighted sum function 40
weights 72–73, 123–124
  calculating parameters 123–124
  non-trainable params 124
  trainable params 124
weights vector 39
width value 122

X

X argument 234
x_test 186
x_train 186
x_valid 186

Y

YOLOv3 (you only look once)
  architecture of 324–325
  object detection with 283–320, 325–337
  overview 321–324
    output bounding boxes 324
    predictions across different scales 323–324

Z

zero-padding 114